MW01534929

HOW TO GET THE MOST OUT OF

DOS 6 UTILITIES

And Beyond

How To Get The Most Out Of DOS 6 UTILITIES And Beyond

David D. Busch

////Brady

New York   London   Toronto   Sydney   Tokyo   Singapore

Brady Publishing
A Division of Prentice Hall Computer Publishing
15 Columbus Circle
New York, NY 10023

ISBN: 1-56686-072-5

Library of Congress Catalog No.: 93-17453

Printing Code: The rightmost double-digit number is the year of the book's printing. For example, 93-1 shows that the first printing of the book occurred in 1993.

96 95 94 93   4 3 2 1

Manufactured in the United States of America

For Cathy. This one was a lot of work, wasn't it?

Credits

PUBLISHER
Michael Violano

ACQUISITIONS DIRECTOR
Jono Hardjowirogo

MANAGING EDITOR
Kelly D. Dobbs

DEVELOPMENTAL EDITOR
Michael Sprague

EDITORIAL ASSISTANTS
Lisa Rose
Julie Volkov

BOOK DESIGNER
Michele Laseau

COVER DESIGNER
HUB Graphics

INDEXER
Jeanne Clark

PRODUCTION TEAM
Diana Bigham, Katy Bodenmiller, Scott Cook, Tim Cox, Mark Enochs, Tom Loveman, Roger Morgan, Joe Ramon, Carrie Roth, Greg Simsic

About the Author

David D. Busch's 40 books include eight that have clarified the mysteries of PC operating systems, including an early Brady best-seller, *DOS Customized*. He specializes in translating confusing computer concepts into simple, yet in-depth descriptions for the average computer user. His books are also favorites among sophisticated DOS users who realize that explanations of complex topics don't have to be cloaked in computer science jargon.

Busch's no-nonsense approach made him the first person to win "Best Book" honors twice from the Computer Press Association. His 2,000-plus magazine articles have been much in demand, too; since 1980, Busch has been a contributing editor and monthly columnist for eight different computer magazines, including *Windows User*.

The President/LocSec of East Central Ohio Mensa is a 1970 graduate of Kent State University. He and his spouse of 24 years reside in their native Ohio with their four children, ages 4 to 23.

Contents at a Glance

Contents

Preface

Don't throw out your old DOS manuals, yet. Everything that's new and exciting about MS-DOS 6 is detailed right here in this book. If you just want to look up the syntax for the **chkdsk** command, your current DOS guide is just fine; Microsoft didn't change the foundation of DOS much. But, if you're looking for the best and most detailed information on new utilities like DoubleSpace, MemMaker, Microsoft Anti-Virus, and Backup, you're holding the key in your hands.

How To Get the Most Out of DOS 6 Utilities and Beyond shows you how to get these utilities to work for you and offers frank advice when they might not be the best solution to your problems. Whether you're a newcomer to DOS or an experienced hand who wants a short-cut to using the new enhancements, this book cuts through the hype and answers all the basic questions plaguing every current and potential DOS 6 user.

Part I:
Utilities, DOS, and Computers

(u-til'-i-ty), *n.* 1. A computer program that optimizes your system's resources until they are all gone. 2. A nonincluded essential software component that must be purchased at extra cost. 3. Any useful feature that the developers of an application program or operating system forgot to include, didn't foresee a need for, or simply elected to skip.

The personal computer industry has nourished the development of utility programs since its beginnings. No operating system or application program ever marketed has ever done everything that every user wanted. When a particular function isn't integrated into software, a utility can be created to provide that feature externally.

Utilities are generally considered programs that perform some housekeeping task or other function not associated with a formal application. A word processing program is not a utility, but a simple text editor like EDIT.EXE, most often used to make small changes in files like AUTOEXEC.BAT or

CONFIG.SYS, *is* a utility. LOTUS 1-2-3 is an application; a program which compiles Lotus spreadsheets into an executable program is a utility.

This first section will introduce you to this book, DOS itself, and the concept of the utility program; will explain how utilities came to be needed; and will discuss what types of utility programs are most common. You'll also learn a little about DOS and how it was developed.

DOS 6 and Its Utilities

For many years, building a complete MS-DOS system was something of a do-it-yourself project. Each computer user started with a solid foundation—Microsoft's basic disk operating system (DOS)—and added the specialized utility programs needed to meet the individual's minimum needs. So-called "power" users actually enjoy evaluating all the available options and picking and choosing the best of them to tailor their own configurations. However, the vast majority of PC users found these extra steps frustrating, confusing, and time-consuming. Why couldn't MS-DOS include all the basic features in a single package?

When Microsoft introduced MS-DOS 6 in March, 1993, many DOS users got the answer they were looking for. DOS 6 is fundamentally a utility-oriented upgrade. You can count the number of new DOS command line functions or options in DOS 6 on one hand. There are a few more new configuration directives (usable only within CONFIG.SYS) and one new batch file command. All the other changes in DOS 6 involve new or enhanced utilities.

These utilities include the following:

➤ Microsoft DoubleSpace, a disk compression utility that boosts available hard disk space by squeezing files into a more compact size.

➤ Microsoft MemMaker, a program that optimizes your system's use of memory by locating areas in upper memory where programs and device drivers can be loaded, freeing up as much as possible of your 640K of conventional RAM.

➤ Improved memory management commands and drivers, including enhanced mem, loadhigh, and devicehigh commands, and a re-vamped EMM386 device driver.

➤ Microsoft Backup, in both Windows and DOS command line versions.

➤ Microsoft Anti-Virus, which can locate and remove more than 1,000 computer viruses.

➤ Microsoft Undelete, also available in Windows and DOS versions, with three distinct levels of protection.

➤ Microsoft Defragmenter, which optimizes the arrangement of the files on your disk to speed access to them.

➤ A much smarter SmartDrive disk cache that stores information from your hard disk in RAM where it can be more quickly accessed by the CPU.

➤ A new Microsoft System Diagnostics program that collects technical information about your computer for use in setting up peripherals and diagnosing problems.

➤ Interlnk, a file transfer program that allows exchanging data between computers through a connecting cable.

➤ Power, a utility that conserves laptop battery power when applications and hardware are idle.

Roughly a dozen utilities and changes encompass most of what is new about DOS 6. That's good news for DOS users in several ways. You don't have to junk your present third-party DOS manuals, tutorials, and tips-and-tricks books and buy new ones. Dozens of new DOS 6 titles hit the bookstores in the same time frame as DOS 6 itself. But you don't need them. All you really need to get the most out of DOS 6's new capabilities is this book, which concentrates only on the real changes, the utilities themselves. If you've ever had to wade through 500 pages of stuff you already knew to find the few nuggets of valuable, new information, you'll understand what I am talking about. *How To Get the Most Out of DOS 6 Utilities* is hundreds of pages of nuggets.

What You'll Learn

You'll learn how to use the new DoubleSpace integrated disk compression utility and how to better manage memory with MemMaker. Simple ways to use Microsoft's greatly improved Backup option and Anti-Virus utility will help you better protect your valuable data. You'll discover why SmartDrive has finally become a disk-caching program worthy of its name.

Instructions on how to use the new MS-DOS 6 utilities are only the beginning, however. This book also explains why you want to use a given utility and provides recommendations on when you might want to go beyond Microsoft's basic offering and choose a third-party utility that offers similar functions, but with advanced options, greater performance, or extended features.

For example, do you really need disk compression—or would you be better off just buying a larger hard disk? Surprisingly, for some users, the latter solution is by far the better choice. The tips in Chapter 14 may save you hundreds of dollars and countless hours struggling with add-on compression options you can't benefit from.

This book, therefore, is more than a complete guide to using the DOS 6 utilities. It's a resource that will let you make intelligent choices about which of these utilities you want to add to your system, which you can safely ignore, and which you should supplement with a few third-party add-ons that can do a better or more suitable job for you. When you finish reading *How To Get the Most Out of DOS 6 Utilities,* you'll be more than a DOS 6 expert: you'll have a rich background in what everyone must know about the hows and whys of DOS utilities.

Who Needs This Book?

How To Get the Most Out of DOS 6 Utilities will appeal to six types of readers:

➤ Curious users who want to know more about DOS 6 before they upgrade or switch from another operating system, such as DR DOS. Is DOS 6 really worth buying, especially if you already have a few of the utilities it now includes? If you're a utilities neophyte, you'll want to know whether DOS 6 is easy to use and that it won't add to your problems rather than solve them. You don't want to wade through explanations of commands you already understand and know how to use. Instead, you want discussions of the new capabilities, so you can evaluate whether MS-DOS 6 is really for you.

➤ Power users trying to tweak their operating system just a little more, perhaps by finding new ways to squeeze out more memory or extra disk space. If you're in this category, you've probably already worked your way through a plethora of third-party utilities and found them less than satisfying. Bleeding-edge memory managers, for example, can deliver every last byte of upper memory but lock up your system in new and unexpected ways. You're sometimes better off with the tested compatibility of something like MemMaker, which at least operates by working closely *with* MS-DOS, rather than by subverting it. This book will show even sophisticated users how to use the built-in utilities—and when to turn elsewhere.

➤ Windows users who want to understand the operating system underlying their graphical user interface (GUI). (See *"Windows Users Note."*)

➤ Corporate decision makers seeking more information before purchasing a new operating system for potential implementation throughout their organizations. Upgrading several hundred or several thousand users from DOS 5 to DOS 6 involves big bucks. This book will help you decide how—or if—you should make the transition.

➤ MS-DOS trainers who need a guide they can use in advanced courses. After you've gotten beyond the "this is a subdirectory; this is the COPY command" stage, you'll want a textbook or teacher's guide that concentrates only on the utilities, which are, after all, the key enhancements of DOS 6. Why teach students who already understand DOS fundamentals from a guide that buries the new information in a rehash of things they are familiar with?

➤ End users who want a reference guide to the DOS 6 utilities—but with more detail and explanation than found in the DOS manual itself.

Windows Users Note

Although the emphasis will be on using MS-DOS 6, this book is essential for Windows users, too. Unlike OS/2 or the impending Windows NT, your current graphical user interface is built on a foundation that is 100 percent MS-DOS. DOS 6's disk-caching capabilities can have a dramatic effect on Windows performance. File compression can let you load more disk-hungry applications (like Corel Draw, which weighs in at 30M!). Viruses can strike Windows applications as easily as DOS applications. Although Windows has its own memory management routines, how you set up DOS memory before you load Windows can affect your ability to run DOS applications within Windows.

DOS 6 includes Windows-oriented versions of its key utilities, including Backup, Undelete, and Anti-Virus, and gives you tools like SmartMon to track the efficiency of others. As a full-time Windows user myself, I know you'll want to read the special notes in this book oriented towards this GUI.

Why Me?

As you might guess, this introduction was written to entice you to buy this book or, if you have already purchased it, to get you to read it instead of putting it on a shelf until the next emergency strikes. I honestly believe this book is an excellent investment, and if I can get you to use it, you'll be more likely to buy my next book when it comes out. After 40 of these books since 1983, I'm in this for the long term.

So, why do I presume to tell you about DOS 6? Do I really know what I am talking about? As a matter of fact, I do, but it wasn't always so. I don't have a degree in computer science. I've never worked as a computer professional, although I've visited with and interviewed hundreds of them in the last 20 years. I love technology, but I don't have technical training.

A DOS User Like You

First and foremost, I am a DOS user like you, and I learned what I know in the same way you might if you didn't have my experiences to draw from. My advantage is that I've been doing this for a long time. I have an inordinate amount of time to spend on it; understanding and explaining computer technology is what I do for a living.

I've expended a lot of effort tweaking operating systems to get them to do what I want. I've run every suite of utilities from Becker and Central Point to Norton and used them in my everyday work for years. I can afford to spend time evaluating all these utilities, because I end up writing reviews for leading publications or books explaining what I've figured out. I'm able to spend days playing "what-if" games with DOS commands, time during which a normal person would be forced to accomplish something useful with a word processing program or spreadsheet. It's been fun, and several of the books that have come of it have sold fairly well.

Foreseeing the Invisible

For example, in 1984 I was probably the first to write an extensive treatise on the use of DOS's "invisible" character, ASCII 255, in what eventually became *PC-DOS Customized*, written for the ancient DOS 2.0 operating system. If you wonder what evil mind dreamt up using ASCII 255 as both the root and extension name for subdirectories, which contained files named ASCII 255, with batch commands that included ASCII 255, look no further. My demented thinking developed invisible commands in invisible files in invisible subdirectories!

Later, I "invented" subroutines in batch files, found new ways to organize hard disks, and turned down an opportunity to write a portion of a book for the industry's largest and most successful publisher because I believed that the topic I'd proposed, the 4DOS command interpreter, deserved a book of its own.

As you might guess, I love finding new tools, like the utilities in DOS 6, and discovering new things that can be done with them. If you share my curiosity or simply want to get more power from your PC at minimal expense, this book is for you.

I should warn you that my very first notoriety in the computer industry was for a series of 1981 articles detailing the fictitious exploits of Kitchen Table, Inc., the world's largest supplier of partially functioning hardware, software, firmware, and limpware. Humor, and a touch of irreverence, manages to creep into my books from time to time, no matter how hard I try to keep it out. I really have no fear of Microsoft or Bill Gates, because neither of them will ever be aware that I was alive. I'm free, therefore, to call 'em in this book as I see 'em.

How To Use This Book

Most computer books have a section that explains how the reader should approach using the book to get the most out of it. These sections generally offer astounding insights, such as recommendations to read the book from front to back, suggestions to skim over the parts you find unbearably boring or irrelevant, and prods to read the difficult parts over and over again, until the information finally sinks in.

Personally, I don't care if you decide to read all the odd-numbered pages first. If this book requires an instruction manual to use, then I haven't done my job. The DOS 6 utilities were designed to be easy to use, and I hope this book will be a painless way for you to get more out of them. There should not *be* any hard parts that require repeated study and yellow highlighting. I'd rather my books become dog-eared from constant reference and pass-along readership than from all-night cram sessions.

If you find there is more background material in this book than you really need, feel free to skim over it; many readers have told me this information is *not* boring or irrelevant.

Chapter Outline

This section provides a brief description of what you'll learn in each section of the book. The Table of Contents and Index can get you to the exact page numbers for specific topics.

Part I: Utilities, DOS, and Computers

1. **DOS 6 and Its Utilities**. This chapter explains the rationale behind this book and provides a preview of what you'll learn in the coming chapters. Brief descriptions of the key new DOS 6 utilities are included.

2. **Utilities or Futilities?** Why DOS 6 users need utilities to best use their resources, improve the performance of their systems, work faster and smarter. What are the major categories of utilities? Which are included in DOS 6? How do the DOS 6 utilities stack up against stand-alone products? How can the user determine which utilities will be of the most use?

3. **Inside DOS and Computers.** If you've been wondering what goes on under the hood, this chapter provides a quick introduction to the basic concepts that make your hardware and software possible.

Part II: Memory Management

4. **Introduction to Memory**. How microprocessors see memory. What is DOS memory, upper memory, HMA, extended memory, expanded memory, etc? How are each of these best used?

5. **Getting More Memory**. This chapter looks at some of the various ways you can add memory to your PC, even before you put MemMaker to work.

6. **Using MemMaker**. This chapter discusses optimizing memory, express mode, custom mode, how MemMaker works, and undoing MemMaker's changes.

7. **Tools for Fine-Tuning Memory**. Learn about some of the commands and directives you'll be using to optimize memory, including the **mem** command and MSD.EXE (Microsoft System Diagnostics utility).

8. **Using Memory Managers**. This chapter details the difference between EMM386.EXE and HIMEM.SYS and how to determine which—or if both—are needed for your system, and looks at third-party managers like QEMM and 386MAX.

Part III: Optimizing Hard Disk Performance

9. **How Hard Disks Work**. You'll find the discussion of sectors and clusters later on a lot less confusing after this description of the evolution and state-of-the-art of hard disk storage.

10. **How Caches Work.** How does it work? Why do I need it? What type of caches work best? This chapter will clear up your cache confusion.

11. **All About SmartDrive**. This chapter describes SmartDrive, and all its options including tips for getting it to work smoothly with Windows.

12. **Using SmartMon**. This chapter looks at DOS 6's Windows-based SmartMon utility, showing how it can be used to track SmartDrive's performance.

13. **Beyond SmartDrive**. A discussion of the leading third-party cache programs, pointing out how they stack up against SmartDrive.

Part IV: Optimizing Hard Disk Space

14. **Do You Need DoubleSpace**? You may not require disk compression at all. This chapter shows you how you can free up 20 to 30 percent of your hard disk space without a special utility.

15. **File Compression Made Small.** Requirements for easy, safe, compression. You'll understand exactly how file compression works after reading this chapter.

16. **Using DoubleSpace**. How to set up and configure DoubleSpace on your hard disk. What happened to MaxCompress?

17. **Compressing Removable Media**. Using compressed disks on "foreign" systems. Your floppies and other removable media can double in capacity, too! Learn how to streamline this procedure.

18. **Defragmenting Disks**. This chapter explains why disk optimization is needed, and how DOS 6's Defragmenter can be used to increase hard disk performance.

19. **Beyond DoubleSpace and Defragmenter.** Non-Microsoft compression and defragmenting utilities, and how they compare to DOS 6's offerings.

Part V: Data Protection

20. **What Is Data Protection?** You'll learn why your data potentially has more value than the computer it's stored on.

21. **Backing Up Your Files**. How to establish a regular, reliable backup schedule

22. **Backup Strategies and Alternatives.** Learn how to set up an efficient backup system and what your alternatives are to DOS 6's Backup software.

23. **What Is a Computer Virus?** What's the difference between a virus and a trojan horse? What are worms? This chapter clears up all the misconceptions about virus infections and their consequences.

24. **Using Microsoft Anti-Virus.** How to detect, disinfect, and prevent viruses. Learn how to thwart both known and unknown viruses. Third-party alternatives are also covered.

25. **Undeleting and Unformatting.** It doesn't take a virus to destroy your files. This chapter shows you how to recover when you accidentally format a disk or erase an essential file by mistake.

Part VI: System Startup Utilities

Part VII: Advanced Utilities

Appendixes

Utilities or Futilities?

There are hundreds, if not thousands, of utility programs aimed squarely at the MS-DOS market. These programs do something better, faster, or more easily than MS-DOS by itself or offer a feature not available within DOS. Some observers like to blame the original developers of the IBM PC architecture and its operating system for the plethora of utilities needed to turn MS-DOS into a complete operating system.

For example, it could be said that file compression is needed only because DOS and its applications use inefficient file formats. We wouldn't need fancy memory managers if all DOS applications didn't have to compete for the same 640K of RAM. Why should you need a special program to restore a file that has been accidentally deleted?

In the real world, hindsight is an excellent tool for pointing out mistakes that often took months or years to become painfully evident. The efforts ongoing since 1987 to produce a workable version of OS/2 have shown how difficult it is to cover all the operating system bases, even when you start from scratch. Utilities offer an excellent way to patch some of the holes in MS-DOS.

Why Are Utilities Needed?

There are three key needs that prompt the creation of DOS-based utility programs: specialized needs, unforeseen requirements, and functions not supported by the original developers.

Specialized Needs

Some features, for example, the capability to convert a word processing file into an obscure or obsolete format, have only limited appeal. A specialized utility, perhaps developed by the author for his or her own use, may become available to serve the users who *do* need it. Utilities can fill an important niche by providing capabilities that most users would not be willing to pay extra for, but others find invaluable.

Unforeseen Requirements

Other utilities are created by clever programmers who thought of doing something the original developer never dreamed of. The grand-daddy of all DOS utilities is perhaps Peter Norton's Unerase, which makes it possible to restore "deleted" files from a disk. In poking around one of the original IBM PCs, Norton discovered that erased files aren't really removed from a disk; only the first character of their directory listing is overwritten. Until the space allocated to a file is actually used by some other file, unerasing is a relatively easy process—if you have a utility like Norton Unerase.

It's probable that the original programmers of DOS elected to erase files in the way they did because it was much faster than physically erasing or overwriting the file completely. If unerasing had been a consideration, we would have seen Undelete included in MS-DOS a lot sooner than Version 5.0. Norton Unerase and its successors are examples of utilities that extend the capabilities of an existing product.

Anti-virus programs also fall into this category. No one could have thought of including anti-virus protection in earlier versions of DOS, because viruses as we know them didn't invade desktop computers in large numbers until relatively recently. Who would have predicted in 1981 that infection-protection utilities would gain such importance only a decade later?

Unsupported Functions

A thriving industry has grown up around utilities that perform obviously useful, widely applicable functions which the developers of an operating system or application have chosen not to support. Disk caching and sophisticated memory management utilities were available long before Microsoft incorporated its first simple versions into MS-DOS and Windows. The initial SmartDrive and EMM386 products were distinctly low-end utilities, lacking the options and capabilities of third-party add-ons. Microsoft was willing to meet the basic needs of DOS users, while allowing other vendors to develop and market more advanced versions.

As you can see, these three rationales generate the vast majority of all DOS utilities and form the foundation of the new capabilities built into DOS 6.

What Kinds of Utilities Are Available?

Utilities fall into several general categories and are marketed in a variety of ways. The most important categories include the following:

➤ **DOS Command Enhancers** These utilities add new DOS commands that either do something not possible with MS-DOS or provide extra options. Some examples follow:

BUFFERS.COM   A utility furnished with QuarterDeck's QEMM memory manager that lets you check the number of DOS buffers and allocate new ones from the DOS prompt. Ordinarily, buffers can be specified only from within CONFIG.SYS.

PCOPY.EXE An enhanced COPY command with many new options.

INPUT.COM A utility that reads a keypress and stores a corresponding value in a register that can be accessed by batch files; similar to the **choice** command added to DOS 6.

4DOS This is a full replacement for DOS's COMMAND.COM, which provides four dozen new or enhanced commands and hundreds of other options.

Recent releases of DOS have included command enhancers of a type: the **mem** command, found first in DOS 4.0, augmented the capabilities of earlier commands, such as CHKDSK (which reports on memory status in a very limited way). The new /c switch for the **dir** command, which shows DoubleSpace compression ratios, is another example of DOS enhancing itself.

➤ **Application-Specific Utilities** These are utilities designed to enhance the capabilities of specific applications or to relieve some of their short-comings. Examples include the following:

DECODER.EXE Removes Ventura Publisher tag codes from files, leaving plain ASCII.

BRKUPDCX.EXE Used with computer fax programs to break up multiple image DCX files into single PCX format files. DOS 6 does not include any application-specific utilities as such.

➤ **Hardware-Specific Utilities** Utilities intended to add some function or to perform a task with a specific piece of hardware. Graphics cards are furnished with utilities that set graphics mode or change the default fonts used. Removable media drives come with special utilities to format or verify cartridges. Other hardware-oriented utilities include the following:

INTRCPT Can be used by the daring to format 360K diskettes to 720K in 1.2M disk drives.

CLOCKWORK A menu-driven clock management utility that compensates for the drift of your system clock

DATASCOPE A utility that captures and analyzes data and signals information from your serial port.

DOS 6's SmartDrive and DoubleSpace could be considered hardware-specific utilities, because they work directly with hard disk drives, floppies, and other media.

➤ **Environment-Oriented Utilities** Microsoft Windows created a whole new class of utilities designed to enhance and support the Windows environment. These utilities include icon editors, screen savers, event schedulers, File Manager and Program Manager replacement shells, and desktop accessories like calculators. Some common Windows utilities include the following:

APPBAR Provides a vertical or horizontal button bar of up to 48 application icons.

PROKEY A macro language that originated as a DOS utility.

CLIPMATE An extension to the Windows Clipboard, which captures multiple text clips for editing, saving, or pasting.

Several DOS 6 utilities come in Windows-specific versions, but none of them are intended solely to add functionality to Windows itself.

➤ **General Utilities** These utilities are general-purpose programs that perform a utility-type function (that is, something other than application-oriented tasks.) In DOS 6, Anti-Virus and Backup are housekeeping utilities. Other common utility programs include the following:

MENUDIRECT GOLD A file/directory/program manager for DOS that speeds access to files and performs functions like copy, delete, edit, find, print, and view on single or groups of tagged files.

BUFFIT Backscrolls your screen so that you can view lists of commands.

MICROLOCK A password-protection system for hard disks.

Almost any utility that doesn't fall into one of the other categories can be considered a general utility.

What Can You Expect from the DOS 6 Utilities?

Microsoft has outlined nine goals for its latest release of DOS and the utilities it contains, each designed to improve the reliability, ease-of-use, and flexibility of MS-DOS. Each of the individual utilities addresses one or more of the following goals:

➤ **Compatibility** Every third-party software developer uses DOS as one of the building blocks of each new application and utility. Therefore, any new DOS component must be compatible with tens of thousands of products that rely on the documented features of the operating system to run. DoubleSpace disk compression, for example, would be useless if it conflicted with a significant number of existing programs. Without a compelling reason to use an incompatible DoubleSpace (e.g., if it were the *only* disk compression utility available), most users would simply ignore it rather than abandon their favorite software.

➤ **Windows Support** It's not enough that MS-DOS let users run Windows. Because both are key components in the future of most users, DOS and its utilities should *add* to the value and functionality of Windows wherever possible. So, SmartDrive disk caching is tightly integrated with Windows, and utilities like Backup, Undelete, and Anti-Virus all have Windows equivalents.

➤ **Easy Setup and Installation** No utility is useful if it is so difficult to set up that the average user will be intimidated or discouraged before he or she even has had the chance to try out the software. So, DOS 6 utilities are designed to be easy to install, through an Express Setup option that requires a minimum of user input. Setup can detect what kind of hardware you have — even if *you* aren't sure — and identify other software you may be running that can conflict with installation. That means you can avoid indecipherable "Oops! We goofed! Installation Aborted! Error code X.25. Please correct and try again!" messages.

DOS 6 Setup is also safe and reversible. If you must halt conversion of a disk volume to DoubleSpace compression halfway through for some reason, you won't lose any data. If you change your mind, DOS 6 can be completely uninstalled and your system restored to its previous operating system environment.

Despite this automation and protection, DOS 6 offers custom installation options for advanced users who understand what they are doing. You can elect to install either DOS or Windows versions of Anti-Virus, Backup, and Undelete — or both versions. You may specify how memory is used, even though MemMaker is capable of setting up most RAM options by itself.

➤ **Hard Disk Management** Your hard disk is the single most common bottleneck that limits your system's performance. RAM handles information thousands of times faster, and your CPU processes data millions of times more quickly. If you ignore the trillions of clock cycles lost while your system waits for you to type something at the keyboard, most components spend a significant proportion of their working capacity waiting for the hard disk to deliver data.

To help crack this ice jam, DOS 6 includes utilities like SmartDrive to replace at least some disk accesses with quick trips to a RAM cache, or Disk Optimizer, to organize the information so that it can be most quickly retrieved from the hard disk. Both have options that knowledgeable users can deploy to optimize their systems even further.

➤ **Memory Management** Memory is relatively cheap, and it's common, especially on systems running Windows, to see 8 to 32M of available RAM. Unfortunately, the underlying design of DOS forces most of your applications to use the same first 640K of it. Memory management provides a way to minimize the bite each program takes out of that precious complement of conventional RAM by shoehorning as many components as possible into upper memory blocks between the 640K and 1024K boundaries and the high memory area in the first 64K after that. MemMaker and commands like **mem, loadhigh,** and **devicehigh** are your first line of defense against RAM cram.

➤ **Workgroup Computing** More users are extending the reach of their systems to other computing resources through networking solutions. The utility Interlnk lets you connect two computers through a cable, of course, but DOS 6's connectivity support goes far beyond that.

DOS 6 has built-in features that allow the addition of components like Workgroup Connection (originally planned to be included as a DOS 6 utility but removed at the last minute) and support for networks including Windows for Workgroups. Although DOS 6 has no built-in network access, the utilities that are included have benefits that are multiplied when you do connect to other users. MemMaker, for example, can be a crucial tool for loading network drivers or other modules into upper memory so that network overhead doesn't exact a heavy penalty in conventional memory usage.

➤ **Data Protection** For most users, the data a computer contains has a value many times that of the computer itself. If a fire struck, would you grab your computer first or your backup tapes and disks? Catastrophes don't always arrive in the form of natural disasters. Equipment can fail; users can erase key files in ingenious and inventive ways; viruses can destroy data intentionally; bugs in application programs can trash an entire hard disk; intruders can accidentally or maliciously tamper with your data.

DOS 6 provides a variety of ways to protect your information from these losses. Anti-Virus can detect and remove viruses before they do damage. Backup, if used religiously, generates copies of data that can reconstruct an image of an entire failed hard disk. Undelete can successfully resurrect an erased file from data limbo in a surprising number of instances.

➤ **System Startup** DOS 6 includes some built-in utilities and directives that streamline and safeguard system startup. Microsoft has added a CONFIG.SYS-less boot option for those times when you've managed to foul up your configuration file to the extent that your system will no longer start. None of the new DOS 6 utilities are likely to create this condition —- inappropriate EMM386 options will simply generate an error message, for example — but the capability to boot "clean" is useful. A second, interactive booting mode allows you to execute, or not execute, each line in CONFIG.SYS, as you prefer.

➤ **Documentation and Help** The Help system established with DOS 5.0 has been continued and enhanced in DOS 6, so you'll be able to easily access help screens describing key features of any of the new utilities from the DOS command line.

What You Won't Find in DOS 6

A number of utilities that were included with previous versions of DOS have been made optional for most DOS 6 users. Files that most users seldom, if ever, need were relegated to a new, non-included Supplemental Disk, which can be purchased from Microsoft for $5, plus shipping. If you purchased an Upgrade kit, a coupon is included in the back for ordering this disk. The deleted utilities and files include the following:

➤ **4201.CPI, 4208.CPI, 5202.CPI** These are code page information (CPI) files used to activate international character sets with certain IBM Proprinter and Quietwriter printers. If you don't need to use international characters with one of these printers, or with a printer that emulates one of them, you have no need for these files.

➤ **LCD.CPI** A code page information file for the PC Convertible liquid crystal screen display.

➤ **ASSIGN.COM** A conflict-prone utility that can swap drive letter assignments among hard and floppy disk drives. It tended to confuse some applications, and its assignments were ignored by others. About the only real use was as a temporary measure to outwit crude software installation programs that refused to operate from any drive other than A. Some software furnished on 5.25-inch diskettes didn't take into account that many users had configured their systems with drive B as their 5.25-inch drive; ASSIGN=A=B could temporarily change the drive letters to fool the installation program. Fortunately, almost all packages today give you the option to specify which drive you want to use, so ASSIGN has few practical applications.

➤ **BACKUP.EXE** This primitive backup program has been supplanted by the new DOS and Windows versions of Backup. You might need the original program to create backup disks for users who haven't upgraded to DOS 6.

➤ **COMP.EXE** Compares the contents of two files, byte by byte. Most DOS users have never bothered to use this utility, which was originally recommended as a check to make sure that a COPY command was completed without error. These days, disk drives are so reliable that these errors are few and far between, indeed.

➤ **EDLIN.EXE** A line-oriented ASCII file editor largely replaced by the much easier to use EDIT.EXE utility. The chief advantage of EDLIN is that its command structure can easily be manipulated by files of commands, called *scripts*, and used to automatically modify ASCII files. Few write EDLIN scripts any more; if you do, you'll want the Supplemental Disk.

➤ **EXE2BIN.EXE** This is a specialized utility that can convert some EXE files to COM files. The speed and size gains so attained are generally not significant with today's faster systems and larger hard disks.

➤ **GORILLA.BAS, MONEY.BAS, NIBBLES.BAS** These are BASIC demo programs that are fun to run once or twice but otherwise occupy a tiny amount of hard disk space to no good purpose.

➤ **GRAFTABL.COM** Enables MS-DOS to display the extended characters (ASCII 128 through 255) of a specified code page when in graphics mode. Few applications need or support this feature these days.

➤ **JOIN.EXE** Tells DOS to include a specified disk drive as if it were part of a subdirectory on another disk drive. Like ASSIGN, JOIN is a confusing and conflict-prone drive redirection command that caused more problems than it solved.

➤ **MIRROR.COM** A DOS 5.0 utility that recorded information about disks that was used by **unformat** and **undelete** to restore a reformatted disk or to recover deleted files. DOS 6's new protection capabilities superseded this short-lived add-on.

➤ **MSHERC.COM** A driver to simulate Hercules monochrome graphics, an early attempt to add graphics capabilities to the original text-only TTL IBM PC monitors.

➤ **PRINTER.SYS** This device driver was used to support code-page switching with the IBM Proprinters and Quietwriter III.

➤ **REMLINE.BAS** Removes REMark lines to reduce the size of a file.

The Supplemental Disk also contains AccessDOS utilities intended to assist persons with disabilities.

The Next Step

This chapter provided an overview of the rationale behind DOS utilities. You learned why DOS needs to be augmented with add-on programs, and some of the most common categories of utilities. Before I go on to explain how to use the individual DOS 6 utilities, it might be useful to offer a little background on how computers and DOS work. You'll find that information helpful in understanding how a given utility operates and why it is needed.

Inside DOS and Computers

It's not necessary to learn all the nitty-gritty details of DOS to use it. After all, an unfortunate number of drivers these days have difficulty identifying any part of their car that isn't covered in fake wood or velour. Most can't tell you anything about internal combustion other than it's probably a good idea. Yet, any driver can climb into any car and use it to drive from one coast to another. In transportation terms, that's power.

So, although you might not need to know exactly how your computer transportation works, you will want to know how to jump-start it, open and close the moon-roof (particularly if your battery is dead), and switch to four-wheel drive when you have to. That's what this book will do for you as you learn about DOS 6's complement of utilities. I promise not to try and turn you into an assembly language programmer.

We'll look at the need for DOS utilities in the larger scheme of things, and that will require dredging up a little microcomputer history. You'll also want to familiarize yourself with the key components of a microcomputer, components that are behind the need for DOS's utilities in the first place.

DOS didn't appear out of thin air as a miraculous complement to the first IBM PC. The genesis of MS-DOS can be traced back to the earliest personal computers, some of which didn't even have an operating system to speak of, at least not in terms of what we think of today as a disk operating system.

First Computers Had No Disk Drive

Some of the first desktop computers didn't have a disk drive. There was no boot-up process to speak of, either. When you turned early Radio Shack computers on, the CRT instantly displayed the message Memory Size?, a prompt to type in a figure to reserve some of the 4K (yes!) of memory for machine language programs. If you just pressed the Enter key, the system displayed some copyright information, the statement READY, and a > prompt.

That's right, no C> prompt. (There wasn't a disk drive, remember?) The prompt indicated that the computer had loaded BASIC and was ready to accept BASIC command line statements (e.g., NEW and LIST) or a series of numbered program lines. BASIC was, in effect, the operating system, and in that computer, it let users do anything that could be accomplished with a very limited set of tiny BASIC commands and 4K of memory. The Apple II and Commodore Pet computers of that era worked in a similar manner.

Based on RAM, CPU, and Peripherals

As different as these early computers were, they all were based on the same components: RAM, a CPU, and peripherals such as a monitor. Although your system may be based on the latest 486 or Pentium chip, it has a heritage that actually dates back to the early 1970s.

For many years, computer systems were built around central processing units, or CPUs, that consisted of transistors and other solid state devices that took up a great deal of space. However, you didn't have to be a computer scientist to read articles in *Popular Science* during the early 1970s about the amazing new computers-on-a-chip. Early microprocessors, developed as controllers for appliances, automobiles, and other consumer items, were also adapted for calculators. Almost overnight, the slide-rule became a curiosity, and bulky mechanical adding machines took their rightful place as doorstops and boat anchors. Everything from microwave ovens to VCRs soon had more intelligence than their owners. Naturally, microprocessors were also included in desktop-sized computer systems.

Early Computers Appealed to Hobbyists

Microcomputers initially appealed mostly to electronics hobbyists, the folks who liked to build their own ham radios and who usually had a couple dozen meters and oscilloscopes to figure out why they didn't work after they were built. These were the perfect folk to figure out ways to take an integrated circuit and make it talk to the outside world.

It was inevitable that among a group of tinkerers smart enough to talk to a machine using nothing but 1s and 0s there would be a few with an entrepreneurial bent. Some of these put their ideas to work within the framework of the corporations that already employed them, resulting in microcomputers like the first TRS-80 Model I from Radio Shack. Others worked out of garages and small shops, producing landmark computers like the Apple II. In either case, these ready-to-run, "turnkey" computer systems brought microcomputer power to a whole new class of users by 1977. This class included, for the first time, the business user.

IBM Enters the Field

"Business is our middle name" rather than "Think" might well be the motto of International Business Machines. As the unmistakable trend toward distributing computer intelligence to the desktop developed, IBM moved in. In 1981, the first IBM Personal Computer popularized the term "PC" and legitimized the micro for use in the largest corporations. The revolution was truly underway.

Since that time, the revolution has been more of an evolution. Instead of dozens of different computer systems, all incompatible to one extent or another, we have only two serious business computer camps: the Apple Macintosh and the IBM PC compatibles. Except for some graphics-oriented applications, such as desktop publishing, the PC has clearly been the more successful. Changes in the PC line have been gradual and individually far from earth-shaking.

In 1983, the IBM PC/XT started the trend toward fast, large-capacity mass storage devices. The following year, the IBM PC/AT heralded a new generation of computers built around a more advanced microprocessor chip. In 1987, we saw the introduction of the Personal System/2 line, which actually didn't offer a whole lot new—other than the Model 80, IBM's catch-up entry in the full 32-bit microprocessor race. From 1981 onward, all the IBM compatible systems ran, for the most part, nothing but continually enhanced versions of MS-DOS.

Inside a Microcomputer

Computers today are sometimes called *Von Neumann machines,* because they are based on concepts pioneered by mathematician John Von Neumann. His model of a computer system was important because it made possible general-purpose computers. Prior to that point, computers were hard-wired together to perform a specific computation and had to be rewired in order to do anything else.

Von Neumann proposed a system that would be *programmable.* Such systems consist of only two basic components, memory and the processor. In the case of binary computers, memory is a huge collection of 1s and 0s arranged in a sort of code that means something to the processor.

Processor Loads Data to Registers

The processor simply loads information from external memory into the processor's own internal memory locations, called *registers.* The data that is loaded tells the processor what to do next. One piece of the binary code may tell it to next load the information contained in an entirely different location to a particular register or to add the contents of one register to a third. Note that in all cases the processor is doing nothing more than moving numbers around according to the instructions it receives. It has no way of knowing whether some of the code in memory is a program or whether it is data. It is the job of the software to keep track of the difference.

All microcomputers, from the Apple Macintosh to the IBM PC, follow this Von Neumann model. As a result, they have several key components in common. One of these is the processor — or microprocessor — that computer-in-miniature that performs the adding, subtracting, and other work that make these machines useful to us.

Processor Also Includes Instructions

The microprocessor not only contains individual memory registers, but also a microcoded, built-in set of programs called *instructions*. All the processing that is done consists of loading values into these registers and performing operations on them based on the microprocessor's instructions. One instruction might tell the microprocessor to move a certain value into one register and then compare it with the value in a second. Based on the outcome of that comparison, the next instruction might ask the microprocessor to add a value to a third register or to do something else.

As an end user, you don't need to be concerned with what the microprocessor is doing at any given moment. The list of tasks to carry out, or the program are put together by the programmer either directly (by programming in "machine language" in rare cases) or through an intermediary higher level language (such as an *assembler* or Visual Basic). In the latter case, the programmers instructions are translated by the assembler, compiler, or other tool into the machine's native language of 1s and 0s.

Family Trees of Microprocessors

Since Motorola and Intel were pioneers in developing microprocessors, most of the chips used in microcomputers today belong to one family or the other. For example, some early microcomputers used either the Motorola MC6800 or a relative, the 6502. Others incorporated a rival, the Intel 8080. Both were 8-bit chips: their registers could handle information only in sets of eight 1s and 0s at a time. That is, they could store all the numbers from 00000000 to 11111111 in binary notation (0 to 256 in decimal) in a single memory location. Because they were limited to 8-bit data paths, these chips used 8-bit memory chips to temporarily store the programs and data that they worked with. In use, each individual bit of information is stored in its own location on a memory chip and moved in parallel over separate lines to other parts of memory or to the computer's registers.

You might think of 8-bit memory as a group of 8 soldiers who move in a single row, side-by-side, from one place to another. They will all arrive at their destination at the same time, which would not be the case if they moved in single file, or *serial* fashion. However, instead of a single path, eight parallel paths (a wider "road") are needed.

Intel and Motorola Still Thrive

Both the Intel and Motorola families thrive today. The Intel line chosen for the IBM computers and compatibles expanded with the 8088 microprocessor, which is a sort of hybrid. Internally, the 8088 is able to handle information in 16-bit chunks. However, to keep costs low, the chip was built to receive data from the outside in 8-bit wide form. Thus, existing 8-bit memory chips could be used. However, two steps must be carried out to fill a 16-bit register, slowing down the operation of the 8088 chip considerably.

The next generation microprocessor chip, the Intel 80286 provided true 16/16-bit operation, with both 16-bit registers and a 16-bit data path. The 80386 microprocessor upped the ante even further with true 32-bit operation. The 486 (nobody uses the 80 prefix anymore) added an on-chip 8K instruction cache, which helps the speedy microprocessor busy with fewer wasted clock cycles and a built-in math co-processor. Speeds went from the pokey 4.77 MHz of the original 8088 to the 50 MHz 486DX chip, which could be considered more than 200 times faster because it processes data through a 32-bit rather than 8-bit path.

Double-Speed Chips Offer Higher Performance

Some recent chips perform their internal calculations at double or triple speed, producing, for example, 33/66 and 33/99 MHz performance in the 486DX2-66 and 486DX3-99 processors. The latest developments at this writing is the true 66 MHz Pentium chip.

Just as a matter of interest, Motorola's 6800 chip has followed a similar evolution to the 68000, 68010, 68020, 68030, and 68040 microprocessors. These microprocessors are used both with UNIX operating systems as

well as in computers like the Apple Macintosh. The Motorola microprocessors have also had a stranglehold on the high-end workstation market
(itself dominated by Sun Microsystems.)

A computer may contain more than one microprocessor. Special chips
can be used to take over part of the processing load from the main
microprocessing unit (MPU) for graphics, display, communications, or
other tasks. For example, 386 systems are sometimes fitted with a 387
math coprocessor. High-end video cards may include a Texas Instru-
ments TIGA chip to handle video processing. The Intel SatisFAXtion
faxmodem line includes internal models with their own RAM and 80186
microprocessor.

Your microcomputer also contains a crystal that the system uses as a
reference in timing the speed of its operations, usually measured in
megahertz (MHz). The oscillation speed of the crystal is set so that the
computer does not operate faster than the microprocessor is designed to
run.

The Role of Memory

The computer's clock speed is only one measure of how fast the computer
operates. Microprocessors today are so fast that they spend an inordinate
amount of time simply waiting for the information requested from
memory, the other key component.

Memory can have its information (often system-level programs that help
the computer operate) stored permanently. This read-only-memory is
called ROM. Of more interest to us is the random-access-memory (RAM)
that can be used to store our programs and data and which must be fast
enough to keep up with the microprocessor chip to be useful.

For example, with the 286 and 386 chips, accessing memory always
requires a minimum of two clock cycles: one cycle for memory to accept
the location of the information to be accessed and a second for it to
provide the microprocessor with the contents of that location. The 486
chips may have the instructions they need already in the internal cache
and thus can keep working at high speed with few, if any wait states.
Ideally, memory should be able to supply the information to the microprocessor within the minimum number of clock cycles.

A 20 MHz 80386 chip has a clock cycle of about 50 nanoseconds, and because two cycles are required to access memory, it can accept data 100 ns after requesting it. Memory that can meet this demand would be rated as 100 ns memory. This is also known as *zero wait states*, because the microprocessor does not have to wait more than the minimum number of cycles for the data. If the memory chip can respond no more quickly than three clock cycles (150 ms for the 20 MHz chip), it is said to operate with one wait state.

Microprocessor Also Affects Speed

Another important factor constraining the speed of your computer system is the instruction set of the microprocessor itself. More advanced microprocessor chips have more powerful instructions, which theoretically can accomplish more work within a given clock cycle. For example, the 286 and higher microprocessors have what is known as *real* and *protected* modes.

In real mode, the computer operates under the assumption that only one *process* will be carried out at one time. A process is simply the name applied to an entire task, such as your application program, and includes all the activities that relate to it, including displaying images on the screen, storing and retrieving information, etc. With only one process underway at a time, the computer can safely assume that all the hardware's available resources, including memory, are available to it 100 percent of the time. DOS always works under this assumption.

Protected Mode Allows Multitasking

In protected mode, the microprocessor allows you to set aside different portions of memory for several different tasks. This protected memory is thus insulated from outside interference from the other processes. Providing memory management of this sort within the microprocessor itself makes *multitasking* as used by Windows much simpler. With multitasking, we can have several processes operating for a single user at one time. The operating system needs only to keep track of how the other resources are being used and does not need to manage the tricky task of partitioning memory.

You might guess that there is a third mode of operation, one that automatically separates not only memory but other resources. That mode, called *virtual 8086* mode does, in fact, exist on the 386 and higher chips. Virtual 8086 mode allows simulating multiple 8086 computers, each with their own memory. A computer using this scheme would in effect give you separate computer systems, each with its own operating system for use in either multitasking or in *multi-user* environments. Instead of having one user carrying out multiple tasks simultaneously, a multi-user system accommodates several users.

Anything Other Than Memory Is a Peripheral

Under the Von Neumann model, you can consider anything other than memory directly accessible to the microprocessor as a *peripheral*. However, we've reached the point where the display screen, keyboard, and even disk drives are scarcely considered peripherals any more. We think of peripherals as the printers, modems, plotters, scanners, and other gadgets that produce some sort of output or provide input from the outside world.

However, all these things and more are peripherals, and they are devices that can have an impact on how efficiently the computer system operates. Even the slowest PC can process information faster than the fastest hard disk drive can supply it or output data much faster than any printer or modem can handle it. As a result, your applications can generally be broken down into those that are limited in speed by the processor and those that are limited by the peripherals.

Who's in Charge Here?

Fortunately, for those of us who found HAL in *2001 A.D.* disquieting, computers don't do anything of their own initiative. Certainly, the microprocessor chip only responds to outside programming — but what is it that tells the disk drive to load a program into memory and then commands memory to send that first bit downstream to the microprocessor?

Von Neumann model computers have only a limited amount of control built in. Designers wanted to avoid the problems of hard-wired systems that had to be literally taken apart and rewired to perform a different set of tasks. Instead, only the minimal amount of controlling logic is built into the computer. The rest of this programming is loaded from other sources and thus can be changed as we like to alter the capabilities of the microcomputer.

IBM compatibles have a basic input/output system stored in read only memory and called the ROM-BIOS for exactly that reason. Some of this system tells the computer what to do when it is turned on — things that we always want it to do and which therefore can safely reside in permanent form in a ROM chip. One of these tasks is the power-on self-test (abbreviated POST). Here, the computer checks itself out briefly, including examining the memory installed in your system. Next, the system activates drive A and tries to load some instructions from the first sector on the first side of that drive. If no disk is there on drive A, or if the door to the drive is open, the ROM-BIOS will be unable to read the information it needs. Instead, it will attempt to find that data on the first hard disk. It goes to a specific location and loads a bootstrap program that enables the system to load the rest of the most-used program in the world: MS-DOS.

Finally, an Operating System

The reason we need a disk operating system is that computers require a software overseer to manage anything more than a limited set of peripherals. The first computers worked fine when the system consisted of a keyboard, a CRT, a cassette recorder, and some memory. After the industry began moving toward more sophisticated types of peripherals, however, BASIC was no longer satisfactory as an operating environment.

Of course, an operating system isn't a strict necessity. Each software program that you run could easily communicate directly with all the components of your PC—from the microprocessor itself to the CRT screen, keyboard, printer, and hard disk. That would be an extraordinary waste of human and computer resources, however. Each time a programmer began developing software for a personal computer, he or she would have to develop routines to handle common chores, such as input/output to the disk and writing to the screen.

Avoiding Reinventing the Wheel

No programmer worthy of the name would reinvent the wheel for each new program. Any software designer would develop code only once and then reuse it again and again within a program. Then the code would go into a software library to become part of that programmer's permanent toolkit. This approach would still involve a great deal of duplication of effort, however, because each programmer would have to develop the same routines others had already written. It's also likely that any given library of routines would not include the best and most efficient examples possible.

In this scenario, programs would be longer than necessary, because many of them would incorporate routines that duplicated those found in other programs. Also, some programs would run much faster than others, because the programmer happened to develop more efficient basic routines.

There's another problem. Hardware configurations of PCs can vary, even among those conforming to the IBM standards. The computer hardware can accommodate some of these differences. In fact, PCs have provisions in their read-only memory (ROM) for handling various types of hard disk configurations, or *geometries*. The CMOS setup program included with your computer probably has up to 48 hard disk types (including one or two user-definable definitions).

But there are other, much more subtle differences between computer systems. Therefore, without an operating system, programs would have to be incredibly complex to accommodate all conceivable hardware differences.

A better solution is to write a program interface that fits between the hardware and the software applications. When a program wants to fetch information from the hard disk, for example, it needn't interrogate the disk to see how it happens to store information or how that information is cataloged. Instead, the request for data can go to the software supervisor, which accesses the hard disk and forwards the information—or perhaps an explanation of why it can't be found—to the program. All the software a user might have can use this method, allowing the common software interface to replace individual program modules.

Advantages of an Operating System

There are several advantages to this scheme, over and above simplifying software applications. For example, the computer manufacturer can change the supervising program to compensate for significant differences in hardware. The commands received from the application programs remain the same; the only thing that alters is the way the interface program puts them to work with a specific hardware configuration.

A standard program interface can easily accommodate all the possibilities, either through built-in routines or by means of add-on modules called *drivers.* Drivers are a kind of utility. EMM386, SmartDrive, and DoubleSpace all work through drivers. Again, the software application doesn't have to concern itself with every detail of displaying text or graphics on the screen if it uses the services provided by the supervising program.

DOS is the most common supervising program in use today. We still employ the term, derived from "disk operating system," even though DOS functions go far beyond supervising disk drives. Much of the interaction between you and your computer system flows through DOS.

Some Software Bypasses DOS

Of course, some software bypasses DOS to access the hardware directly. For example, DOS is notoriously slow in writing to the screen. When all PCs were 4.77 MHz 8088-based models, it was tempting to write to the screen by using routines in the BIOS, rather than those provided by DOS. By doing so, however, the programmer risked creating software that would refuse to run on near-compatible computers.

Most PCs run much faster today, so it is not as necessary to bypass DOS as it used to be. Moreover, the ROM-BIOS found in almost all PC-compatible computers closely duplicates the code of the IBM BIOS. So, compatibility problems have almost vanished.

Some software still does a few tricks to improve performance. Windows 3.1, for example, uses a device called FastDisk, which sends commands such as **copy** directly to the hard drive controller instead of through DOS and your system's BIOS. The downside, of course, is that you must customize FastDisk for each hard disk controller in your system.

Pre-MS-DOS Operating Systems

As you might guess, microcomputer disk operating systems predate the IBM PC by quite a few years. Digital Research, Inc., developed the early CP/M operating systems for 8-bit computers based on the Intel 8080 family of microprocessors. Although other disk operating systems came along, CP/M was the most widely used control program for microcomputers.

Indeed, it was the only common link shared by the many very different computer systems of the day. For example, if you had a Radio Shack (later Tandy) computer, you used TRS-DOS or some variation and could run only the programs written for that environment. Translating software from one operating system to another was extremely time-consuming and usually not worth the bother.

CP/M Allowed Transportable Software

Nonetheless, computers as different as the Radio Shack Model 4 and the Commodore 128 (they were based on entirely different microprocessor families) could be made to run special versions of CP/M. With this common ground, nearly any software package written for CP/M could be transported from one computer to another just by translating from one floppy disk format to another. CP/M was not only one of the first disk operating systems for desktop computers, it was also the most widely used and compatible operating system in an era filled with incompatible products.

It seemed logical, then, to adapt CP/M to the 16-bit 8086 microprocessor, which, after all, was a member of the same 8080 family and upwardly compatible in many ways. But CP/M-86 didn't arrive soon enough to suit Tim Paterson, a hardware engineer and co-owner of Seattle Computer Products. Paterson began developing an operating system called 86-DOS that was designed to look like CP/M to end users, although the program code itself was entirely different.

Microsoft Enters the Arena

At that time, Microsoft Corporation was already well established in the industry because of its de facto standard BASIC. You sometimes see descriptions of a "then-unknown" or "tiny" Microsoft rescued from obscurity simply by providing the initial MS-DOS operating system for the IBM PC.

The actual tale of how MS-DOS won the IBM contract and purchased Paterson's software has been recounted in great detail in excellent books like *Hard Drive* and *Accidental Empires*. It's a fascinating story that I won't repeat here.

However, to put things in perspective, as small as it was, Microsoft was already considered a major player by those who had experience in the industry. The personal computer industry itself was small in those days, with leading systems selling approximately 200,000 to 300,000 units over the course of a year or more. Microsoft BASIC was almost universally used, and, if Digital Research wasn't destined to provide the first PC operating system in 1981, Microsoft was a logical second choice. It is true that when the IBM PC took off beyond anyone's expectations, Microsoft grew with it, into the giant it is today.

Microsoft Licenses DOS

Back in 1980, Microsoft licensed Paterson's DOS, which was renamed PC-DOS and introduced in 1981 along with the first IBM PCs. In the early days of the PC, IBM offered both MS-DOS and CP/M-86. I can remember wondering which would emerge as the winner of the PC horse race. Keep in mind that it was still a wide-open contest. Hobbyists owned most of these machines, even those found in business environments. The relatively large number of CP/M users still represented only a small percentage of the millions of PCs that were to be sold in the years following 1981.

So, CP/M's "head start" didn't do it much good. MS-DOS was priced at a fraction of the cost of the Digital Research offering, so, not surprisingly, MS-DOS became the standard. Meanwhile, CP/M continued to evolve into an MS-DOS-compatible operating system under names such as Concurrent CP/M and Concurrent DOS. If you want to stretch a point, CP/M eventually became DR DOS.

DOS Revisions Since 1981

Since 1981, MS-DOS has undergone almost a dozen major revisions. The first three versions of DOS—DOS 1, DOS 2, and DOS 3—were associated with the introduction of new hardware. After that, IBM's influence over the industry began to wane, and DOS Versions 4.0, 5.0, and 6.0 were driven more by marketing considerations as technology and needs changed. Each new release of DOS included new utilities, generally in the form of new external commands.

Some of these were required by hardware developments. MS-DOS 2.0 was released in March, 1983, with the first built-in support of hard disks, a change that really launched the personal computer as a useful business tool.

MS-DOS 3.0 to 3.31 added useful new commands and support for networking, although it wasn't until the 1990s that desktop networking really began to take off. DOS 3 also moved us from 5.25-inch, 360K floppy disks to the 5.25-inch, 1.2M and 3.5-inch, 720K and 1.44M floppies we use today. These floppy disks first appeared on IBM PC-AT and IBM PS/2 computers.

MS-DOS 4.01 really did not give most of us anything useful, unless you were enamored of clunky shells or wanted an expanded memory specification (EMS) implementation different from that of everyone else in the industry. DOS 4 was largely ignored, with most users sticking with DOS 3.3 during a period of operating system stagnation that lasted from 1987 until DOS 5.0 was unveiled in June, 1991.

DOS 5.0 drew attention largely because it fixed things that should have been done right in DOS 4.0 in the first place and because it added a few sorely needed memory-management features and utilities that had been available from third parties since the late 1980s. Now DOS 6.0 adds more utilities and gains a whole version number, even though the changes to DOS itself are rather insignificant.

Components of DOS

Since even "official" DOS includes utilities, you need to understand how utility programs differ from DOS proper. MS-DOS itself is a fairly small program, augmented by a large group of external utility programs, including FORMAT and FDISK. Only three core programs, called system files, are actually needed for DOS to run. In general, you do not even see two of these programs because DOS makes them invisible on your hard disk and further protects them from accidental erasure. If you ask for a directory of files on your disk, you'll never run across these invisible programs—IO.SYS and MSDOS.SYS, also called IBMBIO.COM and IBMDOS.COM in some versions of DOS. DOS 6 adds a third core program, DBLSPACE.BIN, which is loaded to provide support for DoubleSpace compressed volumes. I lump it in with the others because it is loaded into memory *before* MS-DOS begins carrying out the commands in CONFIG.SYS.

IO.SYS and MSDOS.SYS contain a core of routines that allow the operating system to interface with the PC hardware. These routines include code to handle the clock, the CRT, the keyboard, the printer, and the drive used to boot the operating system.

In addition, MSDOS.SYS contains the *application program interface* (API). You'll see this acronym a great deal in the future, particularly in connection with OS/2. The API provides all the key services required of the operating system by your software. This interface effectively insulates the program from the hardware by accepting and filling requests for disk, file, and CRT services.

COMMAND.COM—One of Three System Files

A third file, called COMMAND.COM in any version of DOS, is also necessary. However, it is stored as an ordinary visible file on your hard disk.

The COMMAND.COM file serves as a command processor. When you type a command such as DIR at the keyboard and press the Enter key, COMMAND.COM intercepts the characters you type. The command processor examines the command line that you typed and tries to make sense of it. It isn't mandatory to use COMMAND.COM with DOS, as long as you furnish a replacement. 4DOS, for example, is an alternative command processor that can work with MS-DOS or DR DOS to provide an enhanced set of commands.

Some commands are *internal* commands, built into and carried out by the command processor itself. Other commands, such as FORMAT or XCOPY, are external commands and, as such, are programs in their own right. External commands were actually the first utility programs for DOS. Instead of rewriting and replacing the entire command processor every time a function was added, the developers of DOS just created new programs that perform the needed tasks. There's really not a lot of difference between DOS's **xcopy** and an add-on utility from a third party, such as the shareware program PCOPY, in logical terms. The real difference is in the functions they perform.

The Next Step

That's all we need to understand how computers and DOS works. You can see that memory forms such a fundamental component of the complete system that memory-based utilities make up some of the most important utilities included with DOS 6. It's time to start exploring individual DOS 6 utilities. We'll start with the memory management components, because so many of the other utilities build on the capabilities they provide.

First, we'll look at how RAM—or the lack thereof—affects system performance, and then we'll look at what DOS 6 can do to help make improvements in the chapters of Part II.

Part II:
Memory Management

The chapters in this section deal with memory and how it is used by MS-DOS. You'll learn about the new MemMaker software and some of the techniques used to squeeze every last bit of utility out of the 640K of memory DOS applications are limited to. You'll also find out about XMS, EMS, HMA, UMBs, and other types of memory that are sometimes needlessly clouded in an alphabet soup of acronyms. Tools like HIMEM and EMM386, which have been available for awhile, will be examined from a fresh perspective.

Memory is easily one of the most important aspects of your computer system, because everything that happens flows through memory. When you look back at the history of computing, much of the progress can be traced to simply removing bottlenecks. Each new breakthrough manages to set the stage for the next barrier we encounter as we move down the road of technology. That's because every software and hardware innovation calls for parameters and boundaries, and these invariably become too restrictive as our needs and capabilities grow by leaps and bounds.

Memory can be one of the tightest bottlenecks in your system or one of your most flexible tools. You'll soon see that it's not how much of it you have, but how you use it.

Introduction to Memory

Our use of random access memory (RAM) in personal computers has been tightly bound by a series of bottlenecks over the years. MS-DOS helps overcome some of them, and operating systems of the future like Windows NT will remove the rest of the barriers. Looking back with the knowledge we have today, it seems impossible that computer and software designers could have been so short-sighted.

Take the 640K barrier (please!). When the IBM PC was introduced, it was offered with 16K of memory in the base model, and 64K of RAM was the upper limit on many of the popular desktop computer systems of the day. And memory was expensive. I once paid $300 for a 16K upgrade for an early system.

Even when incredibly dense 64K-bit chips became available, we could scarcely imagine that 10 sets of them, 640K, would become the standard minimum configuration for most computer users. In those days, IBM

PCs with 256K of memory were considered powerful setups. Folks who worked with large spreadsheets might even have 384K, or possibly a full 512K of RAM. Indeed, it took a ROM upgrade to allow original PCs to access the full 640K that MS-DOS allowed. How could we possibly need more?

It didn't take long to find out. Industry pundits are quick to recall that most early software had to run in 64K and that the surplus of RAM that followed the IBM PC encouraged developers to become sloppy. Suddenly, we had software that required 128K, or even 256K to run.

In truth, software authors didn't suddenly become lazy. Freed from the performance limitations of swapping overlay after overlay in and out of a limited 64K address space, they began writing exciting, more powerful software. Crude graphics were replaced by high-resolution images. Software soon needed all the memory it could get.

Memory for Applications and Data

Keep in mind that some types of programs use memory just to store working files. Large spreadsheets can be manipulated more easily if they can be kept in memory, rather than pulled from disk a piece at a time. The size of these files is determined not by the software writer, but by the end user's application. Given the high-powered capabilities of applications, it's no wonder that 640K soon became a serious bottleneck.

The next thing we decided we needed was a form of multi-tasking. We liked all the different things the computer could do and wanted to be able to switch back and forth between them quickly. Some enterprising programmers discovered a few undocumented DOS calls and invented the terminate-and-stay-resident (TSR) program, or "pop-up" as they were called in those days. TSRs were developed that could do just about anything you wanted: dial your phone, write a memo, provide synonyms for your word processing program. You could pop up one of them right in the middle of whatever you were doing by pressing a hot key combination. When the secondary task at hand was finished, the TSR could be put away and you could return to what you were doing before.

These mini-programs had to co-exist in RAM with your application program, so you had to have enough memory for both. Soon, we were seeing remarkably efficient TSRs that advertised they used "only" 64K of RAM. If you happened to use three or four of these, you quickly found that you didn't have enough memory left to run your applications.

For some of us, that led to a comedy of errors. We might have three or four different system configurations, and reboot using a different AUTOEXEC.BAT file every time we wanted to do another set of tasks; or we used utilities that would allow loading and unloading TSRs in various combinations. Working within the 640K barrier made computer use complex for the average power user who sought to do things that neither the hardware nor operating system were really designed for.

Memory Needn't Be Complicated

By 1985, we had the 80286 microprocessor, something called extended memory, an add-on hardware solution called expanded memory, and even more complexity to worry over. DOS hadn't changed to accommodate these new developments and wouldn't for five more years until DOS 5.0 was released. (DOS 4 tended to complicate memory usage rather than improve it.)

Von Neumann-based computers can deal with memory in different ways. The Macintosh line has always dealt with memory as a huge, flat model that saw all of it (at least the first 8M) on a more or less equal basis. We PC users have not been so lucky. We didn't start out with a nice, clean, 32-bit microprocessor like the Mac did. The first IBM PC was introduced with a chip that processed information internally in 16-bit-wide chunks but had only an 8-bit data path to the outside world. The number of paths available to address this memory also was limited to 20.

The 1M Limit

That means there were, in binary, only 11111111111111111111 different addresses (1,047,575 in decimal) that could be used to specify different memory locations, each of which can store a single byte of data.

The 80286 microprocessor has 24 address lines and can address 16M of RAM, and the 80386 and higher chips have 32 address lines for up to 4G (that's gigabytes) of useful RAM. Fortunately, (or unfortunately, depending on your viewpoint) to allow the later microprocessors to be compatible with the millions of 8088 and 8086 computers in use, Intel built several different modes into the last three generations.

Advanced Processors Play Dumb

In one of these, which you will recall is referred to as real mode, the 80286, 80386, 80486, and Pentium chips pretend that they are unable to directly address more than 1M of memory. In the other mode, protected mode, the more advanced microprocessors can use their full range of memory. As I mentioned in the last chapter, 486 and higher chips also have a third mode, called virtual 8086 (or simply V-86 by programmers), which allows the microprocessor to allocate specific blocks of memory and to run programs as if each were running in a separate dedicated 8086 computer.

However, the most common operating systems used with these chips, MS-DOS and DR DOS, run only in real mode (lacking help from utilities called DOS extenders). Special supervisory programs, called control programs, are used to provide access to the microprocessor's other modes. DOS usually runs under the supervision of the control program to allow you to run your MS-DOS-dependent software.

So, any IBM compatible using MS-DOS generally works within the limitations set up by the original 8088-based IBM PC. The most sophisticated 486 system may operate just as if it were a very, very fast IBM PC.

Conventional Memory

The basic 1M accessible to 8088/86 PCs and the later systems that emulate them is sometimes called conventional memory, but more frequently the term is used to refer to the lower 640K set aside for the use of the operating system and your applications. The remaining 384K is allocated for special system use. Figure 4.1 shows a simplified map of a typical computer system's memory.

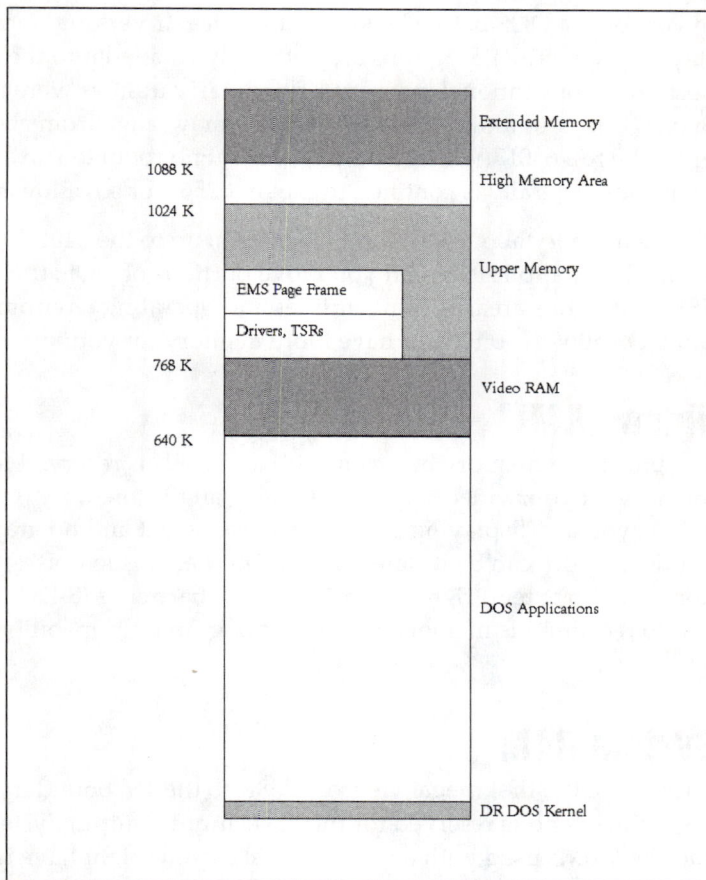

Figure 4.1. A simplified memory map of a computer's RAM.

Conventional Memory: Application RAM

The first 1M of memory is divided into three sections. The lower 640K is called the *application area*. Programmer types sometimes refer to this as the transient program area, or TPA, a term that dates back to the CP/M era or before. The nomenclature is fairly descriptive: program code loaded into this area may be replaced from time to time as an application runs.

In versions of DOS before DOS 5.0, all device drivers and terminate-and-stay-resident (TSR) programs are "officially" loaded into the lowest portion of conventional memory. (Third-party utilities were the first to bypass this limitation.) This low memory may range from about 40K on up to the full 640K (which would leave you no room to run any applications) but generally is confined to the first 256K or so of lower memory.

All the memory above DOS and its drivers, up to the 640K limit, is available for applications. If you move portions of DOS, the drivers, or TSRs out of this area, as some utilities and operating environments like MS-DOS allow you to, you have more memory for your applications.

Video RAM

The portion of memory between 640K and 768K is reserved for video memory. If your video card doesn't need all this memory (if, for example, you are displaying only monochrome text and no graphics), some of this memory can be reclaimed for DOS use. In such cases, the application area can extend right up past the 640K barrier. MS-DOS may allow you to reclaim this memory, at the cost of graphics capability, while it is being used.

System RAM

The area of the first megabyte from 768K to the 1M boundary is called the system area and is reserved for the Basic Input/Output System (BIOS) and the ROMs used with any add-on cards you might have installed in your system. This portion of your memory is also sometimes called adapter RAM because of the video adapters and other boards that may use some of this block.

Usually, the areas occupied are not contiguous; there may be gaps as large as 128K or as small as 4K. This unused address space can be put to work to hold device drivers, TSRs, and other code that would normally reside in low areas of your application RAM. You need a special memory handler, such as EMM386, that can do this for you. The portions of memory used under this scheme are commonly called *upper memory blocks*, or UMBs.

High Memory Area: HMA RAM

I already mentioned the 20 address lines available in the 8088/8086 chip. These are numbered, programmer fashion, A0 to A19. Ordinarily, when you would try to address memory beyond the 1M barrier, the system would "wrap around," taking you automatically from A19 back to A0. However, there is a bug in the system that allows the 21st address line, A20, to be accessed instead. This brings an additional 64K of memory, immediately above the 1M boundary, into view and makes it accessible by DOS and programs written to use it.

This is commonly called the *high memory area* (HMA), and both Quarterdeck and Microsoft claim to have invented it, or at least, of developing early techniques for accessing and using this memory. Quarterdeck put HMA to work with its QEMM memory manager, and Microsoft released a driver called HIMEM.SYS. The best application yet for this free memory has been to enable HIMEM.SYS to put part of MS-DOS itself in this block, removing it from lower memory.

Memory Notation

I've been using decimal notation to this point to mark the various memory boundaries for you. However, it's actually more convenient to divide your megabyte of conventional memory the same way your computer does—into 16 chunks, or pages, of 64K each. Those pages are labeled with the hexadecimal digits 0, 1, 2, 3, 4, 5, 6, 7, 8, 9, A, B, C, D, E, and F.

Using that numbering scheme, DOS is allocated 10 of those pages, from 0 to 9, for a total of 640K. The remaining six, A through F, are set aside for the system to assign to things such as video ROM and other read only memory. Your scanner interface or network adapter may contain a ROM that needs to coexist with your video cards and other devices within that upper 384K. We'll look at possible conflicts in this area in a later chapter.

A and B Pages for Video RAM

As noted previously, the first 128K of high RAM, the A and B pages, are supposed to be reserved for video memory. Depending on the type of video adapter you have, the actual amount required may be as little as 4K or as much as the full 128K. The top end of high RAM, the F page, is also reserved for the system ROM. Again, not all systems use all of this, nor is all of it required after bootup is completed.

Of the remaining pages—C, D, and E—some may be co-opted by various video ROMs and other devices, including, on the PC/AT, an empty ROM socket! Another full 64K page has to be set aside as a page frame for expanded memory specification (EMS) RAM, if you plan to use it. EMS and other non-conventional memory types are explained in the next section.

Other Memory Types

Now that you understand the 1M of memory that is accessible to all 8088/86 and later microprocessors, look at some other types that are made available by special features built into the 80286, 80386, and higher chips or that can be patched onto 8088/86 systems with some hardware add-ons.

The two key types are extended memory and expanded memory, and it's easy to get them confused. As you'll learn in the next sections, you can think of extended memory as extending from the end of conventional memory continuously to the upper limits of your particular microprocessor. Expanded memory, on the other hand, can be visualized as a "balloon" of RAM that expands through a tiny window. Only the portion bulging through the window at any one time is visible to DOS. The analogies are far from perfect, but they can help you keep the distinction between extended and expanded memory clear in your mind.

Extended Memory

Extended memory is memory above 1M—to 16M on 286 machines and up to 4G on later microprocessors. You can think of it as a seamless extension of your computer's memory, starting right where the first megabyte leaves off. Computers using an 8088/86 chip cannot have any extended memory because they are, as we've seen, limited to addressing a single megabyte. Figure 4.2 illustrates the concept.

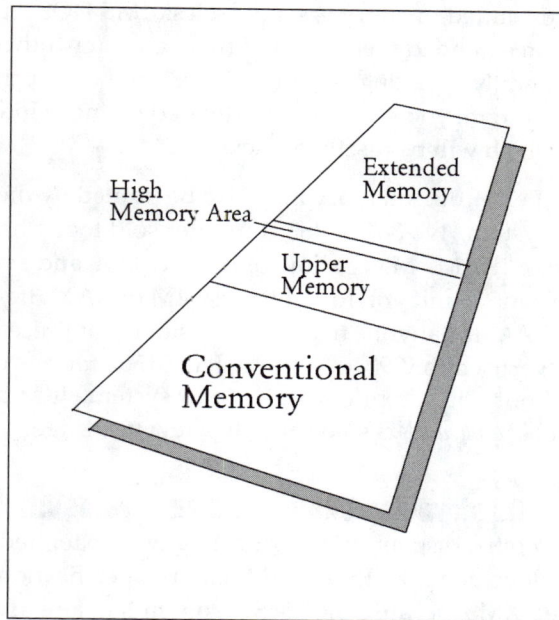

Figure 4.2. Extended memory

Intel 286 and later systems can use all the extended memory installed when they are running in their native modes, called *protected mode*. Unfortunately, most of the time these chips are confined to the real mode that DOS uses. Then they face the same 1M limitations the 8088/86 microprocessors must live with.

The exception is when special protected mode software is used. OS/2 is a protected mode operating system. Microsoft Windows uses protected operation for its Standard and Enhanced modes. Certain DOS extenders, like the one available from Phar Lap, also enable protected mode on 286, 386, and 486 systems.

Your System's Split Personality

You can see that your computer may have a split personality. When running Windows, in Standard or Enhanced modes, extended memory is great. When you run programs outside of Windows or another DOS extender, extended memory is semi-useless. MS-DOS lets you set up a RAM disk in extended memory, and there are a few other things you can do, but generally speaking real-mode DOS can't do much with it. With a 386 or 486 system, you *can* convert extended memory into expanded memory, which will be discussed next.

Your use of extended memory may also be limited by the design of your computer system. No 386 or 486 computer sold today has room to install 4 gigabytes of RAM. Many allow only 16 to 32M, and even top-of-the-line models may limit you to as little as 64M of RAM. If you think 64M is too much RAM for anyone to afford, consider that I recently saw 4M SIMMs advertised for $90; that's less than $1500 for one of the most useful add-ons you can purchase for your system. It's not much more than what 60M *hard disks* sold for only a few years ago.

Microsoft Standardized Extended Memory Specification

There was no fixed set of rules for dealing with extended memory until Microsoft developed the Extended Memory Specification. This is usually abbreviated XMS, because the EMS acronym had already been claimed by the Expanded Memory Specification. Now vendors generally adhere to the guidelines set down by Microsoft.

Expanded Memory

Expanded memory is a special type of memory that is available to any IBM compatible computer, from those using the 8088 microprocessor on up. The Expanded Memory Specification (EMS) bypasses the limitations of the low-end chip's hardware through special hardware of its own. You need this special hardware to use EMS in an 8088/86 or 286 computer. All 386, 486, and higher systems have special memory-handling capabilities built in that allow software developers to write memory managers which can emulate hardware EMS boards using the extended memory you already have. EMS was developed as a way of expanding the amount of RAM available to DOS programs, either to execute program code itself or as a place to store the data that the application uses. Even though addressing EMS is more complicated than using extended memory, you can use EMS in any of your microprocessor's modes. So, EMS memory is available in real mode for running larger applications.

You can think of expanded memory as a balloon of RAM, peeking through a window called a page frame. Figure 4.3 illustrates the idea.

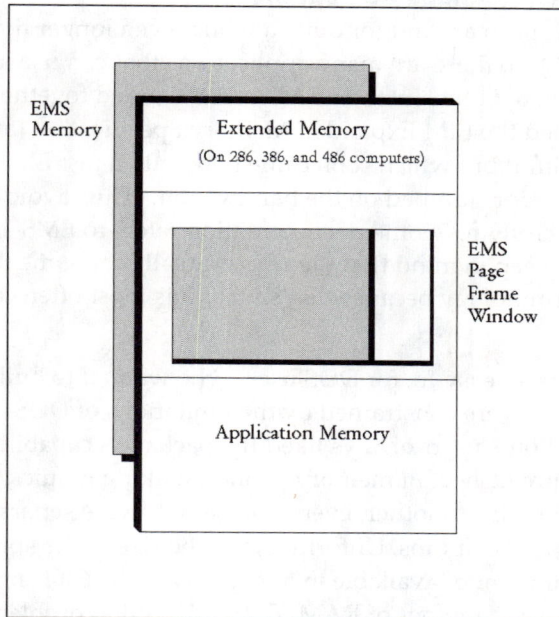

Figure 4.3. Expanded memory.

EMS Helps Improve Performance of DOS Programs

Because even EMS is faster than repeated hard disk accesses, these programs can run faster than they would without expanded memory (although slower than if they were somehow able to use extended memory instead). Memory managers for 386/486 computers can even let you use large blocks of expanded memory to run several programs at the same time.

Unfortunately, only applications written specifically for EMS can use it directly. These applications include spreadsheet programs like Lotus 1-2-3 and Ventura Publisher. Other software can use EMS only when running under a multitasking memory manager like Quarterdeck's QEMM.

Even then, they don't know they are using EMS; the application thinks that it is running in conventional memory.

Many Applications Compatible

EMS has been around for quite a while (even longer than extended memory), so there are many applications that can use it. It was developed when Lotus, Intel, and Microsoft banded together to create what was called the LIM Expanded Memory Specification (after the founding consortium) but which soon came to be called just EMS when AST and other vendors jumped on the bandwagon. (Thus avoiding the ridiculous LIMA acronym.) Some documentation refers to EMS as LIM, so you'll want to keep in mind that the two are really the same thing. I'll use the EMS terminology because that's what it is most often called in everyday use.

EMS was an easy fix for DOS users who wanted to build huge spreadsheets but were constrained by the limitations of DOS memory. Advanced Lotus users always liked the package's capability to keep an entire spreadsheet in memory at once, making it quick and easy to move from one cell to another, even if those cells were separated by hundreds of rows and columns. Unfortunately, the size of the spreadsheet is limited by the amount of available memory. Given the 640K limit of DOS, many users quickly ran out of RAM. EMS solved that problem and opened the door to new applications written specifically to take advantage of the new type of memory.

A Hardware Solution

It's important to note that expanded memory is essentially a hardware solution, requiring special boards that contain the circuitry and firmware that do most of the work in any computer using a chip on the wrong side of the 386. In computer systems with 286 and earlier microprocessors, you can't use just any memory board to get EMS. You must have a board built specifically to comply with one of several EMS specifications.

For 8088/8086 computers, your EMS board must be an 8-bit board for one of your 8-bit slots. All 286 systems require a 16-bit EMS board. Some of these, like the BocaRam AT Plus, can be configured as either EMS memory or extended memory. In a 286 computer, you'll probably want to use such a memory adapter as EMS memory, unless you have a special need for extended memory.

EMS Emulated by Advanced Chips

The situation is different with 80386 and 80486 systems. Those micropro-cessors can simulate expanded memory from the available extended memory and, therefore, do not require a special EMS board. If you use a dual-purpose board like the BocaRam in an 386/486 system, you'll want to configure it as extended memory rather than expanded memory. A special memory manager like EMM386.EXE, QEMM-386, or 386Max can change as much or as little of your extended memory to EMS as you want, but it can't change memory that is defined in hardware as EMS RAM back to extended memory.

EMS 3.2

There have been several expanded memory specifications, but most of today's software supports only the most stable versions—EMS 3.2 and EMS 4.0. We'll look at EMS 3.2 first.

The easiest way to understand expanded memory (EMS) is to visualize a window, or frame, through which your DOS applications can look. With the earliest expanded memory specification still used today, EMS 3.2, this window consists of four 16K pages of contiguous memory, which form a 64K page frame. Under EMS 3.2, your operating system can "see" no more than 64K of EMS at one time. However, a special program called an expanded memory manager, can move various 64K segments in and out of the window rapidly as they are required.

You may have 6 or 8M of expanded memory available and think that your expanded memory manager is working hard to shuffle that vast expanse of RAM in and out of the view of DOS through your tiny 64K window.

Actually, the data isn't moved anywhere. Instead, a bank-switching system is used to move the address of the window itself to the section of memory that needs to be looked at. Hence, EMS memory access can be very fast. Figure 4.3 may help you visualize how EMS memory looks to your microprocessor.

Because of the 64K limitation, EMS 3.2 was good for its intended purpose: providing spreadsheets and other programs with a window to larger data areas. However, it's not really practical to perform multitasking through such a tiny frame.

Expanded memory boards sold for 8088/8086 and 286 systems are furnished with appropriate expanded memory managers, which may support EMS 3.2, the later EEMS, EMS 4.0, or all three, depending on the hardware. You're better off purchasing a board that supports all current EMS versions.

If you want to gain access to EMS memory without buying an EMS board for your 80386, you can purchase a separate memory manger, such as the QEMM-386 and 386Max I mentioned earlier.

EEMS and EMS 4.0

EMS 3.2 was quickly superseded by two new expanded memory specifications—enhanced expanded memory specification (EEMS) and EMS 4.0. These allow mapping of multiple pages of varying sizes into the EMS page frame. Most newer EMS boards and memory managers support these specifications and are backwardly compatible with EMS 3.2 as well. Some applications require an EMS version higher than 3.2.

EMS 4.0 lets you move data in blocks of up to 64 pages (a full megabyte) making it possible with 386 and 486 systems to shuffle the equivalent of an 8088/86 chip's addressable RAM in and out very quickly. In addition, the EMS RAM does not have to be contiguous; the memory manager can use whatever EMS memory it has available with few restrictions. In fact, the page frame is no longer required, although it is retained for backward compatibility with programs (actually, most EMS-aware software) that require it.

How Do I Get EMS?

As I noted earlier, if you have an 8088/8086- or 286-based computer, you must use an add-on EMS board to get this type of memory. MS-DOS can use upper memory blocks with any of these as long has you have EMS that conforms to the LIM 4.0 specification. Because of the limitations of the microprocessors, you must use special hardware tricks to configure memory that is used as EMS in these computers. In fact, it is desirable to bring as much of your computer's memory as possible under the control of the EMS board, so many vendors recommend disabling memory above 256K on your motherboard. The EMS board "backfills" from 256K up to the 640K that is usable by DOS and configures the rest of its memory as EMS.

EMS Page Frame

You'll also need to set aside a 64K block of memory that DOS can use to view a page of EMS. This page frame can reside in DOS memory (the memory from 0 to 640) or be placed above 640K by the memory manager if you have a continuous 64K block of memory there. EMM386 has special commands that let you specify where to place this frame.

Sometimes you can have problems locating a contiguous 64K block, because there might not be enough space between the addresses used by the various adapter cards in your system. Frequently, you can change the addresses used by these cards to free up an upper memory block that can be used as a page frame. Some boards, such as Irma-type IBM 3270 emulators don't have addresses that can be changed, however.

As noted, if you have an 80386, 80486, or Pentium computer, you don't need any special EMS boards. Memory managers like MS-DOS's EMM386 can convert any or all of your extended memory to expanded memory.

Expanded memory can be used directly by some programs. These programs store large files—particularly data or image files—in expanded memory.

What Can I Do with Memory?

MS-DOS enables you to use your memory better in a number of ways. We'll look at them in more detail in the next chapter. However, this summary will help you get started thinking.

MS-DOS allows you to reduce the amount of conventional memory used by your operating system, TSRs, device drivers, and other non-applications programs. This is done by loading parts of them into HMA or UMB. In some cases, a tiny stub of code is left behind in lower memory, but this typically occupies much less space than the full program or utility would have used.

MS-DOS lets you use extended or expanded memory for some utilities, such as RAMDRIVE.EXE and SmartDrive, which would normally use conventional memory.

MS-DOS lets you manage your extended memory and expanded memory better.

The Next Step

With the background about different memory types out of the way, it's time to put that knowledge to work in using DOS 6's memory management utilities. We'll look at MemMaker and how it uses HIMEM, EMM386, and other tools to get the most from the RAM you have.

Getting More Memory

Technology has changed the way we use computers dramatically in the last decade, but as you saw in the last chapter, you can never have too much memory. When hobbyists built their own computers on bread-boards with 256 bytes of RAM, even 4K seemed like a fabulous luxury. The earliest personal computers were furnished with 4K of expensive memory and could be upgraded to an incredible 48 to 64K. Original IBM PCs could be purchased with as little as 16K of RAM and were expand-able to 512 to 640K. Do you sense a pattern, here? Computer technology has continually evolved to support more memory than most users could possibly need or afford, yet we soon outgrow those limitations.

This chapter will show you how to get more memory for your computer, and the next chapter will tell you how to get more from the memory you have, using MemMaker.

Memory Is Cheap—But Can You Use It?

According to one industry reporter, a Microsoft official staging a new product introduction posed a rhetorical question to his audience: "What is Microsoft best known for?"

"The 640K barrier!" shouted a member of the audience. Almost everyone laughed, even though the infamous 640K barrier wasn't Microsoft's fault. Despite the innovations Microsoft has developed (or purchased on our behalf), which include MS-DOS, Windows, and the technology behind many of the DOS 6 utilities discussed in this book, we associate their products first and foremost with the way they use the memory we have available. After all, a programming language or operating system is severely limited if it can work with only 64K at a time, and an upper limit of 640K is a very real barrier when you're dealing with applications that have data files that can average 2 or 3M each.

The demands that modern applications make on permanent magnetic storage (your hard disks and other media) and on temporary storage (random access memory, or RAM) deserve some special attention. It's easy enough to say that the more hard disk space and RAM you have, the better, and let it go at that. But the technology of both sorts of storage is changing so rapidly that you need more specific information. How much storage is too little? How much is a lot? How do you use it when you have it?

Why Memory Is Important

Some software absolutely requires that you have an atypical memory configuration. Some programs won't work unless you have a minimum amount of extended or expanded memory, which is unfortunate for the many users who have allocated all their extra memory in the opposite configuration. For 286 users, expanded memory is more useful. On the other hand, 386 and higher microprocessors can create as much expanded memory as required from extended memory, so it makes more sense to have only the extended variety.

Windows is an especially memory-hungry environment. Theoretically, you can load Windows in Standard mode using just 1M of RAM, but I've never known anyone who lived to tell about it. Enhanced mode on a 386 system absolutely requires 2M of RAM, and 4M is the real bare minimum if you expect to be able to run a program or two. Windows for Workgroups works better with a little more. Windows starts to perform as advertised with 8M of RAM and really hums with 16 to 32M.

With that much RAM, you can load three or four good-sized programs and their data files and switch between them without worrying about Windows swapping RAM out to your hard disk to free up memory space. A decent complement of RAM makes Windows a true multitasking environment.

Those still using Desqview as their windowing, context-switching, multitasking shell also benefit from extra RAM. Like Windows, Desqview can load a large number of programs and switch between them. Programs can operate in the background, too.

Fortunately, memory is exceptionally cheap these days. In 1988, I paid a discounted price of $895 for a 2M add-on memory board for an IBM PS/2 computer. I considered myself very lucky, because memory prices doubled shortly thereafter. The 386 motherboards designed in this period usually allow for only 8M of on-board RAM and may limit you to an- other 8M of 32-bit memory with an add-on board (if that board is even available). With memory selling for $1,000 a megabyte, who in their right mind would conceive of needing more than, say, $16,000 worth of RAM?

Unfortunately, that short-sightedness affects us today when RAM can cost as little as $25 a megabyte. There are still some 486 motherboards being sold that are limited to 32M of RAM. That's only $800 of cost-effective memory, an expenditure that can boost performance more dramatically than almost any purchase in that price range.

With prices this low, it's hard to justify buying other peripherals for your system if your motherboard still doesn't have all the memory it can handle.

Adding More Memory

MemMaker will find better ways to use the memory you already have, but first you need to make sure that you've added enough to your system in the first place. There are several ways to expand the amount of memory available for MemMaker to work with.

Additional Motherboard RAM

Always add memory to your motherboard first. RAM installed on the motherboard can be accessed by the CPU at the full speed of the microprocessor itself, which is likely to be 25 to 50 MHz. Such RAM is installed in banks, which generally deliver information in blocks as wide as the data path of your microprocessor; with 386DX and higher chips, that's 32 bits. Motherboard RAM will always be the fastest memory your computer can use, excluding internal and external CPU RAM caches (which are discussed in Chapter 10.) Most motherboards today allow 32 to 64M of RAM to be installed, using 4M memory modules.

Proprietary Memory Cards

Some motherboards that accept only a limited amount of RAM can be fitted with proprietary cards that fit in a special 32-bit slot. This configuration still allows your CPU to access this RAM with the same speed as memory installed on the motherboard. However, you must have the special board developed for your motherboard; these are not available from third parties. The slot itself is usually a standard ISA-type motherboard slot, with an additional connector behind it for the 32-bit memory. This may look much like the newer VESA local bus (VL-bus) slots found on many computers these days. Because VL-bus cards also can be accessed by the CPU at its full speed, it is possible that VL memory cards will be developed to allow additional RAM expansion of systems that have fully populated motherboards.

Sixteen-Bit Memory Cards

For users of 386 and higher microprocessors, 16-bit memory cards, such as the BocaRAM AT Plus, are your last choice. They deliver memory to the CPU using a measly 16-bit data path and are limited to the ISA bus speed of 10 MHz. So, such RAM is likely to be five to ten times slower than motherboard RAM. The penalty is not quite so great for 286 and 386SX systems, which use a 16-bit memory path anyway. However, the 10 MHz bus speed is likely to be slower than the 16 to 33 MHz CPU speed of 286 and 386 systems; for them, motherboard memory is still the better choice.

The advantage of these cards is, for 286 systems, the capability to configure the RAM as either EMS or extended memory, whichever is most advantageous for the end-user. The BocaRAM AT Plus, for example, can be software configured for these modes, with no need for jumpers or DIP switches.

Non-System RAM

One clever way to "add" memory to your system is to reduce the amount required of your system RAM. For example, you may wish to dedicate 4M of your RAM to SmartDrive. If you happen to have an older 386 limited to 8M of motherboard RAM, that can be impractical. Instead, you can use a caching disk controller that accepts its own RAM. You can buy an extra 4M for the disk controller, freeing all your 8M of motherboard RAM for other purposes. Of course, the disk cache RAM cannot be used or reconfigured for other purposes, but in this situation, it's your best bet. Both IDE and SCSI caching controllers are available.

If you're using PrintCache or another utility to speed up printing, you may have configured several megabytes of RAM to store files as they are being spooled to the printer. Instead, consider buying more RAM for your printer; it can get double duty to store both fonts and pages. Or you can switch PrintCache to use your hard disk as virtual RAM in place of real RAM.

Indeed, there are many instances in which you can substitute hard disk space for RAM, thus freeing up silicon memory when performance isn't an issue.

Buying RAM

Only a year ago, the question of what RAM to buy would have been complicated by a bewildering variety of RAM speeds, configurations, and other options. Today, things are a great deal simpler. Nearly all the most common IBM PC clones take standard single in-line memory modules (SIMMs) in either 1M or 4M sizes. Only a few older computers require individual memory chips (commonly called dynamic RAM or D-RAM chips), SIPPs, or other types. Many newer systems can also accept 16M SIMMs.

Your motherboard will have four to eight slots for these SIMMs, allowing configurations of 4 to 8M of RAM (if you use 1M SIMMs) or 16 to 32M (if you use 4M SIMMs). However, one of my 486 computers has 16 memory slots, allowing up to 64M of RAM on the motherboard. And, my latest 486DX2-66 VL-bus system boasts only *four* slots. For this high-powered machine, you're expected to use only 4 or 16M modules, for a total of 32 or 64M of RAM.

A few computers require special memory modules, but in general, the only other thing you need to worry about is the speed of the RAM, measured in nanoseconds. Even that is not a complicated consideration. You can check your system's manual or view the RAM modules already installed (the part number will end in -6 or -06 for 60 ns, -7 or -07 for 70 ns, etc.). Most vendors sell 60 ns RAM for no more than a dollar or two per megabyte more than for slower memory, so I always buy the faster variety. In fact, I've sometimes asked for 100 ns or 80 ns RAM, found it out of stock, and been offered 60 ns memory for the same price.

Because 60 ns RAM works fine in computers that need only 70 to 80 ns memory, the extra few dollars are a good investment. By standardizing on the faster speed, you will be able to switch RAM to a newer computer in the near future, if you need to. I have one 486 that calls for 53 ns RAM and another that needs 70 ns memory; I use 60 ns in both and can mix and match modules.

These days, it makes the most sense to purchase 4M SIMMs, because they make the best use of your RAM slots. If you have eight slots and fill up four of them with 1M SIMMs instead of a single 4M module, you have only four more for future RAM expansion, unless you sell your 1M RAM (invariably at a loss.)

If you're buying a 16-bit RAM card, look for add-ons that take SIMMs instead of D-RAMS, which are much more difficult to install and use up the space on the card faster. Because of the slower bus speed, however, you'll rarely need RAM that is faster than 80 ns for these cards.

Getting the Most from Your Memory

I realize that my discussion of cheap memory in the first section of this chapter provides little comfort for those on a restricted budget. People who use their computers in businesses should easily be able to cost-justify the expenditure of a few hundred dollars when the payback is so imme-diate and dramatic. However, I recognize that smaller businesses and individuals who want to use scanners may not be able to toss off money in $100 increments. Fortunately, there are some things you can do to stretch the memory you do have. I mentioned some of these applications in the previous section.

If you have an 80386 or 80286 computer, use a memory manager like DOS 6's EMM386 or Quarterdeck's QEMM or QRAM to make the best use of the memory between 640K and 1M on your system. These utilities allow you to load memory resident programs (TSRs), device drivers, and DOS buffers into spare "holes" in this memory, freeing precious DOS memory. We'll explore ways to do this in the following two chapters.

Make sure that your memory is the fastest you can use. If your computer requires 60 ns RAM and you load it up with 80 ns memory, performance suffers. Today, the difference in price between the fastest memory and the slowest is likely to be only a few cents per chip. Don't skimp. You might wonder who would be foolish enough to try to get by with slower RAM. You might if you didn't know the speed of the memory you had or needed or what speed memory would be of use to you.

The Next Step

You understand how memory works. You know how your applications use it. You have explored all the ways to maximize the amount of system RAM available to the system. Perhaps, you've even added a little RAM to "top off" your computer. Now it's time to look at how MemMaker can help you best use this memory.

Using MemMaker

Given the RAM restrictions and bottlenecks outlined in the last chapters, it's little wonder that the memory management improvements found in DOS 6 have garnered the most attention. Whenever recent versions of DOS are compared, it's usually the memory features that are analyzed first. The last chapters explained some of the concepts you need to understand how to manage memory effectively with DOS 6. This chapter will explain how you can implement them effectively as you customize your configuration.

What Is MemMaker?

MemMaker is a utility that works with DOS's memory-oriented device drivers, such as EMM386, to help you find the optimal way to use your available memory. Owners of 386 and higher microprocessors have the most options, because of the advanced memory-management capabilities built into their CPUs. MemMaker works only with these systems, when equipped with extended memory.

The real goal of MemMaker and all memory-management techniques is to *free up conventional memory*. After all, you have 640K of conventional RAM, which is quite a lot if all you need to do is load DOS itself and a brace of drivers to control your mouse, scanner, network card, SCSI hard disk, or a few other devices. These drivers generally take only 2K to 64K of RAM, and you can fit quite a few of them in conventional memory and still have 200-300K left over.

Unfortunately, very few programs will run in even 300K of conventional RAM these days. Many powerful programs, and more than a few games, require 480-550K just to load. If you fill up conventional RAM with drivers or TSR programs, there's not a lot of useful work you can do with what's left.

Windows applications aren't limited by the amount of conventional RAM you have available, as long as you have enough to load Windows itself. Thereafter, they all draw from whatever extended memory is available in your machine, plus the virtual memory created by setting up a permanent or temporary swapfile on your hard disk. Even so, when you go to run DOS programs from within Windows, each and every one of them will be limited to the maximum amount of conventional memory that was available *before* you loaded Windows. So, Windows users who also run DOS programs under that environment also can be victimized by RAM cram.

Conventional memory can be freed up by loading as many device drivers and TSR programs as possible into other types of RAM. Some modules, such as part of the DOS kernel, can be placed in the high memory area (HMA) block of about 64K immediately above the 1M boundary. Other programs can be installed in upper memory blocks between 640K and 1M.

MemMaker is a tool that helps locate the best areas for these programs, determines the optimum combination of programs that can be relocated, and inserts the appropriate routines in your CONFIG.SYS and AUTOEXEC.BAT files.

Do You Need MemMaker?

You don't need MemMaker if you meet any of the following criteria:

➤ You are using a 286 or lower microprocessor.

➤ You have a 386 or higher microprocessor, but have only 1M of RAM installed. (You don't have any extended memory).

➤ You run only Windows and Windows-based applications. If you don't run any DOS applications, the amount of conventional memory available is no constraint. However, you *do* need as much extended memory as possible, and memory-management techniques reduce the amount of free extended memory.

➤ You want to use a third-party memory manager such as QEMM. These managers are furnished with their own memory diagnostic and management utilities, with names like Optimize.

Preparing To Use MemMaker

Before you run MemMaker, you should perform the following checks on your system:

First remove any unnecessary start-up programs from CONFIG.SYS and AUTOEXEC.BAT, particularly those which use memory of any type. MemMaker cannot distinguish between programs and device drivers that are essential to your system and those which are no longer needed, redundant, or optional. Some candidates to look for include the following:

➤ **Device Drivers for Devices You No Longer Use.** Some users have directives in their CONFIG.SYS files for hand-scanners they don't own anymore, disk compression schemes they've outgrown, or network drivers for workstations that have been removed from the network. Some drivers don't announce their presence when the computer reboots, so a busy or careless user may not be aware they are still being loaded.

➤ **Device Drivers You Don't Need.** If you now run only Windows programs or run DOS programs under Windows that don't need mouse support, you don't need to load a mouse driver from CONFIG.SYS or AUTOEXEC.BAT. It's usually a better idea to launch these DOS programs from Windows with a batch file that loads MOUSE.COM or some other driver, making mouse support available only to the DOS sessions that really need it. In other cases, your software selection can eliminate an extra driver. For example, ZSoft's image-editing products require HPSCANER.SYS to provide scanning capabilities with the HP ScanJet IIc, even if the SJII.SYS driver is already loaded. You can save RAM by doing your scanning, at least, with another program, such as the DeskScan software furnished with the ScanJet, and saving ZSoft's PhotoFinish, or Publisher's Paintbrush for image editing. TWAIN scanner support can also eliminate the need for extra drivers.

➤ **Device Drivers You Need Only Occaisonally.** If you rarely use a particular device driver, it makes little sense to load it every time you boot your computer. Disable it by placing a remark (REM) statement at the beginning of the line. You can remove the remark when you want to use the driver, and then reboot your system.

➤ **Device Drivers for "Luxury" Programs.** You really don't get much benefit from these drivers. Do you load an anti-virus TSR each time you boot your computer—yet you rarely download software, use other people's disks, or otherwise expose yourself to computer viruses? For most users, simply scanning each new disk and conducting periodic checks of your hard drives may be all the virus protection needed. Why have a virus-checker in memory all the time? Scan your CONFIG.SYS and AUTOEXEC.BAT files for programs that aren't really needed.

Next, make sure that all the memory-resident programs that you do need are loaded and running. If you normally are logged onto a network, make sure that you're logged on when you run MemMaker. On the other hand, you should unload any programs that aren't normally in memory. Perhaps you've loaded a screen-capture TSR or some other tool that sees only occaisonal use. Exit that program and free up the RAM it uses.

Tools That MemMaker Will Use

MemMaker is only a configuration utility. To optimize your use of memory, it makes use of several commands and device drivers. These are described in the following sections.

EMM386.EXE

This driver can be used only with Intel 386 or later microprocessors. At this writing, that includes what is commonly called the 386DX , 386SX, 386SL, 486DX, and 486SX chips, as well as equivalent chips offered by AMD and Cyrix. These all have a similar basic architecture, and all accept the same basic set of instructions. They are full 32-bit chips, meaning that data is processed 32 bits at a time, and include the same modes:

➤ **Real Mode,** which emulates the 8088/86 microprocessor and its 1M memory limitation.

➤ **Protected Mode,** which emulates a mode found in the 80286 micro-processor and allows accessing extended memory.

➤ **Virtual 8086 Mode,** in which the microprocessor emulates multiple 8086 chips, each of which can address its own 1M of memory and function as if it were a separate computer.

The 386DX is the basic microprocessor in this group, with 32-bit internal processing and a 32-bit data path to the outside world. The 386SX is a lower cost, "286-killer" that provides exactly the same features as the 386DX, but with a 16-bit data path that allows using lower cost (and slower) memory boards. The DX version is also somewhat faster, as it is marketed in 25 MHz, 33 MHz, and (from AMD) 40 MHz versions, but the SX is available in 20 MHz and 16 MHz speeds only (at this time, the 16 MHz versions are also being phased out.) The 386SL is a low power version of the 386 chip intended for use in lap-top computers.

386 Chips Can Use 387 Math Coprocessor

Any of these chips can work in tandem with an appropriate 80x87 math co-processor, which can greatly speed up floating point operations with CAD software and other applications specifically designed to use these features.

The 486DX chips have the math coprocessor built in and, consequently, perform math operations even faster. Indeed, the 486 chip performs many instructions much faster than the 386 chip. In addition to the math coprocessor, it includes a built-in 8K instruction cache. So, a 20 MHz 486 chip is actually 10 to 15 percent faster than a 33 MHz 386 microprocessor in most cases.

486 Doesn't Require Outboard Math Coprocessor

In the 486SX microprocessor, the math coprocessor has been disabled (in early versions) or is entirely absent, providing Intel with a way to market the equivalent of a very fast 386 microprocessor at a lower, more competitive price. Contrary to what you might expect, the 487 chip does not provide the 486SX with an external math coprocessor; that would defeat a key design consideration of the 486 chip. Instead, when you plug a 487 chip into a 486SX computer, the old 486SX chip is entirely disabled. The 487 chip is actually a fully functioning 80486 DX chip.

Because of the special features of these chips, EMM386.EXE can be used to provide several important new features. It will

➤ Create EMS 4.0 memory, or expanded memory, without the need for special hardware.

➤ Move most of the central portion of the DOS operating system, called the kernal, into HMA memory. You'll recall that upper memory blocks are to be found between the 640K and the 1M boundary, but HMA memory is the 64K block of extended memory immediately above the 1M boundary.

➤ Provide the management required to use UMBs for device drivers, TSRs, and data used by the operating system.

➤ Allow you to copy data from ROM into RAM.

➤ Automatically load itself into upper memory (or into conventional memory if you prefer).

➤ Provide an additional 64K to 96K of conventional memory (on top of the 640K normally available) if you have a monochrome display adapter (MDA), Hercules card, CGA adapter, or EGA/VGA card which is being used in non-graphics, text mode only.

MemMaker can do some of these things for you, and I'll explain how to do these things manually in Chapter 8.

HIMEM.SYS

If you have a system using an 80286 microprocessor or an 8088/86 system, you can't take advantage of the built-in memory-management capabilities of the 386 and later chips. However, if you have any 286 system, DOS will let you do some tricks with extended memory.

MemMaker Commands

MemMaker can also make use of several commands in CONFIG.SYS and AUTOEXEC.BAT that allow loading specified device drivers into UMBs. After you've run MemMaker, you'll see lines in both these files that make use of them.

DOS=HIGH,UMB

This command for CONFIG.SYS relocates part of the DOS operating system into the high memory area and makes upper memory blocks available.

DEVICEHIGH

This is used in CONFIG.SYS to load TSR programs and device drivers into upper memory. This command will be discussed in more detail in the next chapter.

LOADHIGH

This is the command line utility that can be used to load TSRs into upper memory after your system has booted, either in AUTOEXEC.BAT or from the DOS prompt. You'll find complete instructions for using this command in the next chapter.

Using MemMaker in Express Setup Mode

MemMaker is loaded by typing **memmaker** at the DOS prompt. You'll be offered the choice of Express and Custom Setup. We'll look at Express Setup first.

Express Setup

You'll want to use Express setup if you don't want to activate special options, such as using part of video RAM for DOS or to troubleshoot specific device driver problems. Express setup provides a basic, reliable memory configuration that works for most users. You can always run Custom setup later to make additional changes or edit your CONFIG.SYS and AUTOEXEC.BAT files yourself.

1. When you select this option, the first screen that appears asks you to specify whether you use any programs that require expanded memory. If you use only Windows programs, you don't need expanded memory, as all Windows programs use only extended and virtual memory. If you use DOS programs from within Windows, Windows' own memory management routines can simulate expanded memory.

   If you run DOS programs outside of Windows, you need expanded memory only if those programs require it. Software like the GEM version of Ventura Publisher or Lotus 1-2-3 are among those that use expanded memory. You should check the manuals of the programs you use frequently and see whether they need EMS. Specifying EMS uses up a 64K block of conventional memory or upper memory for the EMS page frame, so you definitely don't want EMS if you don't need it.

   However, if you do need EMS or are unsure, tell MemMaker Yes by pressing the spacebar then press Enter. If you don't need EMS, just press Enter. MemMaker may ask you some additional questions if you use Windows, in reference to your need for EMS outside the Windows environment.

2. MemMaker now needs to reboot your computer. It has saved some information about your system and needs to reboot to test out various memory configurations. Usually, you can reboot at this point by pressing Enter when asked. Some systems may intercept MemMaker's rebooting command; in that case, press Ctrl-Alt-Del or turn your system off and then back on again.

3. When the system reboots, MemMaker tries to fit the needed device drivers and TSR programs into the available UMBs as efficiently as

possible. This task is a lot more difficult than it sounds. The first complication is that the available UMBs probably don't form a contiguous space. Certain devices, such as scanners, SCSI controllers, or network cards may contain a ROM that is *memory-mapped* into a portion of upper memory. That is, the code contained in that ROM is assigned addresses corresponding to particular UMBs. That memory cannot be used for other drivers. In addition, the EMS page frame usually is slotted into upper memory somewhere. Video adapters and system ROM also eat up blocks.

```
================================Memory================================
Legend:  Available "█"  RAM "▓"  ROM "▒"  Possibly Available "█"
   EMS Page Frame "PP"  Used UMBs "▓▓"  Free UMBs "██"
1024K FC00                       FFFF  Conventional Memory
      F800                       FBFF                  Total: 640K
      F400                       F7FF              Available: 500K
 960K F000                       F3FF                       512096 bytes
      EC00  UUUUUUUUUUUUUUUU      EFFF
      E800  UUUUUUUUUUUUUUUU      EBFF  Extended Memory
      E400  UUUUUUUUUUUUUUUU      E7FF                  Total: 31744K
 896K E000  ----UUUUUUUUUUUU      E3FF
      DC00                       DFFF  MS-DOS Upper Memory Blocks
      D800                       DBFF             Total UMBs: 59K
      D400  PPPPPPPPPPPPPPPP      D7FF        Total Free UMBs: 0K
 832K D000  PPPPPPPPPPPPPPPP      D3FF     Largest Free Block: 0K
      CC00  PPPPPPPPPPPPPPPP      CFFF
      C800  PPPPPPPPPPPPPPPP      CBFF  Expanded Memory (EMS)
      C400                       C7FF             LIM Version: 4.00
 768K C000                       C3FF     Page Frame Address: C800H
```

Figure 6.1. A typical upper memory block configuration.

When MemMaker starts optimizing, your upper memory area may already look like the map shown in figure 6.1. It will try to fit different combinations of drivers and programs into the available blocks, leaving the smallest unused portion possible. For example, assume that you have one 48K and one 12K UMB available. If your CONFIG.SYS file loads drivers that require 8K, 32K, and 16K, in that order, you would end up with the 8K and 32K drivers going into the 48K block, with 8K left over. The remaining 16K driver would not fit in that space, nor in the 12K UMB. MemMaker would recognize this and reorder CONFIG.SYS to load the 32K and 16K drivers first, leaving the 8K module for the 12K block that remains. You would save 16K of conventional RAM with this highly simplified example.

In the real world, fitting drivers into UMBs is a lot more complicated. Some programs require more memory to load than they do to operate, so a particular TSR might need an UMB that's 32K in size to load, but only 24K thereafter. The physical size of the driver file can be misleading.

In only a few seconds, MemMaker may consider thousands of different combinations of drivers and locations before settling on one. Then it's ready to reboot again.

4. Press Enter to reboot your system when asked. Then watch the screen carefully to see that all device drivers and TSRs load properly. Most will display an error message if their installation is halted prematurely. If something bad happens, note the problem. After this initial boot-up, MemMaker will give you the opportunity to undo the changes it has made and will return to your original configuration. When asked if your system is working properly, either reply Yes by pressing Enter or undo the changes by pressing the spacebar, followed by Enter. Then note the instructions on the screen.

Custom Setup

Custom setup is not much more complicated than the Express setup described previously. You'll need to know a few extra facts about your computer and can select special options to minimize problems. Let's run through Custom Setup quickly.

1. When you select Custom setup, MemMaker first asks whether you use any programs that require expanded memory. Review step 1 under "Express Setup" if you have any questions about whether you need EMS.

2. Next, the advanced options screen appears. The questions you'll be asked are as follows:

   ```
   Specify which drivers and TSRs to include in the opti-
   mization?
   ```

   The default is no. If you followed my recommendation earlier and removed all unneeded device drivers and TSRs from CONFIG.SYS and AUTOEXEC.BAT, you won't need to specify which modules to include in the optimization step. If you still have some drivers and memory-resident programs you would like to exclude, change the response to Yes and specify which to include.

`Scan the upper memory area agressively?`

The default answer is yes. MemMaker will look for upper memory blocks that don't appear to be in use, but it may not spot all of them with this agressive approach. You may have to exclude those areas manually later on to avoid problems.

`Optimize upper memory for use with Windows?`

The default value is no. If you select yes, MemMaker will base many of its decisions on how much extended memory remains free after optimization for Windows' use.

`Keep current EMM386 inclusions and exclusions?`

The default is yes. You have already discovered that it is necessary to tell EMM386 not to use the upper memory addresses claimed by some devices or to include other areas it won't normally touch. You may specify upper memory block areas for EMM386 to include under its control and others that it should ignore. You may have found, for example, that you need to manually specify the upper memory addresses of your scanner interface or SCSI controller to avoid conflicts. An exclusion using the syntax x=D800-DC00 on the EMM386 line will prevent the memory manager from attempting to use that area. On the other hand, you may also have discovered that certain areas of upper memory, such as the first 32K of system ROM, aren't used after boot-up, and you would like that block included in upper memory blocks. You can add that area by adding a statement like i=E000-EFFF. We'll look at these options in more detail later, in Chapter 8.

`Move extended BIOS data from conventional to upper memory?`

The default response is to move this portion of DOS into upper memory, where practical.

3. Next, MemMaker checks to see whether you have Windows installed and asks you to confirm the name of its directory. After that, the utility reboots your computer and attempts to determine the best combination of TSR and device drivers to load into upper memory, as described in step 3 under "Express Setup."

4. It is possible that in trying different combinations of driver and TSR locations, MemMaker will cause your computer to lock up or hang. Don't be alarmed. Restart by pressing Ctrl-Alt-Del or turning the power off and then on again. If MemMaker provided some instructions before it halted, press F5 to skip CONFIG.SYS and AUTOEXEC.BAT and do what was suggested. In one of my tests, MemMaker reported that EMM386 hadn't set aside enough memory for a DMA buffer and suggested I add a DMA=128 instruction to the EMM386 line in CONFIG.SYS.

In other cases, you won't have the foggiest notion what went wrong. When MemMaker loads again, you'll be offered the opportunity to try again using the same settings, try again using more conservative settings, or to cancel all changes and return to your original configuration. It's always worth trying again with the same settings, just to see what happens. If the system still hangs, you can always tell MemMaker to use a less aggressive approach. If all else fails, you can return to the configuration you had before you ran MemMaker.

Canceling MemMaker's Changes

Even after you quit MemMaker, you can undo the changes it has made, because it stores copies of the original AUTOEXEC.BAT, CONFIG.SYS, and Windows SYSTEM.INI files. If several days have passed and you have made additional changes to any of those files, those changes will be lost, because MemMaker uses the copies that it made when it last reconfigured your system. So, if you have installed several new Windows programs or done some other work with those files, you'll either have to redo that work or go into the files and try and determine what MemMaker did on your own. In most cases, however, you'll know right away that the new MemMaker setup doesn't work for you, so you can just go ahead and switch back to the most recent version of those files.

To restore the original versions, quit any programs that you might be running, and type

```
memmaker /undo
```

at the DOS prompt. The screen that pops up asks whether you would like to restore your original files or quit and leave the present configuration intact. Press Enter to accept the restoration; then, after MemMaker confirms the process, press Enter again to reboot your computer.

Using MemMaker with Multiple Configurations

If you've set up your system with multiple startup configurations, you'll need to perform one annoying extra step before using MemMaker. The utility isn't smart enough to sort out all your different configuration options, so you should create a separate CONFIG.SYS and AUTOEXEC.BAT file for each configuration, with the menu items and `goto config` lines removed. Then run MemMaker once for each setup and save the new CONFIG.SYS and AUTOEXEC.BAT files it produces. After you've optimized each configuration, create a new set of files that incorporate all the recommendations. The Microsoft MS-DOS 6 User's Guide has some very nice step-by-step instructions for doing this that I can't improve on, so I refer you to that section of Chapter 6 in the Guide.

The Next Step

MemMaker highly automates the process of configuring your computer's use of memory. This utility is an excellent first step toward really fine-tuning your system. However, you can do additional things to squeeze a little more conventional memory out of your available RAM and to use extended memory more efficiently. We'll look at some of those options and other tools you can use in the next chapter.

Tools for Fine-Tuning Memory

Although MemMaker is a fine utility, it can't possibly cover every possibility or explore every option available to you. This chapter will help you understand how upper memory blocks work in a little more depth and will provide the information you need to further fine-tune your use of conventional RAM, UMBs, extended memory, and expanded memory.

You can always manually edit your CONFIG.SYS and AUTOEXEC.BAT files to fine-tune your system's use of memory. You can do this with or without running MemMaker first. I recommend at least trying MemMaker, as it uses some sophisicated routines to determine where device drivers and TSRs can be loaded and to test them for conflicts. After MemMaker has done all it can, you can use the tips in this next section to make some changes and possibly gain a little more memory.

Your Assignment

The changes you'll make to CONFIG.SYS and AUTOEXEC.BAT fall into the following categories:

➤ Making UMBs available. You do this in three steps, activating HIMEM.SYS, telling DOS that you want UMBs to be available, and defining which areas of upper memory are to be included or excluded from use by EMM386.

➤ Setting aside special UMBs for an EMS page frame, if required.

➤ Loading device drivers and TSRs into available UMBs.

➤ Defining other memory parameters, such as the size of a direct memory access (DMA) buffer.

Why Use Upper Memory?

At this point, you might still be wondering why this exercise is necessary. You learned in Chapter 5 that UMBs can help free upper memory. But why is this possible in the first place?

The key thing that makes UMBs possible is that the upper 384K of RAM where your computer system's ROMs reside share addresses with RAM. To quickly review what you've learned in earlier chapters, PCs have a basic 1M of RAM located between the 0 and 1024K addresses. This RAM occupies addresses 0000 through FFFF in hexadecimal, and DOS uses just the first 10 pages of it, up to A000 or the 640K boundary. That memory is there in your system, even if you can't ordinarily use any of it above A000.

You also have ROMs in your computer, including the video ROMs at the lower end of upper memory (starting at A000) and the system ROM that ends at FFFF. These use some of the same addresses as the RAM you have between A000 and FFFF. Ordinarily, your system will ignore the RAM and address only the ROMs. The RAM, in effect, stands "behind" the ROM at the same address, like a person's shadow.

Two Ways To Access Upper RAM

There are two ways in which the RAM between A000 and FFFF can be accessed. One way is through a procedure called RAM shadowing, in which ROMs are copied to the RAM that stands behind them at the same addresses. Then your system is told to use the RAM, which contains the same code as the ROM twin, instead of the original ROM. Because RAM is generally much faster than ROM, the shadow RAM technique can help speed up operations involving those ROMs. Video functions can be carried out much faster when video ROMs are shadowed, and shadowing system ROMs can speed up any ROM calls that your operating system or software makes.

Shadowing can be provided either by the computer system chip set or by the memory manager. EMM386 won't do this, but Quarterdeck's QEMM is one memory manager that can. Some chipsets (the basic components used to provide support for your microprocessor) have shadowing built in. You don't want both hardware and software attempting to shadow your RAM, so you'll want to specify one or other other, but not both methods. You turn off hardware shadowing through your system's CMOS setup system (activated by pressing Ctrl-Alt-Esc or another sequence during boot-up, generally after the power-on-self-test (POST) and memory check but before DOS starts to load).

Converting RAM to UMBs

The second way of using upper RAM is by converting the free blocks not used by ROM to UMBs. That's what I'll address in this chapter and the next. But first, you need to learn about your most valuable tools in your battle against the IBM PC's memory architecture.

The MSD.EXE Utility

Microsoft's MSD.EXE (Microsoft System Diagnostics utility) provides a comprehensive look at your system. It includes several reports you can view on-screen or direct to your printer or a file. Versions of this utility have been available for some time, but it is now being bundled with DOS 6 as part of its comprehensive utilities package.

Some of the data MSD reports is just a general overview of your system, as shown in figure 7.1.

```
----------------------- Summary Information -------------------------

          Computer: Zeos/Award, 486DX
          Memory: 640K, 31744K Ext, 1024K EMS, 1024K XMS
          Video: TIGA, Phoenix
          Network: MS Workgroup Client
          OS Version: MS-DOS Version 6.00, Windows 3.10
          Mouse: InPort Mouse 8.20
   Other Adapters:
       Disk Drives: A: B: C: D: E: F: G: H:
       LPT Ports: 2
       COM Ports: 2

----------------------------- Computer -----------------------------

        Computer Name: Zeos
        BIOS Manufacturer: Award
          BIOS Version: \' CA486 Modular BIOS v3.10
          BIOS Category: IBM PC/AT
          BIOS ID Bytes: FC 01 00
          BIOS Date: 11/22/89
          Processor: 486DX
       Math Coprocessor: Internal
          Keyboard: Enhanced
          Bus Type: ISA/AT/Classic Bus
       DMA Controller: Yes
       Cascaded IRQ2: Yes
       BIOS Data Segment: None
```

Figure 7.1. MSD data report.

Other data is more specific to your use of memory. For example, it can show you a general map of your system's upper memory, like that in figure 7.2. That data can be invaluable when you start planning areas to load drivers or TSR programs into upper memory.

```
     -
     ------------------------- Memory -------------------------------

     Legend:  Available " "  RAM "##"  ROM "RR"  Possibly Available ".."
       EMS Page Frame "PP"  Used UMBs "UU"  Free UMBs "FF"
     1024K FC00 RRRRRRRRRRRRRRRRR FFFF  Conventional Memory
           F800 RRRRRRRRRRRRRRRRR FBFF                  Total: 640K
           F400 RRRRRRRRRRRRRRRRR F7FF              Available: 492K
      960K F000 RRRRRRRRRRRRRRRRR F3FF                          503888 bytes
           EC00 UUUUUUUUUUUUUUUU EFFF
           E800 UUUUUUUUUUUUUUUU EBFF  Extended Memory
           E400 UUUUUUUUUUUUUUUU E7FF                  Total: 31744K
      896K E000 ....UUUUUUUUUUUU E3FF
           DC00             DFFF  MS-DOS Upper Memory Blocks
           D800           . DBFF          Total UMBs: 59K
           D400 PPPPPPPPPPPPPPPPP D7FF     Total Free UMBs: 0K
      832K D000 PPPPPPPPPPPPPPPPP D3FF   Largest Free Block: 0K
           CC00 PPPPPPPPPPPPPPPPP CFFF
           C800 PPPPPPPPPPPPPPPPP CBFF  Expanded Memory (EMS)
           C400 RRRRRRRRRRRRRRRRR C7FF          LIM Version: 4.00
      768K C000 RRRRRRRRRRRRRRRRR C3FF   Page Frame Address: C800H
           BC00 ............... BFFF                  Total: 1024K
           B800 ............... BBFF              Available: 928K
           B400             B7FF
      704K B000 ...........   B3FF  XMS Information
           AC00 ............... AFFF          XMS Version: 2.00
           A800 ............... ABFF       Driver Version: 2.05
           A400 ............... A7FF   A20 Address Line: Enabled
      640K A000 ............... A3FF   High Memory Area: In use
                                              Available: 1024K
                                    Largest Free Block: 1024K

                                    DPMI Information
                                        DPMI Detected: Yes
                                            Version: 0.90
```

Figure 7.2. MSD-generated memory map.

In this map, each line represents 16K of RAM, and each R, P, space, or dot represents 1K of memory. The UMBs are further marked off in 64K sections. That is, starting from the bottom of the map (the 640K boundary), the A page extends from A000 upward to AFFF; B starts at B000 (704K in decimal) and extends to BFFF, and so forth.

Any area marked with a space or dot is possibly available for use as a UMB—at least, as far as MSD is concerned. We may know better, however, based on our knowledge of, say, our system's use of video RAM in the A000-BFFF range.

Each R represents an area claimed by ROM of some sort, and each # indicates a RAM area. An upper memory block already in use by a device driver is noted with a U on the map, and the EMS page frame is marked by 64K worth of Ps. Unused and free UMBs are shown with Fs.

Learn how to read this map, because you'll find it valuable in searching for free UMBs later on.

The Mem Command

Some of this same information can be gleaned in a different format, using the **mem** command, which was introduced with DOS 4.0. It can report memory data in three different formats, depending on what switch you use.

The /C (Classify) switch shows the most complete report, listing loaded programs by how they use memory. The other switches, /D (Debug) and /F (Free memory), are less useful for our purposes. The /D switch shows the status of the modules in memory and can be used to determine the size, in hexadecimal notation, of a program you may want to load into an UMB, but /F just shows the amount of free memory. One additional switch /M (Module), new to DOS 6, reports on how memory is used by a specific program. You can use it to obtain the size of a module when loaded, where it is in memory, and other information. This can be helpful, because, as you'll learn, **devicehigh** can load drivers and TSRs into specific locations in upper memory. When you do this, you need to allow enough room.

A typical display generated by the **mem** command using the /C switch is shown in figure 7.3.

```
Modules using memory below 1 MB:

  Name          Total      =    Conventional  +   Upper Memory
  --------   -------------     -------------     ----------------
  MSDOS       18205   (18K)      18205   (18K)        0    (0K)
  SETVER        784    (1K)        784    (1K)        0    (0K)
  HIMEM        1152    (1K)       1152    (1K)        0    (0K)
  EMM386       3120    (3K)       3120    (3K)        0    (0K)
  DOSOAD      16880   (16K)      16880   (16K)        0    (0K)
  SATISFAX     3968    (4K)       3968    (4K)        0    (0K)
  PROTMAN       128    (0K)        128    (0K)        0    (0K)
  WORKGRP      4368    (4K)       4368    (4K)        0    (0K)
  EXP16        8944    (9K)       8944    (9K)        0    (0K)
  SJII         6992    (7K)       6992    (7K)        0    (0K)
  COMMAND      3008    (3K)       3008    (3K)        0    (0K)
  win386      41904   (41K)      10208   (10K)    31696   (31K)
  CASMGR       5520    (5K)       5520    (5K)        0    (0K)
  TIGACD      41872   (41K)      41872   (41K)        0    (0K)
  HPSCANER     3824    (4K)       3824    (4K)        0    (0K)
  MOUSE       16912   (17K)      16912   (17K)        0    (0K)
  WIN          1712    (2K)       1712    (2K)        0    (0K)
  4DOS         3664    (4K)       3664    (4K)        0    (0K)
  SMARTDRV    28816   (28K)          0    (0K)    28816   (28K)
  Free       503888  (492K)     503888  (492K)        0    (0K)

Memory Summary:

  Type of Memory        Total      =       Used      +       Free
  ---------------     -------------     -------------     ---------------
  Conventional        655360  (640K)     151472  (148K)    503888  (492K)
  Upper                60512   (59K)      60512   (59K)         0    (0K)
  Adapter RAM/ROM     393216  (384K)     393216  (384K)         0    (0K)
  Extended (XMS)    32445344 (31685K)  31396768 (30661K)  1048576 (1024K)
  ----------------    -------------     -------------     ---------------
  Total memory     33554432 (32768K)  32001968 (31252K)  1552464 (1516K)

  Total under 1 MB   715872  (699K)     211984  (207K)    503888  (492K)

  Total Expanded (EMS)             1048576  (1024K)
  Free Expanded (EMS)               950272   (928K)
  Largest executable program size   503872   (492K)
  Largest free upper memory block        0     (0K)
  MS-DOS is resident in the high memory area.
```

Figure 7.3. Using the /C switch with **mem**.

The upper portion of the display is a table that lists each driver and TSR
that resides in conventional or upper memory and shows how much
RAM it occupies in either location. Below that is a summary, showing
how much conventional and upper memory you have, how much is in
use, and the amount that is still free. The total amount of adapter RAM/
ROM (memory between 640 and 1024K, whether it is allocated to UMBs
or not), and whether extended (XMS) memory is installed, used, and free
is also shown. The summary at the bottom lists the amounts of EMS, the
largest executable program size (how much conventional RAM is available for DOS programs), and the size of the largest free upper memory
block.

You can use this information to locate likely candidates for loading into UMBs, simply by matching the size of the largest free UMB with a driver or TSR that is smaller than that. As I noted, some programs require more upper memory when they load than their size would indicate, so this manual procedure doesn't always work.

If you want a hardcopy of the output of either MSD.EXE or **mem** for reference, they are easy enough to obtain. MSD's File menu has a Print choice. You can print directly to an attached printer, or, if you use a PostScript device that doesn't like plain ASCII, you may print to a file and then load that into your favorite application or utility for printing at a later time. The **mem** command can be redirected to a file using this syntax:

```
mem /c>filename
```

Filename is an ASCII file that you can edit or print as required.

The **mem** command with the /M switch, followed by a specific driver name, produces a report showing how that driver uses memory.

Using DEVICEHIGH

The DEVICEHIGH directive is the command that actually loads a device driver into an upper memory block. It functions exactly like the DEVICE directive if no UMBs are available, so you can use it without fear that an essential driver will be skipped if you miscalculated the amount of upper memory you have. The syntax for this directive is:

```
DEVICEHIGH [drive:][path]filename [parameters]
[[/L:region1[,minsize1][;region2 [,minsize2]
[/S]]=[drive:][path] filename [parameters]
```

In this case, the nesting of the optional items in brackets is important, so read the syntax above carefully. Descriptions of each item follow.

➤ *drive: path*   This is the drive and full path to the device driver being loaded.

➤ *filename [parameters]*   This is the filename of the driver itself, along with any parameters that you want to pass along to the device driver.

➤ */L:region1[,minsize1]*   Use this switch to specify a region of upper memory to load the driver. DEVICEHIGH will otherwise load the driver into the largest free UMB, and make all the other UMBs available for the driver to use. The /L switch can explicitly load the driver into the largest UMB within the specified region, and/or specify which regions the driver can use. (Some drivers use more than one area of memory.)

You can enter more than one region, separated by semicolons. To specify regions 2, 3, and 4, you would enter:

    /L:2;3;4

➤ In addition, you can specify a minimum size that must be available in a region before DEVICEHIGH will use it. That protects drivers that require more memory to load than their file size indicates. The *minsize* is separated from the region number with a comma:

    /L:2,16;3;4

➤ */S=[drive:][path] filename [parameters]*   This switch shrinks an UMB to its minimum size as a specified driver loads and is used only with the /L switch with regions for which a minimum size was specified. It is a way of testing to see that a given driver can, indeed, fit into a given UMB and to ensure that the driver will take up no more of the UMB than necessary. The drive, path, filename, and parameters are the same as those used with the command proper.

Note   The syntax for DEVICEHIGH under DOS 5.0 was somewhat different. While DOS 6 recognizes and supports the older syntax, you should use the newer syntax whenever possible. For the record, the original directive worked like this:

    DEVICEHIGH [SIZE=*hexsize*] [*drive:*] [*path*] filename [*parameters*]

LOADHIGH

The equivalent of DEVICEHIGH outside of CONFIG.SYS is the LOADHIGH command (usually abbreviated LH). Its syntax and usage is exactly the same as for DEVICEHIGH. If an appropriate UMB is not available, LOADHIGH will simply load the TSR or driver into conventional RAM.

The Next Step

In addition to the tools that DOS 6 gives you, there are others that may prove helpful. QEMM is furnished with MFT.EXE, and other utilities ranging from Norton's System Information to WinSleuth Gold and Checkit all offer information about memory. Now that you know what tools you have available, it's time to look at the DOS 6 commands and the directives they are used with. We'll do that in the next chapter.

Using Memory Managers

The actual work of memory management is done by two deceptively simple programs, HIMEM.SYS and EMM386.EXE. You need to know what both of them do and how they work if you want to truly master memory management on the PC. This chapter will tell you more than you expected to know about either of them.

What Is HIMEM.SYS?

HIMEM.SYS is an extended memory manager. It manages DOS 6's use of memory above the 1M boundary; you must have it or a third-party program that provides the same services if you plan to use any of your extended RAM. Even EMM386 needs to have HIMEM.SYS loaded before it can work, so a line like the following one should appear before your EMM386 directive in CONFIG.SYS.

```
DEVICE=HIMEM.SYS
```

In most cases, that's all you need to use HIMEM.SYS. Most users place it at the very beginning of their CONFIG.SYS file, just to be on the safe side. But, strictly speaking, it only needs to be included before any other directives that use extended memory. In a few rare cases, you'll be explicitly told to place a particular driver before HIMEM.SYS. Some drivers for SCSI controller cards need to be loaded before any extended memory utilities, for example.

HIMEM.SYS does not need to reside in the root directory of your boot drive; only CONFIG.SYS and AUTOEXEC.BAT must be there. So, you can append a path to the directive, telling DOS where to find the extended memory driver. There are also nine optional switches that are useful under certain circumstances, such as to help DOS remain compatible with certain applications, operating systems, or hardware conditions. These switches are as follows:

➤ /A20CONTROL:ON or OFF

This switch tells HIMEM whether to take control of the A20 address line, even if the line was already on when HIMEM.SYS is loaded. You'll recall that the A20 line is that 21st address line that DOS can access because of a bug in the original Intel 8088/8086 microprocessors. This address line provides control of the first 64K of extended memory (minus a few bytes), which is called the high memory area, or HMA.

This switch is **on** by default. If you want DOS to grab A20 only if it is not already being controlled by another operating system or device, use /A20CONTROL:OFF to re-establish compatibility. It's unlikely you'll need this switch.

➤ /CPUCLOCK:ON or OFF

This is another compatibility option. Normally, it is switched off, but if you find that your computer's clock speed changes when you load HIMEM.SYS, you can try to resolve the problem by specifying **off.** HIMEM.SYS will slow down somewhat, so use this switch only if your computer's technical support staff tells you that you must use it, or you find through personal experimentation that it's the only way to restore compatibility.

➤ /EISA

If your system has an EISA (extended industry standard architecture) bus and more than 16M of memory, HIMEM.SYS will be unable to allocate all your extended memory unless you use this switch. You don't need it if you have an ISA bus system, or another variation, including VL-Bus (local bus) or MCA (IBM's MicroChannel Architecture).

➤ /HMAMIN=nn

DOS 6 is not the only software that can use the HMA area; the 4DOS command interpreter and quite a few other programs can be loaded here. Unfortunately, only one program can use HMA, even if it requires only a small portion of it. By default, HIMEM will turn over control of HMA to the first program that asks for it.

In most cases, that isn't a problem. If you have a DOS=HIGH or DOS=HIGH,UMB line in CONFIG.SYS, DOS 6 itself will grab HMA, and that will be the end of it. However, if HMA is still free by the time the DOS prompt shows up, you might want to put some restrictions on which program gets a shot at it. You may substitute for *nn* any value from 0 to 63, which translates to the number of kilobytes an application must require before HIMEM will allow access to HMA. Enter 0, and the first program that comes knocking gets it. With a value of 63, only a program that needs all of HMA can gain control. Because most users will go ahead and load DOS high, this question becomes moot for the majority.

Note that because Windows in Enhanced mode uses its own memory management routines, this specification has no effect when Windows is running.

➤ /INT15=*xxx*

Some older applications use DOS interrupt 15h instead of HIMEM.SYS to access extended memory. You can substitute for *xxx* the amount of RAM you want reserved for these applications, from 0 (the default) to 65535K. Anything less than 64K is considered 0.

➤ /NUMHANDLES=*n*

This switch is used to specify the maximum number of extended-memory block (EMB) handles that can be in use simultaneously. The default is 32; the maximum is 128. This parameter is ignored by Windows in Enhanced mode.

➤ /MACHINE=*xxxx*

HIMEM is not always able to detect what kind of computer you're using. If not, it will default to its PC/AT compatible specifications. A few systems won't work properly when this happens. Your system vendor will let you know what code you should enter to get HIMEM.SYS to operate properly. Alternatively, you can view a list of available machines by typing **help himem** at the DOS prompt.

➤ /SHADOWRAM:ON or OFF

You probably recall the discussion of ROM shadowing from the last chapter. If your system uses ROM shadowing and has less than 2M of RAM, you may be better off allowing HIMEM.SYS to reclaim the small amount of extended memory used when this option is active. HIMEM can do this itself on some types of systems, using this switch. Consider this a temporary measure only; if you really want ROM shadowing turned off, you're better off doing it through your computer's CMOS setup program or by adjusting jumpers on the motherboard (if that's how it's done with your system.)

➤ /VERBOSE

HIMEM.SYS usually encounters few problems in loading and won't normally display any error messages when it does. If you'd rather see these messages—say, to trouble-shoot a suspected extended memory problem—you can hold down the Alt key as HIMEM loads or add the /VERBOSE switch.

Using EMM386.EXE

EMM386.EXE, which works only with 386 or higher processors, has two chief functions. It provides access to upper memory blocks, so commands like DEVICEHIGH (in CONFIG.SYS) or LOADHIGH (in

AUTOEXEC.BAT, in other batch files, or from the DOS command line) can place device drivers and TSR programs in UMBs. The second function of EMM386 is to use extended memory to simulate expanded memory (Windows' own memory management routines can do this, too, but only within Windows.)

DOS sets up EMM386.EXE for you when you run Setup. You can simply specify what features you want or do not want (such as EMS), and the correct switches will be placed on the directive line in CONFIG.SYS for you. This memory manager also has a number of default parameters that it will use if no appropriate switch is used, so you could, conceivably, get by with a directive as simple as this one:

```
DEVICE=C:\DOS\EMM386.EXE
```

EMM386 can also be run from the DOS command line, to turn its functions on or off, and to disable or enable Weitek coprocessor support. We're most concerned with its use within CONFIG.SYS and the various switches and parameters that can be used with it.

I should warn you that, particularly if you are inexperienced in working with 386/486 memory managers, you may need to experiment somewhat to arrive at the settings that will work best for you. EMM386.EXE isn't always able to detect ROMs or other memory addresses that may actually be in use. You may need to exclude certain areas and include others. You may find that your system works best when you allocate certain amounts of memory to EMS or extended RAM. Your EMS page frame may be moved to keep it from splitting one larger UMB into two smaller ones. These are all things you can determine for yourself with a little experimentation.

This next section will explain each of the parameters and switches EMM386.EXE recognizes and how to use them. The full syntax for the command is as follows:

```
DEVICE=[drive:][path]EMM386.EXE [ON] or [Off] or [AUTO]
[memory] [MIN=size] [Mx] or [FRAME=address] or [/Pmmmm]
[Pn=address] [B=address] [A=altregs] [H=handles]
[D=nnn] [RAM=mmmm-nnnn] [NOEMS] [NOVCPI] [HIGHSCAN]
[VERBOSE] [WIN=mmmm-nnnn] [NOHI] [ROM=mmmm-nnnn]
[NOMOVEXBDA] [ALTBOOT] [W=ON] or [W=OFF] /X=nnnn
/I=nnnn
```

You won't need all of these, of course; most likely, you won't need even more than a few parameters and switches. Some of them (separated by *or*) are mutually exclusive—that is, you may choose one of them but not use any of the others at the same time.

drive: path EMM386.EXE, like HIMEM.SYS, does not have to reside in the root directory of your boot drive. If you have located it elsewhere, substitute the correct drive and path for *drive:path*

ON or Off or AUTO When set to ON (the default), expanded memory support and upper memory blocks are enabled; OFF disables these features. If you specify AUTO, the device driver supplies these services *only* when a program requests them.

Sizing Your EMS

memory This value specifies the *maximum* amount of extended memory that can be converted to EMS by the driver. You can substitute for *memory* any value from 64K to 32767K (32M). If you leave this parameter off, EMM386 will convert all available extended memory to EMS. So, if you need a smaller amount, say 512K for a DOS program, your directive would look like this:

```
DEVICE=EMM386.EXE 512
```

Because EMS is assigned only in multiples of 16K, whatever odd value you enter will be rounded down to the next lowest multiple of 16. To keep EMM386 from allocating any EMS, you must use the NOEMS parameter, below.

l=minXMS This is the opposite of the **memory** command; it specifies the *minimum* amount of extended memory that will remain after EMM386 loads. Use it to specify how much XMS you want to reserve when the driver converts available extended memory to EMS.

NOEMS Tells the driver not to set up an EMS page frame. Because EMM386.EXE will, by default, always try to establish an EMS page frame, you must use NOEMS if you don't want EMS but do want to use other features of the memory manager.

MIN=*size* Specifies the minimum amount of EMS that will be provided. If you have less than *size* extended memory available, EMM386 converts all available XMS to EMS. The default is 256K. If the value of MIN is greater than the amount specified by *memory* (in other words, if you've set up a conflict in which the least amount of EMS provided is more than the maximum allowable), EMM386 uses MIN instead.

If you use a value of 0 for MIN, EMM386 won't *reserve* any memory for EMS; however, that doesn't mean EMS won't be available. (To turn off EMS entirely, you must use the NOEMS parameter.) Instead, EMM386 can still create EMS as required by programs that request it, if any extended memory remains. If other programs have already grabbed all the XMS that is available, subsequent requests for EMS will be ignored. The MIN parameter is a way to make sure that at least *some* extended memory will be set aside for EMS.

Setting Up an EMS Page Frame

If you do use EMS, you must set aside a 64K block of memory that can be used as the page frame (the "window" DOS will use to look at each block of EMS memory as required). EMM386.EXE allows you to specify the address that will be used for the page frame or will find one for you.

Ideally, your page frame should not be in memory below the 640K boundary. A contiguous block of 64K of memory must exist starting at that address for the page frame to be installed. For example, you might enter /FRAME=C800 to place the page frame at address C800h in upper memory.

You might want to do this if the address selected automatically by EMM386 is inappropriate for some reason. You might conceivably have a ROM or some other program using the selected address that EMM386 failed to detect . On several occasions, I've relocated the EMS page frame to better use the available upper memory blocks. It happened that the automatically selected address split a large UMB into two pieces. By adjusting the page frame downward in memory just a bit, I was able to locate the beginning of the page frame in the lower UMB, leaving a larger block above.

Some Programs Confused by Frames Higher Than DFFF

Keep in mind that some programs, notably Ventura Publisher, get confused if you locate the EMS page frame too high in upper memory. The range C000 to D000 includes the most common addresses. I've had a few scanner interfaces also try to use that range but was able to avoid conflicts by moving the page frame up or down a little to leave room for the scanner board's ROM.

There are four ways to specify where the page frame resides: the M*x*, FRAME=*address*, or /P*mmmm* parameters.

M*x* If you use the M*x* parameter, substitute for *x* a value from 1 to 14, representing addresses from C000h to 9000h as follows in table 8.1.

Table 8.1. Mx Parameter Values

Value	Address
1	C000h
2	C400h
3	C800h
4	CC00h
5	D000h
6	D400h
7	D800h
8	DC00h
9	E000h
10	8000h
11	8400h
12	8800h
13	8C00h
14	9000h

The first nine of these values are all upper memory locations, and the last five are located near the top of conventional RAM. You should use these five only if no UMBs are available for your page frame.

FRAME=*address* Instead of using M*x*, you can specify an exact base address for the page frame, using any of the valid addresses listed in table 8.1. You can also enter NONE instead of an address to provide expanded memory *without* a page frame. EMS 4.0 doesn't really require a page frame to function, but some applications don't work properly without one.

/P*mmmm* The third way to specify the base address for the EMS page frame is with the /P switch; for *mmmm* substitute any of the addresses in table 8.1.

/P*n*=*address* You may also break up the 64K page frame into four 16K pages and specify base addresses for each of them individually. However, if the four pages are not contiguous, you lose Version 3.2 compatibility. You cannot use this switch if you specify a base address with the M*x*, FRAME, or /P*mmmm* switches. You might need this option if you find it impossible to locate a single 64K block in upper memory or if you have a group of 16K pages you'd like to use efficiently. Just be certain that all your applications which need EMS adhere to the Version 4.0 standard.

You can use the /P*n* switch four times, substituting 0 to 3 for n and any valid address listed in table 8.1 above, in increments of 400h.

Other EMS-Related Parameters

B=address This parameter specifies the lowest address in conventional RAM that can be used for swapping 16K pages. The default is 4000h, but you can use an address from 1000h to 4000h.

I=*mmmm-nnnn* Specifies addresses that EMM386 should include in the RAM it uses for EMS page frame or UMBs. You can use this parameter to force the driver to take control over areas of upper memory that it would normally leave alone but which you know can be safely used.

If you know, or think you know, that an area of upper memory is available, you can tell EMM386.EXE by using the /I switch. You should substitute for *mmmm* the beginning address of the block you want converted to an UMB or possible EMS page frame address, and for *nnnn*, you can substitute the ending address of that block.

Reclaiming System ROM

I use this command on my system to reclaim an UMB block that supposedly belongs to the system ROM. Although EMM386 will avoid using the whole 64K of system ROM in my computer, 32K of that is used only while the computer is booting up, to perform diagnostic tests. After the tests are finished or bypassed, the system starts looking for CONFIG.SYS, and that 32K of ROM is never, ever used again until the computer is rebooted. So, I include it in my UMBs and get an extra 32K for device drivers.

X=*mmmm-nnnn* This specifies the addresses that EMM386 should exclude from use for the EMS page frame or UMBs. If the driver is unable to detect an adapter, you can manually enter the memory address of that device to protect that area of upper RAM from being used.

Multiple X= and I= entries can be used on a single line to define the boundaries on as much memory as you need to. If entries conflict or overlap, the X switch takes precedence; EMM386 assumes that you really mean it when you say not to use a range of upper memory. Values for *mmmm* and *nnnn* must be in the range A000h to FFFFh, in 4K increments.

RAM=*mmmm-nnnn* This parameter specifies the range of segment addresses available for UMBs and EMS support. Use this parameter to keep EMM386 from using all available upper memory.

Some Specialized Parameters

Most of these parameters won't be needed by the average user. If you do require one, you'll either know it, or the instructions for your application will tell you. For example, don't worry about whether your system has a Weitek coprocessor. They generally aren't plugged into a motherboard just to keep dust out of the socket.

W=ON or W=OFF Turns support for a Weitek coprocessor on or off. Many motherboards have a socket for this specialized coprocessor, and some graphics- or math-oriented programs are written to use it, if present. You can toggle support for the processor with this parameter or from the DOS prompt with the command **emm386 w=on** or **w=off**.

A=*altregs* Fast alternate register sets are used for multitasking. This parameter lets you specify how many register sets EMM386 should allocate if the default value of 7 is not enough. Each extra register uses up 200 bytes of RAM

H=*handles* Defines how many handles EMM386 can work with. The default is 64, but you can specify a value between 2 and 255.

D=*nnn* This parameter defines how many kilobytes of memory should be set aside as a buffer for direct memory access. Certain devices, such as a bus-mastering SCSI controller card, some hand scanners, and other components that move large amounts of data very quickly "talk" directly to your memory without going through the CPU. Sometimes this exchange can take place faster than your system can handle it. A direct memory access (DMA) buffer provides an intermediate location for the data to reside during the process. The default value is 16K. If you have problems—say your system lags behind your hand scanner—increase this value to 32K or more. The installation or diagnostics programs furnished with some devices will advise you when you need a larger DMA buffer.

NOVCPI The virtual control program interface (VCPI) specification was formalized in 1988 as a standard way for multitasking programs that use extended memory to communicate with each other. Desqview and several products called DOS extenders use this specification. As you might expect, Microsoft independently developed its own extended memory specification, called DOS Protected Mode Interface (DPMI). Today, most new software is DPMI compliant, but you may still have some VCPI programs. These may cause problems under Windows. You can switch off support for VCPI programs with the NOVCPI parameter.

This parameter must be used with NOEMS—that is, no VCPI and no EMS under DOS. When both are used, EMM386 also ignores the MEMORY parameter and MIN switch.

HIGHSCAN This switch tells EMM386 to use an additional check of upper memory to determine whether particular blocks are available. This switch has no effect on some computers and may help lock up others by marking as available blocks that are already allocated. For most of us, however, it's a valuable tool for squeezing the most UMBs out of that first megabyte.

VERBOSE Forces EMM386 to display status messages when loading; normally messages are shown only if the driver has a problem carrying out a specific directive. This switch can help in debugging errors, because it keeps you informed about what is working as well as what is not working.

WIN=*mmmm-nnnn* This parameter reserves a range of addresses for Windows rather than EMM386, over-riding the RAM, ROM, and I switches, if necessary. However, the X switch takes precedence over this one. You can substitute for *mmmm* and *nnnn* addresses in the range A000h to FFFFh, in 4K increments. You may need this parameter if conflicts develop between EMM386 and Windows.

NOHI Forces EMM386 to load itself into conventional memory. This will decrease the amount of conventional RAM but increase the memory available for UMBs. You might use this parameter if moving EMM386 down to conventional RAM would let you load a larger driver into the bigger UMB that results, giving you a net gain in conventional memory.

ROM=*mmmm-nnnn* This parameter specifies the addresses used for ROM shadowing. You can use this if you want ROM shadowing, but your system doesn't implement it in hardware. Substitute for *mmmm* and *nnnn* the addresses of the ROMs you want shadowed.

NOMOVEXBDA The extended BIOS data area is normally at the top of conventional memory. EMM386 usually moves it into an UMB. Some programs won't work properly if you allow EMM386.EXE to move this data area to upper memory. This switch will override EMM386.EXE's default setting and keep the extended BIOS data where it normally resides.

This is an advanced switch that you'll need only to solve a rare problem. Note that using this switch will prevent DOS from accessing conventional memory below the BIOS.

ALTBOOT This switch tells EMM386 not to respond to Ctrl-Alt-Del but to use a different boot handler instead. Some systems lock up or do other weird things when EMM386 is loaded and the user presses Ctrl-Alt-Del.

Note for Windows Users

When EMM386 is used, its I, X, NOEMS, M*x*, P*nnnn*, and FRAME switches override the EMMINCLUDE, EMMEXCLUDE, and EMMPAGEFRAME settings used in Windows' SYSTEM.INI file.

Using EMM386 from the DOS Prompt

EMM386.EXE has limited applications from the DOS prompt. You must always load it and specify its switches from CONFIG.SYS. However, thereafter you can perform two functions from DOS. The ON | OFF | AUTO parameters and Weitek coprocessor support can be used. In addition, typing **emm386** on a line by itself will display the current status of the driver's EMS support.

Using What You Know

Here are some tips, some already discussed briefly, on using what you've learned about HIMEM.SYS and EMM386.EXE. You can often squeeze out a little extra conventional memory by following these steps.

Tip

Try disabling EMS with the FRAME=NONE switch. The worst thing that can happen is that a DOS program that optionally uses EMS will find itself limited in the amount of data it can handle or will operate at a slower speed. Programs that require EMS will alert you immediately with an error message along the lines of EMS Page Frame Not Found. If either of these things happen, you can always re-enable EMS. Otherwise, you've gained at least 64K in usable UMBs.

Tip

See whether you can grab the upper memory addresses normally reserved for monochrome video. If you use an EGA or VGA monitor, the video card may not use the addresses between B000 and B7FF. Include them with an I=B000-B7FF parameter on your EMM386 line. This won't work if you have a super VGA monitor or if Windows tries to grab this area, too (enter DualDisplay=True in the [386 Enh] section of SYSTEM.INI to counter this).

Tip Experiment with the loading order of your drivers and TSRs. If your UMBs are limited or are split up into several contiguous areas, you may want to experiment with the loading order in order to pack the most drivers into the available UMBs. For example, if you have a 32K UMB followed by a 24K UMB and three device drivers that require 12K, 26K, and 10K, respectively, you shouldn't load the 12K or 10K drivers first. They will go into the 32K block and not leave enough free upper memory for your 26K driver. If you load the 26K driver first, it will go into the 32K block, leaving 6K left over, and both of the other two will load into the 24K UMB nicely.

Tip The best approach to take is usually to try loading the larger drivers first, but sometimes you'll need to change the order to get everything to fit properly. The MEM command with the /C switch can help you by showing exactly how much memory each driver that is loaded requires. You can use this information to juggle the loading order appropriately.

Using Third-Party Memory Managers

Until DOS 6 was released, there were some very good reasons to use third-party memory managers such as QEMM, 386Max, NetRoom, and others. All these programs were much more sophisticated than EMM386 and had many more options. That made sense; each of these offerings made up the better part of the vendor's product lines, and a lot of specialized talent went into designing them. Microsoft's busy programmers, on the other hand, had Windows NT, Word for Windows 3.0, and other things to worry about.

So, third-party memory managers were the state-of-the-art offerings for a long time. They were better at seeking out available UMBs and performed tricks like QEMM's Stealth attack, in which system ROM is copied to extended memory, freeing up that area for UMB use.

Today, EMM386 is a lot smarter than it used to be. There are many more compatibility switches and special options. HIGHSCAN does a better job of locating available UMBs. Most importantly, EMM386 is guaranteed to be 100 percent compatible with DOS 6 and Windows. That's not to say that bugs won't pop up, but Microsoft can't blame them on a third party and will quickly move to fix them.

Still, you might want to use a third-party memory manager to stay abreast of the bleeding edge of technology or for compatibility with other software that you use. QEMM works better with Desqview than EMM386 does. The following section will describe some of the leading products and detail why you might want to consider them.

Quarterdeck's QEMM

This is the most popular third-party memory manager. It replaces both HIMEM.SYS and EMM386. It is furnished with Manifest (MFT.EXE), which generally does a better job than MSD.EXE of mapping out your memory. It's most striking feature is the Stealth capability I mentioned earlier.

Stealth relocates your ROM BIOS, which resides above F000h in upper memory, to extended memory after your system boots. You can then use those addresses for UMBs. QEMM manages any requests for ROM BIOS calls at their original location, redirecting them to the new address.

QEMM is compatible with Windows, because Windows is quite happy to do its own memory management. You may need to use some extra switches outlined in Quarterdeck's comprehensive but confusing documentation to keep the two from conflicting with each other. In addition, you will need the WINHIRAM.VXD virtual extended memory driver that enables Windows to perform the functions of HIMEM.SYS, because QEMM handles those services itself outside of Windows.

This memory manager has quite a few options not available with EMM386, such as memory sorting; if your add-in memory board has RAM of a different speed from that on your motherboard, QEMM will use the faster memory first. (This feature is disabled when Windows starts. QEMM "remembers" what regions of memory are accessed after it has been loaded, so you can type a **qemm accessed** command from the DOS prompt to see what UMBs really are available under actual working conditions.

Qualitas' 386Max

This memory manager has long been number two and really seems to try harder. It has some special features of its own, although you can never expect any product in a competitive market to remain unique for very long.

If you have an IBM PS/2, you'll be especially interested in a version of this utility called BlueMax. True IBM machines have a 128K system ROM instead of the 32K to 64K found in most clones. That's because PCs include a version of the BASIC programming language right in their ROMs. BlueMax knows how to create UMBs in this area.

Another unique capability is Qualitas' support for multiple instancing of device drivers under Windows Enhanced mode. Each DOS session that you run can access its own device drivers, rather than share a common pool of memory. You can run mouse drivers in all your DOS sessions, or even unique combinations of driver settings in each DOS window (say, special ANSI.SYS settings to change keyboard definitions or screen colors).

At this writing, 386Max is the only third-party memory manager to fully support DPMI and is one of the easiest products to use (there's even an online tutorial).

Memory Commander

This utility takes an unusual approach to increasing conventional RAM. Not only will it move ROMs, drivers, and TSRs to free up as much as possible of your basic 640K, it can add to that, producing up to 842K of conventional memory on a VGA (not super VGA) system! There's no automatic optimization available, but if the absolute maximum amount of conventional RAM is important to you, check out this program. You'll need to use it with **mem** and MSD.EXE to get the information you need.

NetRoom

Although created to free up RAM on systems running network drivers, this utility also works well on stand-alone workstations. It includes an automatic optimizer and does a good job of freeing conventional memory.

QMAPS

This memory manager is slow, doesn't provide a system analysis utility, and has difficulty calculating the size of some types of drivers. However, it is very cheap for network users and is furnished with several utilities, such as a RAM disk and cache, that DOS 6 owners probably don't need.

The Next Step

At this point, your system's RAM should be under control, eliminating one performance bottleneck. Now it's time to take a look at one area that has the most room for improvement for the typical user: mass storage. Hard disk drives and floppies are one of the easiest components of your system to fine tune, particularly with the tools that DOS 6 gives you. We'll look at disk caching, file compression, and disk optimization in the next section of this book.

Part III: Optimizing Hard Disk Performance

This section will explore the ways in which DOS 6 can help you fine-tune and improve the performance of your hard disk drive. Because hard drives are inherently thousands of times slower than RAM, the most important thing you can do is reduce the number of times your system must look for data on the hard disk, rather than memory. You'll learn how to put DOS 6's SmartDrive disk caching utility to work in Chapters 11 through 13. We'll also look at some alternative caching programs that may do a better job for you.

File compression is another way to increase the performance of a hard disk. The extra capacity you gain through utilities like DoubleSpace can effectively double the size of your hard disk. You may even notice some speed gains; the system can read compressed files more quickly than the noncompressed version, and if the decompression step takes less time than the time saved in reading the file, the result is a net decrease in access time.

Defragmentation is the third way to fine tune a hard disk. DOS 6's disk defragmenting utility can arrange the files on your drive so that the sectors are arranged in consecutive order. On a fragmented disk, DOS must skip all over the disk surface to collect all the pieces of a file. That can quickly add up to several additional seconds each time you access a large file on your disk.

To help you understand how these utilities operate, we'll start off with a description of the technology behind hard disks.

How Hard Disks Work

This chapter will serve as your introduction to hard disks and will serve as a basis for understanding how they operate and how they work with DOS 6 and its utilities. There will be some nuts-and-bolts discussions, but nothing really too complex. Hard disks are, in fact, easy to understand. In theory, they resemble the familiar floppy disk. In practice, there is a lot more to them.

After all, more than almost anything else, hard disks are what make desktop computing as we know it possible. Most of what we now do with computers wouldn't be practical if nearly every system didn't have at least a small hard disk attached. Indeed, if you look at the directions the industry is taking, it almost seems as if some manufacturers would like the floppy disk to go away.

NeXT Had No Floppies

Steve Jobs, for example, introduced his NeXT computer with no floppy drives. If you wanted removable storage, you used optical disks or nothing. He's since backed off from that radical stance and, indeed, NeXT has gotten out of the hardware business entirely. Today, the only computers you can buy without a floppy disk are ultraportable notebook systems. Even though the hard disk has been unable to banish the floppy directly, in recent years the floppy disk has become a lot more hard disk-like. Ordinary 3.5-inch disks can hold up to 2.88M of data. Floptical disks can store 20M or more. Many users have 90 or 150M Bernoulli drives, and some hard disks come in removeable cartridges, too, so that you can take them from computer to computer. Some day, perhaps, the chief difference between what we think of as hard disks today and what we think of as floppies will be how difficult they are to get out of the computer.

Hard Disks Predate Floppies

Actually, hard disks predate floppies by a number of years. Old-time hard disk drives for mainframe computers held about 20M and were roughly the size and weight of a washing machine. They weren't convenient for transporting software, and punch cards and tape had drawbacks of their own. So, IBM tucked an 8-inch floppy disk drive away in the innards of some of their big iron behemoths, giving technicians a convenient random access media that was transportable and could hold a megabyte or so of programs or data.

When personal computers came around, few early hobbyists could afford even used washing-machine Winchesters or had any way to connect them to their systems. We had the same bad feelings about paper storage media and magnetic tape that the mainframe folks did. I actually used a computer with an 8-inch floppy drive that could hold a megabyte of information for about three years at the turn of the last decade, and in those days of character-based applications, a megabyte was a lot of storage.

It was a step backwards to get an IBM PC that could store only 160,000 bytes on a floppy. Most of us were relieved to step up to a genuine IBM PC-XT in the mid-1980s and astounded at how quickly an 85 ms hard disk drive could access information.

What Is a Hard Disk?

The hard disk itself is like a floppy disk in that a circular magnetic surface is used to record information and that a read-write head something like the heads found in tape recorders is used to record and retrieve information.

However, on closer comparison, a floppy disk and disk drive are relatively large, imprecise components. That's the case, in part, because floppy drives and their disks must be built to tolerate wide variations in operating environments and in the components themselves. Floppy disk drives must function in somewhat dirty surroundings (such as the dust in ordinary room air) and allow repeated mounting and dismounting of cheap, mass-produced disk media.

Hard Disk Media, Electronics Single Unit

With hard disk drives, the media, read-write heads, other drive components as well as interface circuitry are built as a single integrated unit. In "intelligent" drives such as IDE, or SCSI models, the controller is also built into the drive. This allows a higher degree of precision in fitting together the components that make up the hard disk drive. As a result, some special techniques can be used that result in much higher information densities.

One such technique is to have the read-write head *fly* over the surface of the disk at a very small distance, supported by a cushion of air, instead of resting directly on the disk surface as is the case with floppy disks. The heads do not touch the hard disk surface, except when the disk is stopped, or because of an accident called a head crash. As a result, the disk surface does not wear, and rotational speeds can be much higher. Just as speed-reading techniques allow you to absorb information faster, simply making a hard disk rotate faster allows the read-write heads to access data more quickly. Where floppy disk drives rotate at 300 revolutions per minute, hard disks commonly revolve at 3600 rpm or higher, with correspondingly higher data transfer rates.

There are other differences between a floppy disk and a hard disk. The magnetic coating of a floppy disk is applied to a flexible polyester support or *substrate*. Fixed disks, in contrast, use a rigid aluminum platter. This platter is diamond-turned. Then a magnetic coating is applied by one of several methods.

Thin-Film Media Predominates Today

Originally, this was done only by applying iron oxide particles onto the media in a very smooth layer. Today, so-called *thin-film* techniques are used to coat the media with a much thinner (and tougher) layer that has smaller, denser magnetic particles. The thin films can be applied either by plating (something like the way paint is applied by a roller) or sputtering (similar to using a paint spray can).

Both thin-film techniques allow placing more tracks per inch of radius and recording more bits per inch of track, when compared to the older iron oxide coating method. This is because the newer coating methods provide higher values of *coercivity*, which is a measure of the strength of the magnetic field required to switch the magnetic patterns in a material. As coercivity increases, the size of the particles that can be practically used in magnetic media grows smaller. Thin films allow densities up to 60 million bits per square inch using normal linear recording techniques and track densities between 1500 and 2000 tracks per inch.

Because even a particle of dust can loom as an impassable object given the low flying height of a hard disk read-write head, the platters and heads must be sealed inside a mini "clean room" that provides an environment free of contaminants. If this protection is breached, the user is exposed to the dreaded head crash. A grain of dust, or sometimes external vibration, can cause the read-write head to strike the disk platter forcefully instead of gliding over smoothly. Should the head crash take place when the head is passing over an information-containing area, data can be permanently lost. In the worst cases, damage can occur in the directory track whereupon the disk controller no longer knows where to find *any* of the information on the disk. When a catastrophe of this type occurs, you'll be glad you made regular use of DOS 6's Backup utility (you *do* plan to back up your data regularly?)

Trend Toward Smaller Form Factors

Gradually, we've moved from hard disks with 5.25-inch aluminum platters to those with 3.5-, 2.5-, or 1.8-inch diameter surfaces. There are many advantages to the smaller form factors, and these apply not just to laptop computer designers pressed for space.

Smaller drives require smaller components, which can in turn be made more rugged. In addition, smaller drives allow faster access to the data, because the read-write head has to travel a smaller distance to reach a given track. Thin-film media are making these smaller drives possible with no sacrifice in storage capacity.

With all magnetic disks, information is recorded on the magnetic surface by a read-write head that causes changes in the orientation of the particles or *domains* on the surface. Before the data is recorded, all the magnetic particles on the disk are aligned in the same direction. As information is written, electric currents in the read-write head produce appropriate flux changes in the magnetic orientation of these particles. When the data is read back, these changes in the disk *induce* electrical currents in the read-write head, producing electrical signals that can be amplified and interpreted by the controller and passed on to the computer system.

Measuring Density

The distance between these flux changes on the disk determine the density of information that can be recorded on the disk. The distance can be measured both radially out from the center of the disk (how many different tracks can be fit on the disk, or tracks-per-inch) as well as along the track itself (bits-per-inch). In general, the flux changes are recorded along the surface of a given track. This is called *linear* recording. However, another recording method, called *vertical* or *perpendicular* recording, allows storing information even more densely. With this technology, the particles are positioned vertically, rather than horizontally. The disk media must be coated in a special way. The magnetic layer must be soft on the bottom and hard on the top, to allow the particles to move in the desired direction, yet resist damage at the surface of the disk. In addition, the read-write heads must be specially designed and fly closer than ever to the disk surface.

Much Narrower Heads Required

These narrower, denser tracks require read-write heads that are much smaller than those found in floppy disks. The heads are moved across the surface of the disk by a head-positioning device. Cheaper systems of the past used a stepper motor. Today, most drives use more precise positioning mechanisms, such as the voice-coil motor. These may use rare-earth elements such as cobalt and neodenium in the track sensors, allowing the heads to be positioned more accurately. That translates into greater potential capacity. Voice-coil motor actuators also boast faster access times.

Hard disks generally have several platters, each with two surfaces, and read-write heads mounted in sets that read all the corresponding tracks of all the surfaces on all the platters simultaneously. Because this arrangement provides a "cylinder" of tracks, one on top of each other, a common way to refer to a hard disk's physical makeup is in terms of these cylinders. However, as we'll see, the physical layout of a hard disk may or may not have anything to do with how the hard disk controller and your computer view the *logical* arrangement of the disk.

Figure 9.1 shows a disk divided into tracks and sectors. Figure 9.2 illustrates how the multiple platters fit together to form a cylinder.

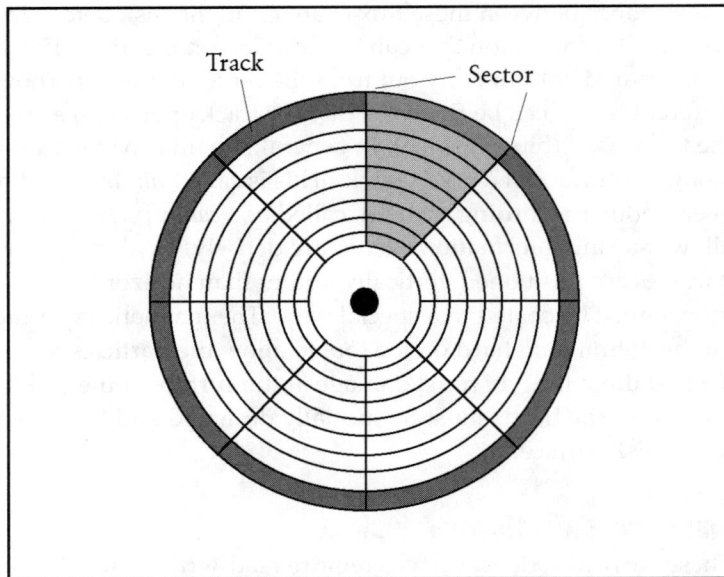

Figure 9.1. A hard disk, divided into tracks and sectors.

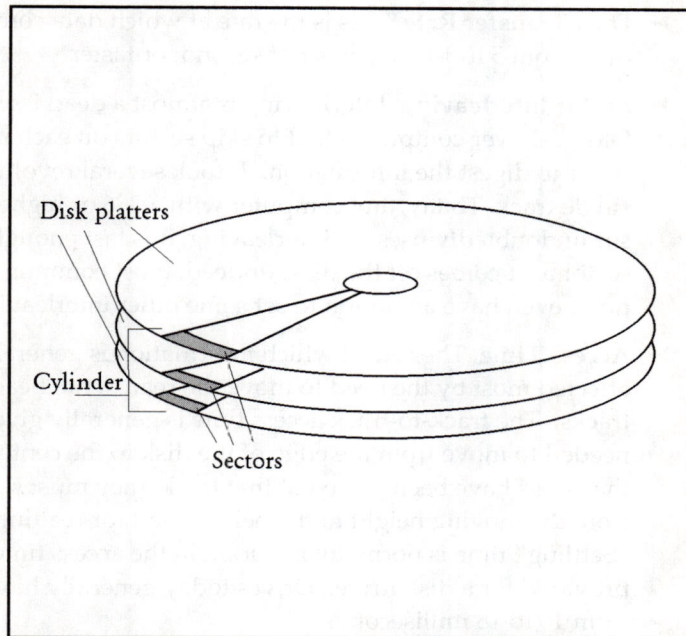

Figure 9.2. Multiple platters form a cylinder.

Factors Affecting Hard Disk Performance

There are five major physical factors of the hard disk itself that affect how quickly a hard disk can write or read data. In addition, there are a number of other factors not related to the disk that can affect disk speed. These have to do with the computer itself, or DOS. Those factors are addressed by the DOS 6 utilities, such as SmartDrive or DoubleSpace. For now, let's look at the physical factors of the hard disk.

➤ **Cylinder Size and Density** This is determined, in part, by the number of surfaces or platters in a hard disk. Cylinder density can also be increased by adding more sectors to each track, usually using a more advanced encoding method.

➤ **Data Transfer Rate** This is the rate at which data comes off the disk, from 5 to 10 megabits per second, or faster.

➤ **Sector Interleaving** Interleaving is almost a dead issue these days. Older, slower computers had to skip sectors on each revolution in order to digest the information. It took several revolutions to read a single track. Today, any computer with a 386 or higher microprocessor undoubtedly uses 1:1 interleaving; it is fast enough to read each sector as it comes off the disk. Indeed, most common hard disks don't even have an option to set some other interleaving factor.

➤ **Access Time** The rate at which information is generally read is affected most by the need to move the read-write head between tracks. The track-to-track access time is generally given as the time needed to move from the edge of the disk to the center track. When the heads have been placed at that track, they must settle down from the moving height to the height used for reading and writing. "Settling" time is normally included in the access time figures provided for a disk drive. Drives today generally have access times from 10 to 18 milliseconds.

➤ **Average Latency** When a head has finished seeking and settling, the disk drive controller must wait until the desired track spins the rest of the way around to the first sector before the read or write can actually take place. This nonproductive period is called *latency* and is, on average, half the time needed for the drive to spin around.

Disk Controllers and Interfaces

A device interface is a standardized way of communicating between two components, in this case the hard disk drive and the computer system. There are a number of standard and quasi-standard interfaces between hard disks (and other peripherals) and IBM PCs and compatible computers. The ST506/412 interface, developed by Seagate Technologies, was one of the most popular but has generally been supplanted by other types.

Device-Level Interfaces

The ST506/412 was a *device-level* interface. In hard disks, such an interface links the controller and disk directly with a large collection of signal lines, each of which carries a separate value. Because the operation of the hard disk and the controller are so tightly linked together, such an interface can be very efficient when the two are well matched. On the other hand, to upgrade the performance of one, you frequently have to replace both. Such drives furnish the controller raw data bits containing both data pulses and timing pulses called clock bits. Data separator circuitry is built into the controller to sort out these two. Unless special encoding techniques are used, this type of interface is generally limited to 5-megabits-per-second data transfer rates.

Another device-level interface is the enhanced small device interface (EDSI), which enjoyed a period of popularity a few years ago. This interface puts the data separator circuitry in the drive and not the controller. Although more expensive to implement, EDSI is potentially much faster than ST506, with the capability to run at 10 to 15 megabits per second.

There has been a trend in recent years to skip the device-level interface entirely and to put the controller circuitry right in the disk drive itself. The drive then connects to the computer with a *system-level* interface.

System-Level Interfaces

Unlike the device-level interface, in which information is carried on dedicated lines, system-level interfaces convey information in logical terms. As a result, multiple devices (for example, more than one hard disk drive) can use the same connection in parallel fashion. More intelligence is required to decode requests from the computer (the drive has to decide that the request is for itself and not some other drive on the connection, for instance).

So such system-level interfaces are termed *intelligent*. One well-known example is the SCSI (Small Computer System Interface.) Although there was a battle among proponents to refer to the SCSI acronym as "sexy," lack of true standardization, until SCSI-2 arrived, led to the more common reference of "scuzzy."

A SCSI device has circuitry on-board that receives requests for information from the PC and intelligently handles finding the data, retrieving it, decoding it, and passing it along to the computer on predefined data lines (ideally) common to all SCSI devices. Because the computer does not have to be concerned with the nuts-and-bolts of operating the peripheral, a SCSI can be a hard disk drive, a tape drive, an optical disk drive, or another peripheral. Such devices are intelligent, so the difference is transparent to the computer system. The SCSI interface has been applied to devices other than storage devices, such as printers and scanners. Unfortunately, manufacturers have had considerable flexibility in terms of what features they include or leave out of their SCSI interfaces while ostensibly still adhering to the "standard." As a result, there are SCSI interfaces and there are SCSI interfaces, and devices may or may not be compatible among computer systems implementing them. Fortunately, the SCSI-2 specification and the standardized advanced SCSI programing interface (ASPI) have helped alleviate the problems. Today, you can use any ASPI-compliant SCSI controller and universal driver software, such as CorelSCSI, with just about any SCSI device, including hard drives, CD-ROMs, scanners, and cartridge drives.

The IDE Interface

The IDE interface first appeared as a direct connection to the PC/AT bus, under the aegis of Compaq. Fast like ESDI, and intelligent like SCSI, IDE drives look to the system as if they were ST506 units, so no ROM changes or drivers are required.

IDE drivers contain their own controller. The outboard interface card has little more than some bus buffers and address decoding circuitry. That support can easily be built into many motherboards. Vendors also offer interface "paddle" cards, some with their own cache memory, that usually also include controller circuitry for floppy disks as well as parallel and serial ports.

The Next Step

The description of how hard disks work will be useful in the following chapters. For example, now that you know how disks are arranged in sectors and cylinders, it's easier to understand why read-ahead caches are so useful. The huge time lags caused by moving from one track to another make it clear that disk defragmentation can provide significant improvements in performance. Clearly, DOS 6 can be an important tool for optimizing mass storage components.

How Caches Work

In the real world, a cache is a place where you store objects to keep them handy. Computers also have need for such convenient storage places. This chapter will provide an introduction to disk caching.

A cache improves performance by preventing your computer from wasting valuable clock cycles when it could be busy doing useful work. Your system's microprocessor runs at a fixed clock speed such as 25, 33, or 50 MHz (although it may have a lower speed that we hardly, if ever, use). Any time the CPU doesn't have instructions to carry out, it just sits there, wasting time. Those clock ticks are gone forever and can't be retrieved later on when your microprocessor is overloaded with things to do. It's best, then, to keep the brains of your system supplied with a steady diet of instructions and data to work on. The less time wasted, the higher performance of your computer.

Computer Systems Have Bottlenecks

Unfortunately, as you learned in Chapter 3, there are several bottlenecks in any computer. Faster microprocessors can almost always handle instructions quicker than they can be fetched from memory. For that reason, most recent computer systems have a sort of buffer that feeds instructions into a queue for the microprocessor. This buffer can be accessed much more quickly than ordinary RAM in the computer, because it often resides in high-speed memory located in a special area that can be quickly accessed by the CPU. In fact, in 486 chips, the memory holding area, 8K in size, is located within the chip itself.

This memory buffer is a type of cache and helps smooth out the bottle-neck between relatively slow RAM and the relatively fast CPU. However, if you think RAM can be slow, you haven't compared the speed of memory with that of even the fastest hard disks. Memory speeds are measured in nanoseconds (one billionth of a second); whereas hard disk transfer rates are measured in milliseconds (one thousandth of a second). The difference between a nanosecond and a millisecond is a lot. It would be like saying "Wait a second" and then not replying for 31.7 years. Few of us have that much patience when we're seated at our computers.

Disk Caches

A second popular form of caching is the disk cache. Important data is kept in faster RAM, making it available to the CPU a few million times faster than if it had to be fetched from the hard disk drive.

Don't confuse RAM caching with disk caching. If your computer is a 486, you have an 8K RAM cache built in and may have more in a secondary, external CPU cache. Other systems, particularly 386 models, may also have external caches supplying data to RAM. However, these do nothing to improve disk performance.

How a Cache Works

SmartDrive and other caches work because computer systems tend to use the same memory locations over and over and access disk drives in predictable ways. That is, if the CPU happens to need a certain sector on your drive, odds are good that it doesn't need only that sector. It will also require the next sectors of that particular file which, on an optimized disk, will often be the next physical sector.

Some Programs Load All Code and Data Simultaneously

Some types of applications benefit from caching more than others. Some programs always load the entire program and its data into memory at once and never need to access the disk again until you save the data file or exit the program. These are generally very simple applications, easily identified because they require a minimum amount of RAM to operate or have a fixed or limited file size. Older spreadsheet programs or barebones text editors are typical examples of this type of software. Because such programs don't generate frequent disk accesses, they don't benefit from caching.

Others Load in Sections

Other programs are loaded into memory only in small sections called overlays. They may work with very large data files read from the disk a little at a time. When the software goes to load its next overlay or needs another block of records, it may find them in the cache.

Caching is effective because a whole group of sectors can be read at one pass and stored in memory until they are needed. You'll recall from the last chapter that jumping around on a disk from one track to another takes a great deal of time — as much as 28 milliseconds, or 1/35th of a second. Because most people can count from 1 to 10 in about a second, that's obviously a period that relates more closely to the human scale of time, rather than the computer's.

Hits and Misses

If your system needs disk information and it already resides in the cache, this is known as a cache hit. Otherwise, a cache miss occurs, and your microprocessor waits for a while until the needed data can be obtained from the disk. Obviously, the higher percentage of cache hits, the better SmartDrive performs.

How Caches Differ from Buffers

The way in which caches are different from the buffers (set in CONFIG.SYS using the BUFFERS directive) can be found in the software built into caches like SmartDrive to improve the hit rate. DOS's disk buffers are relatively dumb; they simply store the most recently read and written information. When it comes time to search through a buffer, DOS does it in a rather brain-damaged manner: it will look through the entire cache in sequential order. With a large number of buffers, it can actually take longer to search through memory than to retrieve the data from disk. Moreover, there is no special likelihood that the next information required will be data that is already in memory.

A cache, in contrast, organizes the data to improve the chances that it contains the required information. In addition, a disk cache uses more intelligent techniques to find needed data, so much less processing time is spent looking through memory. A good rule of thumb is that caches manage data, but buffers merely store data.

Cache Beginnings

Caches have been with us since the 1960s, when a fellow named Belady introduced an algorithm called The Greatest Forward Distance, which is used as a basis for comparison of all later methods. (It's interesting to note that this particular method can't be applied to most real-world systems, because it works only when you know how the operations involved are going to turn out. In effect, it optimizes how the information is used after the fact. Unless a system repeats itself—is cyclic—the Belady algorithm can't be used.)

Least Frequently Used and Least Recently Used Algorithms

Instead, two other methods, called Least Frequently Used and Least Recently Used algorithms are put to work in the most common disk cache systems. The names of each algorithm offer a quick summary of how they work.

Because most caches are fixed in size, when the available memory is full, some information must be discarded to make room for the new data. Under one system, the least frequently used information in the cache is deleted, under the theory that retaining information that is accessed at frequent intervals is most likely to produce a high hit rate. The caching program must keep track of the number of times a given block of information is used.

Data Not Used Is Less Likely To Be Accessed

The other system calls for discarding the oldest information—that information which has not been accessed for the longest time. It's thought that data that hasn't been accessed for awhile is less likely to be used again. The DOS 6 buffers use this method, and SmartDrive also follows a first-in-first-out scheme. In its simplest form, it's fairly easy to implement, since the operating system needs to keep track of just one piece of information for a given block of data: when was it last used by the CPU? However, data that has been used many times can be discarded simply because it hasn't been used as recently as other information which may be needed only once. In the worst case, this data will be used once, "age" its way out of the cache before it is used again, and then be loaded back into the cache a short time later when it is next required. This condition is called *thrashing* and definitely will affect performance.

There are flaws in both theories, of course, but each has strengths in handling certain types of data. Because the information we work with tends to vary quite widely, everything evens out in the long run, and the actual difference in performance between the two algorithms is typically less than 10 percent.

Another cache technique is called look-ahead, in which the cache reads more sectors than requested by the application. Usually, only one or two sectors are demanded by a program at any one time. If the cache is able to look-ahead, it will load more information than needed immediately but will have the sectors required for the next request. That can greatly improve the "hit" rate of the cache.

Other Cache Factors

You might assume that the bigger a cache, the better it will perform. That's not always true, because the way caches treat data can have a significant impact on performance. And, as a cache grows, it will reach a point of diminishing returns.

Direct Mapped Caches

There are three ways to design a cache: direct mapping, fully associative, and set associative. In a direct mapped cache, each data "cubbyhole" or data line corresponds to real data storage addresses on a one-to-one basis. One piece of information in the cache represents one piece on your hard disk, or, in a CPU cache, one external memory location. The cache software can look for data and retrieve it very quickly; either the information is there in the cache, or it is on the disk or external RAM and must be read.

Unfortunately, you'd need 40M of cache to provide an unshared direct line to all the data on a 40M hard disk, or 8M of cache to correspond to a system with 8M of RAM. So, each cache location actually represents more than one disk location or memory location. If overlapping requests are made (the program needs the data stored in locations *a*, *d*, *g*, and *h*, and one cache location happens to serve all four of them) only one of the four will actually be in the cache. The other three collections of data will have to be loaded from the external storage. You can end up with the ironic situation of having a cache that is only half full but be unable to service specific requests from memory because the particular information must all squeeze through the same cache addresses.

Fully Associative Caches

Fully associative caching doesn't use fixed mapping of specific cache locations to external storage. Instead, any cache data line can represent any storage location. Your available cache memory can be fully used; any request can be plugged into any available address. That complicates the retrieval process however. Instead of darting immediately to the assigned cubbyhole for specific data, the cache software must look through a list of tags to determine where, or even if, the information resides in the cache. So, each and *every* request for data, even those for information that is not in the cache, must go through this process.

Set Associative Caches

The best compromise between direct mapped and fully associative caches may be set-associative designs. Under this scheme, the cache is divided into blocks of memory called sets. Each set corresponds to a specific area of storage. However, within the set, the cache software has the freedom to assign data locations in an associative fashion. That reduces the chance of overlapping requests. When the cache looks for specific information, it needs only to check all the addresses in the appropriate set, rather than every address in the cache.

You can see why huge caches don't necessarily provide the best performance. When a cache is large enough that 95 or more percent of the requests for data result in a hit (this happens around 2M for disk caches), additional size has very little effect on performance. Indeed, the extra time needed to check for data can actually slow down your system. A 16M disk cache might result in no better than a 99 percent hit rate (the same as, say, a 4M cache), but one percent of the time the system would be looking through 16M of data fruitlessly before it could finally access your hard disk.

Caching Can Improve Write and Read Performance

In theory, disk caching can provide performance improvements when writing to the disk, as well as when reading. If information is held in memory for a short time, some of it may be changed again before it is written to disk, eliminating a redundant write. In addition, a cache program can be set to use *staged writes*, in which data is written during pauses that would otherwise not be used efficiently.

In practice, most caches use a *write-through* technique. Earlier versions of SmartDrive did this, and the DOS 6 version can also be set to this mode for any or all of the disks it is caching. When write-through caching is activated, disk reads are buffered, but any information sent to the cache is immediately written to the disk. This reduces the possibility that a power outage or accidental, poorly-timed rebooting will occur when important information (including your updated file allocation table) is being written to the disk.

Disk caches can be built into hard disk controllers as physical RAM. This memory can't be used for anything else, however, so hardware disk caches tend to be fairly expensive solutions for most of us. SmartDrive's solution — using the memory we already own — is generally much more economical.

The Next Step

Now that you know why you might want to use a disk cache and how they can affect your system's performance, it's time to learn about SmartDrive itself. You'll learn how to set up SmartDrive and how to best choose from among the available options. You may even want to opt for a third-party cache instead, and I'll explain how to choose one of them, too.

All About SmartDrive

The original SmartDrive, up through Version 3.x, did a lot to sour many DOS users on disk caches. It was slow, not very powerful, and had significant limitations. Most of us either skipped disk caching altogether (a definite mistake) or purchased a third-party cache such as HyperDisk.

Starting with Version 4.0, SmartDrive has gotten a lot smarter. Version 4.1, provided with DOS 6, is a virtual genius. Earlier editions did little more than buffer an entire track as it was read. As you discovered in the last chapter, that's not particularly efficient. A file's clusters may be scattered all over a disk, causing the cache to fill up with a huge collection of tracks that may each have only one or two sectors of useful information. Even on an optimized disk, a track-buffering cache of this sort stupidly accumulates large numbers of sectors that will never be used.

No Track Record

SmartDrive doesn't care about particular tracks. It deals with blocks of data and, therefore, tends to gather from the disk only the information that you really need and may tend to need again soon. SmartDrive is, therefore, much more efficient in its use of the memory you set aside for it.

A 2M SmartDrive 4.x cache should produce hit rates higher than that scored by a SmartDrive 3.x cache that is twice as large.

As a block-oriented cache, SmartDrive can be used with any block device that DOS can read and write to (block devices are, usually, those assigned a drive letter), including floppy disks, Bernoulli drives, floptical disks, and WORM (write once, read many times) optical disks. The two exceptions are CD-ROM drives or drives connected to your computer over a network. Some recent CD-ROM driver software includes its own caching capability, and network drives often have a caching system built into the networking software.

Usable with More Devices

This change to block orientation alone makes SmartDrive 4 a significant improvement over earlier versions, which were compatible only with drives that used the PC's built-in ROM-BIOS through something called DOS Interrupt 13. Although that limitation did not include most hard disk drives, it specifically *excluded* many other mass storage peripherals that can benefit from caching. If you had a Bernoulli drive, you used Iomega's version of PC-Kwik cache. Owners of some other drives were not so lucky.

Large DOS Partitions OK

Because the latest SmartDrive isn't concerned with the logical structure of the disk, it works fine with non-DOS partitions larger than 32M. Prior to DOS 4.0, many users relied on hard disk drivers like OnTrack Disk Manager or SpeedStor to create large disk volumes. These disk management utilities continued to see use after DOS 4, too, because most users skipped that release and went directly from DOS 3.3 to DOS 5.0. So, many hard disks partitioned under these schemes are still in daily use; disk managers are an excellent way to get hard drives to work in computers not designed to support them. (Older computers may not include a user-definable hard disk definition and will recognize only disks listed in their ROM-BIOS tables.)

The original SmartDrive sometimes would not work with these older disk managers. The utilities often bypassed DOS's 1024-track limitation by combining several physical tracks into one larger logical one. SmartDrive

3.x and earlier versions stubbornly refused to work properly with drives that had more than 1,024 physical tracks. Today, neither DOS nor SmartDrive cares much about how many tracks your hard disk has, nor are they even able to tell, in most cases.

Caching Reads and Writes

Another improvement in SmartDrive 4.x was the change from a read-only cache to caching of both reads and writes. Caching reads is useful, because if the information is already contained in the cache, no disk access is needed. But caching writes can also save time; SmartDrive can be configured to write information to your disk only when it has changed. The timing of the write step can also be delayed until there is a pause in activity, reducing the chance that the disk activity will interrupt productive computing.

SmartDrive does not cache writes to removable media, such as floppy disk drives, because it is possible to remove the disk before SmartDrive has finished writing to it. Instead, it functions as a write-through cache for these drives.

Data Lost in RAM?

Some panic at the idea of their valuable data, which they *thought* had been written to disk, floating around instead in RAM until SmartDrive gets around to performing a staged write. In practice, the danger is no greater than the potential loss you might suffer from a power outage or other accidental reset. It may actually be less, because in the latter case, you could lose everything in memory—under a multitasking environment like Windows.

First, SmartDrive won't let unsaved data "age" more than five seconds before writing it to disk. That's a lot less time than most of us let pass before we save working files manually.

In addition, SmartDrive recognizes when you press the Ctrl-Alt-Del keys to reboot or when an application requests the same action and writes the contents of its cache to disk before turning the rebooting process over to the PC. You could still goof and press the reset switch or turn off your system's power, but the only data you would lose would be that which is less than five seconds old. If you include the **smartdrv /c** switch at the end of the batch file you use to run a particular application (which can include Windows), you don't even have to worry about that in many cases.

That particular command tells SmartDrive to empty its cache by writing its contents to disk. By including it at the end of the batch file, the cache will be flushed automatically any time you exit that application. All you need to do is remember to be looking at the C: prompt before you turn off your computer.

Later, I'll show you how to turn write caching on and off for particular drives, so you can disable this feature fully or partially if you're really concerned.

The final enhancement made to SmartDrive 4 was an improvement in the way it responds to being loaded into upper memory blocks. Where older versions often couldn't be loaded high, the latest edition loads itself into any suitable UMB automatically, if it can.

Double Buffering

Double buffering is a technique that SmartDrive requires for compatibility with some disk controllers. Most, including all MFM, RLL, and IDE controllers, as well as many ESDI and SCSI models, do not need double buffering. Those that do use a process called bus mastering, under which the disk controller takes over the computer's bus to transfer data to or from the system's RAM. The Adaptec 1542B SCSI controller is an example of this type of interface. Other models from UltraStor and Always fall into this category.

On a 386 or higher system using virtual 8086 mode (either under Windows or with a memory manager), the read or write address the controller passes along to DOS may not be the same as the actual physical address. Microsoft's Virtual DMA services standard is designed to avoid this problem, but not all bus-mastering controllers support it.

Double buffering solves the problem neatly by creating a special memory 2.5K buffer in conventional RAM, in which physical and virtual addresses are identical. The only "cost" is the small amount of RAM, and the overhead required to shuffle data in and out of the new buffer. SmartDrive can examine your system and determine whether or not you need double buffering for a particular drive. I'll go over this in more detail in the section on using SmartDrive that follows.

Using SmartDrive

SmartDrive is no longer a SYS file loaded from CONFIG.SYS using the **device= directive** syntax. Instead, it is an executable file that is loaded from AUTOEXEC.BAT, called SMARTDRV.EXE. This new approach gives you added flexibility. After SmartDrive has been loaded, you can run it again from the DOS command line, with optional switches that perform a function, such as flushing the cache. SmartDrive recognizes that the cache portion has already been loaded and won't try to load itself again.

If your disk controller requires double buffering, SmartDrive must also be executed from CONFIG.SYS, but, in this case, only the special buffer is set up, not the cache itself. Even if you have a SmartDrive directive in CONFIG.SYS, you must still include another in AUTOEXEC.BAT to activate the cache.

DOS 6's Setup program will add an appropriate line to AUTOEXEC.BAT (and, if required, to CONFIG.SYS), but you may also create or modify this line yourself. The AUTOEXEC.BAT command line looks like this:

```
C:\dos\SMARTDRV C+ D E- 1024 512
```

The drive letter specifications tell SmartDrive what sort of caching to do with each drive. In this example, the plus sign following drive C means that both read and write caching will be used for that drive. Drive D will have read caching only, and drive E will not be cached. If you don't enter any drive letter information, SmartDrive defaults to read-only caching of removable media drives and read/write caching of other disks, excluding RAM disks, CD-ROM drives, and network drives.

Don't Cache Compressed Volumes

If you use DoubleSpace or another disk compression utility, you'll want to *exclude* caching of the driver letters that represent the compressed volumes but cache the host drives that physically store the compressed file. In addition, your SmartDrive command line must appear in AUTOEXEC.BAT after any other commands that set up or define the compressed drives. We'll look at this topic again in Chapter 16 when we discuss DoubleSpace in some detail.

The first number on the command line represents the size of the cache, in bytes when DOS is running alone, and the second number stands for the cache size when Windows is loaded. The reason the number is higher for DOS is simple. DOS generally doesn't use the extended or expanded memory that SmartDrive allocates for its cache. Windows *can* use extended memory and, usually, the more you have, the better. SmartDrive is unable to loan memory not being used for the cache to Windows (other caches, such as HyperDisk, are able to do this, however), so, to be on the safe side, Microsoft recommends allocating less RAM to SmartDrive when Windows is active. In all cases, you should never leave Windows with less than 2M, and preferably 4M or more of extended memory to work with.

If you don't specify an amount of memory for DOS and Windows, SmartDrive defaults to the values shown in table 11.1.

Table 11.1. SmartDrive Cache Size Defaults

Extended Memory	DOS Cache Size	Windows Cache Size
Up to 1M	All	None
Up to 2M	1M	256K
Up to 4M	1M	512K
Up to 6M	2M	1M
Over 6M	2M	2M

In my case, I have 32M of RAM on my main machine, and run Microsoft Windows more than 99 percent of the time, so I specify 4M for SmartDrive under both DOS and Windows. No study has shown that a cache larger than 4M provides any measurable performance gain, or even that 4M is useful. I've got enough extra RAM that 4M makes a good, "it can't hurt" figure.

Unless you, too, have 32M of RAM, you'll probably want a smaller cache, particularly if you are running Windows. When Windows depletes all available extended memory, it simulates more RAM through temporary or permanent disk swap files. It's likely that the disk accesses caused by the premature need to use a swap file will exceed the savings by those eliminated because of your larger cache. That's because most of the "hits" a SmartDrive cache will generate come from the first megabyte. An extra megabyte, or two, or three, provide only a small improvement. In contrast, a memory-starved Windows installation may access a disk swap file repeatedly as portions of a program are swapped in and out of real RAM. A smaller SmartDrive cache can help eliminate this *thrashing*.

SmartDrive Switches

You can customize SmartDrive with several switches, some of which are useful in AUTOEXEC.BAT. The others are used from the command line to force some action after SmartDrive has started or to elicit information. You already know about one of the switches.

Command Line Switches

These switches can be used from the DOS command line to force SmartDrive to take some action immediately. You can also insert them in batch files.

/c tells SmartDrive to flush the contents of the cache to disk. Use this switch when you want to be certain that all your files have been safely written to disk, as when you are getting ready to turn your computer off or reset.

/s asks SmartDrive to display its current status, as shown in listing 11.1.

The listing shows that drives A and B (both floppy drives) have read caching enabled, but not write caching. The no next to all the other drives except drive K indicates that SmartDrive has determined that double-buffering is not needed for these drives. The hyphen in the fourth column for drive K indicates that SmartDrive is unable to determine whether this drive needs double buffering or not. You should probably add this line to your CONFIG.SYS file as a precaution:

```
DEVICE=c:\dos\SMARTDRV.EXE /DOUBLE_BUFFER
```

Listing 11.1

```
Microsoft SMARTDrive Disk Cache version 4.1
Copyright 1991,1993 Microsoft Corp.
Room for    256 elements of   8,192 bytes each
There have been   40,113 cache hits
      and   3,437 cache misses
Cache size:  2,097,152 bytes
Cache size while running Windows:  2,097,152 bytes
          Disk Caching Status
drive   read cache   write cache   buffering
--------------------------------------------------------
   A:        yes          no          no
   B:        yes          no          no
   C:        yes          yes         no
   D:        yes          yes         no
   E:        yes          yes         no
   F:        yes          yes         no
   G:        yes          yes         no
   H:        yes          yes         no
   I:        yes          yes         no
   J:        yes          no          no
   K:        yes          no          -
For help, type "Smartdrv /?".
```

/R clears and restarts SmartDrive.

/? displays help information about SmartDrive.

Startup Switches

The following SmartDrive switches are used when you start up the cache, and, therefore, are most often found in AUTOEXEC.BAT.

/L tells SmartDrive to load into conventional memory. SmartDrive will automatically try to load into extended memory unless you use this switch. If you have only a limited amount of XMS RAM and want to save it for some other purpose, you can use the /L switch to use conventional memory instead.

/Q disables SmartDrive's startup message display, activating "quiet" mode (this is the default). Use this switch with caution, only after you are certain SmartDrive won't encounter any roadblocks you should know about!

/V enables startup message display, activating "verbose" mode.

/E:*size* specifies the number of bytes in the chunks SmartDrive moves with each operation. The default is 8192 bytes, but you can use any power of two (512, 1024, 2048, 4096, etc.).

The larger the chunk, the faster SmartDrive operates, because it doesn't spend time reading and managing smaller bits of RAM. However, that also means that fewer individual chunks can be fit in a cache of a given size. Large clusters of information are easier to handle but may contain more wasted or unneeded data. Smaller clusters take more overhead to manage but are more likely to include the exact sectors you need. It's a little like filling the trunk of your automobile with basketballs or golf balls. You can load and unload the basketballs a lot more quickly, but the golf balls fill up the available space more efficiently.

Tips for Using SmartDrive

Tip

If you have extended memory, don't use both SmartDrive and FASTOPEN together. FASTOPEN is a TSR program that stores the location of recently used files, so DOS can locate them more quickly. SmartDrive performs a similar function but also stores the files themselves, making FASTOPEN a bit redundant.

Tip

If you have only conventional memory, or conventional and EMS memory, you may want to use both SmartDrive and FASTOPEN. Your SmartDrive cache will be very small because of the limited amount of conventional RAM available for it. FASTOPEN can provide additional performance gains, especially if you load it into EMS using the /X switch.

Tip

SmartDrive may also eliminate most of the need for a RAM drive. RAM disks are virtual hard disks created using conventional, EMS, or XMS memory. Some users create one to store frequently used programs and data or to store temporary files. The latter application is particularly useful, because these temporary files are automatically erased when the computer is switched off. However, SmartDrive almost always is more effective in boosting speed than a RAM disk. The latter speeds access only for files that you have copied to it; SmartDrive stores *any* recently used file.

Tip

If your SmartDrive cache is smaller than the recommended optimum for your RAM configuration, you're better off deleting the RAM disk and dedicating the memory to SmartDrive instead. If you already have a 2 to 4M cache and still have a megabyte of RAM you can spare, a RAM disk may improve the speed of some applications. Note that if your program uses a temporary file because it has run out of extended RAM, you're better off skipping the RAM disk and letting your application use the RAM directly.

Tip

Don't forget to embed the **smartdrive /c** command in any batch files followed by system reboots or power-down cycles. These would include batch files you use to load Windows or a menuing program and batch files that change your configuration and then call a program (like the shareware BOOT.COM) to perform a warm boot automatically.

Tip

Do not manually remove SmartDrive's double-buffering command from CONFIG.SYS unless you are positive that your hard disk does not require it. You wouldn't do anything so foolish? Recently, I was trying to reclaim as much RAM as possible to test a memory-hungry program and inserted REMarks before every CONFIG.SYS and AUTOEXEC.BAT line I felt was superfluous. I certainly could do without SmartDrive during the tests. However, when restoring my files later on, I reactivated SmartDrive in AUTOEXEC.BAT but forgot to turn double buffering back on. The computer involved had an advanced local bus SCSI card with high-powered bus-mastering capabilities. Guess what happened?

The Next Step

SmartMon is a Windows-based tool that lets you monitor SmartDrive. Because DOS users will have little interest in this utility, I've broken out the discussion of it into a separate chapter. After that, I'll look at disk-caching options available from third-party sources.

Using SmartMon

SmartDrive Monitor (SmartMon) is a Windows-based utility that provides a visual indication of SmartDrive's activities. You can use this information to modify the cache mode of each drive and to monitor how your changes affect cache efficiency. SmartMon functions as a useful "instrument panel" that offers insight into how SmartDrive works, while letting you fine-tune its settings.

SmartMon is activated like any Windows application: by double-clicking on its icon, in Program Manager or in File Manager, by highlighting its icon and pressing Enter, or by choosing Open from the File Menu. You can load SmartMon automatically each time you run Windows by inserting **load = smartmon.exe** in WIN.INI. If you like, SmartMon can be set to remain Always on Top by checking that option in the Control menu (press Alt-spacebar or click once on the Control box in the upper left corner of the SmartDrive Monitor window). Because the window is not sizeable, you may find it a little intrusive and prefer to let it fall behind other panes as you work. SmartMon can also be minimized; in iconic view it shows only the current cache hit rate.

The SmartDrive Monitor window looks like figure 12.1. The display is divided into four sections: cache memory options, options and logging,

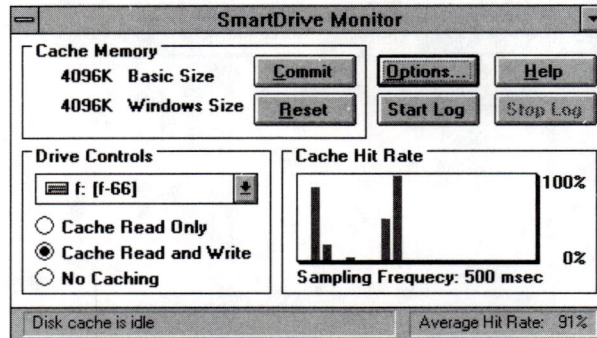

Figure 12.1. SmartDrive Monitor window.

drive controls, and cache hit rate display. A status line at the bottom of the screen reports whether the cache is active and shows an average hit rate.

Cache Memory Controls

The cache memory controls display the size of the SmartDrive cache under both DOS and Windows. You can't change these values from SmartDrive. To do that, you must exit Windows and restart SmartDrive from the DOS command line.

Two buttons are available to direct SmartDrive to flush its cache to disk. Unfortunately, SmartMon uses confusing, non-intuitive terminology that tells nothing about what the buttons actually do. In plain English, here's what each button does:

➤ **COMMIT** tells SmartDrive to write to disk any sectors that have changed but have not yet been previously updated on your hard disk. You generally won't need to use this button because SmartDrive always writes these sectors to disk after they've aged no more than five seconds. In other words, by the time you decide to use the COMMIT option and move the mouse cursor to the button, SmartDrive has already written its sectors.

➤ **RESET** tells SmartDrive to write un-updated sectors to disk and then to clear the cache completely. At the same time, the cumulative average cache hit rate, shown on the status bar at the bottom of the window, is reset. You would use this control to periodically reset SmartMon so that you could measure its effectiveness over a new period. Perhaps you have finished using a particular application, noted the average hit rate SmartDrive generates while using that application, and now want to monitor a different program. The Reset button can be used to restart the calculations at that point.

Drive Caching Controls

Immediately below the Cache Memory controls are the Drive Caching controls, which let you modify the cache mode of any cachable drive on your system. First, select a particular drive from the pull-down selection box. One of the radio buttons will be highlighted, indicating either read, read/write caching, or no caching. To change the caching status of a drive, click on the appropriate radio button.

These changes affect SmartDrive's operation for the *current session only*. To permanently modify the cache settings of a given drive, use the Drive Control setting in the Options menu. If you don't make this change, SmartDrive will return to the default settings specified in AUTOEXEC.BAT (or another program you use to load SmartDrive).

Note that while noncachable drives are shown, you cannot change their status. Such drives include CD-ROM drives, shared network drives, and "fake" drive volumes created by DoubleSpace, Stacker, or other disk compression utilities.

Cache Hit Rate Display

To the right of the Drive Control panel is the Cache Hit Rate display, which shows a histogram that graphically illustrates the instantaneous cache hit rate. SmartMon samples SmartDrive's activity every half-second (500 milliseconds) and logs the number of times the requested data is found in the cache (a hit), compared to the total number of accesses. The percentage of hits in each sample is displayed as a bar in the chart. If 100 percent of the accesses score a hit, the bar will reach maximum height. If the hit rate during that period is only 50 percent, the bar will be only half as tall. The last 30 samplings are displayed, so you can see how effectively SmartDrive performs over a period of time. When SmartDrive is idle, this display is not updated.

You may use the Options menu to change the sampling rate to another frequency (more often or less often than every 500 ms) and to alter the number of intervals shown. If you select more than 30, each bar in the histogram will be shown much thinner; with fewer intervals, they grow fatter. You sacrifice a little readability with more frequent intervals, to gain a broader picture of SmartDrive's performance.

Options and Cache Activity Logging

You'll find four buttons in the upper right corner of the Smart Monitor window. **Help** offers a few screens of explanation about SmartMon. **Start Log** initiates saving information about SmartDrive's performance to a disk file. The **Stop Log** button halts a current logging session. A portion of a sample log file is shown in table 12.1.

The first column shows the number of timer ticks since the beginning of the current Windows session. The second column records the number of accesses to the SmartDrive cache since it was loaded. The third figure is the number of hits since the cache was loaded.

Your log file can contain information over a long period of time, because SmartMon will append any new data to the end of the existing log file, unless you specify a new one. However, any given logging session can be set automatically to stop after eight hours. The default "shut-off" time is two hours and may be set to some other period from one minute to eight hours, using the Options menu.

Table 12.1. A Sample Log File

Ticks	Total	Hits
8031243	59746	55732
8036516	59762	55734
8036735	59763	55734
8043052	59877	55824
8043326	59878	55825
8043876	59879	55826
8046292	59882	55829
8051016	59897	55844
8054861	59916	55855

For most DOS 6 users, the SmartDrive logging capability is a curiosity, providing some interesting statistical information that is only moderately useful, at best, to get a longer term picture of how SmartDrive is performing. The Cache Hit Rate display is a more practical way of monitoring your cache. Logging options can be set using the Options button, described in the next section.

Options

The Options dialog box can be used to modify SmartDrive's settings. The parameters you enter are stored in WIN.INI under the [smartmon] section. There are three different controls you can modify: Cache Hit Rate, Log File, and Drive Control. The Options dialog box is shown in figure 12.2.

Cache Hit Rate is used to specify the sampling frequency, in milliseconds, and the number of display intervals used for the histogram. A frequency smaller than the default 500 ms value can provide additional accuracy, and a larger number offers a picture drawn in coarser increments. As mentioned earlier, you can modify the number of intervals shown in the histogram to change the number of hit rate samples viewed at one time.

```
┌─────────────────────────────────────────────┐
│ ─      SmartDrive Monitor Options             │
│ ┌─Cache Hit Rate──────────────────────────┐   │
│ │ Sampling Frequency (in msec)   [500]    │   │
│ │ Histogram Display Intervals    [30]     │   │
│ └─────────────────────────────────────────┘   │
│ ┌─Log File────────────────────────────────┐   │
│ │ File Name  [smartmon.log]               │   │
│ │ ☒ Automatic Stop (in minutes) [120]     │   │
│ └─────────────────────────────────────────┘   │
│ ┌─Drive Control───────────────────────────┐   │
│ │ ☐ Save Setting in DOS Batch File        │   │
│ │ File Name  [c:\autoexec.bat]            │   │
│ └─────────────────────────────────────────┘   │
│    [  OK  ]      [ Cancel ]      [ Help ]     │
└─────────────────────────────────────────────┘
```

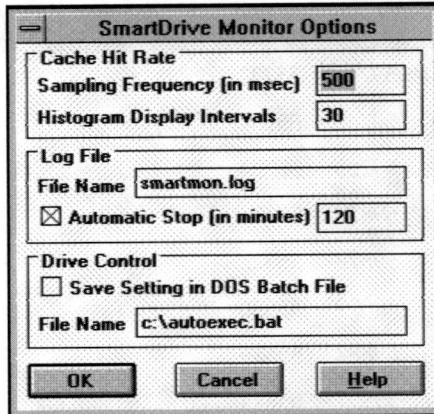

Figure 12.2. SmartMon Options.

Log File allows you to enter the name of your SmartMon log. If you want the utility to use the same log file every time Windows loads, be sure to specify a full pathname for the file. Otherwise, it will look in the current directory of the current drive and create a new file with that name if an existing log file is not found. The length of a logging session, including one currently underway, can be specified by setting a value for Automatic Stop. You may enter from 1 to 480 minutes (eight hours) or uncheck the box and allow logging to proceed continuously.

Drive Control can be used to store any changes you make to drive status during a SmartMon session to the batch file used to load SmartDrive. When the Save Setting in DOS Batch File box is checked, the changes will be stored in the file listed after **File Name**. The actual SmartDrive command line in the file is changed to reflect the new settings. For most users, this is AUTOEXEC.BAT, but you can specify any file you want. If you do not use this option, SmartDrive will return to its previous settings the next time it loads.

Iconic Display

You may want to keep SmartMon minimized as an icon most of the time. When minimized, SmartMon shows the hit rate as a percentage. Either the hit rate for the last sampling period (if the cache is active) is displayed, or the average hit rate (if the cache was idle) is displayed. A little red light blinks on the hard disk bit map when the cache is active.

Tips for Using SmartMon

Tip

If you want to track SmartDrive's performance visually, reduce the window to an icon, set it for Always on Top, and drag it to a corner of your display where you can keep an eye on it. You'll see a display that is updated from time to time. If the average hit rate drops to a low value, you'll be able to make a correlation with whatever activity you were carrying out at the time.

Tip

Use the Options menu to create new SmartMon logs for sessions with individual software packages, so you can compare the disk activity and SmartDrive efficiency under different applications and combinations of applications, and at various cache sizes. You should quickly be able to determine whether you can benefit from a larger cache (you're getting very low hit rates) or whether you can safely reduce your cache to a smaller size (changing to a smaller cache has no effect on hit rates).

Tip

SmartDrive Monitor can also be used to gauge the way DOS applications use SmartDrive. Just run the DOS programs under Windows and use SmartMon as you would for a Windows application.

The Next Step

SmartDrive may not be the answer to every DOS 6 user's need. Third-party vendors offer their own caching programs, frequently as part of full-featured utility packages. The next chapter outlines some of these packages and details their key features.

Beyond SmartDrive

Although SmartDrive has been improved significantly, it is still less flexible than several third-party cache programs. For example, other caches can be set to use memory in different ways.

PC-Kwik can load entirely into conventional memory, use a combination of conventional RAM and upper memory blocks, or divide itself between either extended or expanded memory and UMBs. These combinations are for the program code itself; the actual cache still resides in conventional, extended, or expanded memory as you prefer. This flexibility can help if other caches have a memory lending feature, which allows the cache to load up to half its memory—or more—to other programs that need it. This section discusses some of the pros and cons for using SmartDrive or abandoning it for another disk caching program.

SmartDrive has guaranteed MS-DOS 6 compatibility, whereas other cache options may, or may not, function under all circumstances with DOS and Windows. That's not to say SmartDrive is guaranteed bug-free, but if Microsoft discovers any incompatibilities between it and other Microsoft products, including DOS and Windows, you can bet they'll be fixed in a hurry and at no cost to you. You have access to Microsoft Technical Support. Microsoft is also good about fixing problems that relate to other commonly used products. Double buffering, for example, was introduced to ensure reliability with bus-mastering disk controller cards. Third-party vendors also want their caches to work smoothly with DOS, Windows, and other software, but don't enjoy Microsoft's ability to develop both a new version of its operating environments and the utilities that run under them simultaneously.

Other disk caches are likely to lead SmartDrive in new and useful features. Because SmartDrive is not sold as a separate product, Microsoft has little incentive to improve it beyond a basic level of reliability and competence. Third-party vendors, on the other hand, can't expect you to buy their cache products unless they have something extra to offer. The designers of the cache programs described in this chapter are highly motivated to give you a little extra speed, better usage of memory, or a few other tricks that make their products a better value.

Since SmartDrive can use only conventional memory or extended memory for its cache, you'll need to turn to third-party products if you have a lot of expanded memory and want to use that instead. EMS is slower for caching, because DOS can only glimpse a tiny 64K window of it at one time (see Chapter 4), but it may be your only or most economical option if EMS is what you have.

Third-party caches are a good choice if you're purchasing an entire toolkit, since the components in the package are likely to work best together. Some caches can share memory with RAM disks offered in the same bundle, so RAM can serve double duty.

Take a look at some quick descriptions of a few of the leading cache programs.

PC-Kwik Cache

Long regarded as one of the leading caching programs, PC-Kwik cache works smoothly with DOS 6 and Windows. It includes the options listed earlier, plus many more advanced switches. You might prefer PC-Kwik Cache over SmartDrive if you have a 286 or other computer with a lot of expanded memory that you'd like to use for caching. You also might enjoy playing with the dozens of options this program offers for customizing and fine-tuning the cache.

Copy Sectors in Batches

For example, you can tell PC-Kwik to copy sectors in batches. That may reduce the number of times DOS needs to access the disk. The only drawback is that this mode may interfere with telecommunications when the cache is located in extended memory. The batch reads delay your CPU from looking for other interrupts, such as those required for communicating at 2400 bps or higher. Expanded and conventional memory caches don't suffer from this effect, so you can safely use /B+ with them or with extended memory caches if you don't do much telecommunications. You can also temporarily disable an extended memory cache when you start to telecommunicate, using the /D switch described previously. You might put it in the batch file you use to load your telecommunications software.

Read Ahead Buffering

PC-Kwik can also be told to read all of a track into memory whenever an application requests any sector of it. This parameter will improve performance if your applications or data files are large ones and if you've optimized your disk so that as many sectors of each file as possible reside in contiguous sectors within a track and those that follow. Then reading whole tracks will prove very efficient and provide higher hit rates. However, if your files are small ones scattered randomly throughout your disk, and your disk is highly fragmented, this switch can decrease performance.

Sectors Per Track

You may specify how many sectors per track to allocate. Most hard disks allocate 17 or more sectors per track. PC-Kwik will allocate 17 sectors for the track buffer or fewer if your disk uses smaller tracks. If you happen to have a disk with a higher number of sectors per track, and you also have memory to spare, you can tell the cache to use more sectors for track buffering, up to a maximum of 72.

Advanced Diskette Support

PC-Kwik also has advanced diskette support and changeline support. (Changeline support automatically tells the cache when you've switched media. That way, the cache doesn't need to read the disk to tell if it is a new one. Instead, it can immediately read the next sectors required.)

Fast Return to DOS Prompt

Another useful feature is called fast return to DOS prompt. The cache can return you to the DOS prompt even while it continues to read or write to the disk. That way, you can type another command without waiting. While the switch affects both hard disk and floppy disk usage, you're likely to notice the quick prompt more when using a floppy disk. It tends to take longer to read files from such disks.

Other advanced parameters include some that you may never need to use. They include switches to tell the cache to give priority to disk reads over writes and the capability to set the lowest extended memory address the cache will use. The latest version of this program disables write caching to floppy disks automatically, as an added safety measure.

NCache

Ncache is provided with the Norton Utilities. It, too, works well with DOS 6 and is designed to release memory that Windows may need when Windows loads.

Its strong points include ease of use. For example, to set up the cache, you can enter:

```
NCACHE OPTIMIZE/choice
```

Choice should be selected based on whether you'd like to set up the cache for optimum speed, efficiency, or memory usage. The *speed* option gobbles up as much memory as possible to provide the best performance. If you choose *efficiency*, Ncache puts limits on advanced options like the size of the write-ahead buffer, giving you a good compromise between speed and memory usage. Pick the *memory* option, and Ncache drops its read-ahead and write-ahead buffers to minimize the program's use of RAM.

Use Extended or Expanded Memory

Like PC-Kwik, NCache lets you specify whether the cache will be set up in expanded or extended memory—useful if you have a lot of one or the other and can't switch. You may also enter the size of the data blocks used for storage within the cache buffer, as well as the size of the read and write ahead buffers.

If you'd like to specify the maximum amount of time data can age in the cache before it is written to disk, an NCache switch can be set for delays of up to 60 seconds (if you are brave, or have an uninterruptible power supply attached to your system).

HyperDisk

HyperDisk has generally proved to be much faster than SmartDrive, so you'll want to consider it for that reason. It has one advantage over the previous two caching programs: you can try it out to see whether it meets your needs before you pay for it. HyperDisk is available as a shareware program through many PC user groups, local electronic bulletin board systems (BBS), or online information services like CompuServe and America Online.

Shareware Evaluation

The version you receive is fully functional and includes a documentation file you can print out. After a 21-day evaluation period, you are expected to register the program with HyperWare for $70 or to stop using it. HyperDisk is one of the fastest and most flexible disk caching programs available and was among the first to use conventional, extended, or expanded memory. The program itself can be loaded into upper memory blocks with some systems.

HyperDisk is furnished in several versions, suitable for 286, 386, and higher computers, and systems that use some memory managers, such as Quarterdeck's QEMM. Separate conventional, extended, and expanded memory versions are used.

It can be set to use staged writes, like SmartDrive, or to write directly through to your disk for safety. You can specify the delay (in milliseconds) before it writes "aged" sectors to disk. A media check rate (the interval at which the cache checks to see whether removable media such as floppies and cartridges have been changed) can also be specified.

Speed Cache +

Speed Cache + is a very fast cache that has been rated by *Windows User* magazine as 50 to 75 percent faster than SmartDrive in DOS mode and 10 percent faster under Windows. It comes with its own Windows-based control panel and monitoring tool, too, so this utility may be the first choice of Windows users looking for a better cache than SmartDrive.

That program, Windows Assist, lets you modify cache settings on the fly, like SmartMon, and view information like the number of disk reads and writes, and hits for each, as well as the amount of your cache that has been used. That makes it easy to decide whether you'd benefit from a larger cache.

Unlike PC-Kwik, you don't need to set a multitude of switches to get it to work with Windows. Unlike SmartDrive, it can be used to cache CD-ROM reads. You may find that your CD-ROM drive seems a lot faster when you're using Speed Cache, and if you use these drives extensively (say, to access information or on a BBS that stores user-downloadable files on CD-ROM), that may be reason enough to consider this product.

The Next Step

In addition to the cache programs described in this chapter, similar offerings are available with PC Tools and as standalone programs such as FAST!, Vcache, and Flash. These lesser known programs also offer speed, low cost, and flexibility. One of them could help you optimize your hard disk's performance.

Other ways to improve hard disk performance is covered in the next section of this book, which deals with increasing available storage space through compression, using DoubleSpace or another utility. Disk defragmentation is also addressed. Both let you use your hard disk more efficiently and often allow you to access data more quickly.

Part IV:
Optimizing Hard Disk Space

Parkinson must have been thinking of hard disks when he created his famous law. No matter how large your hard disk is, the available files will invariably expand to fill it up, usually within six months. Along the way, something else will happen: the files that do reside on your disk will gradually become scattered over a wider expanse of real estate, as DOS 6 works harder to find small clusters of sectors to fit individual pieces of files.

Neither condition helps your machine perform at top levels. Full hard disks mean smaller areas for swapfiles or temporary files, forcing applications to thrash back and forth between memory and data files on disk. A fragmented file can take 10 times as long to access as one stored in contiguous sectors on your hard disk.

DOS 6 addresses these concerns with its new DoubleSpace compression utility and Defragmenter. The two work hand-in-hand; file compression works only with volumes that have large areas of contiguous sectors. The next chapters will show you how to use these two utilities and some other techniques you can use to multiply your available hard disk storage.

Do You Need DoubleSpace?

This chapter explains some alternatives to consider that might eliminate your need for DoubleSpace entirely, or you can use these methods *with* compression to gain more free disk space than you ever dreamed of. DoubleSpace is a great utility, but many users have a lot more free space on their hard disks than they thought they had. If you can pick up 80 or 90M without DoubleSpace, you can save Microsoft's file compression utility for a rainy day, when you really need it.

Like any disease, a full hard disk displays any of several different warning signs. These tipoff signs can include slow operation, as your applications find inadequate space to swap temporary files to disk (some may refuse to run at all). Other applications may behave erratically or inform you that a certain operation you have requested cannot be undone (because there is no room to store a copy of the original). Install programs that check for sufficient hard disk space won't install. You may find you have a lot less hard disk space than you thought when you run Windows, because Windows itself grabs up to half of the remaining amount for its own temporary use.

The most blatant indicator is when you use the **dir** command and see that only a few megabytes of space remain. Hmmm...disk is almost full. What to do next? Assuming that you have files that compress well enough to make it worth your while, DoubleSpace is a definite option.

Keep in mind, though, that DoubleSpace adds an extra layer of operating system between you and your data. You must go through the steps of compressing and decompressing drives and maintaining your compressed drives. There are little things you keep in mind, such as remembering not to erase those funny, invisible DBLSPACE.xxx files you encounter on your hard disk. You can avoid all these by increasing your available hard disk space *without* using DoubleSpace.

Erase Unused Files

The first and smartest thing you can do when your hard disk fills up is look for files that have no business being there. You may be able to recover one-third to one-half of your hard disk storage simply by erasing files you don't need. Here is a quick checklist of possible candidates for removal:

Tutorials and Informational Files. These files are not necessary for applications you already know how to use. Many programs install huge tutorial files that can eat up a megabyte or two of hard disk space. README.DOC and similar informational files are often not needed after you've read them once. Zap 'em!

Sample Files. Ventura Publisher includes massive sample chapters. Image editors like PhotoStyler and PhotoShop fill up disk space with sample TIF files. Even word processing programs may include sample documents and templates you don't need. You'll be surprised at how much hard disk space you can reclaim by removing them.

Clip Art and Other Rarely Used Resources. Clip art is nice to have, but storing your whole library online is a waste of hard disk space. Move resources you don't use very often to floppy disks or other removable storage.

Individual Files That Belong in a Library or Archive. There are utilities that will combine image files, Windows icons, or other file types into libraries that can store the same information in a much more efficient format. We saw in the last chapter that 1,000 Windows icons could take up 8M of disk space, using a worst-case scenario. Collected into a data link library (DLL) or similar format, the same icons require less than a megabyte.

Duplicate Files. It's easy to install the same program twice and to forget about the other installation. Many Windows programs can share DLLs, like the Visual Basic library VBRUN200.DLL, yet install them into their own subdirectory, instead of your Windows directory. Both Image Pals and PhotoStyler install the Image Pals Album module on your hard disk; you don't need two copies. Most Aldus products are pretty good about sharing resources found in the \ALDUS subdirectory, but it doesn't always happen that way. Some Microsoft programs can share modules, such as the spell checking dictionary, so you might have extra copies. If you own both Corel PhotoPaint (created by Zsoft) and ZSoft PhotoFinish, you may find they are enough alike that you don't need both.

Shareware utilities like QDUPE.EXE (available on many electronic bulletin boards) can search out your hard disks for duplicate files, list the sets along with file sizes and creation dates (to let you spot true duplicates), and erase the unneeded versions.

Old TEMP Files. Applications generally erase their temporary files when the program finishes, but if your system locks up and you reboot by switching off power or pressing Ctrl-Alt-Del, a few can remain behind. Over the course of several months, a lot of hard disk space can be eaten up. Look for files with TMP, TEM, or SWP extensions, or which contain odd characters like dollar signs or tildes (~) in their file names.

Applications and Utilities You Never Use. Do you still have drivers on your hard disk for a video card you no longer own? Is your DOS directory full of files like DOSSHELL.EXE, POWER.EXE, or NLSFUNC.EXE? If you're not using the DOS 6 shell, you certainly don't need any of its related files; a desktop machine has little use for the laptop power management utility; if you don't need foreign language support, you certainly don't want NLSFUNC.EXE and several other code page-oriented programs on your hard disk. You don't even know what a CGA monitor is? Then you don't want GRAFTABL.COM.

If you do a thorough inventory of your hard disk (the command **chkdsk /V>FILE** will create an ASCII file called FILE listing every program on your disk), you'll find megabytes of free space at your disposal.

Lost Clusters. Some of your unused files may be invisible to you. You may have megabytes of usable space on your hard disk occupied by lost allocation units or clusters that have been abandoned by an application that unexpectedly quit. To reclaim these sectors, first close all currently running applications, including Windows and DOSSHELL, and then type the following:

```
chkdsk /f
```

If **chkdsk** finds any lost clusters, it will display a message like this one:

```
20 lost allocation units found in 6 chains.

Convert lost chains to files?
```

Enter Y to save the lost clusters as files. They will be stored as consecutively numbered files in your root directory, using names like FILE0000.CHK, FILE0001.CHK, etc. In nearly all cases, these files will not contain any information useful to you. It's remotely possible that you can collect some data from them after certain types of applications have halted, but usually you'll just want to erase them (**del *.CHK**) to reclaim the lost clusters. Run **chkdsk** any time you have to reboot your computer with an application running that has temporary files.

Buy an Additional Hard Disk

Most systems have at least one extra drive bay that can be used for a second hard disk. Large drives have dropped significantly in price: a 200M drive can cost as little as $375, 330M units $600, and 550M drives can be purchased for $900 or so. Although paying even $375 instead of $0 (the additional cost of DoubleSpace) may not seem cost-effective, there are factors that may make this a good choice for you.

You want to keep many files online that don't compress very well. If you work with image files, particularly 24-bit color image files that can amount to 4M *each*, you probably already store these files in compressed form. You need real hard disk space, not the imaginary storage that a compressed volume would provide in this case.

You need a large permanent swapfile for Windows. Windows swapfiles can't reside in a compressed volume. Some users can benefit from huge permanent swapfiles—perhaps 100M or more. For example, even though I have 32M of RAM on my main machine, I find that isn't nearly enough to work with three or four 24-bit color images at once. I've set up a 100M permanent swapfile on a 200M hard disk that is used primarily as a "scratch" disk. The permanent swapfile is slower than real RAM but much faster than a Windows temporary swapfile.

You want to use a hard disk volume as a backup for another hard disk, perhaps over a network. Because DoubleSpace disks are stored as one huge file, if something happens to that file so that DOS 6 can't access it, *everything* in the compressed volume is lost. DOS has safeguards built in to keep this from happening, but you still might not want to rely on a compressed drive for backup. Because backup software compresses files anyway, you should be able to fit the same amount of data on your backup hard disk in either case.

When adding a second (or third) hard disk to your system, remember that you can always compress the new drive with DoubleSpace later on, to gain even *more* disk space, so you haven't really lost anything.

Add Open-Ended Storage

In the best of circumstances, DoubleSpace is only a temporary solution. Even a compressed volume will fill up eventually, and then you'll have to resort to one of the other solutions in this section.

If you tend to accumulate files and/or applications as your needs or responsibilities change, no hard disk will be large enough. It's a trait of human nature to abhor a vacuum. If you suddenly have 100M of free space, you'll decide that now, at last, you can keep your income tax preparation program permanently installed, even though you use it only every three months or so. Or, you'll keep more data files online simply because you have room for them. Before long, your hard disk will fill, no matter how large it is. I know users who are shocked at how quickly their 1 gigabyte hard disk filled up. My measly 550M drive must be constantly pruned of old programs that have been reviewed for magazines and are no longer needed or it, too, would be full by now.

Only an infinitely large hard disk drive would satisfy all storage needs, and that's what you get with removable storage like floptical disks, optical disks, and Bernoulli or SyDOS cartridge drives. Each stores from 44 to 150M or more, and you can remove one and insert a new one in a few seconds. In effect, you have a drive "window" that can look at gigabytes of data in 44 to 150M increments. As long as you keep buying new cartridges, you never have to worry about running out of hard disk space or expansion bays.

SyDOS cartridges are true removable hard disk drives, but Bernoulli cartridges resemble extra-thick 5.25-inch floppy disks. Floptical disks look like 3.5-inch floppies but store 20M of data. Drives for these three options typically cost around $500-$600, and the media costs less than $1 per megabyte. That's not a lot less than for fixed disk drives, but these units have that unbeatable advantage of being open-ended.

Optical disks are generally cheaper to use per megabyte, but the drives cost much more—$2000 and up. Removable media drives are generally slower than hard disks; you can use them as expanded primary storage, but you're still better off storing your most frequently used applications and data on a real hard disk.

If your hard disk space requirements never seem to end, removable storage may be the answer.

Network Two or More Computers

If you own two or more computers, a simple network can combine them into one big computer that has access to any of the hard disks installed on either machine. Windows for Workgroups, for example, has made it ridiculously easy to string two computers together. If you have two computers, each with a 330M hard disk, you gain two systems that each can access 660M. Since you can erase programs and data duplicated on the two systems (any application or file can be accessed from either machine), you'll end up with a lot more free disk space. In addition, you can share other peripherals, such as CD-ROM drives and printers over the network.

In my case, I have a 550M drive in my main machine, two 330M drives in a backup, and a 330M drive in a third. I also have roughly 2G of Bernoulli cartridges, and three separate Bernoulli drives, all of which are available to all three 486 systems through a Windows for Workgroups network. Each system has access to 1.5G of hard disk storage and an additional 224M window to Bernoulli cartridges amounting to an additional 2G. My needs and resources are a bit unusual, but you can see why networking makes sense for me.

The Next Step

If you've decided you can benefit from DoubleSpace, you'll want to continue to the discussion of file compression in the next chapter. There is still one more consideration to think about: certain files don't compress very well, and therefore don't benefit from DoubleSpace compression. However, to understand why, you'll need to know a little about how compression works. Then we can move on to installing and using DoubleSpace, in Chapter 15.

File Compression Made Small

Of all the utilities included with DOS 6, its DoubleSpace file compression scheme has attracted the most attention, generated the most controversy, and, after memory management, is often the least understood by the user.

DoubleSpace has attracted attention because it seems to be truly a case of something for nothing. In theory, you take a 80M hard drive, perform some magic on its contents, and end up with 160M of capacity. Because the cost differential between 80 and 160M drives can easily amount to a few hundred dollars, the savings can seem irresistible.

This utility has produced controversy on two levels. No one could have escaped noticing the ugly Microsoft/Stac Electronics legal flap in early 1993 as Goliath and David traded lawsuits and accusations over who owned what patents first and which technologies formed the basis for Stacker and/or DoubleSpace. Most industry observers had been expecting to see Stacker included as part of DOS ever since Windows press materials and ads started relentlessly including references to the product. What we didn't expect was the last-minute addition of DoubleSpace, which, as you'll see, is not the best file compression product available. The price *is* right, however.

The second area of controversy concerns the amount of disk compression you can expect to get. As you'll learn from this chapter, you shouldn't expect your 80M drive to magically grow to 160M. You might gain only 40M of capacity or, even, as little as 10M. This chapter will tell you why and how to maximize the performance of any disk compression utility.

The often-optimistic schemes used to project file compression are a key reason why DoubleSpace and similar programs are so poorly understood. Although Microsoft has streamlined installation, you just can't install DoubleSpace and forget about it. There are some important things to keep in mind as you set up and use DoubleSpace. I'll help you navigate these tough waters, too.

This chapter serves as your introduction to file compression, and the next one will detail exactly how to use DoubleSpace. Even though you can't get something for nothing, you can get something valuable—extra file storage—for very little cost.

Running Out of Space Is Inevitable

Whether your computer has a 40M hard disk or a 660M monster, sooner or later, you'll run out of space. DOS includes a compression utility, DoubleSpace, that can help you postpone the inevitable. When you consider that you may be gaining, in effect, a "free" 40, 60, or 80M hard disk simply by squeezing your existing files smaller, DoubleSpace may seem like a bargain. However, we rarely get something for nothing, and even the best file compression utilities involve some tradeoffs that you should know about. This section will explain how file compression programs work and why they may not help you with some of the files that you use most.

Making Your Hard Disk Go Farther

Actually, you may find a bit more than you wanted to know about this topic in the following section, but file compression is an important technology, so I want to explain it in some detail. I've simplified the topic considerably: you won't find any discussions of discrete cosine transformation as it applies to image compression, because I don't understand the math myself. However, you may have more detail than you need for everyday use. If you're curious or willing to follow a detailed explanation, read on. This information will help you use DoubleSpace intelligently.

File Compression Adds Effective Space

In one sense, file compression is possible because most applications use inefficient file formats to store their data. Word processors that save files as straight ASCII, perhaps with some formatting code embedded, are the worst culprits, because ASCII text is about the most inefficient way to store information. Image editing programs may store files in what is called *uncompressed TIFF*, another horrid waste of hard disk space (the rationale being that almost any other program that works with images can read these files).

On the other hand, these same programs usually offer a *compressed TIFF* option, in which the files are shrunk down, using an industry standard method, or algorithm. You may save as much as 80 percent of the disk space normally required by standard files when an efficient, compressed file format is used.

Data files are the chief wasters of hard disk space, and the amount varies by file format. However, there is also some slack in executable programs and other files on your disk. DoubleSpace, Stacker, and similar packages make it possible to transparently compress all the files in a particular volume by compressing everything in the volume itself, rather than manually squeezing individual files.

Backup Programs and Archiving Programs Also Compress

There are other programs that can be used to compress files that can't be automatically squeezed by an application program. Back-up programs like Fastback II automatically compress files as they are transferred to the backup media. The shareware program PKZIP is one of the most widely known utilities of this sort. You cannot only use it to compress files, but you can collect a number of related files together in a single archive. This can be an especially effective method for storing many small files, because DOS has a minimum amount of disk space that is set aside for even the tiniest files. It may be possible to archive 20 or 30 tiny files into the disk space formerly occupied by only one or two of them.

There are limitations with either file compression option. As I noted, some programs use compression schemes that make their files unreadable by other ordinarily compatible programs. After a file has been squeezed into a PKZIP archive, you can't ordinarily read it or use it until you uncompress it again. In addition, you must remember to compress your files and take the time to do it.

DoubleSpace Is Transparent

DoubleSpace's strength is that it is nearly transparent. DOS's installation program will install it for you so that DoubleSpace will be activated every time you turn your computer on. You can define any or all of your hard disk volumes, or just parts of them as DoubleSpace volumes. You access each of these by drive letters, just as you did before. If you elect to set aside all of a given hard disk for file compression, you'll even access that disk by the same drive letter that you did before.

The most noticeable difference will be that you'll suddenly have a lot more apparent disk storage space available. If you're very observant, you may notice that it takes a little longer to load or save files. That's because DoubleSpace is automatically decompressing and compressing them as you work. However, when a file must be loaded from the hard disk itself, rather than from the SmartDrive cache, there may be no performance penalty. That's because DOS can read a compressed file from the disk more quickly than an uncompressed one. The time saved in disk access may be *more* than the time spent decompressing, giving a net savings.

Some of the gains are illusory. That's because certain files (for some people, that may be *most* of your files) may not be very compressible. To understand why, we need to look at how file compression works.

Compression Works on Codes

When a computer is working with a program, a data file, or a bit-mapped image, it stores a binary number representing each piece of program code, data, or part of the bit map in a separate memory location. In the case of programs, the numbers stand for instructions for the microprocessor, memory locations, or text strings. In data files, the numbers represent a mixture of control codes, text, and formatting information. In an image file, numbers represent values in the bit map and other information.

For example, if the computer encountered the two binary numbers 10110100 and 00001001 in a machine language program, it would inter-pret them to mean that it should load a value of 9 decimal, or 1001 in binary, into a special memory location on the microprocessor, the reg-ister AH.

The same two numbers in the middle of a 256-gray scale bit map would mean something quite different. The 10110100, which is 180 in decimal, might represent a fairly dark gray pixel (because it has a value of 180 on a scale of 0 to 255). The 00001001, on the other hand, would represent a very light, almost white, tone.

Such divergent values might be common in a computer program but rare in something like a scanned image. Therefore, when the ultimate amount of compression is desired, different types of compression methods are usually used for programs and data than for image files. That's why you see claims of 20:1 or better for JPEG (Joint Photographic Experts Group) image compression, when DoubleSpace can rarely produce much better than 2:1 or 3:1 compression. You'll learn why in the next section.

Data Compression versus Image Compression

All data compression schemes operate by replacing individual streams of bits with shorter streams that convey the same information. When squeezing a program, the compression/decompression process cannot lose a single bit of information. Otherwise, the data or program becomes corrupted and is no longer useful for its intended purpose. Data files are also somewhat critical, although it's sometimes possible to drop a bit here and there and still retain all or nearly all of the data in the file. Still, only the most conservative, so-called lossless compression schemes can be used for these files. That is the sort of data compression that DoubleSpace uses. It can squeeze down your files, yet restore them to their exact original state without losing even a bit. That limits DoubleSpace to a relatively conservative range of compression ratios.

Single Bits Are Not Essential in Image Files

Single bits are rarely so important in image files. An 8 by 10-inch image scanned at 300 dots per inch in binary, black-and-white mode contains 7.2 million individual bits. If some of the black pixels are displayed or printed as white, or vice versa, you may not even be able to detect the difference visually, as long as they aren't clumped together to produce a larger white or black spot on the image. Such an image probably contains large spaces of the same value, as when black line art is drawn on a white background. Most of the file consists of binary 0s interrupted by a few strings of 1s here and there.

If a portion of a given line of the image looks like this:

```
000000000000000111000000000000000001111110000000000000000
0000000001111111111111111
```

Why would you want to use up nine whole bytes to store the information about those 72 consecutive pixels? A simple way to convey the same data would be with a string of numbers like this, which takes up only 4.5 bytes:

```
001110000011010000000011000110001000010000
```

If you divide that string into sections of six bits each and then translate the binary numbers into decimal, you get the following series 14, 3, 16, 6, 24, 16. That happens to represent the length of each string of consecutive bits of the same value in the original number. That is, the line begins with 14 white pixels, followed by 3 black pixels, then 16 white pixels, 6 black, 24 white, and 16 black. What I've done here is allocate a run of six bits to store a value that represents the number of pixels in a row for either black or white.

Because there are only two possible states for each pixel, we don't need to convey any information about what type they are, just the length of the *run* of one type before we need to switch over to the other—that is, only the transition points need to be conveyed. Each group of six bits conveys a number from 0 to 63, so we can represent runs of up to 64 individual pixels in either black or white.

As noted, in 6-bit binary chunks that second string of 0s and 1s translates into 14, 3, 16, 6, 24, and 16. Runs longer than 64, if they occur, can be designated by using two or more sets of 6 bits. The success of my simplified scheme hinges on most of these runs being at least 6 bits and less than 64 bits long on average. Runs of fewer than 6 bits can be more efficiently represented by the unencoded binary string, naturally, of 5 or fewer bits. Runs of longer than 64 bits require 12 bits to represent.

You can see that I've compressed the size of this sample line by 50 percent without losing any information. Actual compression algorithms, although considerably more sophisticated, are based on the same principle.

Image files often have long runs of numbers like these. Program and data files usually don't include strings of the same value, except as filler or placeholders. However, there are other compression methods that can squeeze these files, still without losing any information.

Compression Methods

There are several ways to compress the numbers used to represent programs, data, and images. One method is called Huffman encoding, in which the most frequently occurring numbers are represented by relatively short codes. Overall, if binary numbers, such as 11111111, which require the full 8 bits of a byte, occur frequently enough, they will be represented by much shorter binary numbers. The most efficient Huffman encoding schemes prepare a special frequency table for each file being processed, assigning the shortest codes to the numbers that occur most often. Table 15.1 shows how part of such a table might look. It lists the most frequently-encountered binary numbers in a mythical example file.

Table 15.1. Sample Binary Numbers

Original number	Code
11101110	000
10010111	001
11011001	010
11101111	011
01110111	110
10000111	111

The seven most common values might be binary codes for particular program instructions that are carried out repeatedly or a particular alphanumeric character that appears with great frequency. The actual meaning isn't important. The key is that enough of them are used to generate significant file size savings.

In this example, the seven most common values, which would require 53 bits to store unencoded, can be represented by only 21 bits. That's a savings of about 60 percent. With text files, compression can be impressive, because certain characters—e, t, a, o, i, and n, for example—occur much more frequently than others in our language. Huffman encoding works very well with files that have repeated series of numbers. Programs and data fall into this category. Images are much more random and less susceptible to compression using unadorned Huffman encoding. However, it can be combined with other methods that reduce images to a series of numbers that can themselves be further shortened using the Huffman method.

Huffman encoding is far from the best of all file compression schemes. Because every character requires at least one bit to represent it, there is a maximum upper compression limit of 8:1, and that would be possible only if there were just two characters in the file. In addition, Huffman encoding is unable to compress a file until it has read the entire file and evaluated the characters to produce the optimum encoding table. It's not possible to encode "on the fly," which would be desirable when storing a large file to a hard disk or transmitting it through telecommunications. For that, you need a more sophisticated method.

LZ and LZW Compression

Lempel-Ziv (LZ) or Lempel-Ziv-Welch (LZW) compression replaces frequently used strings of numbers with fixed-length codes. This system uses statistical analysis to determine what sets of numbers appear most often.

Abraham Lempel and Jacob Ziv were mathematicians who released a paper in May, 1977, detailing their scheme for compressing data. Nine years later, another researcher named Terry Welch translated the duo's math into practical algorithms. The concept used is very easy to understand.

Picture a black box that we'll call a *data compressor*. Information flows into it one character at a time, is processed, and then flows to a history buffer and out for disposition (say, to your hard disk as a compressed file). When a character is received, the compressor examines its history buffer to see whether this character has been received before. If not, it is released for output. If the character has been received before, it is held until the compressor examines the next character that comes in. It then looks to see whether this *pair* of characters has been previously received.

The process always continues with the compressor trying to build strings of one or more characters that have already appeared in that exact combination previously in its history buffer. When it has the longest string it can accumulate, the compressor releases not the string itself, but a small coded token that tells where in the history buffer the particular string occurs.

Using text as an example for clarity, you can see that strings like *the, they, theater, theaters, theatrical*, could all be represented by progressively shorter series of tokens. This type of compression starts out by not performing very well, because as the initial bytes come in, there are not many instances of each string of characters to point to in the history buffer. But, as files get longer, the odds of a string having occurred somewhere in the file increases, so compression becomes more efficient. Note that this sort of compression works with image files as well as data and program files, because even the random collections of bytes found in image files must repeat to an extent; there are only so many combinations of numbers available to describe an image.

Lossy Compression Schemes

You should probably understand about so-called *lossy* compression methods so that you can appreciate why DoubleSpace produces so much lower file-reduction ratios. The Joint Photographic Experts Group (JPEG) has developed a compression scheme that works particularly well with continuous tone images. It is efficient but still retains most of the valuable image information. Note that I said *most*.

JPEG uses three different algorithms—one called discrete cosine transformation (DCT), a quantization routine, and a numeric compression method like Huffman encoding.   JPEG first divides an image into larger cells—say 8 by 8 pixels—and performs the discrete cosine transformation on the information. This mathematical mumbo-jumbo simply analyzes the pixels in the 64-pixel cell and looks for similarities. Redundant pixels—those that have the same value as those around them—are discarded.

Next, quantization occurs, which compresses the number of tones included in the cell. Some of the pixels that are nearly white are represented as all-white. Then the gray scale and color information is squeezed down by recording the differences in tone from one pixel to the next, and the resulting string of numbers is encoded using a combination of Huffman and other schemes. Each separate block or cell is treated the same way. Because adjacent pixels in an image tend to have values similar to those around them, this area-oriented approach works well with image-based files. Although the overall information in the file may be relatively random, in computer terms, the data in a given cell is almost predictable when taken as a whole.

So, a full-color image section (8 bits used to record each pixel in red, green, and blue colors—24 bits in all), measuring 8 by 8 pixels and originally requiring 192 bytes of storage, can often be squeezed down to 10 to 13 or fewer bytes.

The success of the scheme depends on the subject matter of the image. Pictures with large areas of the same color or those with not too many details can be squeezed quite well. Will you really notice if the sky's gradient from dark blue to light blue isn't exactly the same or as smooth in the original image? In fact, JPEG allows you to specify various compression ratios. The higher the ratio, the more information that is discarded. The end-user may evaluate the results and switch to a lower compression ratio if the reconstructed image is less than satisfactory.

What This Means for DOS 6 Users

The implications of the various file compression technologies available may already be clear to you from the previous discussions. If not, here's a brief summary in simple terms.

First, DoubleSpace has no way of telling whether it is dealing with image files, data files, or program files, so it must use relatively conservative, lossless data compression schemes. This leads to compression ratios on the order of 1.5:1 to 3:1 for most types of files.

Because DoubleSpace needs to compress files with no practical upward limit on size, on the fly, it needs to use compression that works with a continual stream of data.

Some types of files will compress more efficiently than others. You may find that TIF and PCX files, as well as EXE and COM files, may already have been compressed or are already stored in a very compact form. DoubleSpace can't perform magic; there's no way of squeezing out extra space that just isn't there. If most of your files fall into these categories, you won't gain much extra disk space with DoubleSpace.

When I was writing this book, I installed DOS 6 on my backup 486-33 system, which is equipped with a 220M hard disk drive. It was loaded with EXE and COM files and had quite a few image files. I averaged about a 1.31 to 1 compression ratio with that disk, a saving of less than a third. My 220M hard disk became a 290M drive through file compression.

ASCII, EPS, and PostScript Files Are Compressible

Conversely, some other types of files are eminently crunchable. ASCII text files are particularly so. PostScript files and Encapsulated PostScript (EPS) clip art consist primarily of PostScript instructions in ASCII form and are themselves very suitable for compression. You might wind up with compression ratios of 2 to 1 or even 3 to 1 if you have many such files. An 80M hard disk could store as much as a 240M drive under such conditions.

Which Files Should I Compress?

Because some files compress well, and others don't, you need to decide when and how to compress your files. Fortunately, DoubleSpace allows you to set your system up in such a way that you need compress only the files that can benefit from squeezing and without requiring a lot of work and thought on your part. All you need to do is compress part of your hard disk and leave another part uncompressed.

You can easily experiment by copying files into a DoubleSpace partition, and using **dir /c** to see how much they were compressed. As I noted, you'll find that some files will compress more than others. Those are the ones you'll want to keep in a DoubleSpace partition.

Tip

Let image application programs compress image files for you. Rather than store uncompressed (or worse, compressed) TIFF images in a DoubleSpace volume and gain no further useful squeezing, let your image program store files in the most efficient format it supports. Keep these on an uncompressed portion of your disk. You can also store them on a DoubleSpace disk, if you want, realizing that no actual compression is done. Your image-editing program may support JPEG file compression, for example, which will provide much higher compression ratios than DoubleSpace can possibly achieve. You may still achieve some space saving from the more efficient use of disk space, described in the "Transparent Disk Compression" section.

Tip

Don't compress files that are accessed frequently, especially if their compression is modest. If you run Windows all day long, it's probably not a good idea to load Windows into a DoubleSpace partition. Each time your computer accesses a file in the compressed area, DoubleSpace has to uncompress it. That takes a little extra time. The performance penalty might not be important with a program you run only occasionally but can quickly mount up for applications and data files that you work with constantly or on a regular basis.

Tip Don't compress temporary or swap files. These include temporary files that your software may use as a scratch pad or as virtual memory. For example, some programs allow you to specify a disk drive or directory to use as temporary storage if you run out of memory. Others use disk space to swap out portions of memory. Windows 3 is one such package (you can use either a temporary or permanent swap file with Windows).

Tip Don't specify a DoubleSpace volume for these temporary or swap files. There are two good reasons for that. First, when hard disk space is used in this manner, it is generally as a replacement for silicon memory or RAM. Performance always suffers when a slower hard disk substitutes for speedy RAM. Because of the compression and decompression involved, DoubleSpace disks are sometimes even slower than your regular hard disk volumes.

Second, by their very nature, temporary and swap files are transient residents of your disk. Your application will usually erase them if you exit gracefully (that is, without rebooting your computer). So, you really aren't saving any hard disk space. You might be able to store a *larger* swap file in a DoubleSpace volume, but your long-term savings are nil.

Tip Don't compress files that will be accessed rarely or never. If you don't use a file with at least some regularity, it probably doesn't belong on your hard disk. You'd be better off storing it on a floppy and retrieving it on one of those rare occasions when you do need it. Think of this as the ultimate file compression technique: instead of compressing a 400K file down to 200K, you can reduce its claim on your hard disk real estate to virtually nothing by moving it to other media.

Transparent Disk Compression

Oddly enough, there is one way to increase the amount of usable space on your hard disk without compressing the information. It's based on the fact that DOS tends to allocate hard disk space using rather large minimum "chunks" called clusters. These can vary in size, depending on the capacity of your hard disk, but the largest commonly used cluster measures 8192 bytes.

On such a hard disk, a 766-byte file would use 8K of disk space, roughly a 91 percent waste of that space. Ah, you don't have many files that small? If you're a Windows user, think again. 766 bytes happens to be the size of each and every separate .ICO icon file you store outside of a library. If you downloaded a shareware package of 1000 Windows icons from a BBS and stored them all on a hard disk with 8192-byte clusters, you'd have roughly three-quarters of a megabyte of useful icon data. Unfortunately, you'd need 8M of disk space to store them all individually. Have I gotten your attention?

Disk sectors are most often 512 bytes in size. However, earlier releases of DOS had some limitations on the number of different sectors they could keep track of at one time because a three-digit hexadecimal number, or only 12 binary digits, were used to assign a unique number to each disk storage unit. So, the number of unique numbers DOS allowed was 0 to FFF in hex, or 000000000000 to 111111111111 in binary. Both of these translate to 4096 different clusters in decimal notation.

With only 4096 numbers available, that adds up to a measly 2MB (!) of data if each unit were 512 bytes long. Instead, DOS used a different method. Instead of assigning one of these valuable 4096 numbers to a single sector, it grouped them into groups of sectors called clusters. By making a cluster represent 16 sectors—8192 bytes—DOS could refer to 4096 by 8192 bytes of data—the infamous, now vanquished 32M barrier. In DOS 3.0, the file allocation table was changed to allow both 12-bit and 16-bit representations of cluster ID numbers (the latter gives 512M with 8192 byte clusters), and DOS 4 and beyond have effectively given us unlimited disk volumes. Even so, cluster sizes larger than 512 bytes remain the standard.

As a result, hard disks that store many smaller files, such as Windows icons, will have a great deal of wasted space. If most of your files are large, you still waste some space, because few files exactly require a whole number of clusters. Each and every file that is 100 bytes too long needs one additional cluster, wasting up to 8K in disk space.

Transparent disk "compression" schemes reduce this waste by using smaller allocation blocks, typically as small as a single 512-byte sector. Those 1000 Windows icons mentioned earlier would magically be "compressed" to a single megabyte, *before* any additional file compression was done. These methods are called transparent because the operating system is unaware that they are going on. DOS continues to use the same cluster size it always did. A huge file that represents the volume to be allocated is set up, and the files *within* that file are stored using the smaller, 512-byte units.

When combined with the compression methods outlined, significant space savings can be achieved, even with otherwise noncompressible files.

The Down Side of Compression

I've already explained that some types of files don't compress very well, so the amount of compression you get from DoubleSpace may be less than you expected. If that isn't enough, there is one additional down side you should be aware of. Because the amount of compression is difficult to predict ahead of time, free space estimation is always a matter of guesswork.

On an uncompressed disk, the amount of free space is shown as the last line of output from the **dir** command, and the size of the file (*not* the amount of space consumed) is displayed next to the filename. Except in the case of very small files, these figures are fairly accurate. That is, DOS 6's COMMAND.COM file is listed as using 52,925 bytes but actually occupies 13 full clusters on my hard disk with 4096-byte clusters—53,248 bytes. That's less than a one percent difference. With files averaging 100K or more, even those that waste most of a cluster will be listed at about 96 percent of their true size. Free space estimation is not much of a problem on uncompressed disks.

The situation is much different when you're dealing with compressed volumes. You may have 20M of uncompressed space free on a given hard disk, all allocated to a DoubleSpace volume. You don't want to know that you have 20M of real space; you want to know how many extra files you can store on that disk. Unfortunately, without knowing what files are targeted for the disk, there's no way of telling for sure. You may be able to put 60M (uncompressed) of text files in the remaining space or 22M of compressed TIFF files.

The customary solution is to provide an estimate of the available space, based on the compression ratio achieved so far (or, worse, based on optimistic ratios established by the vendor). Luckily, the projections tend to average out over the long term, so you'll usually have a fairly good idea of how much space remains on any given compressed disk. The problems kick in when you attempt to copy in a single session files that represent a significant portion of the remaining space. If there's sufficient space, you may be shocked at how little space actually remains when you are finished.

In other cases, installation programs look to see how much disk space remains before they proceed. An inaccurate free space estimate can cause the installer to fail spectacularly. If you're updating an existing program, you may even lose your current configuration files, templates, or other data—all because you or your software were "fooled" into thinking you had more hard disk space than you really had.

In the chapter that follows on using DoubleSpace, you'll find some suggestions for avoiding most of the pitfalls discussed in this chapter.

The Next Step

It was important for you to learn about file compression before you set up your DoubleSpace volumes, as you needed to make some decisions about what files to compress with DoubleSpace and which files to leave in their natural state. With this background information out of the way, the next step is to look at DoubleSpace itself and to learn how to install, fine-tune, and use it.

Using DoubleSpace

This chapter will show you how to use DoubleSpace, Microsoft's file compression utility. You'll learn how to use both the Express and Custom install options, and you can read about what happens during the installation process *before* you subject your hard disk to the procedure.

What DoubleSpace Does

It's important to know exactly what DoubleSpace is doing when it creates a compressed drive. The utility can operate in one of two modes:

DoubleSpace can create a new compressed drive using some or almost all of the free space on an existing drive. In this case, the new compressed drive will be assigned a drive letter following the last current drive assignment in your system. If you have drives C, D, and E and compress the free space on drive D, your "new" drive will be assigned the drive letter F. The space formerly free on drive D will then be occupied by a hidden, invisible file called a compressed volume file (CVF) with a name like DBLSPACE.000. That file on your original "host" drive will actually contain all your compressed data.

DoubleSpace can also compress an existing drive. In this case, the new compressed drive retains the drive letter assignment it had before. So, if you have drives C, D, and E and decide to compress *all* of D, the resulting compressed drive will still be recognized as drive D by your system. However, DoubleSpace will create a new uncompressed host drive that follows the current drive assignments—in this case as drive J (see the rules for assignment in the next paragraph). The host drive is an uncompressed volume that contains the hidden, invisible DBLSPACE.xxx compressed volume file, plus any files that must remain uncompressed, such as permanent Windows swapfiles.

You need to know about these "ghost" host drives, because they can affect drive assignments that you or your software have come to expect, under certain conditions. To summarize, *creating* a compressed drive puts the new drive after the last drive letter already assigned in your system. Compressing an *existing* drive keeps the same drive letter but moves the original, uncompressed "host" drive after the last drive already assigned in your system.

Compressed volume files are not real disk drives, of course. DoubleSpace fools most applications into treating them as if they were actual drives. But what you really have is a CVF that is assigned a drive letter, and the host drive on which the CVF resides.

When DoubleSpace creates its first new drive, it skips the first four available drive letters and assigns the next one to the compressed drive. For example, if your system currently has hard disks C and D, DoubleSpace will skip E, F, G, and H and assign drive letter I to the first DoubleSpace drive. After that, it works backwards from the first drive letter (drive H would be next assigned) until it reaches a letter that is already being used by a logical or physical drive. DoubleSpace is also able to reassign its drive letters if a conflict develops between a DoubleSpace volume and a drive created by a RAM disk, network logon, or another device driver.

How DoubleSpace Works

DoubleSpace has been so tightly integrated into DOS 6, at least from the user's perspective, that it may not be clear exactly what must happen to give you access to compressed drives. That's not surprising; some interesting things happen as your computer starts and begins to boot DOS.

In Chapter 2, you learned how DOS loads its two basic system files, IO.SYS and MSDOS.SYS, into low memory before it begins to process your CONFIG.SYS and AUTOEXEC.BAT files. To use DoubleSpace, a third file, DBLSPACE.BIN is loaded as well, but into the very top of conventional memory, rather than in low memory.

The reason for that is simple. DBLSPACE.BIN must be present in memory *before* you can access any files stored on compressed volumes, so DOS needs to load it as early as it can in the boot process. After all, it's entirely possible that some of the device drivers that need to be loaded from CONFIG.SYS are themselves located on compressed volumes. If DBLSPACE.BIN wasn't loaded before CONFIG.SYS was processed, there would be no way to access those drivers. It would have been too danger- ous to expect users to remember to place a line loading DBLSPACE.BIN as the very first in their CONFIG.SYS file *without fail*. So, DOS loads this driver all by itself, without your help, into the top of conventional memory.

Why the top? Conventional memory is not the best place for any device driver to reside, but until CONFIG.SYS loads device drivers like HIMEM.SYS and EMM386, which provide access to upper memory, DOS has no access to that RAM. Conventional memory is the only place DBLSPACE.BIN can go. However, there's no rule that says it has to *stay* there. Once deposited at the top of conventional RAM, the driver can be conveniently moved into upper memory using yet another driver, DBLSPACE.SYS.

You should know that DBLSPACE.SYS does not provide access to compressed disks. That can only be done by DBLSPACE.BIN. The sole function of DBLSPACE.SYS is to move DBLSPACE.BIN from high conventional memory to its final location, which can either be the bottom of conventional memory or somewhere in upper memory.

Are you confused yet? Things might be a little clearer if you follow the wandering driver from your hard disk through each of its three possible locations.

Upper Conventional Memory

DBLSPACE.BIN is automatically loaded here during the boot-up process, providing access to any compressed volumes (if any) on your hard disk(s). DOS doesn't automatically put this driver into lower memory along with the rest of the DOS system files, because it would be difficult to move it later without leaving unsightly and wasteful holes. However, top of RAM isn't such a hot location either, as some programs require access to the top of conventional memory. As the system begins loading CONFIG.SYS, the driver should be either moved or removed.

If you don't happen to have any DoubleSpace disks, this driver can drop dead and vanish for all you care. In that case, you won't have a DBLSPACE.SYS line in your CONFIG.SYS file, which loads next.

Lower Conventional Memory

If you do have DoubleSpace disks, are using a 286 or lower microprocessor, or don't have any available upper memory for some other reason, you'll want to move DBLSPACE.BIN to a permanent home in lower conventional memory using a line like this one

```
DEVICE=C\DOS\DBLSPACE.SYS /MOVE
```

You'd substitute the actual path to the DBLSPACE.SYS file on your system, of course. This command tells DOS to move the DBLSPACE.BIN driver to lower memory.

Upper Memory

If you have Double Space disks, a 386 or higher microprocessor, and some available upper memory and want to free up as much conventional RAM as you can, you'd move DBLSPACE.BIN with the **devicehigh** command

```
DEVICEHIGH=C\DOS\DBLSPACE.SYS /MOVE
```

In this case, the driver would be moved to upper memory, if available.

The appropriate **device=** line will be inserted in CONFIG.SYS for you by DoubleSpace Setup and, possibly, changed by MemMaker to move the driver to upper memory. Once DBLSPACE.BIN is happily installed in memory, it "hooks" into DOS to intercept commands targeted at your compressed volumes and automatically performs the necessary compression and decompression steps on files as they are loaded from or written to those disks.

Installing DoubleSpace

Although DoubleSpace can be used to compress removable media, like floppy disks, we'll look at installing the utility and compressing your hard disk(s) first.

It's best not to install DoubleSpace when you first upgrade to DOS 6. After you've used DoubleSpace to compress your hard disks, you'll be unable to use Uninstall to go back to your previous version of DOS. That's not as unlikely as you might think. It is possible that you have a mission-critical application that is not compatible with DOS 6 for some reason (particularly if you are upgrading from a version prior to DOS 5.0). Although the SETVER command takes care of most such incompatibilities (by "lying" to programs that look for a specific DOS version before they will run), other problems can occur.

If they do, you may decide that your application is more important to you than DOS 6 right now. Uninstall quickly and cleanly will restore your early operating system, as long as no DoubleSpace volumes are involved. You can always copy the data on your DoubleSpace disks back to normal hard disk volumes and reinstall your earlier DOS, but the procedure is needlessly time-consuming. So, it's best to wait until you are confident that DOS 6 is the environment you plan to stick with before installing DoubleSpace.

Pre-Installation Checklist

There are several things you should do before you install DoubleSpace.

Back up Your Hard Disks

DoubleSpace will not harm your existing files even if the installation program is interrupted (by, say, a power failure) halfway through.

However, it's better to be 100 percent safe. It's not really DoubleSpace that concerns me. I've learned in the last 15 years that curious end-users can do some amazing things without meaning to do themselves harm. Deleting some of the hidden, normally invisible files that DoubleSpace uses (DBLSPACE.INI, DBLSPACE.000, etc.) can produce the interesting side effect of eliminating all your files in that volume. Back up any hard disk you consider important before installing DoubleSpace.

Run chkdsk /f

Run **chkdsk /f** one last time to find and eliminate any lost clusters. You don't want any of them included in your compressed volume.

Use Express or Custom Setup

Decide whether you want to use Express or Custom setup. Express setup compresses the existing files on drive C. If you have only one hard disk or want to compress only your drive C, this is the way to go. If you want to compress any other drive, you'll need to use Custom setup.

Compress or Create a Drive

Decide whether you want to compress an existing drive, or create a new, blank one from the remaining space on one of your hard disks. The reason you want to do this now is that you may decide to move some applications and files to another drive to make as much room as possible on your new DoubleSpace drive. It's often easier to do this reorganization before you install DoubleSpace, because you're able to estimate more closely what will fit where when working with uncompressed drives and files. A quick example will clarify things a little.

You have three hard disk volumes of 30M each: drives C, D, and E Each is about half full, with 15M free. You plan to compress all three using DoubleSpace. You might want to copy the contents of drive E to Drive D permanently, leaving drive E empty. Then you can use DoubleSpace to compress the data on your first two existing drives. Under average conditions, drive C will end up with about 45M of estimated free disk space from its new 60M capacity; drive D will have roughly 30M free, and drive E will become a spanking-new 60M drive, ready for that whopping big application and its associated files that you never could find enough room for on a single disk.

Starting the Installation

1. To start the installation process, close all running programs, including Windows and DOSSHELL, and return to the DOS prompt. If you use a network and want to keep the same network drive letter assignments that you currently have, log on and connect to any of the networked drives you normally use. DoubleSpace will assign a new drive letter to any uncompressed drives it creates, using the next letter that follows your current assignments. If you don't log onto the network, DoubleSpace may use a letter you normally apply to a networked drive, and you'll have to use another.

2. Type **dblspace** at the DOS prompt. The Welcome screen appears. You can exit by pressing F3 at any time during the process. For now, press Enter to continue. You'll next be asked to choose from Express and Custom setup. Make your selection by pressing the up and down arrows to highlight one choice and press Enter. If you've selected Express setup, skip to step 6.

3. Your next decision is whether to compress the files on an existing drive or to create an empty compressed drive. Highlight your choice and press Enter.

4. Before DoubleSpace goes to work, it will tell you a little about what it plans to do to your disk drive. If you elect to compress an existing drive that contains files that must remain uncompressed (such as a Windows permanent swap file), DoubleSpace will set aside sufficient space for those files and compress only the remaining files. When you've absorbed this information, press Enter to continue.

5. Next, you can select the drive you want to compress. A screen appears, giving current free space on a particular hard disk and projected free space after compression. Use the up and down arrows to select a drive and press Enter.

6. Finally, DoubleSpace will provide an estimate of the time needed to build the compressed file (if you are compressing an existing disk)

or to create a new, empty compressed volume. Press Enter, and DoubleSpace will restart your computer, load the DBLSPACE.BIN module of DOS 6, and start the compression process. If the computer doesn't restart by itself, you can turn it off and then on again. DoubleSpace always defragments the drive as part of the process, because the CVF must reside on contiguous sectors. (For more information about defragmenting, consult Chapter 18.)

That's all there is to installing DoubleSpace and creating your first compressed drive.

Managing Compressed Drives

Most operations with compressed drives are carried out exactly as you would with an uncompressed drive; you can copy files to and from them, run programs, create subdirectories, and do most other tasks. Some functions can't be done using existing DOS commands. The **chkdsk** command, for example, won't work as you might expect on a compressed drive from the DOS prompt; it only checks the underlying MS-DOS directory structure and file allocation table (FAT). To check the compressed disk for file errors, you need to run the DoubleSpace utility. In addition, housekeeping functions and creation of additional compressed drives all need this special utility.

You can load the DoubleSpace utility by typing dblspace from the DOS prompt, as you did for the original installation. DoubleSpace can also be used in command line mode by following the **dblspace** command with any of a series of switches, which are discussed "DoubleSpace's Command Line Mode."

If you enter just **dblspace**, the utility enters its menu-oriented mode. Any existing compressed drives and their hosts will be shown. You can highlight one of these to perform functions such as defragment, change size, and so forth. These functions are described later. You can also create a new compressed drive or compress an additional one. Let's look at each of DoubleSpace's four menus in turn.

Drive Menu

The Drive menu includes eight commands, Info, Change Size, Change Ratio, Mount, Unmount, Format, Delete, and Exit. Like all the menus, you can activate the Drive menu by pressing the Alt key and then using the arrow keys to scroll down through the choices. The functions of the individual selections are as follows:

Info This command shows information about the currently selected drive. The listing includes the drive's free and used space, the name of the compressed volume file (CVF) for that disk, and both the estimated and actual compression ratios.

Change Size You can use this command to enlarge or reduce the size of the selected drive. Compressed drives, unlike real ones, exist as files that can be adjusted upward or downward in size. You might need to reduce the size of a compressed drive in order to increase the amount of uncompressed space on the host drive.

For example, you may find that you need a larger permanent Windows swapfile to improve performance or increase the number of programs you can load at one time. The CVF on the disk where the swapfile resides can be shrunk to free up the space you need—providing there is free space on the compressed disk volume itself. Obviously, you can't make a DoubleSpace disk so small that it can no longer contain its files.

On the other hand, if you later decide that you don't need some of the uncompressed space on a disk, the CVF can be expanded to include a larger proportion of the host drive.

You may also adjust the relative size of compressed disks that reside on the *same* host drive. You might have started with a single 330M hard disk which was partitioned as only one logical drive, C. You might have created two compressed drives within C which were assigned drive letters D and E. Later, you decide that you made D too large and E too small. If you'd partitioned your main drive using **fdisk**, you'd be out of luck. The only way to resize the drives would be to back them up, remove the logical drives completely, and then create new logical drives in the desired sizes.

With DoubleSpace, you can dynamically change the size of your drives without affecting their contents.

Change Ratio DoubleSpace uses the estimated compression ratio when it displays the estimated free space left on a drive. This best-guess figure may or may not provide an accurate picture. If you plan to use a given compressed drive to store files that typically compress at a different ratio, you can change the figure DOS uses for its own estimates. For example, you may designate one compressed drive to store ASCII files that compress about 3:1. In that case, you might want to change DoubleSpace's ratio from the default 2:1 to the higher figure. Conversely, if you will be storing many non-squeezable files, you can revise the ratio downward.

Mount This command makes a CVF available to DOS 6 by assigning it a drive letter. Generally, all your hard disk CVFs will be mounted automatically when DOS boots. You might want to unmount one for security or other reasons, and later remount it with this command. However, Mount is most often used to enable DOS to use compressed volumes that have been stored on removable media, such as floppy disks.

Unmount Disconnects a CVF, rendering it inaccessible.

Format Formats a compressed drive, erasing all the file information it contains. You won't usually need to format a CVF, but it is a fast way to "clean out" a compressed drive of all its files, without deleting them one by one.

Delete Removes the selected compressed drive and its CVF, erasing all the files it contains. You can use this command to convert a compressed drive back into its uncompressed state. Drive C cannot be deleted. Because the CVF is simply a file, if you accidentally delete a compressed drive, you may be able to recover it with the DOS 6 **undelete** command, particularly if you try immediately before any new files have been written to the former host drive.

Exit Quits the DoubleSpace utility.

Compress Menu

The commands on this menu can be used to create a new, empty compressed drive from the free space on an uncompressed drive (including a formatted floppy disk) or to compress an existing drive.

To compress an existing drive, choose the Existing Drive menu item. DoubleSpace will display a list of drives that can be compressed. Excluded are drives that are too full, RAM disks, network drives, CD-ROM drives, Interlnk drives, and paths assigned drive letters by the **subst** command. By too full, DOS means at least 1.2M of free space on a hard disk used to boot the system, and .65M (650K) of free space on other disks, including floppies. (This obviously means that DoubleSpace cannot compress 360K floppy disks.)

You may select a drive, make any setting changes you want, and direct DoubleSpace to compress the drive. You'll be shown the amount of uncompressed space that will remain (the default is 2M). You can change this by highlighting the figure with the up or down arrow and pressing Enter. You can then type in a new amount of uncompressed disk space that should remain when DoubleSpace is finished. The process is identical to that carried out when you first installed DoubleSpace.

To create a new compressed drive, choose Create New Drive from the Compress menu. You'll be shown a list of drives that can contain your new drive. Change the parameters (amount of free space to remain uncompressed), if necessary, and press Enter to proceed.

Tools Menu

The Tools menu includes commands used to fine-tune and maintain compressed drives. The choices include the following:

Defragment This command organizes all the files in the compressed volume so that they are located in consecutive sectors within the CVF. That makes it possible to reduce the size of the compressed disk, because all the free sectors will be located at the end of the file, rather than scattered throughout the CVF.

Chkdsk This command searches a compressed drive for errors and, optionally, corrects them. If an application ends abruptly, it can create cross-linked files and unallocated clusters in a compressed volume as easily as on an uncompressed disk. The Chkdsk tool can fix these problems.

Options This choice displays the DoubleSpace Options dialog box, which lets you specify the number of additional drives that are mountable after you boot your computer and the last drive letter you want DoubleSpace to use.

Help Menu

The Help menu provides additional information on using any of the DoubleSpace commands.

DoubleSpace's Command Line Mode

The commands available from the DoubleSpace utility's menu mode can also be invoked directly from the DOS command line or from batch files that use the correct syntax. The allowable switches and their parameters are as follows:

```
dblspace  /chkdsk [/F] [drivE]
```

Checks the validity of a compressed drive's internal file structure, as described earlier. You may add the optional /F switch, which forces DOS to fix any errors it finds, or a drive letter specification. If you don't specify a drive, the current drive will be used.

```
dblspace /compress drive1: [/NEWDRIVE=drive2:]
[/RESERVE=size]
```

Compresses a hard disk or floppy. You must specify *drive1:*, which represents the drive letter of an existing drive you want to compress. Optionally, you may use the /NEWDRIVE switch, followed by the drive letter you would like DoubleSpace to apply to the original—host—drive. If you omit this switch, DoubleSpace assigns the next available drive letter to the new drive, using the allocation rules described earlier.

The /RESERVE switch can be used to specify how many megabytes of space on the host drive to leave uncompressed.

```
dblspace /create drive1: [/NEWDRIVE=drive2:]
[/RESERVE=size] or [/SIZE=size]
```

Creates a new compressed drive in the free space of an existing drive. The syntax is similar to the /compress switch described previously, except you may specify *either* the amount of uncompressed space to reserve *or* the actual size of the new compressed drive (you can't use both the /RESERVE and /SIZE switches at the same time.) If you enter 0 as a value for /RESERVE, DoubleDisk will make the compressed drive as large as it can. There must always be some uncompressed space set aside for the host drive and for any files that DoubleSpace encounters that *must* remain uncompressed. If you omit both /RESERVE and /SIZE switches, DoubleSpace uses all but 1M of the available space.

```
dblspace /defragment [drivE]
```

Defragments a compressed drive. You may enter a drive to defragment; otherwise DoubleSpace will default to the current drive.

```
dblspace /delete drive
```

Deletes a compressed drive. Note that you must specify which drive to delete. DoubleSpace will not delete the current drive unless you explicitly enter that drive letter, nor will it delete drive C. Use **undelete** to restore an erased compressed drive. Complete instructions are in "Undeleting a Deleted Compressed Drive" later in this chapter.

```
dblspace /format drive:
```

Formats a compressed drive. You must enter the drive letter of the compressed drive to be formatted. DoubleSpace provides an additional layer of protection by not allowing you to format the current drive simply because you forgot to type in a drive name. You cannot format a compressed drive C under any circumstances.

```
dblspace /info
```

Displays information about a compressed drive. Note that the /info switch itself is optional. If you enter the **dblspace** command followed by a drive letter, the informational list will be shown.

```
dblspace [/list] drive:
```

Shows a list information on all drives on a system, both compressed and uncompressed, except for network drives.

```
dblspace /mount [=CVFname] drive1: [/newdrive=drive2:]
```

Mounts a compressed volume file. You must specify the drive in which the CVF file can be found (*drive1:*). If you omit *CVFname*, DoubleSpace will default to the name DBLSPACE.000. If you want to mount a CVF with some other name, you may specify it. You can also enter the drive letter you want the mounted drive to use. If you don't enter a letter, DoubleSpace will use the next available letter, using the rules described previously.

```
dblspace /unmount [drive:]
```

Unmounts a compressed volume file. If you omit *drive:*, DoubleSpace unmounts the current drive.

```
dblspace /ratio[=r.r] [drive:] or [/ALL]
```

Changes the estimated compression ratio of a compressed drive. Substitute for *r.r* the ratio you want, from 1.0 (1:1) to 16.0 (16:1). Note that the figure you enter is the value used on the *left* side of the ratio; 3.2 would produce a ratio of 3.2:1, *not* 3:2. The decimal point and trailing zero are optional if you enter a whole number. If you omit *r.r*, DoubleSpace will use the actual compression ratio for all the files currently on the drive. To specify a drive, either omit any further switches (DoubleSpace will use the current drive), enter a drive letter, *or* use the /ALL switch (DoubleSpace will apply the ratio specified, or the default ratios to all the compressed drives on your system.) You cannot enter a drive letter *and* use the /ALL switch.

```
dblspace /size[=size1] or [/RESERVE=size2] drivE
```

Alters the size of a compressed drive. For *size1*, substitute the new size of the drive, in megabytes of uncompressed space on the host drive. That is, if your host drive has 20M free, you could add half of it to the CVF on that drive by specifying 10 as the *size1* parameter. The amount of new compressed space would depend on the ratio in effect for that drive.

Alternatively, you can specify a size for the new drive by using the /RESERVE switch to specify how much space to leave uncompressed on the host drive. If you used 10 for *size2*, all but 10M of the indicated drive would be included in the CVF. Note that you cannot use both *size1* and /RESERVE. Enter 0 as a value for /RESERVE to make the compressed drive as large as possible. If you use neither, DoubleSpace will resize the compressed drive to make it as *small* as possible. You must enter a drive letter to indicate which drive you want resized.

Abbreviating Switches

Some of the switches described can be abbreviated to a shorter form:

/COMPRESS	/COM
/NEWDRIVE	/NEW
/RESERVE	/RES
/CREATE	/CR
/SIZE	/SI
/DEFRAGMENT	/DEF
/FORMAT	/F
/LIST	/L
/MOUNT	/MO
/UNMOUNT	/U

Undeleting a Deleted Compressed Drive

If you accidentally delete a compressed drive that you intended to keep, *immediately* go to the DOS prompt, log onto the host drive where the CVF resided, and type **undelete.** You'll be shown a list of available files to restore, which should include one with a name like ?BLSPACE.000. Reply Y when asked whether you want to undelete the file and supply the missing first letter, usually D. You must then remount the drive using the **dblspace /mount** command.

The Next Step

Compressing hard disks is a relatively painless process when you understand how DoubleSpace works. This utility can also be used to compress removable media, such as floppy disk, Bernoulli or SyDOS cartridges, and floptical disks. There are some extra considerations you need to be aware of, and I'll address them in the next chapter.

Compressing Removable Drives

DoubleSpace isn't limited to compressing your hard disks. It works equally well with any removable media you might have, including floppy disks. If you use floppies for simple backups (achieved by copying files, rather than through DOS 6's Backup utilities), setting up DoubleSpace volumes on these disks is an easy way to provide compression and stretch your media even further. DoubleSpace can also stretch the capacity of other media, such as rewritable optical disk drives. This chapter will discuss some of the special issues you need to be aware of and will provide tips for using DoubleSpace with all types of removable media.

Why Compress Removable Media?

The most pressing reason to compress any type of storage is to save money. It's always less expensive to add 100M of hard disk space by compressing an existing 200M drive than by buying a new 100M unit. Removable media is expensive, too. A 150M collection of 3.5-inch, 1.44M floppy disks can cost $100; a 150M Bernoulli cartridge sells for around $140 through most mail-order outlets. Doubling the capacity of either of these can save significant amounts of money.

The downside is that compressed removable media are not quite as convenient as compressed hard disks. That's because DOS 6 is unable to automatically mount a CVF it finds on a removable disk, even if only one is present. You must manually mount any such disk you care to use, each and every time you switch from one disk to another. Because DoubleSpace cannot be run from within Windows, that means that Windows users must exit their operating environment each and every time they want to use a different removable compressed disk.

There are technical reasons why this is necessary. Because no DOS command is activated when a disk is simply inserted or removed from a drive, DOS has no way of knowing that a new disk has been inserted until you try to do something with that disk. To automount a disk, each and every DOS command and DOS service would have to examine every removable disk accessed to see whether a CVF were present, but un-mounted. If so, DOS would then have to ask you whether you wanted the disk to be mounted or would assume that you did. It's clearly simpler and safer to require the user to mount removable disks and to allow DOS commands to assume that the system files and drivers that have been loaded will take care of recognizing valid drives and drive letter assignments.

The bottom line is that using compressed removable media is less conve-nient but still might be an excellent solution for some users. Here are some examples of good applications for this technology:

> **For off-line storage of PostScript clip art, text files, and other highly compressible types of information.** These files can typically be compressed 2:1 to 3:1 or more, so it's a shame to store them in uncompressed format. If you archive them in PKZIP files, you must go through the extra step of unzipping them before use. Still, you wouldn't want these files cluttering up your hard disk, so a com-pressed floppy or other removable media is an excellent compro-mise. You can store perhaps 3 or 4M of EPS files on a 1.44M disk, but still as individual files that can be viewed and retrieved easily.

➤ **For storage of large collections of small files**. The reason for this is different than you might think. Floppy disks already use 512 byte sectors, so small files waste no more space on an uncompressed floppy as on a compressed disk (which can use smaller allocation units than a hard disk). However, managing large numbers of files is easier when you can get more of them on a single disk. It's easier to locate, say, a font file when you need to look through only four or five disks rather than eight or ten.

➤ **As an informal backup system**. In between regular backups, you might want to place working files on a floppy disk just for added protection. You've nearly finished a crucial report and have to leave the building for a few hours. Compressed floppies or other removable media can hold twice as much data, so you can carry more of your essential files with you. A single compressed disk can probably hold everything an individual can accumulate in a short period of time between regularly scheduled backups.

➤ **A way to exchange files efficiently with another DoubleSpace user**. If you must use "sneakernet" within an organization, or need to send disks back and forth between sites, DoubleSpace compression is a good way to reduce the number of disks required. You could always use a stand-alone program like PKZIP to squeeze files, if you know the other person has PKUNZIP, but you would run into problems if you wanted to recreate a specific directory structure to keep the files separate. PKZIP has this capability, of course, but you need to remember or look up the syntax to fold subdirectory structure into the archive file. With DoubleSpace, logging onto the source directory and typing **xcopy /s** does the trick. The recipient uses the same command to copy the files to a hard disk using the same subdirectory structure.

Creating Compressed Removable Disks

At first, DoubleSpace's menu-oriented mode is probably the easiest route to take, as you can clearly see what your options are. Type **dblespace** from the DOS prompt to load the DoubleSpace utility. Then choose Compress and Existing Drive from the top menu.

You must always use Existing Drive rather than Create New Drive with removable media; that way, the new floppy disk will always have the same drive letter. Although it's one thing to have "new" hard disk volumes taking on new drive letters, it would be very confusing if you discovered your floppy disk drive was suddenly drive N instead of drive A or drive B. DoubleSpace doesn't give you the option of compressing only part of a floppy; it's all or nothing, and the compressed volume retains its original drive letter.

That's not true of other type of removable media. Disks with larger capacities can be fully or partially compressed, and DoubleSpace will assign a new drive letter to the compressed volume. However, whether you are working with floppies or other removable media, DoubleSpace can create only one CVF per disk.

With non-floppies, you can compress existing data on the disk to create the DoubleSpace volume or make a new compressed volume on an empty disk. Even if the CVF you create is relatively small (say, it uses 4M of a 90M removable cartridge), you can't go back later and create an additional compressed disk (as you can on a fixed disk). You can enlarge the existing CVF, reduce it, or delete it. But DoubleSpace won't allow you to put more than one compressed volume on a single removable disk. Therefore, the Create New Drive dialog box will never even show removable disks as an option.

After you select Existing Drive, DoubleSpace scans your available drives and shows a list of any that can be compressed, as shown in figure 17.1. Note that if your floppy disk or other removable media have data already but don't have sufficient free space, they won't show up on the list. So, a 720K, 1.2M or 1.44M disk must have at least 650K free for DoubleSpace to consider it for compression. A 360K floppy won't appear at all. A Bernoulli or SyDOS cartridge or other media must have 1.2M free.

The current amount of free space and the projected free space after compression will be shown. Select the removable drive you want to compress and press Enter. If you're compressing a floppy disk, no other options are available. You can respond to the prompts and start the compression process, which takes about a minute. DoubleSpace automatically defragments, compresses, and mounts the disk.

```
 Drive  Compress  Tools  Help

                                    Free          Total
        Drive  Description      Space (MB)     Space (MB)

        P    Compressed hard drive      13.34        13.34  ↑



                                                            ↓

        To work with a compressed drive, press the UP ARROW or DOWN
        ARROW key to select it. Then, choose the action you want
        from the Drive or Tools menu.

        To quit DoubleSpace, choose Exit from the Drive menu. For
        help, press F1.

 DoubleSpace  │  F1=Help  ALT=Menu Bar  ↓=Next Item  ↑=Previous Item
```

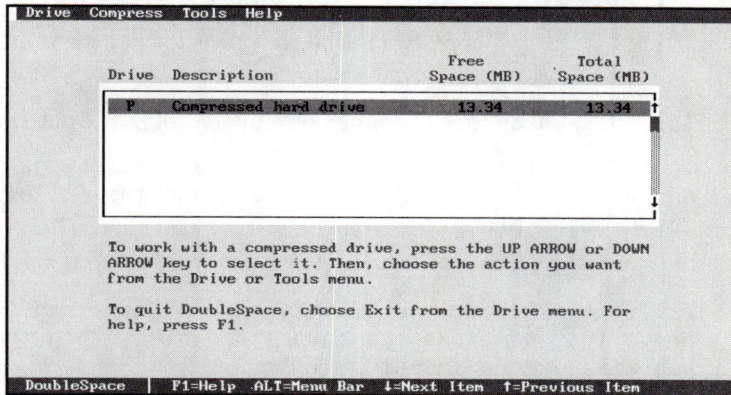

Figure 17.1. List of available drives for compression.

When compressing removable media with larger capacities, you are shown the amount of free space that will remain when DoubleSpace is finished (2M is the default), as shown in figure 17.2. You may highlight this value with the up or down arrows and change it. You can thus leave some uncompressed space available for other purposes. Although you cannot add a second compressed volume to a removable disk, you can expand the one you are creating now at a later time.

Deleting a Compressed Removable Disk

A special note is required because DOS 6 won't automatically mount these compressed disks. To delete one, you must first mount it. Thereafter, DoubleSpace will recognize the volume and allow you to delete it normally.

Using Compressed Removable Disks

When you insert a compressed disk into a drive, DOS treats it as if it were unmounted. That is, DOS commands "see" the uncompressed portion of the disk. The DoubleSpace volume and its data is hidden away in the

DBLDSPACE.xxx CVF. In case you're absent minded or the disk falls into the hands of someone who is not familiar with DoubleSpace, a file called READTHIS.TXT is placed in the root directory of the removable disk. This file reads as follows:

```
This disk has been compressed by MS-DOS 6 DoubleSpace.

To make this disk's contents accessible, change to the
drive that contains it, and then type the following at
the command prompt:

DBLSPACE/MOUNT

(If this file is located on a drive other than the
drive that contains the compressed disk, then the disk
has already been mounted).
```

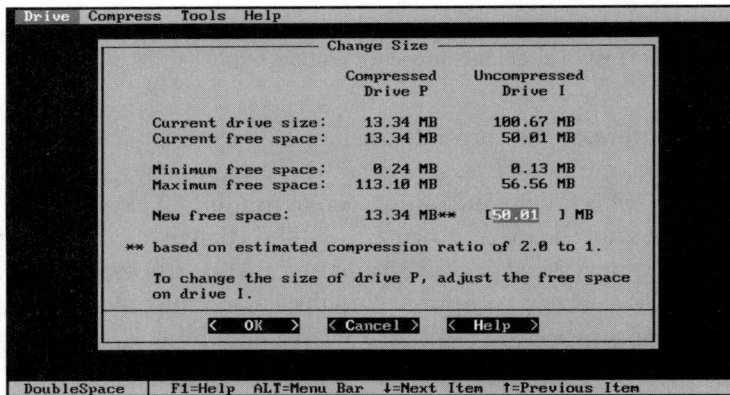

Figure 17.2. Amount of free space that will remain.

Of course, these instructions will work only for users who have already installed DoubleSpace on their systems. Others will be dumped into the first-time-user DoubleSpace installation routine, which can be confusing at best and alarming at worst.

DoubleSpace automatically mounts a removable disk when it is first compressed. Thereafter, you must mount it manually when it is first used in any working session. If you change disks or reboot your computer, you must remount the disk again. As noted earlier, for Windows users that means exiting Windows, mounting the disk, and then loading Windows again.

Although the mounting command is easy to remember and not very lengthy, you still might want to create a batch file to mount disks inserted in a particular disk drive. One typical such file might look like this:

```
@ECHO OFF

dblspace /mount a:
```

This file would mount the disk in drive A:. If you named it MTA.BAT, you could quickly mount any disk in that drive by typing MTA at the DOS prompt. (Remember to place this batch file in a subdirectory included in your DOS PATH.)

The Next Step

I almost exhausted the possibilities DoubleSpace has to offer. If you're looking for something more in a disk compression utility, you'll want to read Chapter 19, which discusses third-party alternatives to DoubleSpace, including the leading contender, Stacker. But first, we need to look at one of the tools DoubleSpace uses to create its compressed volumes, Defragmenter. It happens to be a utility that can be useful even if you aren't compressing hard or removable disks.

Defragmenting Disks

As disks, particularly the hard variety, are used a great deal, files tend to get scattered throughout the disk. It's not just *associated* files that may be located a great distance from one another on your disk. Individual parts of one file may be spread over a large amount of hard disk real estate, so your disk must move from track to track searching for all the bits and pieces you need to load the file into memory. In the worst case, your disk may go from the innermost track for one sector, then to the outermost for the next, and then back again. As you might guess, this can impact performance quite seriously. Even with a hard disk with an average track-to-track access time of 20 ms, that means you must wait an extra second each 50 times your hard disk must seek out a new track unnecessarily. Considering the hundreds of sectors in a file, that lost time can add up quite quickly. It also means extra wear-and-tear on your hard disk.

DOS Can Access Scattered Sectors—Slowly

Disk fragmentation is possible only because of the way DOS stores files. A given sector includes a pointer telling the operating system where to find the next sector if it isn't the next contiguous one on the disk. So, DOS has no problem locating all the sectors of a file, no matter how widely scattered they are—it just takes a great deal more time to do so.

This characteristic is actually an important feature of DOS. If DOS couldn't use your hard disk in this way, a great deal of disk space would be wasted. That's because, in use, your hard disk tends to become fragmented as files are erased, leaving holes that must be filled with new files.

When you write files to a fresh hard disk, DOS selects a set of sectors that are logically consecutive on the disk surface, starting with a single track and then moving to adjacent tracks as necessary. Note that the sectors aren't necessarily physically consecutive, because your disk's interleave factor may have been set higher than 1:1 if you have an older, slower computer system such as a 286. For example, if your interleave is set for 2:1, DOS may try to write a file to sectors 1, 3, 5, 7, 9, 11, and so forth on a disk. When it reads them back, it will skip every other sector (as required by the 2:1 interleave) and access each of these *logically* contiguous sectors in the most efficient manner.

DOS Uses Oldest Sectors First

DOS 6, like other recent versions of the operating system, uses the oldest sectors first, that is, those that haven't been used the longest. Under that scheme, the operating system will use all the sectors on your hard disk at least once before trying to assign any that have already been used but are now free because the files they were allocated to have been erased.

This scheme helps ensure that sectors which belonged to recently erased files won't be immediately assigned to a new file. Freed-up sectors are allowed to "age" awhile, which makes it possible to unerase files for a period of time. DOS doesn't actually erase the information the files contain; it removes the first character from the file name in the file allocation table (FAT), and returns the sectors involved to the available pool (putting them at the end of the line, as I said).

Eventually, all the sectors on a hard disk will have been used once, so DOS goes back and starts reassigning the oldest freed-up sectors next. However, it's unlikely that the next set of sectors to be used will be exactly as long as the file which now needs to be written.

Varying File Sizes Create Holes

If the file happens to be shorter than the one that previously occupied the allocated space, DOS will use some of the contiguous sectors and leave a smaller "hole" in the available pool. If the new file is longer, DOS will use up the contiguous sectors and then jump to the next set to write the remaining sectors. Often, it will need to use a third or fourth set of sectors to write all of a file. Invariably, the last set used will have a few extra sectors, leaving another small hole.

As more and more files are written and erased, this mismatch of file sizes ends up creating a maze of small groups of sectors scattered all over your disk. Before long, nearly every file will require four or five, or many more additional groups of clusters, and your hard disk starts working overtime retrieving them.

There are two ways to relieve this problem. You can copy every file on your hard disk to another hard disk or a set of files, using a file-by-file copy command such as COPY, XCOPY, or MOVE. You may then erase your hard disk and copy the files back. They'll automatically be placed in contiguous sectors on your disk. As you might guess, this procedure can take a long time.

Disk Optimizers Are Not New

Disk optimizers have been around for a long time. They essentially perform the same task but do it within the confines of a single hard disk. That is, they copy each of the sectors of a given file to an unused portion of your disk and then write those sectors back in another section, using consecutive sectors.

If your disk is very full, this process can take awhile, because the optimizer can work with only a small number of sectors at one time. For safety reasons, a given file is not erased from its temporary holding location until it has been properly written to its new site. That way, if the optimization process is interrupted no files will be lost. The only bad thing that happens after an interruption is that your disk isn't as optimally reorganized as it could have been.

In addition to rewriting all your files into contiguous sectors, optimizers use some other considerations to enhance performance: directory organization, file order, and file priority.

Directory Organization

Subdirectories on your hard disk are actually a special type of file, and DOS searches for them in the same way it looks for files. So, your subdirectory "files" should be defragmented and placed where DOS can find them quickly. To locate a file called C:\DATA \1993\MYFILE.DAT, DOS first looks in the root directory of C for a subdirectory listing called \DATA. It then reads that file looking for another subdirectory file, 1993. It must open that file to see whether MYFILE.DAT is included. An optimized directory structure can improve access to every file located within a subdirectory.

File Sorting

DOS stores files in the order in which they were written. You may prefer to list all EXE files first so that DOS can find applications more quickly. Or, if you don't switch between programs very quickly, you might prefer to have all your data files stored first for faster access. DOS 6's Defragmenter provides simple sorting order options for files.

File Priority

Third-party defragmenters may let you prioritize files that should be placed at the front of the hard disk.

Defragmenter Is Easy To Use

Defragmenter is easy to use and does the job, even if it is less flexible than some of the optimizers sold by third parties, such as the Norton SpeedDisk program (upon which the Microsoft version is based). Before you use it, you should keep several things in mind.

Because you'll be rewriting every file on your disk, you won't want any other program to write to that disk during the process. Therefore, Defragmenter should be the only program running at that time. You'll have to exit from Windows, since Defragmenter will refuse to run inside it. If you have a memory resident program (a TSR or "pop-up") that may write to the disk, don't use it during optimizing. If you're not sure, you may want to unload the program or disable it in your CONFIG.SYS and AUTOEXEC.BAT files through REMarks and then re-boot.

Defragmenter will not move system files, which can include files written to your disk by copy-protected programs. That's generally a good idea. However, you may have set the system attribute of some files yourself, in order to hide them or protect them from accidental erasure. For example, I have a large-screen monitor that uses special drivers and always looks for a certain configuration file in the root directory of one hard disk when the monitor is activated. I like to keep my root directories clean of extraneous programs, so I set the system and hidden attributes of this configuration file. The driver can find the file just fine, and I don't have to see it or worry about accidentally erasing it when I remove other, more temporary files from the root directory of that drive using wildcard commands.

Other programs create system-type files that can be moved safely during the optimization process. You just need to remember to change their attributes and then change them back after your disk has been reorganized.

Before You Run Defragmenter

Just prior to running Defragmenter, there are several things you can do to increase its efficiency and effectiveness. You won't need to run Defragmenter very often (unless your hard disk experiences an enormous amount of activity)—perhaps once a month—so these extra steps should present no hardship.

Tip

Make sure that you won't need to undelete a file. Normally, only a file's directory entry is altered when you delete a file. Until DOS happens to use the actual file clusters for another file, the original file is available for resurrection through the **undelete** command. However, when you fully optimize a disk, sectors can be be written to new locations that overwrite those formerly allocated to deleted files. Make certain that you don't have files you may want to undelete later before you run Defragmenter.

Tip

You might want to run **chkdsk** with the /F switch before optimizing a disk. I experiment with software and hardware quite a bit and often manage to lock up my system for one reason or another. Over the course of a month, it's almost guaranteed that I'll reboot while programs are running often enough to create quite a collection of lost chains of clusters on my hard disks. These won't interfere with Defragmenter, of course, but it makes little sense to include misallocated sectors among those you reorganize. When you do finally run **chkdsk**, you'll create some instant holes in your otherwise nicely defragmented hard disk.

Tip

Many experts recommend backing up your disk before optimizing it. Indeed, they recommend backing up your hard disk before doing almost anything that might somehow destroy your disk and data if you goof it up in some unlikely way. However, disk optimizing is very safe, and a backup is probably a needless waste of your time. The experts who recommend backup just want to protect themselves from phone calls from idiots who ignore all the other recommendations and manage to do some harm to their hard disk.

You should already be backing up your disk and its files on a regular schedule, anyway. If you've done that, you don't really need to do a backup before running Defragmenter. However, to protect myself legally, I must add that I recommend skipping the backup *only* if you adhere closely to the other recommendations (e.g. don't try to optimize while you're copying files to and from the disk under another Desqview window) and you're *not* one of those idiots I mentioned earlier.

Running Defragmenter—Menu Mode

DOS 6's Defragmenter can be used in command line or interactive, menu-oriented modes. If you type **defrag** at the DOS command line you can immediately begin to defragment the current hard disk or press tab to select the Configure button and Enter to activate the Optimize menu.

The menu bar at the top then provides only two choices: `Optimize` and `F1=Help`. The graphic display represents the sectors of your hard disk. This is known as the Disk Map. Any Xs show where unmovable sectors are, which are generally those that contain system or hidden files but can also be bad sectors that the operating system has locked out. The other marked sectors are those that contain files. On a typical disk, there will be many blanks representing files that have been deleted with sectors not yet allocated to new files. At the bottom of the screen is a box showing the current status of any defrag operation underway and a legend that explains what the blocks in the graphic display mean.

There are seven choices on the Optimize menu, but your real options are fairly limited. Let's look at them quickly.

Begin Optimization If you select this choice, Defragmenter will being optimizing your disk, using the currently selected drive and optimization method.

Drive... This choice brings up a scrolling box that lets you choose which drive to optimize. It shows your local hard disks and removable drives.

Optimization... Select this item to specify whether you want Full Optimization, which reorganizes files so that each file resides on contiguous sectors on your disk. In addition, all the files are rewritten starting at the beginning of the disk to eliminate any unsightly gaps that will quickly fill up with newly fragmented files. You can choose Unfragment Files Only, which rewrites your files to contiguous sectors but does not necessarily fill in all the "holes" in your hard disk.

File sort... This item lets you specify the order in which files should be written to your disk directory. You can specify unsorted, or sorted by name, file extension, date and time, or size, and in either ascending or descending order. If you happen to use your newest files more frequently than older files, you'll want to sort by date and time, or, if you carry out many operations that look at files by their alphabetically arranged file names, you may gain a little extra speed if the files are written to the disk in order of their filenames. Remember that a few days after files are arranged in *any* order, it's likely that new ones or rewritten versions will be present on the hard disk anyway.

This step doesn't actually change the order of the files on the disk. Instead, it rewrites the disk directories in the order selected so that they can be read more quickly.

Map legend... This choice pops up a longer description of the graphic disk display.

About Defrag... Is an information box about the utility.

eXit... Exits the program.

As Defragmenter runs, you can watch the graphic display change when files are read and rewritten to your disk. A bar display shows what percentage of your hard disk has been optimized, so you can estimate how much time remains.

Running Defragmenter—Command Line Mode

After you've used Defragmenter a few times, you may become comfortable enough to run it from the command line. Instead of selecting options from menus, you can specify them as switches on the input line. There are a few options available in this mode that you cannot use in interactive mode. The syntax for **defrag** is as follows:

```
defrag [drive:] [/F] or [/U] [/S[:]order] [/B]
[/SKIPHIGH] [/LCD] or [/BW] or [/G0] [/H]
```

If you don't specify *drive*, **defrag** will use the current drive. You can enter either /F (full optimization) or /U (defragment files only), but not both, to choose the optimization method, as outlined previously.

If you use the /S switch, you may specify the order in which files are sorted prior to rewriting them to your hard disk. For *order*, substitute N (alphabetic order by name), N- (reverse alphabetic order by name), E (alphabetic order by extension), E- (reverse alphabetic order by extension,

D (date and time, earliest first), D- (date and time, oldest first), S (size, smallest first), S- (size, largest first).

If you add the /B switch, **defrag** will have DOS reboot your computer when optimization is finished. If you needed to reboot without loading certain TSRs or other programs, change your AUTOEXEC.BAT and CONFIG.SYS files back to the way they were after you've rebooted, but *before* you run **defrag**. Use the /B switch, and you can walk away while the defragmentation takes place. When you come back, your system will have rebooted back to its normal state.

The /SKIPHIGH switch loads **defrag** into conventional memory, instead of upper memory (where available). You might want to do this if you've encountered conflicts before running the utility in upper memory.

If you have trouble seeing Defragmenter operate on your screen, you can specify one of three switches that may help in specific instances. The /LCD switch starts the utility using a color scheme that is more legible on liquid crystal display (LCD) screens. The /BW screen forces a black-and-white color scheme, and /G0 disables the graphic mouse and graphic character set, producing an ANSI-oriented block mouse cursor and character graphics instead.

The /H switch will enable you to move hidden files as part of the defragmentation process. You can do this when reorganizing drives other than drive C, where you know there are hidden files that can be safely moved. Windows swapfiles do not fall into this category, but there are other kinds of hidden files, such as the 4DOS DESCRIPT.ION file description files. (4DOS is a replacement for COMMAND.COM with extra commands and capabilities.)

How Often Should You Run Defragmenter?

The first time you optimize a particular disk, you may find that even with total neglect, only 20 to 30 percent of your disk is defragmented. That can be partly traced to the fact that a large proportion of the files on most disk drives will be applications or utility programs which are never rewritten after they have been installed. Moreover, we tend to install software first, on clean hard disks that are naturally unfragmented. Most later disk activity comes from writing and rewriting files in the space that remains. Sometimes, applications are updated or deleted, leaving holes and creating more fragmentation. But, in general, only about a third of your hard disk, at most, will be subject to fragmentation over any period of time.

Still, because data files are frequently accessed, and the degree of fragmentation can be severe, you lose nothing by defragmenting any disk that displays less than 92 percent unfragmented files. Some users like to defragment before their hard disks reach that state. You can run Defragmenter once a week, simply to examine the state of each of your hard disks from the report issued when you select each drive in turn.

The Next Step

If you noticed the Symantec credits that pop up when Defragmenter runs, you guessed that Microsoft's utility is actually a version of the SpeedDisk optimizer furnished with Symantec's Norton Utilities. If you also guessed that the Norton program has more options and flexibility, you're right again. In the next chapter, we'll look at some third-party optimizers and disk compression utilities that take you a bit beyond where Microsoft has ventured with DOS 6. You'll see when and why you might want to lay out the extra bucks to purchase one of these add-ons.

Beyond DoubleSpace and Defragmenter

For most DOS 6 users, DoubleSpace and Defragmenter provide all the disk compression and optimization you'll ever need. Yet, you may want to explore other options that provide special features you don't get with the basic DOS utilities. Stacker 3.0, for example, is much more friendly to Windows users and has a special feature that lets you use compressed "stacked" floppies on any computer, whether it has Stacker installed or not.

Similarly, the disk defragmentation utilities available from other sources offer features not included with DOS 6's **defrag** command. This chapter will outline a few of your options and explain why you might want to consider them.

Other Compression Utilities

Disk compression utilities have been around for a long time, under names like Squish Plus, SuperStor, and Stacker. Digital Research incorporated SuperStor into its own DR DOS 6.0 in 1992, and updated versions of that utility have been duking it out with Stacker in the advertising wars ever since. They share many features, but Stacker has gotten the most attention because of its on-going lawsuit with Microsoft. This next section will detail some of the features of the two market leaders.

Stacker 3.0

Stacker has consistently scored the highest marks in terms of compression ratios and speed when compared with SuperStor in various magazine test drives. It also scores high in ease of use, Windows compatibility and—not surprisingly—compatibility with DOS 6. (DoubleSpace can convert Stacker drives to DoubleSpace volumes.)

Unlike DoubleSpace, Stacker can be installed either from Windows or the DOS prompt. It has both express and custom modes. You can choose between best speed and best compression so that Stacker will either use its most aggressive compression algorithms, at a slight speed penalty, or use slightly less efficient squeezing techniques that are marginally faster. Because the best compression choice usually doesn't produce much in the way of space savings, but the best performance setting *can* shave ten percent off the time needed to load a compressed file, I recommend always using the letter setting.

Stacker is furnished with DOS and Windows utilities that simplify maintaining your compressed drives. The Windows Stackometer utility, shown in figure 19.1, is especially slick, showing compression ratio, free disk space, and fragmentation in easy to read graphics displays. The capability to access this information, mount drives, and change parameters from within Windows makes Stacker an excellent alternative to DoubleSpace.

You can also password-protect "stacked" disks with read-and-write or read-only privileges. Separate passwords can be assigned for each compressed volume.

Like DoubleSpace, Stacker can compress floppy disks. However, the resulting disk can be read and written to by any computer, even those without Stacker installed. A miniature version of the Stacker driver is included on any stacked floppy. When you use the **dir** command to view the contents of one of these disks, only a readme file appears. The file contains instructions to enter the Stacker command that loads the driver into the host computer's memory. Thereafter, that computer can read any stacked floppy until the DOS session is ended or the computer is rebooted. (Very clever.)

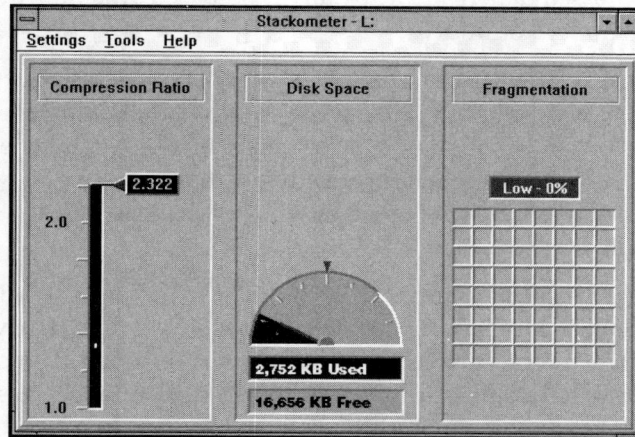

Figure 19.1. Stacker's Windows-based Stackometer.

Because compressed disks always work best with optimized file structures, Stacker includes its own defragmenter. This fast-operating utility functions like DOS 6's Defragmenter. You can elect to put each file into a single contiguous area but leave free space fragmented, or you can choose full optimization that moves all free space into contiguous blocks.

Stacker is a particularly good deal because the older Version 2.0 is often furnished free with hard disks, removable cartridge drives, or bundled with other software. You can upgrade to Version 3.0 for $49.95 or less, a significant saving from the $149.95 list price for this utility. Now that DOS 6 includes DoubleSpace, look for disk compression technology to improve and come down in price as the competition heats up.

SuperStor

Now available in SuperStor and SuperStor Pro versions, this utility was the first to offer the Migrating Floppy trick, including a feature called Universal Data Exchange (UDE) to allow standard floppy disks to hold compressed data readable by any DOS-based system, with or without the main SuperStor utility.

Each floppy contains a 20K TSR driver that includes all of the codes necessary to read but not to write to SuperStor-compressed floppies. That's a serious limitation compared to Stacker's implementation, because data transport using compressed floppies is a one-way trip with SuperStor—unless the target system also has the full SuperStor utility installed.

In other respects, SuperStor does a workman-like job of disk compression. You can't install it from within Windows, and disk volumes being compressed must have 1M of free space. Both existing disks and new compressed volumes can be squeezed. Instead of DOS 6's **dir /c** command, you use a special **xdir** command to view ratios on compressed volumes. It shows the bytes used, number free, actual bytes used, and actual amount of disk space free. The total compression ratio for all the files currently stored on the disk is also calculated.

SuperStor does automatically recognize whether a disk is compressed or not and offers an automounting capability that DOS 6 lacks.

Like other disk compression utilities, SuperStor uses 512 byte clusters (Microsoft now calls these allocation units) internally, which optimizes the use of the available space. You can define up to eight different partitions per disk, each of which must be 512M or smaller.

SuperStor's disk optimizer offers the traditional full and partial defragmentation of both uncompressed and compressed disk space. Disk Tuneup also includes a feature for adding a second level of disk compression. The utility will scan an already-compressed volume to search for additional pattern matches that can be replaced by shorter codes. This extra step can squeeze the disk down an extra 5 to 25 percent. It is similar in concept to the Max Compress option originally slated for DOS 6, but deleted by Microsoft at the last minute.

The basic SuperStor version includes compression, defragmentation, diagnostics and repair utilities, automatic mounting of compressed drives, and the recompression feature. SuperStor Pro adds its own disk caching routine, special Windows support, JPEG image compression, and a previewing feature. The Pro version also has an uninstall utility if you change your mind.

Other Disk Optimizers

Not all disk defragmenters are furnished as part of file compression utilities. Users who plan no disk squeezing can still gain performance benefits from optimization. So, you'll find some stand-alone utilities in this category included as part of packages like Norton Utilities and PC Tools. The third-party utilities often have features not included with the DOS 6 version.

For example, although nearly all defragmenters let you choose between full optimization or optimizing only the files (leaving free space fragmented), Norton Utilities and PC-Kwik Power Disk provide the option of consolidating all your free space at the end of your hard disk, without defragmenting the files themselves. Because optimizing files can take a great deal of time, this ultra-quick option can be a quick way to defragment your free space, reducing the number of newly fragmented files that have to be created on a daily basis. This step, if done regularly in a minute or less, can reduce the need for full optimization.

Some additional performance can be gained by placing selected files and directories at the front of the hard disk, where the heads can find them more quickly. Most third-party defragmenters let you place EXE and COM files at the front of the disk. Files that never change are best placed at the front. Data files that tend to grow can be put at the back of the disk, where they can add clusters as needed without excessive fragmentation. Here's a quick rundown of the top contenders.

Norton Utilities SpeedDisk

SpeedDisk looks a great deal like Defragmenter, right down to some of the menu displays. But, where Defragmenter has a single menu, plus Help, SpeedDisk boasts two additional menus, Configure and Information, with new options.

The Optimize menu includes four choices found in Defragmenter: Begin Optimization, Drive..., Optimization Method..., and Exit. However, the similarities end there. Instead of two optimization methods, you can choose Full with Directories First, which moves directories to the front of the disk; Full with File Reorder, which reorders files by directory; Unfragment Files Only, which leaves some free space holes; and Unfragment Free Space, the quick optimizer mentioned earlier.

The File Sort options are similar to those provided with Defragmenter: unsorted or sorted by name, extension, date and time, or file size, in ascending or descending order. However, you can also select which files will be placed at the beginning of the disk, using a simple point-and-shoot operation.

Additional options include Read-after-Write, in which SpeedDisk will verify each cluster; Clear Unused Space, which wipes clean all free space as a security measure; and Beep When Done, an alert to let you know when SpeedDisk is finished.

The Disk Statistics window shows the disk size, percentage of disk used, percentage of unfragmented files, number of directories, and number of files. It also reports the clusters allocated to moveable and unmovable files, directories, and clusters marked as bad, along with the number of free clusters on the disk.

Because, like Defragmenter, SpeedDisk fully supports your mouse and is accompanied by a full collection of other utilities in the Norton suite, it's very easy to use. The two share so much in look and feel that, from the standpoint of familiarity alone, SpeedDisk is probably your best choice when you want something more than Defragmenter has to offer.

Disk Optimizer Tools

This utility by-passes an uncommon problem: most defragmenters place an upper limit on the number of files they can handle. Disk Optimizer doesn't. It's also one of the few defragmenters that let you specify whether certain files should be placed at the front or the back of the disk, although you can select them by extension (EXE, COM, DOC, etc.) only. Although slower than most, its $50 list price and compatibility with large hard disks containing many files make it an attractive option.

FastTrax

FastTrax is a bit unfriendlier to use—there's no mouse support, for example—and it handles only hard disks 85M or smaller. That makes its capability to process an unlimited number of directories and files a little less useful; smaller hard disks are unlikely to have huge numbers of either. You can place selected directories and files anywhere you want on a hard disk, using a priority scheme. Unless you have a need to place files that precisely, DOS 6's Defragmenter is a better, cheaper choice.

OpTune

OpTune is very fast, offers extras like surface testing of your hard disk, and lets you place files at the front or back of the disk, as you prefer. Unfortunately, you must use DOS 6's EDIT.EXE utility or another ASCII editor to designate individual file placement in a large file that OpTune uses. If you can master the process, this is a flexible, speedy file defragmenter.

PC-Kwik Power Disk

As mentioned earlier, this is one of two (with Norton) utilities that offer space-only defragmentation. This is also one of the fastest defragmenters available, without any sacrifice in safety. Its automatic sorting capability will optimize file placement for you, but you can override that by creating a special ASCII file.

PC Tools

The full PC Tools collection of utilities is a great buy, but you won't want it for its defragmenter. There is little protection provided to save your files if the defragmenter is halted during operation. Because this process can take so long and with power failures so uncertain, few users who don't have an uninterruptible power source will want to take the risk. Pass on this one.

Vopt

Vopt is very easy to use, because you don't get many options. You run it from the command line by typing **Vopt.** Full optimization is your only choice, although it operates as fast as most defragmenters in their quick mode. To achieve that speed, however, you must turn off Vopt's safety features, using the single available switch, **/s.** This optimizer uses a defragmenting scheme that always copies your sectors to safe areas before erasing them from the old, so even in non-safe mode you won't lose files. Because DOS 6's defragmenter is also easy to use, there is nothing to recommend Vopt as an alternative.

The Next Step

At this point, you've optimized your hard disk to run faster. Now, you'll want to protect your data by shielding your system from viruses, accidental file deletion, hard disk crashes, and a multitude of other catastrophes. Those will be addressed in Section V, which follows.

Part V: Data Protection

What's the most valuable component of your computer system? The system unit, with CPU and RAM, probably costs several thousand dollars. If you have a monitor measuring 20-inches or more, you may have spent upwards of $2200 for it. PostScript printers can cost several grand. True color video cards fall into the same price bracket. Without a doubt, your hardware represents a hefty investment, one that you wouldn't care to lose. If you have any money tied up in your computer system, you undoubtedly have blanketed it with property/casualty insurance to cover your loss in case of fire, theft, vandalism, or natural disaster.

But have you really protected the most valuable component of your computer system? All the insurance in the world won't recover lost data, which represent that most precious of commodities: your time. You can replace a broken computer with a single phone call and install it the next day. But, if you spent two weeks setting up that computer, installing programs, and configuring it the way you like it, you'll spend another two weeks doing everything over again if you don't have a backup. Three months of daily work compiling data may take *six* months to reconstruct, because you no longer have the data readily available.

Some information is impossible to regain after it has been lost. Can you put a price tag on a month's worth of invoices that will never get billed—unless a customer inquires? You can't attach a price tag to such a disaster, because you'll never know exactly how much those lost invoices would have brought in.

The next section of this book deals with data protection and recovery techniques using new DOS 6 utilities like Backup and Anti-Virus. The following chapters deal with probably the most important—and neglected—aspects of working with an operating system. Everyone is quick to tweak their hard disk to make it work faster or to gain a little extra disk space. Few make regular backups, take the proper steps to ensure that deleted files can be retrieved, or guard against virus invasions. DOS 6 makes it easier to protect yourself. Now, there should be no excuse for lost data.

What Is Data Protection?

Nothing is more certain than death, taxes, and data loss. Sooner or later, everyone experiences an unplanned loss of a a file or program. For the careless or overworked, tiny incidents may crop up on a weekly basis. A file gets deleted by mistake. You reformat the wrong floppy disk—the one containing backups of your office memos. Your hard disk finally spins its last. That cute little game you planned to play with during a free moment has eaten up the boot sector of your drive. You gave a new file the same name as an important existing file and managed to over-write something essential with something inconsequential. The ways in which users manage to lose data are limited only by a lack of imagination.

Fortunately, DOS 6 has a brace of utilities that can transform potential disasters into amusing anecdotes. Instead of losing your job, you'll be able to joke about your latest Stupid Human Trick. You'll say, "Imagine that...I managed to erase the final version of our annual report the day before we sent it to the printer...but I just undeleted the file, and Mr. Dithers never had a clue!"

The next several chapters will cover DOS 6's new data protection and recovery utilities in detail, and we'll look at some third-party utilities that pick up where DOS 6 leaves off. But first, it might be useful to list some of the ways in which data can be lost and why.

Unsaved Files

The easiest way to lose important data is to neglect to save it to disk in the first place. You've painstakingly created a spreadsheet, called Untitled1, entered all the data, checked your formulas, and then maybe even printed out a copy. Exhausted, and ready to go home, you begin to exit the program. A dialog box pops up. `Untitled1 has not been saved. Do you want to save your changes?` Just then, the phone rings. You answer it, and while you talk, you finish shutting down your system. One distracted click on the NO button in the dialog box, and you've erased six hours of work. How much is the better part of a working day worth to you?

You don't need to be negligent to lose a file in this way. A split-second brownout that reboots your computer, an accidental bump of a poorly placed power switch or an unexpected system crash (both the Spanish Inquisition and Windows General Protection Faults are *always* unexpected) can trash your RAM in a twinkling of an eye. Nothing can be more heartbreaking than losing an unsaved file, because you're usually right there to witness the tragedy. There is even a Sniglet describing the phenomenon: the *onosecond*. An onosecond is the period of time between when you click on the NO button, realize what you've done, cry "Oh no!" and then watch your file vanish.

There are simple ways to protect yourself from losing files this way. Follow these guidelines to save yourself some embarrassment.

➤ **Save Immediately.** As soon as you create a new file, immediately save it under a valid file name. Then save it again at intervals as you work. That first save seems to help jog the brain into remembering to store a current working file from time to time.

➤ **Activate Autosave.** Use software that automatically saves current files on a regular basis. Word for Windows, for example, can be set to save a file as often as every minute. It has a "fast save" option that stores only the changes, so the disk access takes only a second or two. Even an autostore function does you no good unless you remember to activate it. Set your software so that this feature is part of the default mode.

➤ **Choose Smart Applications.** Favor software that creates temporary files that are automatically recovered when the program is exited abnormally. A power failure can pull the plug on your favorite application before you have a chance to save a file. The really savvy applications notice this and offer to recover unsaved files when you next load the program. These same packages usually erase the temporary files when you exit normally, so they won't protect you if you forget to save your work.

➤ **Create Automatic Backups.** Find applications that automatically store backup versions of files you are working on. When you open a file, a copy of the original version, usually named with a BAK extension, is created. Then, if the revised version is destroyed in some way, you at least have the original to work with.

➤ **Consider Windows.** A few ancient DOS applications let you exit without saving, but no Windows application is that stupid. If you try to exit Windows itself and if any open Windows applications have unsaved documents, you'll be asked if you want to save each and every one of them. Even if your programs have been minimized to tiny icons that you've forgotten about, Windows will remember to prompt you.

Erased Files

The second leading cause of lost files are those that are erased accidentally or intentionally and then needed at some later time. Here are some ways you can accidentally erase files. Keep this list in mind, and you may even avoid some of them the next time.

➤ **Wrong Filename.** You meant to erase DAVID.DOC but erased BUSCH.DOC instead. In trashing E:\MYFILE.DAT, you find that you wanted to erase D:\MYFILE.DAT instead. Don't give your files ambiguous or duplicated file names (although with only eight characters, plus an extension to choose from, that's almost a ridiculous recommendation). Be certain that the file you are erasing is the one you wanted to remove. If you aren't 100 percent sure, open the file to see what it contains. Typing it from the DOS prompt may give you a clue for ASCII files and other files that contain at least some ASCII characters. A tool that applies longer labels to files, such as the 4DOS command interpreter or various Windows utilities, like ImagePals Album, can help.

➤ **Excessively Broad File Specification.** You want to erase COMMENT1.DOC, COMMENT2.DOC, COMMENT3.DOC, and COMMENT4.DOC and type **del COM*.*** at the DOS prompt. Oops! There goes COMMAND.COM! You should have used COM*.DOC or, better yet, COMMENT?.DOC as your file specification. Always use the **dir** command with your planned file spec before you actually type the **del** command. You'll see a list of the exact files which will be removed. You can also use the /P switch to ask DOS to prompt you before deleting each file.

➤ **Wrong Command.** You typed **del** instead of **dir.** It happens. Watch it!

➤ **Bad Timing.** You thought you were finished with a file. You erased it too soon. Consider copying files to a temporary directory when you think you no longer need them and then erase the whole works a day or week later, when you're really sure. If this happens to you a lot, copy old files to a floppy and store them for a month or a year. You never can tell when you'll need to recycle an old file. I prepare a newsletter for a club I belong to. After it's gone to the printer I never, ever need the old files. Except when the printer calls three days later and says he's spilled a can of ink all over my master pages.

➤ **Ready, Fire, Aim!** You copy all the files from one subdirectory to another, then erase the original subdirectory's contents, and then discover you didn't copy *all* the files from the original subdirectory.

Use DOS 6's **move** command and then check to make sure that there's nothing left in a subdirectory before you zap it.

Overwritten Files

Closely allied with erased files are overwritten files, but these are a little more exciting because you can't recover an overwritten file with **undelete**. You'll need a valid backup to recover one of these, so the stakes are a lot higher. Files can be overwritten in the following ways.

➤ **The Copy Command.** There is no provision to check for an existing file with the same name as your **copy** destination filespec. This command will happily overwrite any file you want (or don't want) without so much as a peep. The only safeguard is to check your target subdirectory for files that already have the name(s) you are using. If you're just trying to rename a file, use the **ren** command instead; it won't let you rename a file using a name that already exists.

➤ **Wrong Filename.** You save a file. Your application informs you that a file already exists by that name. Do you really want to overwrite it? You reply Yes. The file is overwritten. Then you realize the older file was a *different* file, not an earlier version of the current file.

➤ **Stupid Software**. Some ancient programs don't check before overwriting files. Don't use them; they're probably lacking other essential features, anyway.

➤ **Stupid Installation Programs.** Another variation on this theme is the installation program that isn't smart enough to check for files you might want to keep before it writes its own on your disk. It needs a data link library for Windows called COMMDLG.DLL and copies an older version into your Windows subdirectory, overwriting the latest and greatest version. Or, the installation program creates a new MYPROG.INI file, overwriting the old one that had all your precious settings. Your only hope is to back up your important files before you install one of these, but by the time you realize you needed to, it's often too late.

Lost Files

Some lost files are *really* lost. They still exist, somewhere, but you don't know where. You've copied them to a different hard disk subdirectory, moved them to a removable disk, or otherwise lost track. You may not be sure whether the file is just lost or completely erased. These files are very difficult to recover, because **undelete** or **backup** won't help you. If you use a cataloging program, or a file finder utility (like Norton's SuperFind), you may be able to keep track of your files more efficiently.

Intentional Vandalism and Theft

If bad people get access to your computer, they may be able to erase or copy sensitive or important files or even steal your computer. Password protection of files and applications (Norton Desktop for Windows offers this), a sturdy chain, or other physical security measures can help. But, above all, you need a backup of important data.

Reformatted Disks

DOS 6 provides abundant warnings before it will let you reformat a floppy disk. Hard disks are even more difficult to reformat; you must also provide a volume label of the logical disk before **format** proceeds. Reformatting a disk is a very good way of losing every single file on it, so this condition is potentially a disaster of major proportions. With all these levels of protection, you would think accidentally formatting the wrong disk would be fairly rare. It's not. That's why DOS 6 includes an **unformat** command and **mirror**, which stores information to help you recover from an accidental format.

Hard Disk Crashes

It used to be common to talk about what to do *when* your hard disk crashes, rather than *if*, since any hard disk will eventually wear out, taking all its data with it. However, hard disks have gotten so reliable and technology is proceeding so rapidly that a much smaller number are actually used long enough for them to wear out. A 20M drive that can run six or seven years before it runs into the *mean time between failures* wall will be obsolete long before a crash takes place. It's probably sitting on a shelf, replaced by a $350 drive with a 200M capacity.

So, the average user may not encounter a hard disk crash, given a modicum of care and a top-quality drive. However, as the bumper sticker reminds us, Anomalies Happen. Any hard disk can fail prematurely or suffer an accident (dropping the computer off a desk, while running, is a good bet). Hard disk crashes are especially tragic because it's easy to lose everything on the drive. The damaged sectors may fall in the boot portion of your drive or ravage your directories or FAT table. It may be necessary to reformat the drive to lock out affected portions. Often, it's not economical to fix a broken hard disk; when it costs $200 to repair a drive and $400 to buy a new one, guess which option most users will choose?

Data recovery services can extract information from crashed disks, and if you haven't made a backup of so-called mission critical information, this may be your only course. However, the hourly rates for such services make recovery an expensive lesson indeed.

Worn Out Media

Some types of media wear out. The magnetic disks in floppies and Bernoulli cartridges can wear out from constant use. You'll usually know when this happens because you'll start getting disk errors. If you don't copy the files to other media, it is possible to lose data stored on worn-out disks. Vigilance and extra backups are your best protection.

Viruses

As you'll see in Chapter 23, viruses are evil computer programs designed to invade your system and, eventually, make themselves known to you by one means or another. Some are relatively harmless and do nothing more than consume extra disk space, pop up with inane messages, or perform some distracting action (such as forcing you to type HAPPY BIRTHDAY before releasing your computer from its clutches.) Others are more vicious; they can reformat your hard disk, destroy files, or perform other mischief.

When you start losing data to a virus, the infection is no longer a joke. Anti-virus programs can help stop these invasions and recover after one has taken place.

Data Protection Concepts

There are various ways of protecting your data and programs to minimize the effects of any of these potential disasters. Some of these are *preventive* measures, designed to thwart data loss before it occurs. You can install TSR programs that spot viruses before they have had a chance to enter your system. Utilities like **mirror** can store a copy of essential information, so you can recover if you accidentally reformat a disk. Backup programs keep extra copies of data, ready for immediate restoration. To benefit from these utilities, you must take the time to use them before a disaster takes place. The prefix *pre* is the key component of prevention; you have to do something ahead of time.

Other data protection measures are actually *recovery* procedures. Data has already been lost or damaged but is not beyond recovery. Deleted files can be undeleted. You can excise the virus-damaged portions of other files, leaving healthy, usable data behind. Recovery procedures can bail you out even if you were ill-prepared for data loss, but only up to a point. After deleted files are overwritten, all the rolled-up sleeves and concerned looks in the world won't bring them back. Let certain breeds of virus run free long enough, and they will destroy everything on your hard disk *and* your backup media. When you have a choice between prevention and recovery, choose prevention every time.

The Next Step

The following chapters will tell you what you need to know to avoid the most common types of data loss. You'll learn how to back up your hard disks easily and reliably and how to keep viruses from darkening your door. But to benefit from these utilities, you have to use them. I hope this chapter has you worried enough that you'll follow through with DOS 6's built-in data protection utilities.

Backing Up Your Files

Backing up your hard disk is a lot like changing the oil in your car. Everyone agrees it's a wonderful idea and a sure bet for avoiding long-term problems. Nobody does it as often as they need to, and a few postpone or avoid the chore entirely. We hate doing it ourselves and would prefer if somebody else took care of it for us. Yet, when your engine or hard disk seizes up, you'll wish you had kept a regular maintenance schedule.

This chapter will explain some general concepts about backups and show you how to use the new Windows and DOS versions of the DOS 6 backup program. You'll find the latest edition much different from earlier versions, so there's much to learn.

Although DOS has had backup capabilities since version 2.0, users haven't liked it much. The DOS **backup** command was strictly command-line oriented. You needed to learn complex syntax to use it. In practice, the command line arguments weren't that difficult to master, but given the sporadic nature of most backups, it was easy to forget how to use the command between sessions. The average user wouldn't memorize the commands and had no impetus to create a batch file to automate the procedure.

The second reason DOS **backup** was unpopular was that it wasn't flexible. You couldn't define certain sets of files to back up, except using a limited number of criteria, such as date, time, and whether that file had been backed up since it was last changed. Most users need a lot more options. They want to back up critical files frequently, and other files on a looser schedule. It's also nice to be able to perform a full backup sometimes and at other times to create backup files of only the most recent versions of a file.

Earlier versions of DOS **backup** had other problems. It was slow, and each new version wasn't always able to restore backups created with earlier versions. There was no special Windows support.

These defects have been largely overcome by DOS 6's Backup program, which comes in both DOS and Windows versions. Each is an easy-to-use menu-based program with lots of options. You don't have to learn a bunch of funny command line switches and can select which files to back up according to your own schedule. Best of all, Backup is now much faster and can use special techniques to operate your hardware at high speed. Backing up may never become fun, but at least now it's not hard to do.

Backup Concepts

Before we jump into a description of how to use Backup, you'll want to learn some of the terminology that applies to the process. Something as simple as deciding what kind of backup you want can be needlessly complicated if you don't understand what each option entails. Here are some of the key concepts you need to understand.

Archive Flag

In addition to directory location information, DOS stores a byte of information about each file called an attribute byte. Each of the eight bits in that byte can be set individually to either 1 or 0, indicating whether that attribute is currently on or off. Some of the bits control whether a file has system, read-only, or hidden attributes. The archive bit is set to 1 whenever a file is changed and then cleared to a value of 0 when that file is copied by a program or command used for archiving. The **xcopy** command and Backup are two utilities capable of resetting this archive flag. DOS uses the flag to track whether a file has been changed, but not backed up or copied. Flagged files are the files you have to worry about losing.

Setup Files

These are files with the definitions for each type of backup that you want to perform. A setup can include the names of the entire disks or specific files that should be backed up, the media or path to back up to, and various options such as verification, password protection, and so forth.

Backup Set

The set of files spanning as many individual disks or other media as required for a given backup. Each backup session produces a separate backup set.

History File / Catalog

All backup programs keep a history file or catalog of backup sets, which tracks what files are included with a given set of backup disks. The restore function uses this file to put the backed up files on the hard disk where they belong. Microsoft Backup, in both its Windows and DOS versions, keeps a master catalog that stores information about all backups you've performed, as well as individual catalogs about each backup set.

Full Backup

A full backup is a complete backup of all selected files, most often all the files on a given hard disk, and frequently all the files on all your hard disks. Strictly speaking, a backup of everything is called a *total backup*. A full backup is really nothing more than a complete backup of the selected files without regard for other factors, such as whether they have been backed up or not.

In other words, this type of backup copies files without regard to whether or not their archive flags are set. That is, even if some of the files have already been backed up, a full backup will back them up again, anyway. After a full backup has been performed, all the archive flags of the affected files are reset to indicate that the files have been safely backed up. A full backup creates a single history file, which can be used to completely restore a subdirectory, hard disk, or set of hard disks.

Incremental Backup

An incremental backup copies *only* the selected files that have been created or changed since the last full or incremental backup. This type of backup is used to quickly copy the new or modified files. These files are added to the full backup history file, giving you, in effect, an updated version of your full backup, which then can be used at any time to fully restore your directories or hard disks. An incremental backup resets the archive flags of the copied files to show that they have been properly backed up. An incremental backup is a little like updating a catalog/price sheet by adding new pages to the end and then changing the table of contents to point to the added pages. The old pages don't have to be ripped out, and you don't need to reprint the whole catalog, but you end up with an up-to-date publication. The downside is that you need to retain your full backup and all the incremental backups to have a complete copy of everything on your hard disk.

Differential Backup

A differential backup copies only the selected files that have been created or changed since the last full or incremental backup. Like the incremental version, a differential backup is fast, because only new or modified files are involved. However, it does not reset the archive flag and mark a file as being backed up. You can use this type of backup to copy the latest versions of files, without affecting any later incremental backup.

Using our catalog/price sheet analogy again, a differential backup is something like receiving a set of updated sheets, but you don't insert them into the catalog or update the table of contents. You can use the updates (the differential backup) to quickly scan what's new, but if you want your main catalog to be fully current, you still need to do an incremental backup at some time. You can restore the full catalog (your hard disk) from the full backup and the differential backup, but they aren't integrated into a single set.

Choosing a Backup Type

How do you select which type of backup you want to perform? I realize the difference between full, incremental, and differential backups can be confusing, so I'll spell it out for you in black-and-white.

Use full backup when you want a complete set of backup files for a hard disk. You'll always need at least one full backup, regardless of how you plan to keep your backup files current. This may be when you back up that hard disk for the first time or at intervals when you want to create a new complete backup of that disk. Because it's always a good idea to have more than one set of backup disks, a good way to obtain them is to do a full backup at intervals.

Full Backups: Pros and Cons

Full backups are an excellent tool for capturing a complete picture of your hard disks and all their files. This type of backup takes much longer than a partial backup but may be a good idea if you are experiencing problems with a system, input large amounts of new data in a short time span, or change your software configuration or hard disk structure frequently. Because a full backup makes no distinction between files that have or have not been backed up recently, it's a good way to collect all your files into a single backup set.

Full backups are usually carried out on a schedule based on regular intervals. For example, you perform a full backup of your hard disk on January 1. Thereafter, you do incremental backups weekly so that on January 31, your first set of backup disks (the original full backup and all the incremental backup disks accumulated since then) are fully up-to-date. Then, on February 1, you do *another* full backup, using a different set of disks. At that point, you have two backups. If you need to restore your hard disk any time during February, you can use the set created on February 1 (and subsequently updated with incremental backups). If that set of disks happens to be defective, you can still fall back to your January set, which was current through January 31, and be only a few weeks behind.

On March 1, take your January disks and perform a third full backup. You still have only two sets of disks—the February and March disks—and can continue throughout the year with a current and near-current set of backups always available. This system takes less time than maintaining two complete sets of backup disks.

Incremental Backups: Pros and Cons

Use incremental backups to keep your full backup set up-to-date between full backups. As you perform incremental backups, you'll need to add disks to your set to hold the new and modified files. After you've gone through two full cycles and begin re-using sets of disks, you'll usually find that each set should include enough disks to hold most of a month's files. That's because you'll be purging files from your hard disk as it fills, so each month's full backup will contain roughly the same number of files.

Incremental backups let you restore files quickly and easily and are very fast because only the most recent changes to files are backed up. Even so, the older versions of files remain in the set. You can still restore those older versions if you need to. Because files that haven't changed aren't duplicated, an incremental backup uses fewer disks than a full backup.

Differential Backups: Pros and Cons

Use differential backups to store a set of the very latest files, without building an expanding collection of disks. A differential backup writes over older files with the newer ones, so you can keep reusing a disk for a longer period before it fills. However, you can't access previous versions of a file; only the newest is kept. Alternate disks used for a differential backup; that way if one set proves to be defective, you'll still have a full backup copy.

The advantage of a differential backup will be apparent to those who work with the same sets of files over and over. Say you modify certain spreadsheets or accounting databases on a regular basis. Those constitute the bulk of the files you work with. You want only the very latest versions of those files; older, versions are useless to you. A differential backup can quickly copy those files, often onto the same media, time after time. Because you aren't creating many new files, you won't accumulate an expanding collection of disks, as you would with an incremental backup. It's easier to keep track of differential backups, because you have only one set, plus the full backup. That comes in handy when you must restore, too, because you won't need a bunch of incremental sets; just the full backup and differential backup are required to fully restore a hard disk.

On the other hand, if you constantly create files, a differential backup won't save you much time, and may even take a little more time to perform than an incremental backup.

Preparing To Use Backup

Before you can use Backup in either version, you'll need to configure the utility for your hardware. In the following section, I'll use the Windows version as an illustration for the discussion and figures. However, the DOS and Windows versions are based on Symantec's "Bedrock" technology, which allows creating applications for different platforms and environments that use virtually the same source code. The two versions look and function virtually identically. Where they differ, I'll point out the things you need to know.

The first time you run Backup, you'll be invited to configure the program for your system. The DOS version lets you specify a preferred video monitor mode (CGA, EGA/VGA, etc.) and mouse type. Windows Backup, of course, uses whatever video and mouse have been installed for Windows and does not require this step. The first screen you'll see will have all the elements shown in figure 21.1.

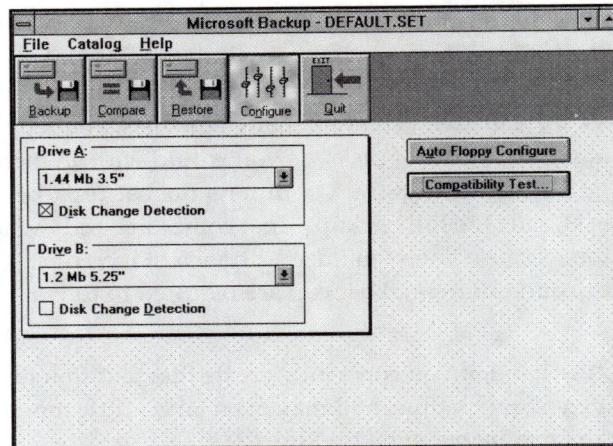

Figure 21.1. Windows Backup Configure screen.

Defining Your Floppy Disks

You'll see a window for each of your floppy disk drives, with the default type shown. Usually, the correct drive will be detected automatically; the drive type defined in your CMOS setup is used as the default. With some computers, the user may swap the drive A and drive B cables to reverse the order of the drives without changing the definitions in CMOS. The drives may still function normally, but software like Backup will be unable to determine the drive type correctly. In that case, you'll need to enter the correct drive type from the pull-down list. Backup checks to see whether your drive provides automatic diskette change information. If so, the utility will be able to detect when you've inserted a new diskette during backup, and you won't need to press Enter each time a requested diskette is inserted.

Next, Backup performs a Compatibility Test to see whether Backup is configured to operate reliably with your hardware. To do this, the program will perform a small backup of some files to several diskettes and then compare the stored files to the originals. When you activate this test, have two diskettes that don't have data you want to retain; all information on the disks will be erased during the test.

As the test proceeds, you'll see a screen like that shown in figure 21.2. It shows the number of disks that will be required for the backup, files involved, how many bytes are being backed up, estimated and elapsed time, and compression ratio—just like in a real backup. After the backup is completed, you'll be asked to insert the disks again for comparison. If everything checks out, you can save this configuration as your default. If your system does not pass the compatibility check, you might want to run some diagnostic programs, such as MSD.EXE, to see whether your hardware is working correctly.

Choosing Files To Back Up

The first step in performing a backup is to select files and/or hard disks to back up, settings, and backup options. After you've made these choices, you can store them in setup files, which may be reused at any time to do the same kind of backup. Setup files include the following information:

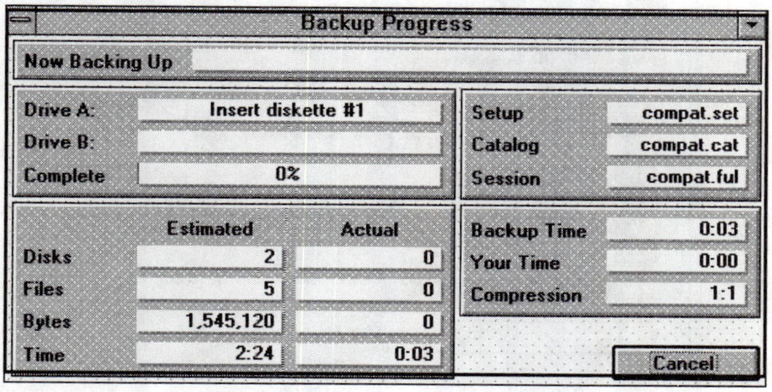

Figure 21.2. Backup Progress window.

Which hard disks and files to back up. You may select one or more hard disks from the Backup From window shown at the lower left in figure 21.3. Choose a drive by highlighting it. You can select all the files on the highlighted drive by pressing the spacebar or clicking on its icon with the mouse. You may also choose specific files stored on that drive by pressing Enter or choosing the Select Files... button. You'll then be shown a screen like figure 21.4, in which you can highlight files.

Click on a directory's folder icon to toggle the backup of that subdirectory on or off. If a plus sign appears in the folder, all the files in that subdirectory and its child subdirectories will be backed up. If a minus sign appears, the files will not be backed up. You can choose by subdirectory or by individual file, if you want, by clicking and shift-clicking on the file names as they appear in the right pane of the window. A filled-in box will appear next to files that have been selected for backup. A hollow box will appear next to files that have as been selected, but which will not be backed up.

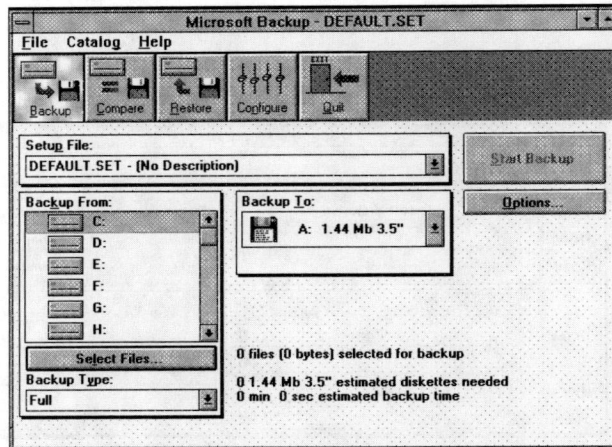

Figure 21.3. Microsoft Backup for Windows screen.

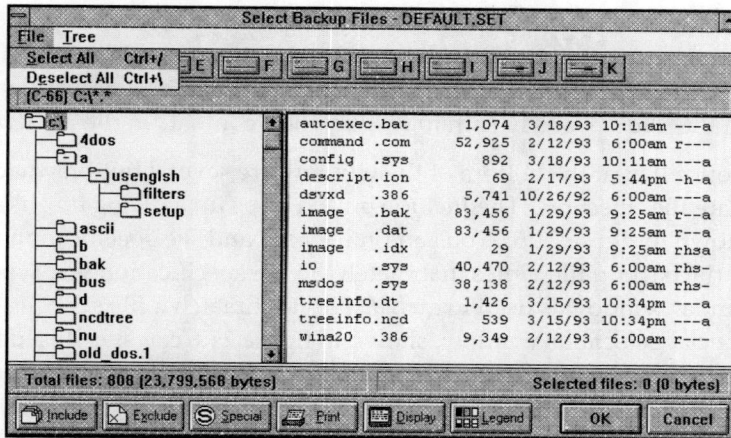

Figure 21.4. Select Backup Files.

Other blocks will pop up next to the subdirectory folders in the left pane. These represent the status of backup for the files in those subdirectories, as follows:

➤ **Black filled box:** All files in the subdirectory have been selected for backup.

➤ **White hollow box:** All files in the subdirectory have been selected, but will not be backed up.

➤ **Gray box:** All files in the subdirectory have been selected, and some of them will be backed up.

➤ **Half black/half white box:** Some files have been selected, and all selected files will be backed up.

➤ **Half gray/half white box:** Some files have been selected, and some of them will be backed up.

➤ **White hollow box bisected by a line:** Some files have been selected, but none of them will be backed up.

You can use these indicators to gauge how much of a each particular subdirectory will be backed up given your current selections. If you want to see exactly which files will be backed up in which subdirectory, click on the folder icons in turn to display their contents in the right pane.

Notice that at the bottom of the window are several buttons that automate file selection. The Include button pops up a dialog box like that shown in figure 21.5. You can type a path and file specification to include in the backup filenames that match the file specification you type. A similar window is used to *exclude* files that match a file specification. The Special Selections window, shown in figure 21.6 can specify a date range and exclude copy-protected, read-only, system, or hidden files, if you prefer.

The Print button can be used to print a list of the file on your current drive, or all drives in your system, and the Display Options button brings up a dialog box that controls the sorting order and toggles on or off the display of certain information about your files, including file size, date, time, and attributes. You can sometimes use this information to decide which individual files to back up.

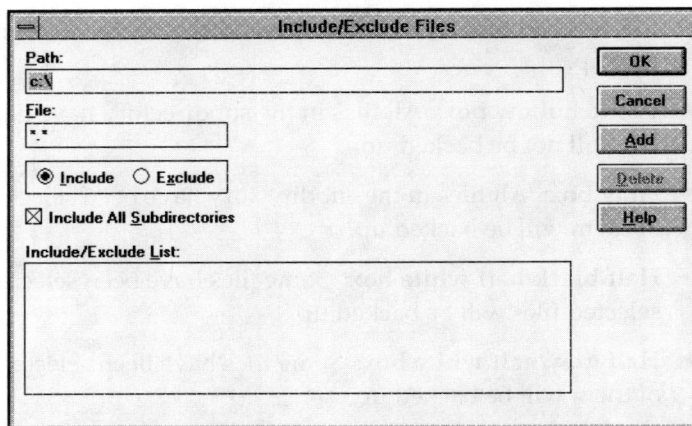

Figure 21.5. Including and excluding files.

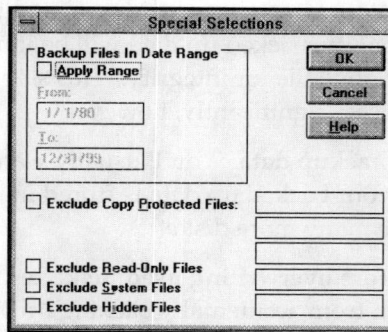

Figure 21.6. Special File Selection window.

You can repeat this process for any or all the hard disks in your system, so a single backup set can contain every file you have, spanning multiple hard disks.

What type of media to back up to. The middle window in figure 21.3 is labeled Backup To:, and it lets you select a specific floppy drive or any DOS device that has been assigned a drive letter and can be specified by a path. For example, instead of backing up drive C to drive A, you could copy the files to D:\BAK (another hard disk), E (a Bernoulli drive), or some other peripheral.

What type of backup is desired. At the bottom left of figure 21.3, you'll see the Backup Type window, which lets you select from Full, Incremental, or Differential backups. Your very first backup must be a Full backup, of course. Later, you can create additional backup sets for the other two types if you want to use them.

Backup options. From a dialog box that pops up when you select the Options button you can choose from among nine additional options for each backup. These options, shown in figure 21.7, are as follows:

➤ **Verify backup data.** This provides an additional level of protection, ensuring that the backed up data will be immediately compared with the original file for integrity. This step will slow down the backup process significantly, however.

➤ **Compress backup data.** You'll usually want to use this option; without it your backed up data is stored in uncompressed form and will require many more diskettes.

➤ **Prompt before overwriting used diskettes.** This check can help prevent you from accidentally backing up over one of your current backup diskettes. You should label each disk carefully, but, even so, it's easy to make mistakes. If you check this box, Backup will prompt you with some information about what's on the current diskette, and you can decide whether to use it or to replace it with a different disk.

➤ **Always format diskettes.** Check this box, and Backup will always format your diskettes before use. This is an extra security and reliability measure. Formatting will wipe out the old information on a disk and double-check to make sure that the diskette is usable.

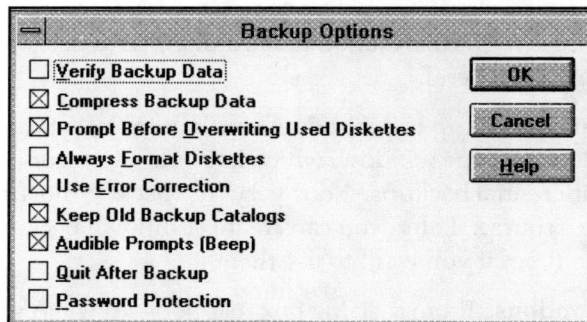

Figure 21.7. Backup Options.

However, time to back up a disk drive will be increased by the extra step of formatting each diskette.

➤ **Use Error Correction.** With this choice selected, Backup will include, along with backed up files, some information that can be used to reconstruct damaged files. Error correction takes up a little extra disk space, but when you consider the purpose of a backup in the first place, the cost for this added security is small.

➤ **Audible prompts.** Backup will beep when it is ready for another disk. This option is useful if you plan to be doing something else while the backup takes place.

➤ **Quit after Backup.** The program will return to the DOS prompt (DOS version) or Windows (Windows version) when finished. If you have set Backup to operate automatically through a scheduler, you'll want your system to return to its normal operation after the backup is completed.

➤ **Password protection.** You can prevent unauthorized persons from using your backup sets by activating password protection with this check box.

Saving Your Setup

After you have entered all these parameters, you can save the settings in a file as a setup. Choose the File menu and Save Setup As... to enter a file name for your setup file. The SET file extension must be used. You can also add a 32-character description of the setup, such as *Backs up C, D, E, F* or *All Word Processing Files.* Your setup files will appear in the drop-down Setup File list, so you can duplicate any backup configuration at a later time.

Starting the Backup

After a setup has been entered or selected from a library of existing setup files, all you need to do is click on the Start Backup button. You'll be prompted to insert new diskettes (or other media) as required, until the complete backup is done. Depending on the options, media, and size of the files to be backed up, the complete backup process may take anywhere from a few minutes to an hour or more.

Comparing Files

If you want an additional check to make sure that your backup was successful and accurate, you can use Backup's Compare option to verify the integrity of your files. The Compare dialog box looks like figure 21.8. You can select the drive to compare from, choose a backup set from the catalog, mark which files to compare, and whether to compare to the original locations or another location. The only other options available are whether you want audible prompts (a beep) when it's time to switch disks and whether Backup should quit when Compare is finished.

Restoring Files

If you're using one of the non-standard applications for Backup described previously, you may find yourself using Restore quite frequently. Others may seldom, if ever, need to restore a file. However, most of us will have at least an occasional need to retrieve a file that was accidentally lost beyond the reach of Undelete or to restore a hard disk that has, finally, failed.

The Restore dialog box is almost virtually identical to the one shown in figure 21.8. You select a backup set from your master catalog, specify source and target drives, and choose only specific files to restore. If you don't choose individual files, Restore will copy all the files in the backup set to the target location. There are seven options, shown in figure 21.9, which you can select by clicking on the Options button.

➤ **Verify restored files.** The utility will read back files it has restored and compare them with the archived versions to verify that they are the same.

➤ **Prompt before creating directories.** Restored files are normally copied back to the same subdirectories they were originally backed up from. That keeps your original directory structure intact and makes it easy to restore an entire hard disk from scratch. However, there are times when you don't want to put the restored files in the

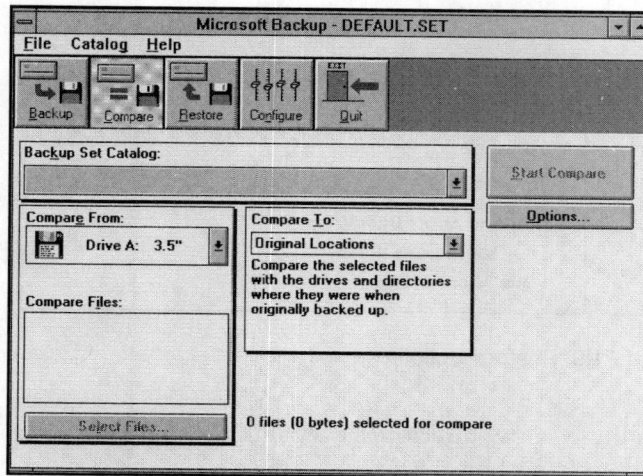

Figure 21.8. File Compare window.

same directories. Perhaps you've renamed the subdirectories since the last backup. For example, \MSDOS has been renamed \DOS to shorten your DOS PATH. You can ask Restore to prompt you before creating new directories as files are copied to your hard disk.

➤ **Prompt before creating files.** When you restore files to a subdirectory, the utility often has to create new files, because some old ones may have been erased since the last backup. If you would rather Restore prompted you before doing this, you can check this box.

➤ **Prompt before overwriting files.** You may want to restore only missing files and to keep the newer versions that reside on your hard disk. This option can force Restore to prompt you before overwriting an existing file with a backup version.

➤ **Restore empty directories.** Empty directories currently have no files in them, but may still be required by certain applications to store temporary files, printer queues, etc. Restore can still create

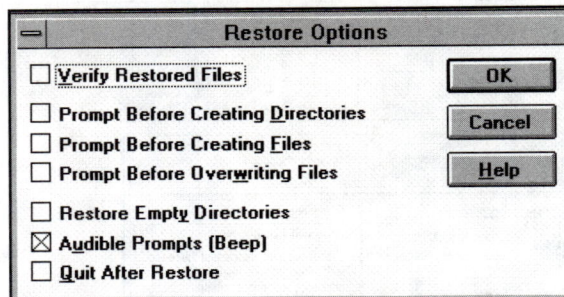

Figure 21.9. Restore Options.

these empty directories even if it has no files to put in them, if you check this box.

➤ **Audible prompts.** Unless you work in a "quiet zone," you'll want Restore to let you know with a beep when it is time to swap disks.

➤ **Quit after Restore.** Tells the utility to quit when finished.

Working with Catalogs

Each backup set is accompanied by its own catalog, which contains information about the files that have been backed up. This includes the directory path of each file; names, size, and attributes of the files and directories that have been backed up; total number of files; date the backup was created; the setup file used; and total size of the backup set.

➤ **Individual backup sets are assigned a unique name**. The extension will always be either FUL, INC, or DIF, depending on whether the backup was a full, incremental, or differential session. The root name will be created using the following formula:

➤ **Drives backed up.** The first two characters of the filename will consist of the first and last drives backed up. If you backed up drives E to G, the characters will be EG. When only one drive is included in a backup, both characters are the same; e.g., a backup of drive D would have DD as the first two characters of its catalog name.

➤ **Year of creation.** The next character will represent the last digit of the year; in all of 1993, this number is 3.

➤ **Month of creation.** The fourth and fifth character in the file name represents the month the backup set was created. (It's interesting to note that the month could have been indicated by a single digit, using hexadecimal notation—1, 2, 3, 4, 5, 6, 7, 8, 9, A, B, C—but decimal numbers were used instead, for *your* convenience.)

➤ **Day of creation.** The day of the month, from 01 to 31, appears in the sixth and seventh positions.

➤ **Multiple backup letter.** The first backup of a hard disk on a given day will have an A in the eighth position. If you happen to back up the same hard disk more than once in a day, the second will take a B; the third will take a C; and so forth. This happens only when you have the Keep Old Backup Catalogs option set to on. If it is off, the first backup will have an A; the second will take the letter B; and each successive backup will alternate between the two.

You can use this code to find the particular backup catalog you want. With every full backup, the utility creates a master catalog, which keeps track of all the incremental and differential backups compiled between full backups. The master catalog is used to restore all the files backed up in the current cycle. You can also select either the most recent version of a file or an earlier version from the master catalog.

Backup catalogs are stored in two places. One copy is kept on your hard disk and is accessible from the Backup program itself. The other is written to the backup media itself. That's a great idea. You can examine your catalogs without digging out the disks used for the backup.

Yet, if your entire hard disk crashes and the master catalog is no longer available, each backup set contains its own catalog that can be used to restore the disk.

Activating Restore

When you've checked off the options and selected the files you want to restore from the catalogs, choose Start Restore, and your files will be copied to the appropriate locations. Again, the process may take from a few minutes to several hours.

If you want to restore a backup created by a pre-DOS 6 version of **backup** (an entirely different program), you'll need the older version of the utility, available on the supplementary diskette that Microsoft sells for a small additional fee. Your manual includes a card you can use to order this diskette.

You can also restore backups made with DOS 6's backup utility with the Norton Utilities version. You must purchase the Norton product separately, however.

The Next Step

Although you understand how to choose a backup procedure and how to use Microsoft Backup, there are some other things to consider, including the best media for backup, how to store your backup sets, and alternative backup software. We'll look at all these topics in the next chapter.

Backup Strategies and Alternatives

We looked at backup strategies in general terms in the last chapter. However, there are quite a few alternatives and options to consider. Can Backup be used for more than data protection? What media are best for backup? Where should you store your backup sets? Do third-party backup utilities provide features not included with DOS 6? This chapter will explore all these topics.

Other Uses for Backup

Although the primary use for Microsoft Backup will be to create duplicate copies of valued files, there are several other things you can do with this program. You might not have thought of these useful applications:

➤ **Copy Large Files to Disks for Transport to Other Computers.** You have a large, 4M image file you wish to share with a colleague. Telecommunications would take too long or incur prohibitive long-distance charges. Neither of you have a tape drive or use other removable media with sufficient capacity. What can you do? If both of you are using DOS 6, you can use Backup to create a compressed backup set of the large file, which will be broken up into as many pieces as necessary to fit on multiple floppy disks. Your colleague can use Backup's Restore feature to reconstruct the file on his or her own hard disk from the backup set.

➤ **Create Libraries of Files.** Backup is a convenient way to create space-efficient libraries of files that can be accessed from a single catalog even though they span multiple disks. Windows icons, clip art, groups of programs, data files, and other files can be collected together through a single backup session. Then you can view the contents of the backup set/library with Backup's Restore function and select individual files for retrieval when you need them.

➤ **Duplicate Computer Configurations.** You've set up one computer in an office with all the software, configuration files, and other settings exactly the way you want them. Now you need to dupli-cate that setup on six identical computer systems in an office. Just back up the first computer and then use Restore to copy a mirror image of the original's hard disk to the other computers. If you use the DOS version of Backup, you won't have to install Windows first; let Backup create your Windows environment for you.

➤ **Create Archives.** Archives are like libraries, except that instead of storing frequently used file resources, they serve as a sort of morgue for old files that you may never need again—but might. As you accumulate data files for certain programs, they can be backed up to removable media and then deliberately erased from your hard disk. That frees up hard disk space. All you need to do is remember not to reuse those disks the next time you make a backup! Check off Keep Old Catalogs under Options so that Backup won't erase them.

What Media Should I Use?

In the last chapter, I assumed that most users would prefer diskettes as their backup medium. Every PC is equipped with at least one floppy disk drive, and most systems sold since 1985 can use high-density media (1.2 or 1.44M disks). Diskettes sell for as little as 25 cents per megabyte of storage, so, with compression, a reasonable number of disks—say, 30 or so—can back up a partially filled 80 to 100M disk drive, at a cost of $7.50 to $30 for media. Juggling 30 disks for a full backup isn't fun, but it's cost-effective. However, there are other media to consider. Here's a brief rundown on each of them:

Bernoulli Drives

Iomega's Bernoulli drives are a more expensive way to back up your system, with some important convenience features that can outweigh the cost penalty. I'll give you the bad news first: a 150M Bernoulli cartridge costs roughly $125 through mail order sources. That's 83 cents per megabyte or roughly three times the cost of very cheap floppy disks. On the other hand, if you're paying $1.25 for a 1.44M brand-name diskette, the cost will be very similar.

The good news is that you won't need to swap 30 of the blasted things in and out to do a single backup. A 150M Bernoulli cartridge can store most of the information on a 200 to 300M hard disk. Iomega also offers cartridges with less capacity (65, 90, and 105M for example), although these cost a little more per megabyte.

Bernoulli drives are something of a hybrid between floppy and hard disks. Like hard disks, these drives use a very low "flying" height to allow writing data very densely on magnetic media. But instead of keeping the read/write head suspended over the disk, Bernoulli drives rely on the vacuum effect produced by the rotation of the flexible media to draw the disk—a 5.25-inch disk—toward the magnetic head. Any accident causes the media to fall away from the head, so crashes are practically impossible. The media does not have to be sealed in an airtight environment, so Bernoulli disks are much more forgiving of storage conditions.

The drives themselves cost $500 to $800 from mail order sources. Currently, you can choose from 90M and 150M drives in internal and transportable (with its own power supply) versions, as well as a "PC-Powered" model that draws power from the PC it is connected to. You may use an ASPI (advanced SCSI programming interface) compatible SCSI card and universal driver software like CorelSCSI, Iomega's own SCSI interface cards, or a parallel port SCSI adapter.

Bernoulli drives make wonderful backup targets if you can afford them. My favorite technique is to just make a mirror-image copy of a hard disk using **xcopy /s**. If something happens to a file or subdirectory (say an installation upgrade went horribly wrong and now Windows won't load anymore), I can just insert the appropriate Bernoulli disk and select files to copy back to the hard disk just as if I were using another hard drive. I partition my hard disks with 105M volumes so that a single Bernoulli cartridge will back up any of them without compression. DoubleSpace could stretch these drives even further.

You can also use Microsoft Backup and back up any disks to these cartridges just as if you were using an enormous floppy. You probably won't have to swap cartridges, however, since you should be able to complete most backups—as well as a few incremental or differential backups—onto a single cartridge.

SyDOS Cartridges

These cartridges are true hard-disks-in-a-box that you can swap. They are currently available in 44 and 88M sizes, and the 88M drives can finally read and write to the older 44M cartridges. Because SyDOS cartridges are actual hard disks, you must treat them with a little more respect than a Bernoulli cartridge, but barring a 20-foot drop, you should experience few problems. The carts can be less expensive than Bernoulli media, but otherwise, you would use one of these exactly as you would a Bernoulli disk.

Tape Backup

Oddly, the one medium designed specifically for backup often receives the least attention. Tape backup is gaining more attention because lower cost, higher capacity drives have become available. In the near future, most users will continue to rely on the floppy drives that are built into their systems. But, $200-$350 tape drives that can store 125 to 250M of data on a $30 tape should become much more common.

Tape is a serial medium, so it is inherently a little slower, especially when it comes time to retrieve a single file that is stored near the end of the tape. You can set your system to back up to tape during idle hours (evenings or overnight), so speed will be of little concern until it comes time to restore a complete hard disk. You can't beat the price of the media: if you can get 250M of data (compressed) onto a $30 tape, you're paying only 12 cents per megabyte. Tape backup makes it practical to do full backups *daily* if you want. All you need are five tapes, which can be reused each Monday through Friday.

Tape systems are available in various formats, with names like QIC-40, QIC-80, Irwin, etc. The format you choose makes little difference unless you plan to swap tapes with other users. The important thing is that your tape drive will obviously have no trouble reading its own format. If you have huge backup needs, there are 4 mm digital audiotape (DAT) and 8 mm helical scan drives capable of storing gigabytes of information. These drives cost more than $1,000 but are an excellent choice if you have mammoth disk drives.

Tape subsystems are often supplied with their own backup software, which you may find more convenient or flexible than Microsoft Backup.

Floptical Disk

Floptical disks are nothing more than special 3.5-inch floppies that have had tiny markings placed on them, often burned by a laser. The read/write mechanism of the floptical drive can then use these markings to track much more precisely and, therefore, record data more densely than with conventional floppy disks. Though floptical disks look a lot like ordinary 1.44M floppies, they can store 21M of data, at a cost of about $1 per megabyte. These drives can still read 720K, 1.44M and 2.88M 3.5-inch disks, and are available in external and internal versions. One $400 drive can easily replace your existing 3.5-inch floppy drive.

At 21M, floptical disks won't let you do full backups of any reasonably sized hard disk, but you won't have to swap nearly as many of them. One of these babies can do the job of 14 regular floppy disks, so three or four of them might be enough. A single floptical can go a long way when doing incremental and differential backups, though.

When you consider the cost of the drive and media, floptical drives probably aren't your best alternative choice for backup. Bernoulli and SyDOS drives that cost only a little more can double as open-ended secondary storage, at a similar cost for media. Floptical disks are strongest when used as a super-floppy for floppy type data storage and exchange applications. If you want to send 20M worth of files to a colleague who also has a floptical drive, these disks are your best choice. Otherwise, look at one of the alternatives at the cost and convenience ends of the spectrum.

Optical Disk

True optical disk drives are destined to become the low-cost mass storage medium of the future. You'll pay $20-$30 for a rewritable optical disk that can hold 128M of information or only a little more for a disk that can hold 600M to a full gigabyte. Today, the drives are rather pricey, listing at $500 to $4000, depending on speed and capacity. The slowest units are pokey indeed, with track to track access times no better than 300 to 600 ms. Even the fastest, at 28 ms or so, are slow by hard disk standards.

If you have other needs for optical disk that can justify the investment in a drive (such as massive storage requirements), one of these drives can make an excellent backup target. Rewritable optical disks are your best choice. Although write once, read many (WORM) disks can have capacities up to 10.2 gigabytes, they can fill rather quickly when used for backup on a regular basis. (Realistically, you could hardly afford one of these mammoth WORM systems for a PC in any case.)

Storing Your Backup Sets

Most discussions of the importance of making backups of your hard disk neglect to cover one very important aspect: where to keep your backup sets. They are no less valuable than any other important business or personal records and should be given the same care.

On one hand, if your hard disk crashes or you manage to erase a file (or subdirectory), it's great to have a set of disks on a shelf a few feet away, ready for a quick emergency restoration. On the other, some disasters call for a bit more distance. If a fire damages your office, your insurance may buy you a new computer but will be of little help in replacing a set of melted backup disks. If you've ever been through a fire (I have), you'll know that thick, inky smoke covers everything with soot, even in rooms that aren't touched by the fire itself. It doesn't take much of a blaze to permanently damage a set of backup disks.

A clever thief who makes off with your computer may decide to scoop up a few hundred disks in hopes of garnering some marketable software in the bargain. A misguided intruder with vandalism in mind may not steal anything, but still manage to wreak havoc by shredding a few disks. There are a variety of disasters that can make you wish that you had stored your back-up disks off-premises.

Proper storage of backup media is not as complicated as you might think. When I worked out of a separate office, I backed up each day's work before leaving for home, threw the disks in a briefcase, and took them with me. The disks never left the briefcase and returned to the office the next morning for the next day's differential backup. If my office burned to the ground overnight, I'd lose zero work. A really smart user could keep two systems—one at home, one at the office—synchronized by restoring each day's work onto the home system in the evening. That way, he or she could continue to work at home, perform another backup before leaving for work the next morning, and then restore the new files to the office computer.

If you don't want to go to these lengths, it's still simple to rotate backups off-site. Your most recent backup remains near your computer, ready for instant restoration if a disk crash or other mishap takes place. The last backup is stored off-site, either at home or another location. I keep a set of disks in a detached garage. When you're ready to back up your hard disk again, take the latest backup off-site, return the second set of disks, and use them for the next cycle.

Of course, this sort of rotation involves some risk. If your latest set of backup disks is damaged, your next-most-recent set will be somewhat out of date, depending on the amount of time between full backups. If you back up once a month, the alternate backup set could be anywhere from one to four weeks behind. You can avoid losing even that amount of data by keeping a copy of your latest backup set off-site. That would include the full backup disks, plus copies of each incremental or differential backup you make. Duplicating the backup disks themselves should take only a few minutes—particularly if you are using a differential backup procedure—much less time than another whole backup. You can do this weekly or as often as necessary.

Regardless of whether your backup disks are stored near your computer or off-site, you should still adhere to some common sense guidelines. You don't want your backups damaged simply from being stored incorrectly. Here are some considerations:

➤ **Avoid Temperature Extremes.** Heat can damage magnetic media. Avoid the trunk of your car or other locations that can get very hot. Cold temperatures by itself shouldn't damage disks, but when you bring them indoors from very cold storage, moisture will tend to condense from humid air onto frigid surfaces. A dripping wet disk is not a good thing to put into a floppy disk drive.

➤ **Stay Away from Magnetic Fields.** Because magnetic fields are used to write data to disks, any sort of magnet is a good way to scramble or erase that information. I've seen folks use kitchen magnets to stick a disk to the side of a monitor for safekeeping, then wonder why the disk doesn't work anymore. Keep magnetic scissors or paper clip holders (common in offices) away from all media. The paper clips themselves can become magnetized, so don't clip notes to disks with them. (Even if the clip is not magnetic, it can damage a 5.25-inch floppy just from mechanical pressure on its jacket.) Don't store your backups near a monitor or an old-style telephone with a mechanical bell. Motors also produce magnetic fields. A disk has to be placed fairly close to a magnet for damage to occur, but don't take any chances!

➤ **Steer Clear of Icky Stuff.** Dust, moisture, and smoke can all damage disks. Those floppies I keep in my detached garage are stored in individual Zip-Loc storage bags. If you must keep your backups in an uncontrolled environment, protect them with decent packaging.

➤ **Consider a Special Storage Location.** A small safe costs around $100, and many are rated to protect against fire for a limited period of time. There are also fireproof file cabinets that can protect your paper records along with your disks. A bank safety deposit box is a good, inexpensive storage location if you know you'll never need your disks during evenings or weekends. One tightwad I know keeps disks in an airtight container kept in a freezer locker. The container is always brought up to room temperature before it is opened, so the disks suffer no damage.

Establishing a Backup Schedule

It's important to establish a regular schedule for your backups and then to stick to it. If you back up only when you get around to it, you never will. Or, you'll back up once every three months and find yourself suddenly relying on an image of your hard disk that is hopelessly out of date. Here are several backup strategies you can use. Select one based on your needs.

Strategy 1: Weekly Full Backups

If you don't accumulate much new data during a week or if the information is a type that is easily replaced, you may want to perform weekly full backups. Those who work with information that is immediately transferred to other users might fall into this category. You can easily retrieve your most recent working files from others (perhaps over a network), and, because you carefully log what you do each day, you know what those files are. In that case, weekly backups are probably sufficient. Each Friday before leaving the office, you can start a full backup cycle.

In order to provide yourself with backups of your backup sets and the ability to store at least one set off-site, it's probably a good idea to alternate between three complete sets of disks, tapes, or other media. On Friday of Week 1, use set 1; on Friday of Week 2, use set 2; on Friday of Week 3, use set 3. Then, at the end of Week 4, use set 1 again and repeat the cycle. You'll never be more than two weeks away from a full backup set, even if your most recent backup set proves to be faulty.

Strategy 2:Weekly Full Backups, Daily Incremental Backups

If you need a little more protection from losing files, weekly full backups and daily incremental backups may work for you. If you frequently need to go back and retrieve old versions of a file, no more than a week old, this strategy is ideal. The downside is that you must make incremental backups daily for maximum security, and you can accumulate a lot of disks over the course of a month. You must keep all these disks safe to provide the protection you need.

At the end of Week 1, perform a full backup. Then, at the end of each day in the following week, do an incremental backup. At the end of Week 2, perform another full backup. Store the disks produced from Week 1 in a safe place, as your backup for the most recent set. Repeat the process at the end of Week 3 and then start the cycle over, reusing the disks from Week 1.

This backup strategy will ensure that you always have copies of every version of your files. You can lose no more than a day's worth of work, unless your backup set becomes corrupted. Even then, you'll never be more than a week behind.

Strategy 3: Monthly Full Backups, Daily or Weekly Differential Backups

If you find doing a weekly full backup is a chore, and you need only the latest version of your files, you may find that this strategy will serve you well. At the beginning of each month, generate a full backup of your hard disk. Then each day (or once a week if your files can be replaced from other sources), perform a fast differential backup. You'll need a large number of disks to store files if you go a month between full backups, but not nearly as many as if you required incremental backups.

For the busy person with lots of disks to spare, this can be the fastest way to ensure complete protection (if you follow the daily schedule.) You can alternate disk sets to provide yourself with a backup to your backup.

Other Backup Software

As you know, Microsoft Backup is a version of the program distributed by Symantec with its Norton Desktop for Windows, Norton Desktop for DOS, and separately as Norton Backup for Windows. You may want to use one of these other versions instead of the DOS. They are almost identical, adding only tape support, a macro capability, and optional fast, direct memory access mode. However, the Norton products are tightly integrated; its Backup automatically appears in the Desktop utilities as a menu choice.

This next section provides a brief overview of the features of competing backup software. You'll find that some programs offer options you don't get with the DOS 6 utility. Read the next section and decide for yourself.

Back-It for Windows

Back-It is a good choice for Windows users who have an odd-ball type drive that currently forces them to use a DOS-based program for backup. (A DOS version of this program is also available). Back-It supports more tape drives than most other Windows utilities. The drawbacks are that it requires reformatting tapes to Back-It's proprietary format, which can take up to an hour, and that you must use a new tape or disk for each new full, incremental, or differential backup, no matter how much free space remains.

Although it provides three different levels of compression, Back-It can be up to three times slower than the fastest backup programs no matter what setting you use. It's not particularly fast when it comes time to restore files, either. However, Back-It includes some nice utilities, including a function to print labels for each disk or tape in a backup set.

Central Point Backup for Windows
Backup for DOS

Central Point's software is bundled with many tape drives, including Iomega's. It's fast, includes drag-and-drop features that make it easy to select files for backup or restoration, and has built-in virus scanning. Another nice feature is a scheduler, which can be set to back up your hard disk at a prearranged time. The scheduler pops up 30 seconds before the backup starts, so you can cancel it or set a snooze alarm to delay the process for five minutes while you wrap up what you are doing.

To drag-and-drop files, open Central Point Backup and File Manager and then drag the files you want to back up from the File Manager window to the Backup window. Password protection is also available.

DOS 6 users might prefer this program if they want to schedule backups automatically and like the idea of easy file selection. Because DOS 6 has virus protection built in, the extra level provided by Central Point Backup isn't especially helpful. The DOS and Windows versions are comparable.

Distinct Backup

There's little to recommend this Windows program over Microsoft Backup, other than a scheduler. It doesn't support tape drives; you must use local floppy drives, or another logical drive, including network drives. You do get to select the level of compression, from none, quick, or efficient.

Distinct does include a nice viewer that can show you the contents of ASCII files and other formats, including Microsoft Excel and Word for Windows. The included screen saver is largely superfluous for Windows users.

FastBack Plus
FastBack Express

FastBack was the only choice for DOS backup for years and still is a formidable competitor, but it has been largely surpassed by newer Windows backup programs from Central Point and Norton. It's fast, but offers fewer options than comparable programs and, at this writing, doesn't support tape drives, unless they have been assigned a drive letter.

Three versions are available: FastBack Plus for DOS, FastBack Plus for Windows, and FastBack Express for Windows. The Express edition is aimed at beginners. It lacks the macro language and scheduler provided with the Plus version but does have automatic compression to pack as much data as possible on your disks. Full, incremental, and selected file backups can be performed.

FastBack Plus also adds data encryption, passwords, and the aforementioned scheduler and macro language. Differential backups are available, along with a novel Full Erase backup option. With the latter, the files you select are first backed up and then erased from your hard disk. It's a convenient way of creating archives of files that you don't expect to need for a while. FastBack can share backup files with Macintoshes, so you can use this program to exchange files between the two platforms in a compressed format.

Norton Backup for Windows
Norton Backup for DOS

These are the "full" versions of Microsoft Backup and Microsoft Windows Backup, if you can call them that, because the DOS 6 versions of these programs don't lack too many essential features. Indeed, the menus for the programs are very similar.

With the Windows version, you can select from preset, basic, and advanced modes, each with more backup options. Preset mode uses predefined backup sets, but with the provision to view which files are included. If you want to depart from the set's definitions, you need to use the basic mode, which offers simple menus and option lists. Advanced mode includes all data compression, verification, and overwrite warning options. At this writing, only tape drives that operate through the floppy controller, rather than a separate card, are compatible.

Where DOS 6's Backup lets you choose only between compression or no compression, the full Norton product has three levels of compression, each taking more time but requiring less disk space. Bonus items include a TapeTools menu for formatting, retensioning, or performing other tape maintenance tasks; a viewer for checking out a file's contents; and a Norton Emergency Rescue disk that doesn't require Windows when the time comes to restore a crashed disk.

The DOS version can automatically run Norton Disk Doctor each time you back up, and a graphical interface mode, complete with icons, makes it as easy to use as a Windows product.

SitBack for Windows
SitBack Lite

Here's a clever idea: a backup program that runs as a TSR and provides continual incremental backups all day long! It's loaded from the DOS command line, takes only 17K of RAM, and runs in the background whether you are using Windows or not.

The strategy is to make a full backup of your hard disk immediately. Then leave a floppy disk in drive B. Because your computer only looks to drive A when booting, a disk in B can remain there all the time, even through multiple reboots. SitBack copies new or updated files to the floppy (or other media) whenever your computer is idle. You can include or exclude files by extension; all EXE and COM files are ignored by default.

SitBack uses no compression or special file formats, so you don't need the program to use or to restore backed up files. The downside is that you don't get as many files on your floppy before you need to switch to a new one. This is a perfect application for DoubleSpace technology. Create a DoubleSpace volume on each disk that you plan to use with SitBack, mount the disk, and let this backup program do its thing. Depending on how many files you create or modify during a day, you may get one or two days' use from a single floppy, or perhaps a little more. When the disk fills, mount a new one. You'll need to prepare your disks in advance whether you use DoubleSpace or not, because SitBack won't format floppies automatically.

You could also have SitBack back up to another hard disk, or you could specify a hard disk as an alternate for the utility to use when the backup floppy fills. SitBack is one of the slowest backup programs when it comes to doing a full backup, but its constant, background operation makes it a logical choice if you want to reduce the possibility that you'll lose even a few minutes' worth of data. There's nothing else like it on the market— other than SitBack Lite. The Lite version sells for 80 percent less ($19.95) and does not use the TSR to automatically back up your files. You must use a Windows application to manually save the files at intervals. The company plans to include data compression in a future version.

Sytos Plus File Backup Manager for DOS

This backup program includes a lot of tape-oriented features, however, oddly, it doesn't support the QIC-40/80 tape formats. It does work well with DC600 tapes, 4 mm and 8 mm DAT, and other formats. You can archive unneeded files, add backups to media already partially filled with previous backups, and back up using several different setups. The downside: the program doesn't support floppy disk changeline signals, so you must tell it when you've replaced a full disk with a fresh one.

The verdict: if you want to use 4 mm or 8 mm tape, this program is a good candidate. Otherwise, DOS 6's Backup programs should do a better job for you.

The Next Step

I've covered everything you need to know about backing up your hard disk, including strategies, the procedures for using Microsoft Backup for DOS and Windows, and alternate backup procedures. But creating backup copies of your data represents only half of the data protection equation. Viruses can also destroy data, and backing up offers little or no defense. The only way to ensure that viruses will not invade your files is to stop them before they enter your system. Failing that, you need to learn how to repair the damage as quickly and as transparently as possible. The next chapters tell you what viruses are, how they work, and how to use Microsoft Anti-Virus to protect yourself.

What Is a Computer Virus?

Not too long ago, computer viruses were not much more than interesting fodder for computer scientists and science fiction writers. It's long been known that computer programs can be written that do "smart" things. We've seen software that can learn to play chess, programs that can "talk" to users in the fashion of a psychoanalyst, and applications based on inexact, but realistic "fuzzy logic" parameters.

As we move toward artificial intelligence, programs that can reproduce—replicate—themselves and that examine our systems for other programs to shelter their code are a natural progression. The ability to damage software or other components is only a minor refinement in this direction.

Computer viruses are the perfect crime. They exist because there is a challenge in creating them, yet there is little fear of retribution. An unfortunate mean streak is alway less restrained when directed at faceless individuals. The same people who cut you off in traffic without a thought go home and brew up computer viruses in their spare time.

It wasn't always so. The first computer viruses were conceived as programming exercises. Early software designers sometimes wrote self-replicating programs designed to erase the self-replicating programs of other programmers on their team. The winner was the designer whose "organism" was the most abundant at the end of the game. There was no chance that such an early "virus" could spread to other systems because all computers were huge, expensive, standalone devices that didn't communicate with other systems.

That changed when computers began to be linked through vast networks, and the PC brought computing power to every desktop. Instead of trying to best your programmer buddies in a friendly contest, other motivations for creating computer viruses were born.

You might want to create a computer virus just to prove to yourself—or others—that you could do it. Designing a virus is also a good way to become famous, if only pseudonominously, among your peers and the computing community at large. An effective virus is a good way to exact revenge for a real or imagined injury. Political activists have found viruses a powerful channel for spreading their messages worldwide. Finally, a good virus makes an excellent practical joke.

Viruses are often misunderstood. You have less to fear from them than you might think, yet the damage they can inflict may be more extensive than you expect. Some are mischievous, little more than a joke that may make you smile. Others are annoying; perhaps you must type Happy Birthday! on a certain date before your computer is freed from the clutches of the virus. Still other viruses are malicious, doing real damage to your data. This chapter should clear up some of the misconceptions and start you on the road to virus protection with DOS 6's Anti-Virus programs and other software.

Types of Bad Software

Computer viruses are one specific type of what I'll call "bad" software. These are programs that are ill-behaved in one way or another, eventually causing some phenomenon that you'd rather not experience, ranging from a system crash to the complete destruction of every file exposed to the errant software. It's even theoretically possible to damage certain types of hardware permanently, although I've heard only unconfirmed rumors of this sort of thing.

It's important not to lump all kinds of bad software together, because they are dangerous for different reasons, and the ways you protect yourself also differ. This next section will describe the main categories of misbehaving software.

Poorly Written or Poorly Used Programs

Some bad software has good intentions. The programmer never intended to do bad things to your computer system, but matters just got out of hand. The most common program of this type is the bug-filled Version 1.0 of anything that hasn't been sufficiently beta-tested. These applications and utilities can crash your disk by using memory or other resources improperly. That's fairly easy to do on an IBM PC; DOS was written with the assumption that every resource on a system would be available to a running program. A program that wants to use a certain segment of memory may have no way of telling whether or not that memory is also being used by another program running at the same time. The result: DOS crashes.

The idea that more than one program could run at once is foreign to the basic DOS architecture. Yet, Microsoft violated that concept itself with PRINT, the very first TSR, designed to print in the background while the user continued to work at other tasks. The DOS-based multitasking solutions since then have been little better than valiant attempts at patching a weak structure. A poorly written program can still generate a General Protection Fault under Windows despite the best attempts by Microsoft to build a sturdy, robust environment.

Other software is ill-behaved because the programmer used non-documented DOS calls that became non-existent DOS calls in later releases, or in an attempt to gain some speed, wrote directly to your system's BIOS instead of working through DOS. Not all BIOS's work the same, so such software can cause crashes or not work at all.

It makes no difference whether the software is badly written or badly used. If it crashes your system or trashes your disk, that program is as dangerous as an intentionally destructive virus. Your lost data doesn't know it has vanished through an innocent mistake.

Examples of bad software with good intentions include any Windows program that generates General Protection Faults or DOS commands and utilities that do bad things when used in a reasonable way (under earlier versions of DOS and Windows, CHKDSK, when run in a DOS window, could "recover" Windows temporary files, with disastrous results). If a program overwrites a file that you want without asking you first, it's bad. If it destroys its own files when interrupted by a system reset (DisplayWrite 4 was adept at this), it's bad.

Your only protection against this kind of software mishap is to identify the culprit and to remove it from your system, or to find a way to disable the improper behavior.

Trojan Horses

Everyone knows the consequences of not looking a gift horse in the mouth. An innocent-looking program can conceal code that can do more damage than the Greeks who used a giant horse to gain entry to ancient Troy.

A trojan horse is code hidden inside an otherwise useful program, which springs into action when the program is run. The main program may function perfectly well while the trojan code does its dirty work. Trojan horse is a very broad term that encompasses many different kinds of programs that do something—harmless or not—that you don't expect them to do. A simple trojan horse stays resident in its host program; when the hidden code actively begins to reproduce itself, it enters the more specialized realm of the virus, described later.

Logic Bombs

A logic bomb is a type of trojan horse, triggered by some logical condition on your computer. Unlike a simple trojan horse that operates every time you activate the host program, a logic bomb remains inert until some specific condition is met. It may wait until you insert a disk in your floppy drive and then erase all the data on that disk. Or, a logic bomb may affect only printer output. Like other trojan horses, a logic bomb can remain with its host program or act as a virus and spread.

Time Bombs

Time bombs are more specialized logic bombs, activated solely by the elapse of time. Some may wait until so many days or hours have passed (thereby disguising the time of entry to your system) or activate only on a specific day. The infamous Michaelangelo virus, which supposedly was to devastate PCs worldwide on Michaelangelo's birthday, is a time bomb.

Worms

Worms are bits of program code that can reproduce themselves and move through programs and systems and even into other systems. Some worms can wander through your PC's memory or hard disk space until all of it is consumed. Others know how to attach themselves to electronic mail or other data that moves from system to system, and thus can actively spread on their own. The 1988 Internet Worm, which affected 6000 computers worldwide is an example of this type of invader.

Viruses

Viruses are so-named because they bear a remarkable resemblance to biological viruses that can infect humans. Like biological viruses, they can reproduce themselves and rely on another entity, such as a computer program or data file to infect another system. Unlike worms, viruses don't actively seek out actual transport to the other system. You must download an infected program, copy it from a floppy disk, run it from a disk or over a network, or otherwise import the virulent code into your system.

How Do Viruses Attack?

Viruses can only invade a system when you run a program that contains their code. Simply having a virus present in a file on your computer isn't enough. Unfortunately, what is considered a program in this sense encompasses a great deal more than just EXE and COM files. Other programs with instructions that your computer executes also can contain viruses.

BIN Files

These are program code executed by other programs or DOS itself, and not from the DOS prompt. You may not even be aware that these files are present on your hard disk. For example, after you've installed DoubleSpace on your system, the binary file DBLSPACE.BIN is automatically loaded each time you boot DOS 6, even if you disable the device statements in CONFIG.SYS. The only way to get rid of it totally is to delete the invisible DBLSPACE.BIN file from your root directory. Look for a virus to attach itself to this file in the near future. Since it's invisible and easily forgotten, DBLSPACE.BIN is the last place you'll look for a virus.

OVL/DLL Files

OVL files are program overlay files, called in by DOS programs as required because there isn't enough RAM to hold the entire program all at one time. The rough Windows equivalent is the DLL (dynamic link library) file, which contains code that can be shared by many different Windows applications.

DRV Files

Driver files tell DOS how to work with specific peripherals. Their code can be invaded by viruses designed to do so.

SYS Files

These device drivers are loaded from CONFIG.SYS and contain program instructions that can be infected by viruses. CONFIG.SYS itself is a simple ASCII list of instructions with rigid and limited syntax and so can't be affected by what we think of as a virus. I suppose a program could be created to change your CONFIG.SYS file so that your system configuration was a little flaky (BUFFERS=1 would slow things down a bit), but such changes are easily detected.

Boot Sectors

The boot sectors of a disk contain the instructions used to start up the system. Some viruses change these instructions so that the virus is loaded into memory before your computer is finished loading DOS. A virus resident in the boot sector of your hard disk is especially difficult to get rid of; you have to reformat your disk and restore all your software and data. An especially insidious kind of virus installs itself in the boot sector of floppy disks that are themselves not normally bootable. If you leave one of these in drive A and restart your computer, it will try to boot from the floppy and instead load the virus into memory, where, in all likelihood, it will install itself in the boot sectors of your hard disk.

In one sense, we PC owners are lucky. We must consciously run a program to activate a virus. On the Apple Macintosh, a Desktop program is run each time a disk is inserted in the floppy drive, ostensibly to gain information about the programs and data on the disk. So, simply inserting a disk can be enough to load a virus into a Mac.

There are two sides to every coin, however. The way the Mac treats floppies makes it easy to write an anti-virus program that checks a floppy immediately when the disk is inserted. Not all PC floppy drives implement changeline hardware, giving DOS a way to know when a new disk has been inserted. PC virus protection schemes must wait until the disk is actually accessed before they can check for viruses. So, you can insert a disk containing a boot-sector virus, never access it, and then reboot your system and install the virus before even the best anti-virus program has had a chance to check for it.

Viruses attack your system using several methods. Those that attack executable programs attach themselves to the end of a COM or EXE file. They are loaded into memory any time that program is run.

Boot sector viruses attack the first sector of a bootable floppy disk or the master boot record of a hard disk. Typically, the true boot sector of a floppy is copied to the last sector of the root directory and is replaced by the virus's code. On boot-up, the virus resets the amount of memory available in your system to some figure about 2K less than the actual amount and loads itself into that reserved area. That way, DOS isn't even aware that this memory exists, so conventional memory-checking techniques won't reveal the presence of the virus.

The next thing a boot-sector virus loaded from a floppy does is check the master boot record of your hard disk and see whether it is infected. If so, the virus copies the original master boot record to some other location, replaces it with some viral code, and then provides a link that sends control to the new boot sectors after the virus has been loaded. From then on, the virus monitors all disk activity, infecting any new floppies that you insert in your drives.

The latest wrinkle in the virus canvas are so-called stealth viruses, which do their best to conceal themselves from anti-virus software. The first step down this road came in the form of viruses that managed to modify files without changing the date stamp. Others were developed that intercepted requests for information about files from the system. They then subtracted their own length from the length of the file reported to the system. No date change, no length change, no virus, right? Wrong.

There are now viruses which don't invade files at all but, instead, reside on your hard disk as hidden files. They lie in wait until the time comes to spring into action and destroy your data. Polymorphic viruses mutate, changing their code at random, making it more difficult for virus-scanning software to look for tell-tale sequences of code called signatures. Viruses also can encrypt themselves in random ways, using only a small unencrypted piece of code that does nothing but extract the rest of the code and load it into memory.

Where Do Viruses Come From?

In the good old days, you needed a decent hacker to create a decent computer virus. Note that the term *hacker* has been applied by the press in a derogatory sense to encompass only those misguided souls who invade computer systems or create viruses, trojan horses, or other intentionally misbehaved software. Within the computer community, hacker has been broadly applied to any dedicated soul with an awesome ability to do amazing things with computer hardware or software. You'll find people without ethics in any group, and hackers are no exception. Some of these wizards directed their energies into creating what we know today as computer viruses; it took that kind of ingenuity to create an effective virus program.

Sadly, today that is no longer the case. There are several software toolkits with names like Dark Avenger Mutation Engine, Virus Construction Set, or Virus Construction Lab that make it relatively simple to create your own personal virus. Thousands of different viruses could easily be generated by these kits in a limited period of time. The vast majority are poorly done and easily countered and, ironically, tend to be of most danger to the creator and those near to him or her. VCL, in particular, tends to crash the machine it is run on.

How Can You Tell When a Virus Strikes?

Fortunately, this doesn't have to be a concern for most users. If you use a good anti-virus program, you can let it take care of ferreting out viruses before or after the fact. Even so, some things may have happened to your system that give you pause. What really caused that crash yesterday? Was it me who erased those missing files? Did that floppy disk develop a defective sector . . . or was it something else? Do I have an IRQ conflict, or is it a virus?

If you're already using virus protection, you can probably eliminate a virus as the cause of any of these events. If not, and you want to run down a list of possible symptoms for yourself, here are some things to look for.

➤ **Unexpected Size or Date Changes.** With rare exceptions, any COM or EXE file should keep the same size and date for as long as it resides on your system. If you notice that one of these files has grown in size, even slightly, or that an existing program suddenly has a recent date, suspect a virus.

➤ **Slow Operation.** If a particular program takes much longer to load or start operating, there may be a virus resident that is doing its work before turning control over to the original program.

➤ **Sudden or Unexpected Decrease in Available Memory or Disk Space.** You type the **mem** command from time to time and notice that you've lost 16K of DOS RAM for some reason, even though you haven't installed any new programs. It might be a good time to run DOS 6's anti-virus software as a first check. One real tipoff is when **mem** or **chkdsk** report less than 655360 bytes total memory. Virtually every 286 and higher computer in use today has 640K of DOS RAM to start with (reported as 655360 bytes), so if you have less total memory (not just memory after all drivers, TSRs, and DOS itself are loaded), you may have a problem.

➤ **Programs Want to Write to Write-Protected Media for No Good Reason.** Your spreadsheet program suddenly reports that it can't write to drive A. You didn't *want* to write to drive A. What's going on?

➤ **Files Vanish or Are Unexpectedly Corrupt.** Go ahead and restore the files or reinstall the software, but write protect your media or, better yet, take the time to run Microsoft Anti-Virus first.

➤ **Unexpected Reboots.** Your computer reboots after it's been switched on for a specific period of time or when you run certain programs. If no other problem is apparent, think virus.

➤ **Overt Virus-Type Behavior.** You get funny dialog boxes demanding cookies, screen-saver type effects when no screen saver is active (bouncing balls, stars, melting screens, etc.) Your computer acts really funny, and you have no other explanation.

Guarding Against Viruses

Your first line of defense should be to not expose yourself to viruses in the first place. You can do that in the following ways.

➤ **Install and Use Anti-Virus Software.** These programs can spot viruses the first time they are run and prevent them from infecting your system. They can also detect viruses in new programs before they are run. If you're too late to stop an infection, anti-virus software can remove the errant files.

➤ **Backup Your Programs and Data.** An extra copy of critical data can minimize the damage a virus can do. Just dispose of the virus and restore all the files that were damaged. Of course, you must be positive that your backed up files have not been infected, too. Microsoft Anti-Virus can check restored files before you run them as a safety measure.

➤ **Check Software Downloads.** Computer BBSs are no more likely to contain virus-bearing software than any other source. Since system operators often check all posted software, they may be *less* likely to let a virus slip by, and because BBSs deal only with files, not disks, they are fairly immune to boot sector viruses. But, you still should be especially wary of software from unknown sources. Be suspicious of software that claims to perform miracles, such as speed up your system or format floppy disks to triple their normal capacity. Download to a floppy disk instead of your hard disk and examine the software with Anti-Virus before you run it.

➤ **Check Any New Diskette You Insert in Your Computer.** Even check disks you receive in a shrink-wrapped software package. There are two reasons for this. First, there have been documented cases of well-known software vendors (does the name Aldus ring a bell?) sending out virus-infected commercial software. Worse, many computer retailers have shrinkwrap machines that can be used to reseal packages that have been opened for demonstration purposes, or even returned by the customer.

➤ *Always* **Write Protect Your Original Program Disks.** *Leave* them write protected under all circumstances. Don't use these disks to install the software. Install from copies of the originals and write protect those, too. If an installation program insists on writing serial number or registration information to a master diskette, you can unprotect the copy and proceed with the installation. Afterwards, immediately make another copy of the original disks for subsequent installations. *Never* reinstall software from a disk that has been written to, even if you are positive there were no viruses resident in your computer at the time.

Remember that write protection is the closest thing to fool-proof that you'll find in a PC. It's a *hardware* measure: when a disk drive sees that a disk is write protected, it won't write to it, no matter what the operating system or a virus tries to tell it. In contrast, making a file "write protected" by setting its archive bit to read-only is useful against only the most stupid of viruses. Any software, including the **attrib** command, can turn a read-only file into an ordinary file in a flash.

➤ **Consider Renaming "Dangerous" Programs and Utilities.** That way, simplistic viruses can't access them. If FORMAT.COM is renamed to FMAT.COM, you can still access it by typing **fmat.** But a fairly dumb virus that uses the DOS **format** command won't find it. You should be aware that more sophisticated invaders won't have any difficult writing directly to your hard disk through DOS calls, so this procedure is limited protection, at best.

How Does Anti-Virus Software Work?

All anti-virus software, including Microsoft Anti-Virus, take some combination of three approaches to protecting you from virus invasions. No one system can do the job all by itself. Your best approach is to use some level of all three, either that provided in DOS 6 or one of the solutions offered by third-part vendors. The three levels of virus protection are discussed in the next section.

Detection

The first thing you need to do when setting up a virus protection system for the first time is to look for any viruses that may have already invaded your system. Detection, a key first step and is carried out in one of two ways: scanning for tell-tale *signature* code segments or checking existing files for integrity.

To scan for signatures, a virus-detection program needs to have a library containing those signature patterns. Being able to match specific signatures with individual viruses makes it possible not only to detect the *presence* of the virus but to *remove* the virus during the disinfection process.

These libraries are not easy to compile. As new viruses are introduced, they must first be identified (usually by some unlucky end-user), at which point they are often uploaded to the vendor of the virus-protection software package that failed to detect the new strain. The vendor dissects the virus, determines a signature, and creates an updated signature file that can be used by all owners of that anti-virus package. These files are often available for downloading over CompuServe, America OnLine, or local BBSs or mailed as part of a subscription service. Programs like McAfee's SCAN.EXE are entirely recompiled to include each new set of viruses, so you must download or otherwise obtain a new copy of the entire program every time you need an update.

Viruses can also be detected by looking for virus-like code within likely files. Because viruses all operate by performing certain functions, such as performing disk accesses, trapping system interrupts, or jumping from one part of a program to another, scanning programs can look for un-usual instances of these functions. The advantage of this type of program is that it can spot new viruses before their signatures are identified, as well as stealth-type viruses that mask or disguise their signatures.

Disinfection

After you've found existing viruses in your system, the next step is to remove, or disinfect them. There are several ways to accomplish this. The easiest thing to do is overwrite only the virus code in the file. To do this, however, you must be able to positively identify the virus. Some strains appear under 30 or 40 different names and varieties. "Fix" the wrong one, and you will probably damage the host file. An anti-virus program with an extensive, frequently updated list of signatures is essential.

The second way to disinfect a system is to replace the virus-ridden file with an uninfected copy. To do that, you must *have* an uninfected backup, and that may not always be practical. Some anti-virus software uses a combination of these approaches, and a few programs collect so much information about a file during a pre-invasion "innoculation" step that a damaged file can be reconstructed from the information file alone.

Prevention

Finally, when you've found and removed all the viruses that reside on your system, you'll next want to take steps to prevent them from ever taking root again. The most common solution is a terminate-and-stay-resident program that constantly monitors your PC for virus-like activity.

They can scan floppy disks as the information they contain is read into memory. You'll learn more about prevention in the next chapter, as you learn how to use Microsoft Anti-Virus.

The Next Step

This chapter showed you how to minimize your chances of encountering a computer virus, even if you don't use Microsoft Anti-Virus or another system of protection. You also learned some of the terminology that is applied to viruses, and we cleared up a few misconceptions about viruses and the people who create them. Now it's time to look at Microsoft's answer to virus protection. You can learn everything you need to know about Microsoft Anti-Virus in the next chapter.

Using Microsoft Anti-Virus

By including Microsoft Anti-Virus for DOS, Microsoft Anti-Virus for Windows, and VSafe with DOS 6, Microsoft has brought a basic level of virus protection to every DOS user. These utilities are most effective if you use them regularly, to eliminate every chance that a virus will invade your system. Luckily, they are easy to use and won't require a lot of your time. Even the initial setup steps will require only a few minutes. This chapter covers everything you need to know about using DOS 6's virus-protection utilities.

Getting Started

The first time you use anti-virus protection, you need to follow the three basic steps outlined in the last chapter: detection, disinfection, and protection. In addition, you need a fail-safe way to restart your computer if a virus does manage to invade your system. You can do this by carefully following these steps:

1. Run Microsoft Anti-Virus for DOS. Even if you plan to rely on the Windows version later on, it's important to run Microsoft

Anti-Virus in its DOS version for your initial sweep for viruses. That's because this version can find some memory-resident viruses that may be missed by the Windows-based program.

There's a simple reason for this: the first thing the virus-scanner does is check the first megabyte of memory for viruses. Under plain DOS, all programs, including viruses, must run in that first megabyte. Extended or expanded memory are used only for data storage, unless you have a special program like Windows or Desqview running. Anti-Virus for DOS and Windows don't check those other regions of memory for viruses, so you must run the DOS version outside of Windows or Desqview to be certain that no viruses are present for this initial pass.

2. Load Anti-Virus for DOS by typing **msav** at the DOS prompt. You'll see a main menu screen like that shown in figure 24.1. Press F8 to bring up a list of options. Make sure that Verify Integrity, Create New Checksums, Anti-Stealth, and Check All Files are checked. Those options will ensure that Anti-Virus performs its most comprehensive examination.

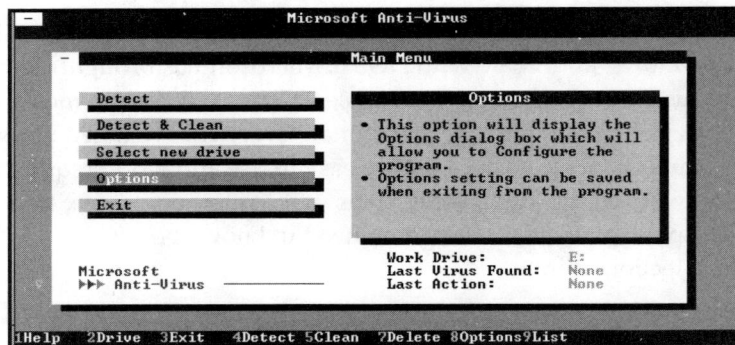

Figure 24.1. Anti-Virus for DOS.

3. Next, press F2 to pop up a list of drives, choose your first drive by typing its drive letter and then start the scan by pressing D (for Detect). Anti-Virus will scan the entire drive and report any viruses it finds. If any are located, a Virus Found window pops up. You can decide to delete the offending file (do this if you know you have a good backup copy or two), or Clean (to remove only the viral code and leave the rest of the file intact). With any luck, no viruses will be located and you can repeat this process for each of your hard disks.

4. Create a clean boot-up floppy. At this point, you can be fairly certain that no viruses reside on your system. This is a good time to make a clean boot-up floppy disk that you can use to restart your system if a virus, including a boot sector virus, manages to sneak in. Insert a new floppy disk in drive A and type **format a: /s.** This will create a bootable floppy that contains the DOS 6 system files, including COMMAND.COM.

5. Copy all the Microsoft Anti-Virus files to the floppy disk by logging into your DOS subdirectory on your hard disk and typing copy **msav*.* a:\.** That will copy the DOS version of Anti-Virus to the disk. Do this even if you plan to use the Windows edition of the product on a daily basis. You want to have a disk that can be safely booted and used to rid your hard disk of viruses in an emergency. If a virus infects your system, you will be unable to safely run Windows until the virus has been cleaned off. So, you must use the DOS version to do that.

6. *Write protect* your bootable floppy disk, make a copy or two of it using **diskcopy,** and put them in several safe places, perhaps with your backup sets.

7. Set up automatic virus detection. You can breathe easier now. Your system is currently safe. To keep it that way, you need to configure Anti-Virus to check your memory and disk drives for viruses each time you turn on your computer.

The best way to do this is with the DOS version of the product, through a line inserted into your AUTOEXEC.BAT file. The wisest thing to do is make this line the first one in the file, so it will be executed immediately after CONFIG.SYS has loaded its drivers and before any other programs are run. Add one of the following commands to AUTOEXEC.BAT (ignore the instructions on page 69 of the DOS 6 manual; they are *wrong*).

msav /p /a scans all drives except drive A and B

msav /p /l scans only local (non-network drives)

The first command shown in the DOS manual, **msav /p,** scans only the boot drive. You'll need to use one of the two shown here to scan all the drives in your system. If you're willing to settle for less protection, you can scan only your boot drive (that's where boot sector viruses settle in) and scan your other drives manually from time to time.

The only problem with this scheme is that it takes some time each and every time you boot up. If you have several large hard disk drives, the process can take a few minutes. You can work around this by making the virus scan optional through a few interactive lines in your AUTOEXEC.BAT file. The lines would look like these

```
choice /T:Y,5 Do you want to scan for viruses?
if errorlevel 2 goto noscan
msav /p /a
:noscan
```

This routine uses the new DOS 6 **choice** command. The first line displays a prompt, Do you want to scan for viruses? [Y/N] and gives you five seconds to enter either Y or N. If any other character is pressed, a beep will sound. If no key is pressed, Y will be used as the default.

The second level checks the DOS errorlevel. If it is 2 (because N was pressed), control of the batch file jumps to the label :noscan, and the other lines in AUTOEXEC.BAT that follow. Otherwise, the file drops down to the next line (because Y was pressed or accepted as the default) and performs the scan. If you're accustomed to turning on your computer at the beginning of the day and then going off to get a cup of coffee, when you come back your system will have been scanned for viruses. But if you subsequently reboot later in the day, you can bypass this step easily.

Using VSafe

If you're willing to accept a little less protection, you can dispense with daily scanning of your hard disks and use VSafe, which is a memory-resident program that monitors your computer's activity for signs that may indicate a virus invasion. VSafe can use as little as 7K of conventional RAM if you let it load most of its code into expanded or extended memory.

The DOS 6 Help file on VSafe notes that you should not use the **vsafe** command when you are running Windows. What Microsoft meant to warn you against was using VSafe from *within* Windows. You can safely load it before you start Windows, although its error messages won't be displayed unless you also run the MSAVTSR.EXE program. I'll explain how to do that shortly. First, let's look at VSafe and what it does. The full syntax of the **vsafe** command is as follows:

```
VSAFE [/option[+ or -]]...] [/NE] [/NX] [/Ax] [/Cx]
[/N] [/D] [/U]
```

For */option*, you can substitute one or more of the following switches, each of which can be accompanied by a plus or minus sign to turn that switch on (+) or off (-).

➤ **1** warns you before low-level formatting of a hard disk takes place. A low level format cannot be reversed by the **unformat** command. The default is on.

➤ **2** warns you when a TSR program loads. You'll be alerted when legitimate TSRs take up residence in memory but also when a virus tries to do the same thing. The default is off.

➤ **3** prevents programs from writing to disk. You can "write protect" all your hard disks temporarily with this command. For obvious reasons, the default setting is off.

➤ **4** tells VSafe to check all executable files that DOS opens. The default is on.

➤ **5** constantly checks for boot sector viruses. The default is on.

➤ **6** warns you when any program attempts to write to the boot sector or partition table of your hard disk. Other than FDISK, SYS, or

FORMAT (with the /S switch), only special disk utilities will need to do this. The default setting is on.

➤ **7** alerts you of attempts to write to the boot sector of a floppy disk. The default is off.

➤ **8** lets you know when an attempt is made to modify an executable file. Except for a few self-modifying files, this should never happen, so you'll always want to know when this happens. The default is off.

Any of these options can be toggled on or off after VSafe has been loaded, by pressing the associated hotkey. The default is Alt-V, but you can change this to another key using the following guidelines. When the hotkey is pressed, a window pops up with the eight options displayed, along with a ninth, Remove VSafe from Memory.

The other switches control how VSafe configures itself initially. Normally, it attempts to load into expanded or extended memory to preserve conventional RAM, but you can prevent this with either of the two following switches:

➤ **/NE** stops VSafe from loading into expanded memory.

➤ **/NX** prevents VSafe from loading into extended memory.

Although VSafe will pop up automatically when a monitored condition occurs, you can invoke it manually by pressing a hotkey. You can set the hotkey as the Control key or Alt key, plus another key, using these two switches:

➤ **/A**x sets the hotkey to Alt plus x.

➤ **/C**x sets the hotkey to Control plus x.

The last three switches perform other functions:

➤ **/N**   tells VSafe to monitor network drives, using the optional parameters described earlier.

➤ **/D**   turns off comparison of checksums.

➤ **/U**   unloads VSafe from RAM.

Using VSafe with Windows

As noted, you should not attempt to load VSafe from within a DOS window loaded after Windows starts. You can load it before loading Windows. You'll need to also run the MWAVTSR.EXE program to see any messages VSafe generates and to access a Windows-based control panel. To automatically load this program each time you start Windows, include the line **load=mwavtsr.exe** at the beginning of your WIN.INI file. It is possible that you already load one or more programs using this command, so if you already find a **load=** line in WIN.INI, just add **mwavtsr.exe** to the end, separated from the other entries by a space.

The Windows control panel for VSafe looks like figure 24.2.

Running Microsoft Anti-Virus for DOS from the DOS Prompt

Although Anti-Virus is easiest to run from its interactive, menu-oriented mode, you can use it from the command line, with a set of switches. The complete syntax for the command is as follows:

```
MSAV [drive:] [/S] [/C] [/R] [/A] [/L] [/N] [/P] [/F]
[/VIDEO]
```

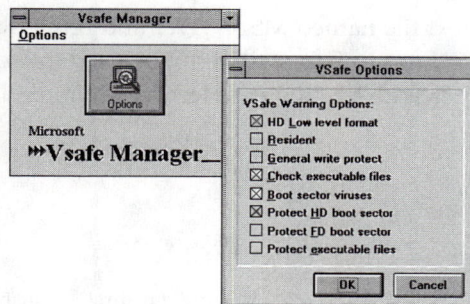

Figure 24.2. VSafe Windows Manager.

For *drive:* substitute a single drive letter that you would like to scan. If you don't enter a drive letter, the utility will scan the current drive.

/S   scans only; it does not remove any viruses that are located.

/C   scans and cleans the specified drive.

/R   creates MSAV.RPT in the root directory of the scanned drive, including information about the number of viruses found and removed.

/A   scans all drives except drive A and B.

/L   scans all drives but network drives.

/P   disables interactive mode.

/F   turns off display of filenames as they are scanned. This switch can be used only with /P or /N.

/VIDEO displays valid video display switches, which can be used to control the number of lines in the screen display (/25, /28, /43, /50, /60), use of color or black-and-white display schemes (/IN, /BW, /MONO, /LCD), and type of display updating (/FF=fast CGA, /BF=use BIOS). Other switches disable alternate fonts (/NF), allow use of a graphics mouse cursor in Windows (/BT), force the use of an ASCII character instead of a graphics mouse cursor (/NGM), swap left and right mouse buttons (/LE), and allow a reset if the mouse cursor locks up (/PS2).

/N displays a text file named MSAV.TXT and returns an errorlevel code of 86 if a virus is found. This switch can be used to create specialized scanning routines with batch files. Here's a simplified example:

```
@echo off
c:
msav c: /n /s
if not errorlevel 86 goto d
choice /C:YNQ /T:Y,20 Virus found!  Remove it? Enter
[Y]es, [N]o or [Q]uit:
if errorlevel 3 goto quit
if errorlevel 2 goto d
msav c: /n /c /f
```

```
:d

d:

msav d: /n /s

if not errorlevel 86 goto quit

choice /C:YNQ /T:Y,20 Virus found!  Remove it? Enter
[Y]es, [N]o or [Q]uit:

if errorlevel 2 goto quit

msav d: /n /c /f

:quit
```

This routine would first log onto drive C and then run Anti-Virus while displaying a custom MSAV.TXT file with a message of your choice. ("Now scanning your drive, please stand by.") If a virus is found (errorlevel is 86), the user is offered the choice of entering Y (remove the virus), N (ignore it), or Q (quit the batch file entirely). The process repeats for drive D.

You can see that various customized scanning routines can be created in this way, either for naive users or for your own specialized needs.

Checksums

As an extra measure of protection, Anti-Virus can compare current information about your files with a log of data compiled earlier. That information is nothing more than a simple checksum, which is a number arrived at by applying an algorithm to certain information about the file. A logfile called CHKLIST.MS is created the first time you scan a directory, when Anti-Virus computes and records a checksum for each infectable program. During subsequent scans, Anti-Virus compares the checksum stored in that directory's CHKLIST.MS against the current checksums for each file. Any change may indicate a virus infection—or that you have modified the file (in the case of data files that happen to have an extension the same as an executable file—e.g., Telix phone lists and some font files both use the FON extension.) You can scrap these checksum files at any time and start over.

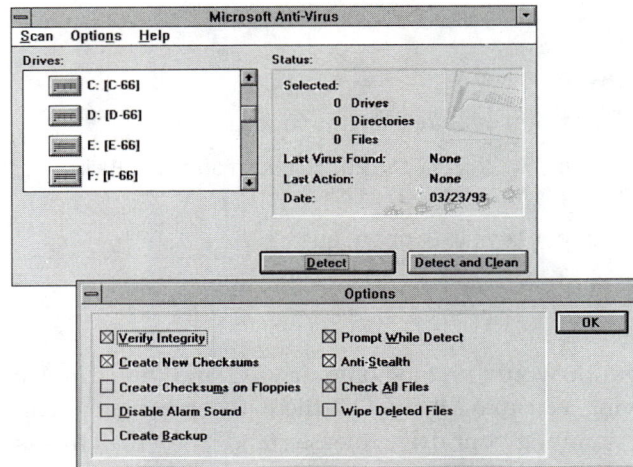

Figure 24.3. The Options menu.

Running Microsoft Anti-Virus for DOS Windows in Interactive Mode

Anti-Virus can be run in a graphical, interactive mode that lets you select options. The Windows version of the program is shown in figure 24.2. Drives to scan may be chosen one at a time from the drive window at left. Click on the Detect or Detect and Clean buttons to activate the scan. The results will be shown in the window at right.

These two modes can also be selected from the Scan menu, which offers the options of viewing the current virus list or deleting CHKLIST.MS files. The Options menu presents the list of options shown in figure 24.3. These options include the following:

➤ **Verify integrity.** When this option is checked, Anti-Virus and VSafe will watch executable files and issue a verify error if any of them change, based on the checksums included in your checklist files. These executable files aren't suppose to change, so this is a sure-fire clue that an infection may have taken place.

➤ **Create new checksums.** When this option is selected, new checksums for each executable file will be calculated and stored in the checklist files.

➤ **Create checksums on floppies.** This option tells Anti-Virus to create a checklist file for each subdirectory scanned on a floppy disk. Both Anti-Virus and VSafe use this information to see whether a file has been changed.

➤ **Disable alarm sound.** Anti-Virus can beep to get your attention, but you may not need this extra noise level unless your computer operates unattended for periods of time.

➤ **Create backup.** When activated, Anti-Virus will create a copy of a suspected virus-infected file before attempting to clean the file. The old file is renamed with the VIR extension. If the cleaning step ends up corrupting your file, and you have no other copies, you will at least have the infected version. The original then can be used with other virus-cleaning tools.

➤ **Prompt while detect.** Tells Anti-Virus to display Verify Error and Virus Found warnings during Detect scans. If switched off, no warnings will be provided, but you'll be given a list of suspected virus-infected files at the end of the scan.

➤ **Anti-stealth.** This option must be used with the Verify Integrity selection. It activates certain low-level techniques to discover viruses that normally intercept DOS calls and report the *expected* file size for infected files, rather than the true size.

➤ **Check all files.** Unless you select this option, Anti-Virus doesn't really check all the files on your disk; it searches only files with the following extensions: 386, APP, BIN, CMD, COM, DLL, DRV, FON, ICO, OV*, PGM, PIF, PRG, and SYS. When Check all files is chosen, Anti-Virus scans every file, including data files. Data files can't be infected by virus code, but they can be altered or damaged. Use this option, along with **Create new checksums,** to build a checksum file that includes checksums for your data files. Then **Verify integrity** will spot changes to data files. These changes are less likely to be caused by viruses (just updating a file will change it) but can provide an additional level of security when you suspect that a virus may be changing your data.

➤ **Wipe deleted files.** When this option is chosen, virus-infected files are no longer simply deleted. Anti-Virus totally overwrites them so that every trace of the infected file is removed from your disk.

Drag-and-Drop Virus Detection

With the Windows version of Anti-Virus, you can check suspected files by dragging their icons from the File Manager and dropping them onto the utility's minimized icon, its open window, or icon in the file list. If you work with File Manager a lot, this is a quick way to inspect new files before dragging them to their permanent homes in other directories on your system.

Coping with Found Viruses

Okay, you've got a virus. Now what do you do? As Anti-Virus scans in interactive mode under both DOS and Windows, and Prompt While Detect is checked, it displays a Virus Found dialog box whenever an infection is found. You'll be given four choices: Clean, Delete, Stop, or Continue. If you select Clean, the file with the virus will be repaired. Choose Delete, and Anti-Virus removes the file from your hard disk. Select Stop, and virus scanning will be halted, and you can take some action manually. Opt for Continue, and the scan will resume. You can note the name of the file and move on.

You may also be alerted to a virus invasion if the Verify Integrity and Prompt While Detect options are active, and Anti-Virus finds that an executable file has changed.

Not all changes are caused by virus infection. You may have upgraded your software, or the file may be a data file rather than an executable file. If you know the change is legitimate, you can update the checksum file by selecting the Update box. If you feel that it is actually a virus-ridden file, you may select Delete to remove it. Choose Continue to ignore the file and go on or Stop to cease the scan.

Other messages you get include the following:

➤ `File was destroyed by the virus.` The file cannot be recovered. You can delete the file, ignore it, or stop the scan.

➤ `Program is trying to modify system memory.` VSafe will tell you when a program tries to directly modify your system memory. This could be a network driver, or a virus. If you're not running on a network, select Stop and run Anti-Virus to look for infections.

➤ `Program is trying to stay resident in memory.` VSafe is alerting you that a TSR is trying to set up shop in your computer. If you are trying to load a TSR at that time, you can ignore the message and continue. Otherwise, stop and run Anti-Virus.

➤ `Program is trying to write to disk.` If you switched on Write Protect, received this message from VSafe, and you want the program to write to the disk, select continue. If you didn't expect a program to try and write to the disk at this time, stop and run Anti-Virus.

➤ `Resident programs were loaded after VSafe.` This isn't a virus alert. TSRs should be removed in an orderly fashion, in the reverse order of how they were loaded. If you try to remove VSafe from memory and had loaded other TSRs after it, you could cause an unstable memory condition. If you can't unload the other programs in the right order, disable the VSafe command in your AUTOEXEC.BAT file and reboot.

➤ `Since a virus was detected.....` It's a good idea to reboot when you quit Anti-Virus after a virus has been detected. The utility offers you this option. Choose Reboot to reset your system.

➤ `The xxxxxx virus is known to infect DATA files.....` When you see this message, Anti-Virus turns on the Check All Files option and can scan every file on the disk, including data files.

Updating Virus Signatures

Any virus detection system based on signatures is only as good as its file of signature codes. The day your copy of DOS 6 was shipped, new viruses were reported and signatures developed for them. You'll need to periodically obtain updated lists of signatures to keep abreast of these changes. These lists let you detect new viruses but don't allow you to clean (remove them.) That's because although Anti-Virus uses externally accessible lists to track virus signatures, the information needed to clean them is built into the program itself. To remove new viruses, you'll need to update the Anti-Virus program, too.

A coupon for an Anti-Virus update offer is included in the back of your DOS 6 guide. You can obtain updates and new signature lists from a special BBS, if your computer is equipped with a modem and telecommunications software. You'll also need a user identification code. Although the procedure is outlined in Appendix D of the Microsoft DOS guide, we can run through it quickly here, with a little more detail. Follow these steps.

1. Load your telecommunications software and change your settings, if necessary, to 8 data bits, no parity, and 1 stop bit (8, N, 1). Choose any speed up to 9600 bps.

2. Dial (503) 531-8100. When your modem connects with the BBS, you'll be prompted to choose between ANSI graphics and no graphics. If your terminal emulation supports ANSI graphics and you want them, select Y and press Enter. Otherwise, select N.

3. You'll be asked for a user code. Type **new.**

4. Next, a check is made to see whether ANSI graphics are in effect. If so, you'll see the word ANSI blinking. Enter Y if you see it blink or N if not.

5. You'll then be asked to enter your name, address, and phone number, computer type, and user identification code (from 3 to 29 characters). You may select a password. Remember the user code and password for future use.

6. From the main menu, choose option D (Download Anti-Virus Signature files). You'll be given a choice of readme files, Windows

Anti-Virus files, or DOS Anti-Virus files. Choose the one you want, select a download protocol supported by your telecommunications package (ZModem, XModem, etc.), and start the download. The readme files contain instructions on using the signature files after you've downloaded them. In most cases, all you need to do is expand the files from the self-extracting archive you just downloaded and then copy them to a specified subdirectory. Both versions of Anti-Virus will use the updated signatures automatically the next time the programs are loaded.

7. When finished, you can press X, followed by Enter, to leave the BBS.

When Microsoft Anti-Virus Isn't Enough

Anti-Virus does an excellent job of protecting your system from viruses, particularly if you follow all the steps outlined in this chapter. However, there are reasons why you might want an additional antivirus product.

Many virus experts recommend using two separate products from different vendors in order to protect yourself from blind spots a single utility might suffer from. It's true that some of these recommendations come from anti-virus program vendors who don't want to go out of business after DOS 6 becomes widely used. Yet, there is a kernel of truth in this advice.

Other anti-virus programs may offer special features, extra convenience, or have other advantages that are attractive to you. For example, Norton Anti-Virus for Windows is currently the only product that scans all your extended memory while in Windows. It can spot viruses that the programs which stop at the 1M barrier miss. Norton also incorporates its cleaning data into the virus signature files, so you don't have to update the application itself to enable removal of newly discovered viruses.

The following section provides an overview of some of the leading anti-virus products.

AntiVirusPLUS

This product includes several features not available in the basic DOS 6 anti-virus package. It can create an emergency disk for you automatically, which includes information about your CMOS settings and partition tables, which can be a life-saver if your system really gets messed up.

The package revolves around three programs, EXAMINE, the scanning utility that looks for virus signatures; PREVENT1, which monitors for virus-type activity, and IMMUNE2, which is a VSafe equivalent that keeps viruses from loading. A fourth program, CURE, is a standalone (non-TSR) scanner. Like Microsoft Anti-Virus, checksum monitoring is available, although in a limited form.

Central Point Anti-Virus for DOS and Windows

This is the full version of the program set included with DOS 6. Upgrade to this package, and you get a sophisticated installation routine that performs the initial scan and clean cycle for you. It also does a better job of protecting from boot sector viruses by including BootSafe, a master boot record protection utility, and a hidden boot-sector file called BOOT.CPS, which can be used to restore a damaged boot record. In addition to VSafe, you also get VWatch, which performs an Anti-Virus-like scan constantly as a TSR. Both Windows and DOS versions are available.

Data Physician PLUS!

For about half the cost of most other virus programs, you get both DOS and Windows versions. It includes automated installation, scanning TSR, and integrity checks against a checksum file. You can attach a "security prefix" to executable files so that they will check themselves before the file loads. Unlike DOS 6's Anti-Virus, one TSR does both continual scanning for virus signatures and for changes in file size.

Panda Pro

This program doesn't find and cure viruses; you can use Microsoft Anti-Virus for that. What it does is lock up your system tighter than a drum so that a virus has no chance to enter. Your master boot record is rigorously protected, and you may even find it impossible to install new executable files on your system without gaining this utility's permission. That's the kind of control that network administrators will favor. Because it has no virus removal features, you should think of this product as an add-on to keep networked systems in tight rein.

Dr. Solomon's Anti-Virus Toolkit

Not easy to use, this product is one of the few that can monitor conventional, upper, extended, and expanded memory. It does a workman-like job of scanning for viruses. The chief advantage of this package is that it's available in DOS, Windows, and OS/2 versions. If your office uses a number of environments and wants to settle on one anti-virus package, this one does the job.

F-Prot Professional

This retail version of the shareware product adds master boot record protection, cyclic redundancy checks (CRC), and either command line or interactive operation. It performs scanning and integrity checking, cleaning, and deleting of infected files. There's not a lot to recommend this program over Microsoft Anti-Virus, but it is a venerable, easy-to-use offering that might make a good "second" anti-virus program to use as a double check.

IBM AntiVirus

At $29.95 this program is probably the cheapest product you can buy with a genuine IBM label. This program uses fuzzy logic techniques to spot both known viruses as well as their mutations. This is one smart program! It also identifies product updates without false alarms. The DOS and Windows versions included with the program have scheduling, a TSR that checks each file as it is loaded, and the capability to disable a virus on the fly. Its integrity checking is also smarter than most; legitimate changes to files are identified and ignored. If you like clever design and unusual features, check out this program. At this price, you can't lose.

InocuLAN/PC

If you have a Netware network, this package automates and extends virus protection to your LAN with little fuss. Its interface resembles Netware's own utilities, in fact. No checksum monitoring is available, but the two TSRs that look for virus signatures and virus-like activities do a good job of finding, fixing, and deleting viruses as they attack. One nice touch: to gain a little speed, you can tell this utility to check only the most common virus signatures rather than its whole library.

Norton AntiVirus

If any program is a worthy upgrade from Microsoft Anti-Virus, this is it. It's a full-featured anti-virus program with some capabilities found in no other package. As noted earlier, the Windows version checks all your memory for viruses, and you don't need to update the program itself to clean viruses; the signature update files contain the necessary information.

But there's a lot more. Like some other packages, Norton creates a rescue disk with CMOS, partition table, and boot-sector information. Its checksum files use a proprietary algorithm and are stored in encrypted and hidden form, making it nearly impossible for a virus to tamper with the database. The NAV TSR also guards over the checksums and blocks any attempt to change the values. Now that's protection!

Strong network support includes automatic updates of user files when they log in and special administrator options, such as the capability to force users to scan when they log into the network. Networked or not, Norton AntiVirus makes an excellent companion or replacement for DOS 6's Anti-Virus program.

NOVI

NOVI is marketed by the same Symantec organization that sells Norton AntiVirus, and there is definitely room for both products. Although NOVI can scan for viruses, its primary approach is a heavy-weight TSR that keeps close watch over any potential virus-infection route and blocks invaders in their tracks. One module performs constant checks on files; another applies locks to the EXE files to keep them from being changed;

and still another guards the boot sectors. You can block attribute changes (so read-only files stay read-only) and write protect specific files. NOVI creates a rescue disk with boot-sector, CMOS, and hidden files copied off-line.

NOVI is exceptionally strict. When it detects a boot-sector virus, it refuses to boot from your hard disk. You must use a clean floppy to start up your computer until the virus has been deleted. NOVI checks compressed files as they are extracted, too. This is a robust alternative to Microsoft Anti-Virus.

PC Rx for DOS and Windows

If you find constantly updating virus signature lists a pain, you might be interested in PC Rx . Although it uses signatures to identify virus type, it does a pretty good job without them. You must be willing to live on the edge, though. Instead of monitoring for changes in checksums or virus signatures, this utility waits until a virus has loaded itself before taking action. It works from a set of rules describing how normal files behave, and when it spots a departure from those rules, a box pops up alerting you that specific files have been invaded or are under attack. You can then reboot and scan and clean your system. Oddly enough, this system works, but won't help an EXE file that has been invaded and can't be disinfected. Keep plenty of backup copies of your software available. Although PC Rx can block virus action without knowing which specific virus is at work, you'll still want to obtain the lists from time to time to aid in disinfecting your system.

Pro-Scan

This DOS program is an offering from the famous McAfee Associates, which offers anti-virus products as a sideline to its main business of promoting John McAfee. It incorporates many of the features of the stand-alone programs VirusScan, Clean-up, and Vshield, which are available through most bulletin board systems. By wrapping a shell around these programs, the system becomes a little easier to use. You get TSR monitoring of checksum changes, but the alert doesn't sound until you attempt to load the infected file. Better late than never, but that's little consolation if your only copy of an executable file is destroyed. An alternative to this TSR is McAfee's own Vshield, which provides signature scanning. Indeed, the only advantage Pro-Scan has over the McAfee products available from BBSs is the menu shell. Check out those programs and pay for them through registration only if you find them useful and want to continue using them.

Untouchable

This DOS-based package's TSR is kind to your memory, requiring just 1K to 5K to scan for viruses and their footprints. It includes a scanner that checks for signatures and a checksum verifier that uses encrypted databases that resist modification. You get the usual rescue disk features (although the rescue disk isn't bootable unless you make it so yourself!), and the helpful capability to scan compressed files if they haven't been protected with a password. Untouchable won't prevent boot-sector modifications, although the rescue disk can repair these infections. A network version of this program is also available.

Vaccine

This program has scanning, file integrity checking, and monitoring for stealth infection techniques. Rather than repair your files, it prefers to delete them, so this program is best accompanied by a vigorous backup routine. Its collection of utilities can be accessed from a single shell program, with the exception of a utility that copies your CMOS settings to an external disk. Vaccine maintains tight control over what programs are allowed to run by letting you build an Authorized Program File. Only programs you enter into this file can run. This can be a lot of work! You're probably better off with an anti-virus program that is a little more automated.

Virex for the PC

Virex is a well-known product that includes scanning, two TSRs, and provision to store the headers of executable files along with their checksums, so you can restore programs that have been infected. The

VirexPro TSR monitors program and system activity and is quite effective at spotting viruses at work. It's also quite effective at recommending what to do when your system is attacked.

ViruSafe

The makers of XTree bring you this anti-virus program that is especially good at reconstructing damaged files. It's one DOS-based program that includes a scheduler to automatically run the virus utilities at times you select. Highly automated, ViruSafe can perform scanning and removal in one step. It can alert you with a beep if a virus is detected while you run Windows. If you use XTree, you'll be comfortable with this program and can purchase it at a sharply discounted price.

Virus Alert

Virus Alert is strict! You can force the program to scan on bootup and disable the control-break and escape keys so that there is no easy exit from the process. A utility called On-Guard can check the root directory, memory and your master boot record and lock up the computer if a virus is detected. The user is forced to boot from a floppy. This program is a logical choice for administrators who want to keep naive users of standalone workstations from bypassing virus checks.

The Next Step

The final piece of the data protection puzzle is the capability to recover deleted files. We'll look at how Microsoft's Unformat and Undelete for DOS and Windows works in the next chapter. By the end of this section, you'll have no excuse for losing a file.

Undeleting and Unformatting

It doesn't take a virus to destroy a file. User carelessness or accidents can delete files as effectively as any virus. Depending on when you discover the error, these mistakes can be difficult to recover from. DOS 6 includes a number of utilities to help protect you from these problems. This chapter will explain how to use the tools that make undeleting and unformatting possible.

Unformatting

Formatting a disk can take place on two levels. A low-level format establishes certain information, including sector size and interleave factor, and marks the disk with magnetic signals so that DOS can use it. Some kinds of intelligent disk drives, including IDE models, can't be low-level formatted by the user.

A high level format—carried out from the DOS prompt—sets up a file allocation table (FAT) that is used to assign individual sectors of the disk to specific files. Under DOS 6, there are several types of high-level format. If you use the /Q switch when formatting a disk, DOS performs a quick format, in which only the FAT and root directory of the disk are deleted. No check is made to verify sectors. This type of format works only on disks that have been previously formatted by DOS. The deleted FAT and root directory information are retained in mirror files and can thus be restored if you later change your mind.

That's not true when you use the /U (unconditional) format switch. This type of formatting destroys all the data on the disk and checks the disk for bad sectors. It's a good choice if you've been having trouble with a disk but feel it would be usable if the bad sectors were locked out. A disk can be unformatted only if it uses 512, 1024, or 2048 bytes per sector. That encompasses nearly all hard disks in use today, even with odd-ball disk manager utilities managing their partitions.

To restore a formatted disk, you must use the **unformat** command. The complete syntax for this command is as follows:

```
UNFORMAT drive: [/J]
UNFORMAT drive: [/TEST]
UNFORMAT drive: [/U] [/L] [/P]
UNFORMAT /PARTN [/L]
```

For *drive:*, substitute the drive letter of the disk you want to unformat. The /J switch checks to see whether the mirror files agree with the system information on the disk. The /TEST switch can be used to check to see whether a disk can be unformatted. The /L switch displays the names of files and directories found or, when used with the /PARTN switch, the current partition tables.

The /U switch attempts to unformat a disk without using mirror files. You can try this if mirror files were not recorded for a disk for some reason (e.g., it was formatted prior to DOS 5.0). The /P switch directs output to the printer connected to LPT1, so you can have a permanent record of the process.

The /PARTN switch can restore a hard disk's partition table from a file stored on another disk. You can create this file by using the **mirror /partn** command. You'll be prompted for a destination for the file.

Sometimes, **unformat** cannot recover a file because it cannot locate all the pieces of the file. When that happens, you'll be offered the choice of truncating the file or deleting it completely.

Undeleting a File

Peter Norton was working as a programmer for a large firm when he became one of the very first people to accidentally delete an important file on an IBM PC. However, Norton did a lot more than just tear out his hair. He dug around in the operating system until he discovered that deleted files aren't really removed; only the first character of their entry in the file allocation table is overwritten. The utility he wrote to recover deleted files was one of the first, and most successful, DOS utilities ever created.

Today, file undeleting has gotten a lot more sophisticated. DOS 6 provides three levels of protection, and two undelete programs (one each for DOS and Windows). If you configure your system properly, it can be very, very difficult to lose a file accidentally.

One way to lose a file is to delete a subdirectory. Undelete for DOS can't resurrect subdirectories, nor can it undelete files that are contained in deleted subdirectories. Please keep that in mind before deleting any subdirectories on your disk. Undelete for Windows may be able to retrieve files from deleted directories, if you first restore the directory.

DOS's three levels of protection are called Standard protection, Delete Sentry, and Delete Tracker. Your system was configured for Standard protection when you installed DOS 6. You can opt for one of the other two levels at any time. Here is a brief description of each level.

Standard Protection

This is the basic level of protection that has been available since DOS was introduced. It operates on the principle that DOS doesn't really erase files—it only modifies their FAT entries. All recent versions of DOS reuse sectors on an "oldest first" scheme, so a file you have deleted won't be overwritten until DOS uses up its allocation of older sectors first. That may not take much time, so it's important to act quickly.

Standard protection does not require any special action on your part, nor the use of any TSR program. To undelete files, use the **undelete** command, which has the following syntax in Standard mode:

```
UNDELETE  [drive: [/LIST] [/ALL] [/S]
```

For *drive:,* substitute the drive letter of the drive containing the files you want to undelete. The other switches have these meanings:

➤ **/LIST** lists all the files available for undeletion, but does not undelete them.

➤ **/ALL** undeletes all possible files. You'll be prompted to enter a first character for each eligible file.

➤ **/S** displays the level of deletion protection for each drive in your system.

Delete Tracker

The next level of protection is offered by Delete Tracker. When this level is activated, each time you delete a file, its location is stored in a hidden file named PCTRACKER.DEL. Delete Tracker uses a TSR that requires 13.5K of RAM, plus a tiny amount of space on your hard disk for the tracking file.

To activate Delete Tracker, use the following syntax:

```
UNDELETE /Tdrive[-entries]
```

For *drive,* substitute the drive letter of the hard disk you want to protect with Delete Tracker. You can optionally provide a value for entries, if you feel you need more than the defaults, which range from 25 entries/ 5K of disk space for a 360K floppy to 303 entries/55K for 32M and larger hard disks. To recover files deleted when Delete Tracker is active, use the **undelete** command followed by the /ALL switch (for all files) or /DT (to recover only files listed in the deletion tracking file created by Delete Tracker). As always, you'll be prompted for the first character of the filename before each file is restored.

Delete Sentry

The highest level of protection is afforded by Delete Sentry. This TSR (also requiring 13.5K) creates an entire hidden subdirectory called SENTRY. When you delete the file, the entire file is relocated into the SENTRY subdirectory and its location kept in the FAT. In effect, you haven't really deleted the file; you've just moved it out of sight. The file still takes up as much space as it did on your hard disk. This is obviously a very safe method.

If left unchecked, Delete Sentry would quickly fill up your hard disk with deleted files. That doesn't happen. Instead, after roughly seven percent of your hard disk is filled by files in SENTRY, the utility begins replacing older files with newer ones. This value can be changed to a higher number with the UNDELETE.INI configuration file described in the next section.

On a 120M hard disk, the amount of space allocated for Delete Sentry is only about 8M. If you work with many large files (such as image files that amount to a megabyte or more each), you can find your older files cycling in and out of SENTRY very quickly, perhaps in only a few hours. So, don't depend on this undelete method too heavily.

To activate Delete Sentry, enter the following:

```
UNDELETE /S[drive]
```

When you specify *drive*, Delete Sentry activates protection for that drive. Otherwise, the utility protects only drives previously activated and listed in UNDELETE.INI.

To undelete files protected with Delete Sentry, use the /ALL switch (for all files) or the following syntax:

```
UNDELETE /DS
```

UNDELETE.INI

This is a file that defines values used by undelete. The default values are as follows:

➤ Use Delete Sentry.

➤ Save all files except those with TMP, VM?, WOA, SWP, SPL, RMG, IMG, THM, and DOV extensions.

➤ Don't save files which have been backed up.

➤ Purge files older than seven days.

➤ Restrict SENTRY subdirectory to 20 percent of total disk space.

This file is usually stored in your DOS subdirectory and looks something like the one following:

```
[configuration]
archive=FALSE
days=7
percentage=20
[sentry.drives]
C=
D=
E=
F=
[mirror.drives]
C=
D=
E=
F=
[sentry.files]
sentry.files=*.* -*.TMP -*.VM? -*.WOA -*.SWP -*.SPL -
*.RMG -*.IMG -*.THM -*.DOV
[defaults]
d.sentry=TRUE
d.tracker=FALSE
```

Under [configuration], the flag that determines whether archived files are to be protected is listed. Change this to TRUE if you want to include these files in your SENTRY subdirectory on each hard disk. You can also expand the number of days to more than the default seven if you feel that additional time would be useful or to a lower number if you don't need deleted files hanging around that long. The default percentage of 20 percent of your hard disk space might be a little high if you are cramped for space. The storage may be better applied to a swapfile for Windows or another use.

The [sentry.drives] section lists the letters of each drive protected by Disk Sentry. You can add or delete drive letters manually if you want to expand or restrict protection. Just type each drive letter on its own line, followed by an equal sign.

The [mirror.drives] section lists the letters of drives protected by Disk Tracker when active. You may edit this section if you like.

The [sentry.files] section lists the file specifications that will or will not be protected. Filespecs preceded by a minus sign will be excluded from protection. Others will be included. The default spec for inclusion is *.* (all files), and the files that are excluded are shown in the preceding example. You can add others if you like. Perhaps you don't want to save ZIP files, or any file meeting a $*.* or ~*.* specification.

The [defaults] section shows the type of file tracking in use. Both Delete Sentry and Delete Tracker methods are shown, followed by True or False, as appropriate. If you change this entry, the new protection level doesn't take effect until the next time you load DOS.

Other Undelete Switches

/DOS recovers only files listed as deleted by DOS; does not include any protected by Delete Sentry or Delete Tracker.

/PURGE [*drive:*] removes all files from the SENTRY directory for the specified drive. If no drive is entered, the current drive is used.

/STATUS shows the type of protection activated for each drive.

/LOAD loads whichever Undelete TSR is specified in UNDELETE.INI.

/UNLOAD unloads the TSR from memory.

Note, you shouldn't try to load or unload UNDELETE from Windows.

Using Undelete for Windows

Windows users can access a special version of Undelete, with an easy-to-use interface, shown in figure 25.1. The main window includes an array of six buttons, plus a pane that shows all the files available for retrieval on the currently logged drive.

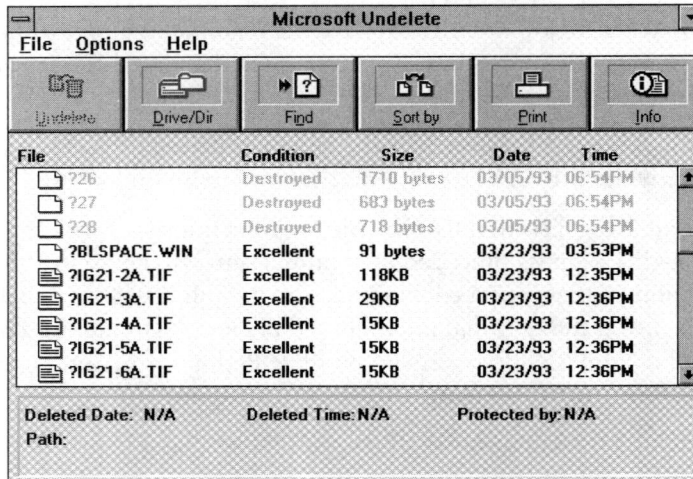

Figure 25.1. Undelete for Windows.

To configure this utility, first load Undelete for Windows and choose Undelete from the File menu. That activates deletion protection, using the mode specified in UNDELETE.INI. To change this level, select Options and Configure Delete Protection. You'll see a dialog box like that shown in figure 25.2. You can check off any of the three levels discussed earlier. When you choose one, a dialog box will appear to let you choose the drives or other options available for that level. The dialog box for Delete Tracker is shown in figure 25.3, and the Delete Sentry dialogs are shown in figure 25.4. The former includes a drive window that can be used to specify individual drives. The latter requires clicking a separate Drives... button to choose individual drives.

To recover a file, access the drive window for the disk drive that contained the file you want to recover. You can change drives by clicking on the Drive/Dir button, pressing Alt-D, or choosing Change Drive/Directory from the File menu.

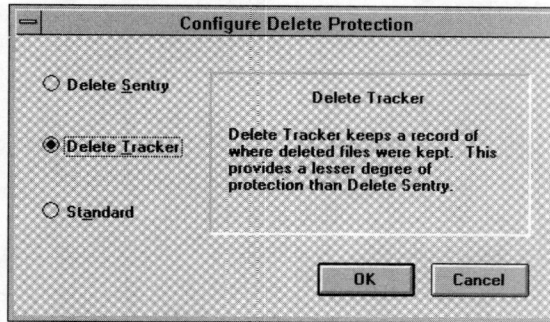

Figure 25.2. Configure Delete Protection.

The files displayed in the pane will be shown grayed out or in black characters, along with their filename (minus the first character), size, date, time, and condition. The condition will be listed as either destroyed (unavailable for recovery), poor (it's unlikely that the entire file can be recovered; at least some of its sectors have been used by other files), good (all or nearly all of the file can be recovered), excellent or perfect (100 percent of the file can be retrieved).

Files listed as Destroyed cannot be recovered, because all of their known clusters have been overwritten. It is remotely possible that a few clusters can still be located using the DOS version of Undelete. If the file is very important, it's worth a try, I suppose.

Files in Poor condition may be partially recoverably by Undelete for DOS. It is likely that the file's first cluster, and probably others, have been reassigned to other files. To regain Poor files, exit Windows and run the DOS version of the program. If the files contained ASCII data, you may be able to reuse the part of the file you resurrect. It's highly unlikely that a program file that can't be completely recovered will be of any use to you.

Files in Good condition may be fragmented and partially overwritten (this is another reason to keep your disk optimized at all times; deleted

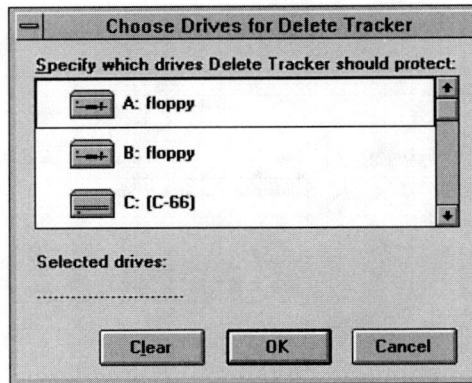

Figure 25.3. Delete Tracker.

files are then likely to reside in contiguous sectors). However, in general, all the file's clusters will be available. This condition is often reported for files not protected by Delete Tracker or Delete Sentry.

Files in Excellent condition are unfragmented and all the clusters are available, but there is a chance that some data has been overwritten. Files protected by Delete Tracker are likely to be in this condition.

Files in Perfect condition can usually be recovered with no lost data. They have been protected by Delete Sentry, and all clusters are available.

The File Info menu and for File buttons provide complete information about each file, including the location of the first cluster.

You can specify a sort order for the files, using date, time, extension, time or date deleted, or condition. It's usually most convenient to sort files by condition, as all the perfect and good files are shown at the top of the list. These are likely to be the ones you want to work with in any case.

You may also click on the Find button to search for filenames by specifications you type.

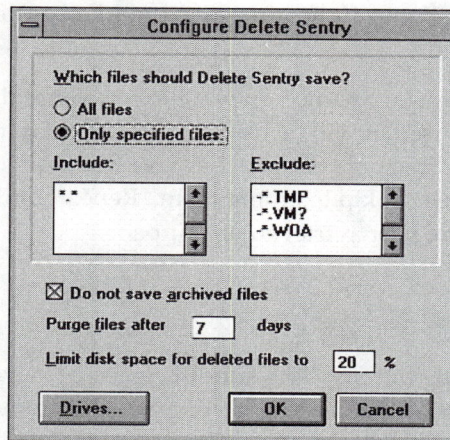

Figure 25.4. Delete Sentry.

Select files by clicking on them with the mouse. If you want to choose a large group of files, you can also choose them by filename specification. For example, if you accidentally deleted a group of 40 TIF files, you can enter *.TIF to choose all of them at one time. Or, you might want to select all deleted files except those meeting a given file specification, such as *.ZIP. You can do that, too.

Recover the selected files by clicking on the Undelete icon or choosing Undelete To... from the file menu (to specify a different drive and directory for the file). You may enter a file name to save the retrieved file to, or Undelete will use its stored information about the file to add the missing first character.

Recovering a Subdirectory

You can restore a deleted subdirectory with Undelete for Windows. Just use the Drive/Dir button to change to the drive containing the deleted subdirectory. Directories are marked as <DIR>. If Undelete can locate the parts of the directory file, it will be marked with one of the recoverable conditions. If the directory is marked as destroyed, you won't be able to recover it.

Highlight the directory name you want to recover and click on Undelete. If it can be recovered, it will be listed as Recovered in the Undelete window. If the directory contains files you want to retrieve, click on the Add button or select Skip to ignore them. Repeat until all the files in the subdirectory have been retrieved or skipped.

Purging Deleted Files

You can clean up your SENTRY subdirectories by purging files that have been saved but which you are positive are no longer needed. Select the drive and directory containing the files with the Drive/Dir button and choose the directory. In the Undelete screen, mark the files to be purged and then activate Purge Delete File Sentry File from the File menu. The selected files will be permanently removed from the Undelete screen.

The Next Step

Undeleting and Unformatting disk files is the final piece of the data protection puzzle. You've learned how to use every DOS 6 tool for data safeguarding and recovery. There are some additional third-party tools you can use, which will be discussed in Chapter 30. The final two sections of this book will look at other DOS 6 utilities available, as well as additional utilities you may want to add to your toolkit.

Part VI: System Startup Utilities

The boot-up process is incredibly important, because that's when your operating system literally assembles itself into the DOS configuration you'll use for the rest of your working session. The drivers needed to operate your hardware load; memory is allocated; and key programs you'll use find themselves niches in RAM. Configured improperly, your system may be crippled. Set up just so—and your computer operates much more efficiently and effectively.

This next section will examine the role of CONFIG.SYS and AUTOEXEC.BAT, and show you how new features of DOS 6 can help you customize your startup configuration. You'll learn how to use the Clean Start feature, multiconfigurations, and interactive startup options. These can all work together to tailor your system to work better.

What Is CONFIG.SYS?

It's easy to forget about the changes Microsoft has made that affect your startup files like CONFIG.SYS file, with all the attention given to DoubleSpace and some of the other all-new utilities. However, you should stop to consider just how essential and central to your computer's operation CONFIG.SYS is.

CONFIG.SYS is the list of instructions DOS uses to build itself at boot-up time. The ways in which you can structure those instructions haven't just been spiffed up, they've been completely made-over and turned into a limited-function programming environment of their own.

No Programming Required

That's not to say that you need to learn how to program to customize DOS with CONFIG.SYS. However, some powerful new features have been added that give you unprecedented flexibility in how you configure your operating system. This chapter will explain what CONFIG.SYS is and how to use each of its features, both old and new.

You've already had some exposure to CONFIG.SYS in earlier chapters; that was unavoidable. If you found some of the discussions puzzling, this chapter and the next one should clear up the mystery. If you're an old hand, prepare to be impressed with the capabilities Microsoft has grafted onto an old friend (or enemy, as the case may be.)

What Is CONFIG.SYS?

In the IBM world, the operating system is at the same time one of the most flexible and least flexible pieces of software we use. That's because DOS deals with our computer hardware on a most basic and intimate level. It needs to be very flexible in order to carry out requests for services that may involve sending information to many different types of printers, using display screens and other output devices, and receiving data from sources as different as scanners (which send streams of bits used to represent images) and keyboards (which transmit codes representing key combinations).

This flexibility wasn't always built into DOS. The first MS-DOS 1.0 and 1.1 and some earlier operating systems could deal only with a limited set of devices, which had to be accounted for at the time the program was written. There was no way to add a new type of printer, or CRT, or other device without releasing a new version of DOS.

DOS 2.0 Added CONFIG.SYS

DOS 2.0 was introduced when the first hard disks became available for PCs and debuted the concept of *installable device drivers*. Simply put, these drivers are special modules that tell DOS how to handle particular types of devices. When the operating system boots, it actually builds a custom version of itself out of the building blocks you specify in a listing called CONFIG.SYS. These blocks are carefully stacked one on top of another during the loading process in a way that does not allow them to be moved, changed, added, or subtracted later during that session.

So, although we have a great deal of flexibility in how we tell DOS to build or configure itself at boot time, we have no leeway thereafter. Once erected, our DOS structure becomes extremely inflexible. If you decide you want to use a different device or want to use it in a way that is not allowed using the parameters you originally specified, your only option is to start DOS over from scratch with a new set of configuration instructions. Some drivers can be added after DOS loads, but you are severely limited in the ways you can do this.

This is a weak link in DOS, but one we have to live with for the time being. DOS makes the situation a lot more livable by providing new and more convenient ways of specifying what configuration we want to use at boot-up time. It does this in several ways.

Ability To Query User at Boot Up

Your CONFIG.SYS file in DOS can contain queries that ask you whether you want to use a particular facility during this session. Thus, just by adding a few question marks to configuration directives, a single CONFIG.SYS file can serve multiple purposes.

Multiple Blocks in CONFIG.SYS

You can separate groups of commands into blocks and choose which sets you want executed from a startup menu.

Files Can Include Comments

CONFIG.SYS files can contain comments, which explain what various functions do, what parameters they expect, and how to modify them. That can help when it is time to use a different configuration. You can also use this capability to "comment out" lines that you want to disable (without being queried each time) but which you don't want to remove entirely.

Bypass Startup Files

By pressing F8, you can bypass CONFIG.SYS and AUTOEXEC.BAT completely. This is useful for times when you want a plain vanilla version of DOS 6 to test software or to debug an errant startup file.

CONFIG.SYS Directives

The easiest way to jump right into discussing how CONFIG.SYS can help you is to explain how each feature works. The CONFIG.SYS commands, or directives, can be broken down into four categories: those that affect operation of your disk drives and other storage media; those that control the various features of your system itself; those that manage installation of device drivers and programs that can be installed from CONFIG.SYS; and a new category, directives that can be used to control and structure how CONFIG.SYS carries out the other commands in the file. Most of the commands in the first two categories are not new. The others, however, can take some getting used to.

Disk Operation Controls

The following commands and programs are used to tailor the performance of your hard disk drives or floppies or to add them to your system. Device drivers, installed through the DEVICE= directive, also can have some effect on your storage hardware.

BUFFERS

BUFFERS are like a dumb disk cache. We already discussed the differences between disk buffers and caches earlier in this book. DOS assigns 15 buffers if you don't include a BUFFERS line in CONFIG.SYS. You can reduce these to as few as three, for example, if you have a cache installed, or as many as 99 if you're really careless. (Too many buffers can reduce performance as DOS spends more time looking through the buffers than it would save by not reading the information from disk.)

FASTOPEN

You can think of FASTOPEN, which is loaded through the INSTALL directive, as a kind of disk buffer for file names. DOS keeps a list of file names and paths in this buffer as you access programs and data files during a session. Then, if you need to use the same file again, DOS does not have to hunt along the subdirectories named in your PATH statement to find it. If you don't think that can save some time, think about how DOS searches for files.

When you enter a command at the DOS prompt, the operating system looks at the string of words you've typed and breaks it up, or parses it, into individual components. At first, it concerns itself only with the first word on the line. Is that word an internal DOS command? If so, the rest of the line is passed on to that command as arguments, and DOS attempts to carry out the command.

It will next look to see whether there is an executable file ending in COM, EXE, or BAT (in that order) in the current directory and try to execute the line. If not, DOS will then look for executable files in each of the subdirectories named in your PATH statement. You probably have a PATH command in your AUTOEXEC.BAT file, which looks something like this:

```
PATH=C:\DOS;C:\UTILS;C:\SYS;D:\WINDOWS
```

A longer path (it can be up to 123 characters long) will give DOS more optional places to look but can greatly increase the amount of time you wait before the command or program is executed—or, in the worst case, the file is not found, and you see a BAD COMMAND OR FILE NAME error message on the screen. DOS, after all, stores subdirectory listings in files of their own, so if one of the subdirectories on your path was C:\WINDOWS\OMNIPAGE, DOS would open the file that represents the C:\WINDOWS subdirectory, hunt through it for a subdirectory name OMNIPAGE, and then close that file and open the OMNIPAGE subdirectory file looking for the command you typed—even if you happened to enter a typo rather than a real command. Think about that the next time you're tempted to add yet another subdirectory to your path.

FASTOPEN creates a table of filenames in memory, and DOS can check this table first when it goes to open a file. If the filename is present, it can directly open the file and not have to hunt through your entire path. You can specify as few as 128 filenames, or as many as 32,768. The table is built anew each time you reboot your computer, so it's unlikely you would ever access enough files in a given session to require 32,768 entries. Setting aside memory for many more entries than you need won't improve performance. Each entry also uses up 2 bytes of memory, so you wouldn't want to dedicate 64K just for the FASTOPEN buffer.

That's a lot less than the memory required by MS-DOS for its FASTOPEN entries, which each require 48 bytes. The default value is 512 (using up 1K of RAM), but you can specify fewer if you want. The syntax for this directive is

```
FASTOPEN = nnnn
```

where *nnnn* is a number between 128 and 32,768.

LASTDRIVE

This directive enables DOS to recognize additional disk drive letters that aren't assigned to physical or logical drives when your computer boots. Ordinarily, the operating system recognizes your floppy and hard disk drives and assigns drive letters to them. A and B belong to the first two floppy disks (if you have only one such drive, A and B will apply to that one alone). Your first hard disk will be assigned C, with each physical or logical drive after that one given the letters D, E, and so forth. Any RAM disks you create using RAMDISK.SYS or a similar program will be assigned the letters immediately following those given to your hard disks.

If you try to use any other drive letters, DOS will report Invalid drive specified. That's a convenience to you, since you won't waste a lot of time trying to access disk drives that don't exist. However, you won't be able to create new logical drives, using commands like SUBST (which assigns a drive letter to a subdirectory name) beyond the valid drive letters DOS recognizes. LASTDRIVE lets you tell the operating system the letter of the last drive you intend to use, so it will make room in its list of valid drives to include additional devices added after the system has booted. The syntax for this directive is

```
LASTDRIVE = driveletter
```

where *driveletter* is a letter from C to Z.

DRIVPARM

The DRIVPARM directive lets you define the physical characteristics for a disk drive that DOS already knows about. It's useful for integrating drives in computers that were designed before that drive type was developed. So, you can use DRIVPARM to tell an 8088-based system that a given 3.5-inch disk drive is a 1.44M unit with 80 tracks. There are seven different parameters you can enter; check your DOS documentation for more information on using this command.

CONFIG.SYS System Controls

These directives set up certain system parameters that are shared by all the software that you use.

BREAK

This command governs when DOS will look to the keyboard to see whether you've pressed Ctrl-Break or Ctrl-C to stop the running program. It does not disable either of these two key sequences; it only changes the way in which DOS checks for them.

When you have this line in your CONFIG.SYS file

```
BREAK = OFF
```

DOS will only stop the program when it reads from the keyboard, writes to the screen, or sends output to the printer. The other option

```
BREAK = ON
```

will tell DOS to look for Ctrl-Break and Ctrl-C each time the program reads from and writes to your hard disk or floppy. This setting will let you break into programs that don't use the keyboard, CRT screen, or printer for long periods of time. For example, you may have a word processing program that performs its global searches and replaces without displaying any progress reports on the screen. You would have no way of stopping the program after it started a long search/replace if BREAK was off.

Many programs disable BREAK entirely so that you must use the method provided by the application (often the ESC key) to interrupt a process. That's often necessary because it's possible to damage files if you stop a program at the wrong place.

COUNTRY

This directive tells DOS how to format date and time information, which currency symbol is in use in your particular country, and which code page should be used to provide the correct characters and symbols used in your country's language. If you live in the United States, you'll probably never have to change this setting. If you work in Europe, Canada, or other places where accommodating a second or third language is a more common part of life, you might have to use this command.

The syntax is as follows:

```
COUNTRY=xxx,yyy,filename
```

You would replace *xxx* with the country code for the time and date format you want to have as the default. The actual code for some countries is, seemingly, related in some way to the international area code used for direct telephone dialing.

You can also specify *yyy*, which is the code page of the character set you want to use, and *filename*, which contains other country data. You can find a list of code pages in your DOS manual. These are organized by language rather than country, so French-speaking Canadians and French computer users would both select the same code page.

DOS

This directive, discussed earlier in the book, is used to tell DOS to load itself high and make upper memory blocks available.

FILES

This directive controls how many files can be opened at the same time by all your programs. The default value is 20, but the installation programs for some applications demand a much greater number, up to 60 or more. Each extra file handle allowed consumes about 64 bytes of memory, so it's best not to have more than you really need. DOS will let you specify from 20 to 255. The syntax is as follows:

```
FILES=nnn
```

FCBS

Some older software uses File Control Blocks (FCBs) rather than the file handles specified with the FILES command. Your documentation will specifically mention that you need an FCBS entry and will tell you how many of these blocks to allow. The syntax for this directive is as follows:

```
FCBS=n1, n2
```

The value specified for *n1* can range from 1 to 255 and represents the number of FCBs that can open at the same time. The value for *n2* indicates how many FCBs cannot be automatically closed to accommodate an application that attempts to use more than the number specified in *n1*.

NUMLOCK

This command specifies whether the numeric keypad is on or off when your computer first boots.

SET

SET is the directive used to place variables into the DOS environment. Prior to the latest version of DOS, the average user could only do this from the DOS command line or a batch file. Now you can set variables you need from CONFIG.SYS. This ensures that all copies of COMMAND.COM loaded after CONFIG.SYS will include the environment variable you specify. Moreover, because users can't abort CONFIG.SYS (unless you write it in such a way that you give them the option), this method eliminates problems that can occur if the user happens to abort AUTOEXEC.BAT with Ctrl-C, or something else happens that keeps the variables from loading properly.

Many programs use an environment variable to determine where they should look for their own program files or to determine what subdirectory will be used for temporary files. Calera's WordScan and QMS's UltraScript are examples of the former type of software.

SHELL

This directive will start the DOS command processor, COMMAND.COM, or another one of your choice (such as 4DOS.COM). You can also use this command to specify a directory other than the root directory for COMMAND.COM. You may also use it to set the size of the DOS environment (we'll look at the environment topic a little later).

The syntax for SHELL is as follows:

```
SHELL = filename [/E:nnnnn] [/P[:filename]] [/R]
```

You would substitute for *filename* the name and subdirectory path for the command processor, usually COMMAND.COM. The optional /E switch can include *nnnnn*, which represents the size of the environment in bytes. Values range from 512 bytes (the minimum, and considerably more than the 160 bytes used by MS-DOS) to 32,751 bytes. If you enter an incorrect value, an environment of 512 bytes will be used.

/P Switch Makes Permanent

The non-optional /P switch makes the command processor permanent and tells DOS to execute AUTOEXEC.BAT when CONFIG.SYS is finished. If you don't use /P, you'll be able to remove the command processor from memory at the DOS prompt by typing EXIT. That's a good way of locking up your system. If you want to use a file other than AUTOEXEC.BAT, you can enter a different file name following the /P switch.

The optional /R switch tells DOS to attempt to load COMMAND.COM into high or upper memory, instead of conventional memory, if there is room. You must have a memory manager like EMM386.EXE or HIMEM.SYS loaded before attempting this, however.

Many people get the SHELL command confused with the DOS COMMAND command and the environment variable COMSPEC. The following section contains a quick description of the difference.

COMSPEC Is Environment Variable

COMSPEC is a variable that tells DOS the name and subdirectory location of the current command processor. That command processor will be used whenever you load a new copy of COMMAND.COM. (This is done whenever you use the DOS prompt from within a program that is already running.) For example, your word processor may allow you to "shell out" to DOS to perform some DOS function, or Windows may load another copy of COMMAND.COM to provide a DOS prompt while Windows is still running.

The SHELL directive sets COMSPEC to equal the command processor you specified when CONFIG.SYS is run. You can change the value of COMSPEC from the DOS prompt, a batch file, or even with a SET statement in CONFIG.SYS that follows the SHELL directive. You would enter the change this way:

```
COMSPEC=filename
```

Substitute for *filename* the name of the alternate command processor you want to use. When would you do this? Perhaps you want COMMAND.COM as your primary command processor but would like to use 4DOS or NDOS as secondary processors to be loaded by Windows or another program. Changing COMSPEC will let you have this flexibility.

The COMMAND Command

The command that loads any additional copies of the command processor is called the COMMAND command (if that isn't confusing enough, as it is). You can exit from the new processor by typing EXIT. A simple way to see that you have indeed loaded a new command processor is through the use of the SET command. From the DOS prompt type this line:

```
SET PROCESSOR=This is the first version
```

Then type SET again with no arguments. You'll see a list of your current environment variables (including COMSPEC) and one like this:

```
PROCESSOR=This is the first version
```

Now type COMMAND. A new copy of COMMAND.COM will be loaded. Type SET and you'll see that your PROCESSOR variable is still there. Change it by typing:

```
SET PROCESSOR=This is the second version
```

Type SET again to confirm that the variable has been changed in your environment. Now type EXIT and type SET one last time. The PROCESSOR variable will again say `This is the first version`.

COMMAND's Parameters

COMMAND has some parameters of its own. The /P switch will make the new version permanent, so you can't exit by typing EXIT. /E:*nnnn* will set the size of the environment in the new version, and the /C command will tell the new command processor to carry out a command, or run a program, and then EXIT automatically. Prior to the introduction of the CALL command, this last switch was the only way to get a batch file to run another batch file and then to return to the original for additional processing.

STACKS

This command sets aside memory for processing hardware interrupts. Each time DOS receives a hardware interrupt request, it allocates one stack from the available number. Some computers operate correctly even if you don't specify a particular number of stacks with this command; others become unstable and require a particular allocation (you'll see a `Stack Overflow` or `Exception error 12` message when this happens). You can enter the number of stacks and the size of each stack. The default values for non-8088 systems are 9 and 128.

SWITCHES

This directive specifies certain special options for DOS. The four allowable switches are as follows:

➤ **/W** Tells DOS that the WINA20.386 file, used only by Windows 3.0, has been moved to a directory other than the root directory.

➤ **/K** Forces an enhanced keyboard to behave like a conventional keyboard.

➤ **/N** Prevents you from using the F5 or F8 key to bypass startup commands. Use this switch if you want to make sure that a user (or intruder) doesn't skip your carefully crafted configuration.

➤ **/F** Skips the two-second delay after displaying the `Starting MS-DOS ...` message during startup. You won't have that built-in pause to press the F5 or F8 keys anymore, but DOS will boot faster.

Device Driver and TSR Controls

This section describes the various device drivers and directives available under DOS.

INSTALL

INSTALL is a command that can be used to load TSRs, which can also be loaded outside of CONFIG.SYS from the DOS command prompt. Placing them in your configuration file is a good way of ensuring that anyone using a given computer won't accidentally or intentionally abort the loading process. If you are installing a system for someone else, this provides extra security. After a TSR has been loaded, it can't be removed without rebooting. You can use DOS's security features to password protect CONFIG.SYS so that no one can change it or replace it to bypass your selection of TSRs.

DEVICE and DEVICEHIGH

The DEVICE and DEVICEHIGH directives allow you to install specific files called *drivers*, which enable your system to use a wide variety of peripherals. You may use Ontrack Disk Manager to partition your hard disk (although DOS reduces the need for this add-on with its own support for large volumes) and will want to load DMDRVR.BIN as one of the very first statements in your CONFIG.SYS file. Your mouse may use a MOUSE.SYS driver, while your hand scanner, RAM disk, or removable storage media drive call for drivers of their own. A "maxed out" computer system may require seven or eight DEVICE or DEVICEHIGH statements in its CONFIG.SYS file.

As you learned earlier, DEVICEHIGH is another version of the DEVICE command, with the added capability of loading device drivers into upper memory blocks if they are available. That's basically the only difference between them.

Most Devices Furnished with Own Drivers

Many of the device drivers you use will be supplied by the vendors of the hardware you've installed in your computer. You'll need to follow the instructions furnished with the device to determine exactly what syntax should be used with a given driver. You'll also want to experiment to see whether the device works properly when loaded high into UMBs.

10 Drivers with DOS

DOS also provides 10 device drivers of its own. Four of them, DBLSPACE.SYS, SMARTDRV.EXE, EMM386.EXE, and HIMEM.SYS, were introduced in earlier chapters and won't be discussed further in this section.

Two more, DISPLAY.SYS and EGA.SYS, are rarely used by most of us. They enable code page switching on EGA and VGA displays and provide a means to save and restore the display when an EGA monitor is used with DOSSHELL or Windows, respectively. After you've set up your system for the correct code page (if you are using a character set other than the default provided for your country with DOS) or EGA operation with the DOS Shell or Windows, you generally can forget about these drivers.

RAMDRIVE.SYS

RAMDRIVE.SYS allows you to specify some of your memory to act as if it were a disk drive. Because memory is so much faster than real disk drives, a virtual RAM disk will operate very quickly. However, the information contained in a RAMDRIVE will disappear when the computer is turned off. Therefore, RAM disks are best used for temporary files, as disks used as virtual memory by programs that can use a disk drive in place of RAM when it runs out of conventional memory (obviously, you're better off if the program can use expanded or extended memory directly rather than through a RAM disk). You can also copy program files to a RAM disk, because these don't change during a session. Any data that you risk storing on a RAM disk should be copied back to permanent media without fail. That's hard to manage, particularly when you may experience a power outage at an unexpected time.

The syntax for RAMDRIVE.SYS is as follows:

```
DEVICE=C:\DOS\RAMDRIVE.SYS [size] [sectorsize] [files]
[/E:sectors] [/X]
```

You would substitute the name of the actual directory where RAMDRIVE.SYS is stored. For size, fill in the size of the RAM disk you would like to create, in the range 1K to 256K if you are using conventional memory. The default is 64K. Even the maximum value is not a significant amount in many cases, until you consider that it is coming out of your precious lower 640K.

Will Use Expanded Memory

If you add the /X switch, RAMDRIVE.SYS will use expanded memory instead, in which case you can specify a size of up to 32M. The *sectorsize* parameter allows you to enter the smallest amount of space reserved on the RAM disk for files. The default is 128 bytes, but you can also use values of 256 or 512 bytes.

Smaller Sectors Efficient for Small Files

Smaller sectors use the RAM disk space more efficiently, particularly with small files. If you don't have expanded memory and are setting up a RAM disk in conventional memory, you'll appreciate this capability. For example, a 32K RAM disk with 512 byte sectors could store only 64 very small files (such as batch files, which run well from a RAM disk) but could handle 250 of them using a 128-byte sector size.

As your RAM disk and the size of the files you store on it grow, the importance of specifying a small sector size decreases. DOS is able to read larger sectors more quickly, so the 512 byte option would improve performance slightly if you are storing large files.

Maxfiles Sets Aside Directories

The *maxfiles* parameter determines how much of your RAM disk will be set aside to hold directory entries. The default is 64 directory entries, but you can specify from 2 to 512. You might want fewer enteries if you know your RAM disk won't be used for many files and if you want to free up some space. You may want a larger number of enteries to accommodate a very large number of files.

The /E:*sectors* switch can be used to load the RAM disk into extended memory. The sectors parameters tell DOS how many sectors, from 1 to 8, should be transferred from the RAM disk to conventional memory at one time. The default value is 8. You might want to specify a lower number if your RAM disk is being used for very small files of less than 8 sectors (3,584 bytes to 796 bytes, depending on the sector size you are using), which can be read in smaller bytes. The performance gains here are likely to be microscopic, so you'll rarely need to specify anything less than 8 sectors.

ANSI.SYS

ANSI.SYS replaces the default screen and keyboard drivers built into your operating system and your computer's BIOS. What ANSI.SYS does is intercept characters received from the keyboard. It either passes them on to DOS unchanged or supplies new, redefined characters or strings of characters.

ANSI.SYS also allows control of the display, including the colors shown on the screen, the position of the cursor, and the characters used to supply the system prompt itself. To activate ANSI.SYS, include this line in your CONFIG.SYS file:

```
DEVICE=C:\DOS\ANSI.SYS
```

When ANSI.SYS is loaded, you can send it escape sequences from your keyboard or a batch file. Frequent applications include redefining the system prompt so that it includes the time, date, current disk and subdirectory, or other information. You can also change screen display modes and redefine your keys. Most previous DOS "supercharging" or "customizing" books, including my own, have had extensive discussions of how to perform these tasks. At this point, I feel the topic has been done to death, and I won't waste your time rehashing techniques that have been covered elsewhere repeatedly.

DRIVER.SYS

DRIVER.SYS isn't used as frequently as it might be. It will enable you to connect an external diskette drive or to assign a second drive letter to a current disk. The latter capability is one that has some broad applications for some users. The syntax for the directive is as follows:

```
DEVICE=DRIVER.SYS /D:ddd /T:ttt /S:ss /H:hh /C /N /F:f
```

The /D:*ddd* parameter allows you to enter the drive number of the drive being affected by DRIVER.SYS. Although it may seem confusing, diskette drives are numbered 0 to 127, and hard disks are numbered 128 to 255 by the system. Of course, no one would have so many drives. Your A drive would be drive 0, your B drive would be drive 1. Any external floppy disk drives would be numbered drive 2, drive 3, and so on. The first hard disk, usually C, is numbered 128, and so forth.

The /T:*ttt* switch indicates the number of tracks per side for the disk. Replace *ttt* with the number of tracks; the default value is 80. The /S:*sss* switch indicates the number of sectors per track, from 1 to 99. Default is 9 sectors per track.

The /H:*hhh* switch allows you to enter the number of read/write heads in the disk drive. The default value is 2. The /C switch specifies support for the diskette changeline, and /N specifies a nonremovable disk (like a hard disk).

Form Factor of the Drive

The final switch is the /F:*f* parameter. The *f* following the color should be a number that indicates the form factor or type of drive. You can choose from 0 for a single- or double-sided 160/180/320/360K, 5.25-inch drive; 1 for 1.2M 5.25-inch drives; 2 for 3.5-inch drives.

If you have an external floppy drive, you might need to use DRIVER.SYS to tell your system about it. However, the driver can also be used to assign two drive letters to a single floppy. Suppose that you frequently format 720K disks in your 1.44M drive A. You could create a new logical floppy drive with 720K characteristics by including this line in your CONFIG.SYS file:

```
DEVICE=DRIVER.SYS /D:0 /T:80 /S:9 /H:2 /F:2
```

The basic difference between 1.44M and 720K drives is that they use 18- and 9-sector tracks, respectively. The preceding command tells DRIVER.SYS to assign a new drive letter to the first floppy disk and to treat it as if it were an 80-track, 9-sector, double-side, 3.5-inch drive. DOS will continue to access Drive A as a 1.44M drive, but a new logical floppy will be created (as drive D if you have only one hard disk; if not, the next available letter will be assigned).

Then, when you want to have a 720K floppy, just refer to drive D. Wait! Won't DOS read both 1.44M and 720K disks in the same drive with no special instructions? That's true, but the operating system will always default to the higher capacity. PS/2 systems will even go ahead and format a lower density diskette at the higher density. If you want to format a 720K disk on any type of machine, you have three choices: you can try to remember some clumsy syntax and type

```
FORMAT A /N:9 /T:80
```

each time you go to format a 720K floppy; you can create a batch file with that line in it and then try to remember what you called the batch file (720FMT.BAT is a good choice); or you can define an extra floppy as a 720K drive and forget about all that. You can use your imaginary disk as if it were a real 720K drive and gain some extra flexibility.

Using Two 1.44M Drives

For example, if you happen to have two 1.44M drives, you can assign either or both of them a new drive letter that represents a 720K disk. You can use the DRIVER.SYS disk to automatically determine how a diskette has been formatted. Because IBM PS/2 machines will format a 720K disk for 1.44M operation, you may not be aware of it unless you happen to look at how many files are on the disk. But put a 720K diskette that has been formatted for the higher density in a virtual 720K drive on a PS/2, and you'll know right away.

Unless all you deal with are other PS/2 computers, and you don't particularly care about your data, it's not a good idea to format 720K disks at 1.44M, even if you punch an extra hole in the disk so that other computers will think it's high-density media. Although some swear by this technique, claiming the disks are identical except for the extra markup applied to high density floppies, others report serious problems. High-density disks are supposed to have greater coercivity, which is the capability to retain encoded information. All I can tell you is that I backed up information to about 50 such disks some years ago, and they worked fine. A few months later, I found that at least some information had disappeared from 60 percent of them. Backup disks are the last place you want to find unreliable operation.

SETVER

The **setver** command loads a table of DOS version numbers into memory so that DOS can "lie" to specific programs that look for a certain version of DOS before they will operate.

CONFIG.SYS Controls

These directives can be used to control how CONFIG.SYS itself is interpreted. We'll look at these in more detail in the next chapter.

REM

This directive tells DOS to ignore the rest of the text on a line. Remarks can be descriptive text that explain what a given section does or a marker to disable a given line for testing or other purposes.

INCLUDE

CONFIG.SYS now allows defining configuration blocks within the file, which can be executed individually, based on your startup menu. The **include** command tells DOS to include the contents of one configuration block within another.

MENUCOLOR

This command sets the text and background colors for the startup menu.

MENUDEFAULT

This command defines the default menu item on the startup menu and sets a timeout value if desired. If you do not use this command, DOS sets the default to item 1.

MENUITEM

This directive defines an item on the startup menu, which can have up to nine choices.

SUBMENU

Defines submenus within CONFIG.SYS.

The Next Step

This chapter has served as your introduction to the commands and directives available in CONFIG.SYS. These included the new commands added with DOS 6, as well as older ones that might have been more familiar to you. The next chapter will explain how to use CONFIG.SYS commands to tailor your system in flexible ways.

Customizing CONFIG.SYS

Chapter 26 provided an introduction to directives and commands you can use to set up CONFIG.SYS for your particular system. This chapter will cover customization in much more detail and will outline some of the special control features offered by DOS 6.

I'll provide some sample CONFIG.SYS files that you can use to create your own version and explain how each of the changes you make can affect the way your system operates.

CONFIG.SYS and Programming

Prior to the introduction of DOS 6, CONFIG.SYS consisted of nothing more than a list of directives (which provide the operating system with parameters, such as BUFFERS=20 or FILES=30) and commands (which tell the operating system to execute some function such as SET PROCESSOR=386). The only options you had were the values entered or the switches applied to particular commands or directives. The only way to alter how one of these was implemented was by manually editing the CONFIG.SYS file.

Options Are Limited

Even then, your options were limited to changing a line or removing it entirely. It wasn't possible to deactivate a directive, even just for testing purposes, without inserting some characters at the beginning of the line, which turned it into an unrecognized command. Most of us used the characters REM for this purpose so that we could tell at a glance that the line in question was intended either as a remark or as a deactivated command, rather than just a typo.

However, inserting REM doesn't make the line a true remark. When the operating system encounters the REM statement under other versions prior to DOS 5.0, it is unable to execute it and displays an error message to that effect. Although the message itself is harmless, if you want to include 10 or 15 different remarked statements in a CONFIG.SYS file, it will become annoying fairly quickly, and will also increase the time needed to boot-up your computer.

A Programming Language

DOS eliminates those restrictions by providing some of the elements of a programming language in a very limited form. If you know BASIC or batch file programming language, you'll understand immediately how to use these features. CONFIG.SYS has been given a limited subset of features that can do a few of the things that a real programming language can do. There are only a few such statements, so if you find the thought of programming somewhat alarming, you can be at ease.

The rest of us welcome the capabilities that have been added, but still miss a few constructions, like the conditional statements that produce IF..THEN..ELSE branching. These would give CONFIG.SYS a frightening amount of flexibility. However, something is better than nothing.

Interactive Directives

The first capability that has been added to CONFIG.SYS is the option of being prompted whether some, or all, of the directives should be carried out. There are three ways to accomplish this, plus a fourth way to bypass CONFIG.SYS altogether.

➤ You can be prompted for each entry in CONFIG.SYS by pressing F8 when DOS starts to load.

➤ You may be prompted only for specific entries by inserting a question mark after the directive.

➤ CONFIG.SYS can be skipped entirely by pressing F5 when DOS starts to load.

➤ You can choose from whole blocks of entries through a menuing system.

The following section will look at each of these options in more detail.

Interactive Booting

The first way to interact with CONFIG.SYS is to press F8 after the `Starting MS-DOS...` prompt appears. You generally have two seconds to do this, unless you've turned off the delay with the SWITCHES= /F directive in CONFIG.SYS. (Make it the first line in your CONFIG.SYS file.) You can still intercept the startup of DOS by pressing F5 or F8, but you must do so *immediately* when the `Starting MS-DOS...` message appears.

When DOS senses that you've pressed F8 in the allotted time, it displays a message: `MS-DOS will prompt you to confirm each CONFIG.SYS command`. Then it processes each line in CONFIG.SYS one after another, prompting you to reply Y or N for each, in this format: `DEVICEHIGH=SJII.SYS [Y,N]?` You must enter a reply for each command in CONFIG.SYS; there is no way to bypass or abort the process after it has started.

After all the directives have been processed, DOS asks you the following: `Process AUTOEXEC.BAT [Y,N]?` If you reply Y, the entire AUTOEXEC.BAT file will be executed. Enter N, and it will be skipped entirely. You won't be queried on each command.

The F8 key is a good way to temporarily disable specific drivers or TSRs when you want to check out your system. For example, to run Intel's SOFTSET.EXE utility for its Ether Express 16 cards (these are bundled with Windows for Workgroups), you must disable all network drivers. You could edit CONFIG.SYS, inserting REM statements at the beginning of each of three network driver lines, reboot, run SOFTSET, then remove the REMs, and reboot again. Or, you could press F8 on the first reboot, disable those drivers just for that session, and immediately reboot after SOFTSET has been run.

Perhaps you have a game or other program that you run occasionally that requires more RAM than is generally available in your full working configuration. Reboot, press F8 to disable a few drivers you won't need for that session, and run the RAM-hungry software.

This technique is also useful for troubleshooting. You can disable all your drivers and add them in one by one just by changing your responses during the boot-up process. Microsoft has given us a powerful tool just with one function key.

Selective Interaction

Perhaps there is only one or two drivers that you want to selectively enable or disable. This could be a temporary need or something you would like included in your CONFIG.SYS file on a regular basis. For example, you may use your scanner about half the time. You always know on a given day whether or not you'll need the scanner. You have so many other essential drivers that when the scanner drivers are loaded, you don't have enough RAM left to operate your CD-ROM drive. So, you would like to be prompted whether or not scanner drivers should be loaded each time you boot up.

That's easy enough to do. Just place a question mark after the command name. DOS will ask you before executing that command. Use this syntax:

```
DEVICE?=SJII.SYS
```

You may place as many or as few of these in your CONFIG.SYS file as you want. Keep in mind, however, that there is no timeout feature; CONFIG.SYS will stop cold until you enter a Y or N response. If you would rather your computer finish its startup without intervention on some occasions, don't use this feature. You must always be present to help complete the process.

There are many reasons why you wouldn't want to hang around while your computer boots. If your system has a built-in faxmodem, it may be unable to receive a fax until its drivers and software are loaded from DOS or Windows. You've probably automated those steps. A momentary power flicker or brownout can cause your system to reboot spontaneously. Ordinarily, the system will start up, and any software you've set to reload automatically will load itself. If you happen to be away from your desk (or gone overnight), you won't miss any faxes. You *will*, however, if your system is stopped and is waiting for you to enter Y or N to a CONFIG.SYS prompt. Computer bulletin board systems and other software that should run around-the-clock are examples of applications that you don't want interrupted by a random reboot.

Skipping Startup Files Completely

If you press F5 when the `Starting MS-DOS...` message appears, both CONFIG.SYS and AUTOEXEC.BAT will be skipped. This is an excellent tool to use when you've managed to mess up either one so badly that your system locks up or refuses to boot. It's possible to do things with EMM386.EXE that can freeze a system (*including* important areas of ROM), and many other drivers can conflict with each other or DOS in new and interesting ways. Prior to DOS 6, it was impossible to bypass CONFIG.SYS, so your only recourse was to boot from a floppy, which can take a very long time. When you're impatiently awaiting the chance to go fix whatever fouled up your system, the delay can be excruciating.

Now those long waits are over. Press F5, and DOS immediately drops to the DOS prompt. Keep in mind that because none of the commands in CONFIG.SYS and AUTOEXEC.BAT have been processed, you may be missing a few capabilities you need or expect, including the following:

➤ If you require special drivers to access a device, that device will not be accessible. Forget about accessing files from your Bernoulli drives until you've fixed your system. Your mouse is dead.

➤ Your PATH command in AUTOEXEC.BAT hasn't been processed. If you want to edit CONFIG.SYS with the EDIT program, you need to preface the command with the pathname to your DOS files.

➤ If you've been really clever and moved COMMAND.COM out of the root directory (but pointed to it through a SHELL command in CONFIG.SYS), DOS may not even be able to find its command interpreter. Look ma! No C:> prompt! All is not lost; you can type a path to COMMAND.COM, and DOS will finish loading normally.

Environment variables will be set to their default values, but you probably won't be running Windows or other software that requires environment variables until you've fixed your startup files, anyway.

The F5 key can be your best friend when you need to recover from a startup blunder you've made while trying to "enhance" your configuration.

Setting Up a CONFIG.SYS Menu

If you have several different configurations you would like to choose from each time you start up DOS, CONFIG.SYS can be set up with a menu that lists up to nine variations you can choose from by pressing a single key. This way, those rarely used drivers can be loaded only when you need them. If you have conflicting sets of drivers, they can be batched together in different configurations, or you can have a bare-bones configuration used just for testing purposes. The system is flexible enough to meet many different needs. The next section will tell you how to set up multiple configurations using a single CONFIG.SYS file.

Using Configuration Blocks

A configuration block is a set of commands that are carried out together. Each block begins with a *block header*, which is nothing more than a single-word name surrounded by brackets. You may use up to 70 characters, but no spaces (use an underline to separate "words"), slashes, commas, semicolons, equal signs, or square brackets.

You can name the blocks by the function they carry out, for specific users, or for any other logical category you want to set up. When DOS begins processing a particular configuration block, it carries out all the commands after the block header until it encounters another block header. Here are some sample configuration blocks that illustrate the sorts of commands you can include in them:

```
[scanner]
devicehigh=SJII.SYS
devicehigh=HPSCANER.SYS

[network]
device=G:\W\protman.dos /i:G:\W
device=G:\W\workgrp.sys
device=G:\W\exp16.dos

[iomega]
device=C:\u\oad\DOSCFG.EXE /L=001 /M1 /V
device=C:\U\OAD\DOSOAD.SYS

[unused]
REM device=C:\UTILS\STAC\STACKER.COM /EMS /P=9 J: A:
REM device=C:\MTMCDSA.SYS /D:MSCD001 /P:300 /A:0 /M:2 /I:3
REM device=g:\ndw\NAV&.SYS /b

[david]
files=40
shell=C:\D\COMMAND.COM C:\D\   /p
include=scanner
include=iomega
set user=david
set temp=c:\davtemp
```

```
[cathy]
switches= /w /f /n
files=60
shell=C:\4DOS\4DOS.COM C:\4DOS\
set user=cathy
set temp=c:\cathtemp
```

Each of these examples illustrates a point. The [scanner] block might be set for execution only under some configurations and the [network] block only when networking capabilities are desired. Perhaps some users of the system need access to a Bernoulli drive, with drivers loaded in the [iomega] section. You might find it convenient to group unused directives in an [unused] block just for reference purposes.

The real power of configuration blocks is shown in the next two examples, for [david] and [cathy]. David prefers to use COMMAND.COM as his command processor and needs scanner functions and access to the Bernoulli drives. The **include** directive tells DOS to execute all the commands in the [scanner] and [iomega] blocks. Note that the brackets are not needed following the equal sign. Moreover, the **set user** directive creates an environment variable in the master environment block called *user* that stores the name of the particular user. Batch files written for this system can use that environment variable to determine who is using the computer and to modify its behavior accordingly. AUTOEXEC.BAT, for example, can include special setup options based on the *user* variable.

The configuration block for Cathy is a little different. Cathy prefers to use 4DOS as her command interpreter. She typically has more open files than David, so the **files** command is set for 60. She's a relative neophyte, so the administrator has set the **switches** directive so that she can't bypass CONFIG.SYS by pressing F5 or F8. The *user* variable is set to Cathy's name.

Note that both David and Cathy have separate temporary file directories. Many programs use the environment variable TEMP (or TMP) to determine where to store their temporary files. By separating David and

Cathy's temp files, I've made it easier to determine what happened to whom if the system crashes and temporary files are left behind.

You can place any groups of commands in configuration blocks. You may find it simple to place commands that should be shared by all configurations in a block named [common]. DOS will always execute all the commands in a [common] block, and you may use more than one. It's probably a good idea to put a final [common] configuration header at the end of your CONFIG.SYS file. Programs that modify CONFIG.SYS when they are installed usually place their special commands at the end of the file. Placing a [common] header there ensures that these statements will not be appended to the end of another, more exclusive block, and will thus be shared by all configurations.

Selecting Configurations

Now you understand how to set up different configurations. How do you select between them? Four new CONFIG.SYS commands are available which control how configuration blocks are selected. They are **menuitem**, **menudefault**, **menucolor**, and **submenu**.

Menuitem

This command defines a specific entry in your startup menu and can include menu text to help you select the item you want. The syntax is as follows:

```
MENUITEM=blockname[,menutext]
```

Substitute for *blockname* the name of a single block you want executed when the user selects this menu item. Remember that this blockname can branch to several other blocks using the **include** statement, so if you want [david] to also share the statements in the configuration blocks named [scanner] and [iomega], just include them in his block. DOS will also carry out commands at the beginning of CONFIG.SYS, before it encounters the menu, as well as any commands included in [common] blocks.

To help your user select a menu item, you can include menu text of up to 70 characters. Spaces and other characters are allowed. Here are some example **menuitem** entries:

```
MENUITEM=scanner, Load scanner drivers

MENUITEM=network, Load network drivers

MENUITEM=david, David's Configuration

MENUITEM=cathy, Cathy's Configuration
```

If you mistype the name of a menu item, CONFIG.SYS won't display it at startup.

Menudefault

This command is the default menu item that will be selected if you fail to choose one in the time allotted. This command avoids the startup lockup I described earlier. The syntax for the command is as follows:

```
MENUDEFAULT=blockname[,timeout]
```

If you don't specify a default menu item, CONFIG.SYS defaults to menu item 1. However, if you don't enter a time, CONFIG.SYS won't proceed until you press Enter. For *timeout*, you can substitute any value from 0 to 90 seconds. When 0 is specified, CONFIG.SYS immediately branches to the header specified by menu item 1, with no chance to enter an alternate. Ninety seconds is a little long to wait but can be used to make sure that you have plenty of time to make a choice in case you've wandered off for a bit, without the risk that your computer will halt the reboot process if your return is delayed.

Menucolor

This option specifies the foreground and background colors for your menu text. The syntax is as follows:

```
MENUCOLOR=textcolor[,background]
```

For *textcolor* and *background,* you can substitute one of the following values:

0	Black	8	Gray
1	Blue	9	Bright blue
2	Green	10	Bright green
3	Cyan	11	Bright cyan
4	Red	12	Bright red
5	Magenta	13	Bright magenta
6	Brown	14	Yellow
7	White	15	Bright white

On old style TTL monochrome monitors, colors 8 through 15 blink. If you don't enter a value for *background*, the *textcolor* is displayed on a black background.

Submenu

Although you can have only nine main menu items, each of them can call up a submenu of additional items. The syntax is the same as for **menuitem**. A system that uses submenus might look like this one:

```
[menu]
    MENUITEM=main, Main Configuration
    SUBMENU=scanner,Scanner Configurations
    SUBMENU=users,User Configurations

    [main]
    DOS=HIGH,UMB
    DEVICEHIGH=MOUSE.SYS

    [scanner]
    MENUITEM=scanjet,HP ScanJet
    MENUITEM=epson,Epson 800C
    MENUITEM=logitech,Hand Scanner
```

```
[users]
MENUITEM=david,David
MENUITEM=cathy,Cathy
MENUITEM=teryn,Teryn
MENUITEM=jonathan,Jonathan
```

Below these would be separate configuration blocks for [scanjet], [epson], [logitech], [david], [cathy], [teryn], and [jonathan]. As you can see, **submenu**, along with commands like **include**, lets you create complex menu structures that will encompass just about any startup configuration you care to create.

The Next Step

You can also create complex AUTOEXEC.BAT files using DOS 6's new capabilities. The next chapter will explain how batch files work, detail the role of AUTOEXEC.BAT, and show you how to use environment variables and the **choice** command to customize your startup files even further.

Customizing AUTOEXEC.BAT

Your second startup file that can be easily customized with DOS 6 is AUTOEXEC.BAT. This chapter will explain what batch files are and what commands can be used with them. Then I'll show you some new—and old—ways AUTOEXEC.BAT can be used to tailor your startup configuration. Along the way, you'll learn a little about the DOS environment and some new commands, like **choice**.

Batch files are files containing lists of commands that DOS will examine and carry out as if you had entered them from the keyboard. DOS 6 adds only one new capability to batch files themselves, the **choice** command. However, the capability to set environment variables from within CONFIG.SYS opens up new possibilities.

What Is a Batch File?

A batch file is a special kind of ASCII text file, which always contains the extension BAT. This extension makes batch files a type of file referred to as a *system file*. Other files lumped in this category are those ending with

EXE or COM extensions. System files have one attribute in common: they may be summoned simply by typing their "root" name — the part of the name before the extension—as long as you are logged onto the drive and directory that contains the file or have instructed DOS how to find it through a PATH command.

When DOS sees a file name consisting of a legal word with no extension, it first looks to see whether a COM or EXE file with that root exists — in that order. If so, it runs that program. Next, it looks to see whether a BAT file has that root. In that case, DOS looks at each line of text and tries to carry it out as if it were entered at the keyboard. There are certain special rules for batch files that apply in this case. If no COM, EXE, or BAT file with the root exists and there is no other file by that name (if there is an extension, such as BAS, it will not match), then the BAD COM-MAND OR FILE NAME error message is displayed.

Batch files are a left-over from the dawn of computing, when mainframes were so big and expensive that the only economical way to operate them was to arrange all their tasks in queues or batches that would be executed one after another with no wasteful pauses between them. These batches were packaged not only as lists of commands to carry out and as programs to run, but with a special job control language that gave the processor some additional instructions as to how to perform each task.

Similarly, DOS has its own batch file language of commands that are generally (but not always) used only within batch files. You can create and edit batch files using DOS's EDIT utility.

The most common use for batch files is to load applications programs that require a series of commands. For example, you may have a memory-resident thesaurus program that you load before your word processing software. The software itself may have command line parameters that don't change, such as which drive and directory to use for document files.

When your PC is powered up, it will look for AUTOEXEC.BAT in the root directory of the startup disk. If AUTOEXEC.BAT is found, its commands will be executed automatically, without your needing to do anything.

AUTOEXEC.BAT is a good way to custom-configure your system the way you want it. You can choose the program that you want the computer to run when it is turned on. For example, if you want the PC to operate as an unattended host computer during certain hours of the night, you may connect it to a timer and autoanswer modem and insert the name of your host communications program in the AUTOEXEC.BAT file. Then, when the timer turns the computer on, the host program will be run automatically. This example shows a typical AUTOEXEC.BAT file:

```
ECHO OFF
SET TEMP=C:\TEMP
C:\SYS\SETSPEED /P3 /FC:\SYS\MOUSEPRO.FIL
PATH J:\EXCEL;C:\BATCH;C:\DOS;D:\WORD
C:\UTILS\FASTATKB 00 NUL
CLS
VERIFY ON
```

Most of these lines tailor some portion of the operating system or the programs that it runs. The SET TEMP line defines a temporary directory, which is used by some programs to store transitional files that aren't needed after a task has run to completion. The line below the SET TEMP line defines the speed and profile for a Microsoft mouse, and the next line defines a PATH for DOS to search when looking for executable files.

Batch Commands

This section will list some of the basic batch file commands, which are often called subcommands because they are most often used only within batch files. However, they are full-fledged DOS commands that can also be used at the command line prompt in some cases. I'll mention these instances as we go along.

➤ **ECHO** displays a line of text, or, with ON or OFF, toggles the display of commands as they are executed. You can type **echo** on a line by itself to see the current **echo** status.

➤ **REM** can be used to insert remarks up to 123 characters in a batch file.

➤ **CLS** clears the screen.

➤ **PAUSE** causes the batch file to suspend execution until the user presses a key. The pause can be used to allow the operator to change his or her mind, insert a disk, or do some other task. Pause ordinarily displays the message `Strike a key when ready...`, but you can follow it with a replacement message of your choice.

➤ **GOTO** sends control of the batch file to a different line, marked with a label. Labels start with a colon, and only the first eight characters are significant. The others are ignored.

Conditional Statements

IF sends control to a specific label only if a condition is met. Batch file language's conditional statements provide a means of control over what the batch file does, similar to program branching instructions like GOTO in BASIC. In fact, batch files can include GOTO and IF, which are used much like they are in BASIC. However, these commands are somewhat limited. There is no ELSE statement (this deficiency can be overcome with programming techniques, just as in BASIC), and IF can only test for three different types of conditions:

➤ Whether one string of characters equals another

➤ Whether a file by a given name exists

➤ What the current ERRORLEVEL is

Test Strings for Equality

The first two are easy to understand. String comparisons must match in case (upper- or lowercase) to be considered identical. For example, look at these lines:

```
IF "AAA"=="aaa" ECHO AAA is equal to aaa
IF "AAA"=="AAA" ECHO AAA is equal to AAA
```

If you execute both lines, only the second one would cause the message to be echoed to the screen. Note that a double equal sign must be used. This convention is borrowed from languages that, unlike BASIC, make the proper distinction between using the equal sign used to assign values and the equal sign used to express equivalence. If this isn't clear, consider these examples:

```
SET A=B
IF A==B GOTO END
```

Single and Double Equal Signs Are Different

In the first case, A will always equal B after the line is run, because the value of B is assigned to A by that line. In the second case, no such assignment takes place. Instead, the line merely checks to see whether the two are equal, and, if so, performs some other task. Variables are assigned in batch files using the single equal sign. These are variables stored in the DOS environment and will be discussed in more detail in the next chapter.

For now, just remember that for comparisons, the double equal sign is required. You can follow IF with NOT to check to see whether two strings are not the same. Look at the following examples:

```
IF "Hello There"=="Hello There" GOTO END

IF NOT "Hello There"=="Hi" GOTO END

IF "Hello There"=="Hi" GOTO END
```

In all three cases, the batch file would branch to the label :END, because the comparison would test as true in each case. Now look at this comparison:

```
IF Notice No Quotes==Notice No Quotes GOTO END
```

This comparison is also true. Quotation marks are not required for string comparisons in batch files. It's a good idea to include them for clarity; you'll always know exactly what is being compared on either side of the equal sign. If you wanted to, you could use other characters to delineate the strings being compared. This line is the equivalent of the preceding one:

```
IF (Notice No Quotes)==(Notice No Quotes) GOTO END
```

I like quotes because the meaning is instantly clear to anyone who is looking at a batch file. There is another reason for using quotes that will be explored shortly.

Test To See Whether a File Exists

IF can check to see whether a file already exists within the current directory or one you specify. The most common use is to avoid overwriting a file that you may mean to keep.

Test for ERRORLEVEL

The third thing IF can check for is the **errorlevel**, which is a code set by DOS after the execution of certain commands, such as **xcopy** or **choice**. You can check to see whether **errorlevel** is 0, 1, 2, and so forth to determine whether the command was carried to completion, or some problem was encountered. Not all DOS commands set an **errorlevel**, but most DOS manuals will list them for you.

Note that **errorlevel** tells whether or not an **errorlevel** is equal to or greater than the value specified. If you had a line like either of these

```
IF errorlevel==200 GOTO END

IF errorlevel 200 GOTO END
```

the batch file would go to label :END if **errorlevel** equalled 200 or more. So, 200, 201, 202, and any higher number up to the maximum 255 would test as true. Note that the double equal sign is optional when you are using **errorlevel**.

The usual procedure to test for the exact **errorlevel** is to nest IF statements like this:

```
IF errorlevel 200 IF NOT errorlevel 201 ECHO It is
exactly 200.
```

If **errorlevel** 200 tests true, then the level is 200 or higher. If it is not true at 201, then it cannot be 201 or any higher number and, therefore, must be equal to exactly 200.

It's more useful to use **errorlevel** tests with **choice**, which was used earlier in this book.

Using Parameters

The first two uses of IF hinge around a third feature of batch files, the use of *parameters*. When applied to DOS and batch commands, a parameter is additional information that you supply on the command line when you type the command. This information is used by the command to determine how the file acts. When you type: **diskcopy** A: B:, the data following the external command name are parameters. Each parameter is separated by a space.

Command Line Can Include Parameters

When you type the root name of a batch file, you may also follow that name with a series of parameters. When the batch file is called, DOS will substitute the parameters that you type on the command line for special parameter variable markers that you insert in the batch file. The variables are typed sequentially on the command line and are substituted by DOS in the same order. In the batch file, the variables all start with a percent sign and are numbered %0, %1, %2, etc.

The first, %0, is always the filename of the batch file itself. The other parameters, %1 to %9, are all available for replacement with values you type on the command line with the batch file name. The first parameter on the command line is substituted for %1; the second will be assigned to %2; and so forth.

DOS allows up to 10 parameters (%0 to %9) but includes a **shift** command that allows typing more than 10 parameters on a single command line.

The FOR..IN..DO Command

This is the closest thing batch file language has to the FOR...NEXT loop of BASIC. A variable, designated by double percent signs, is sequentially assigned a value, and then the operation specified after DO is carried out. The syntax is

```
FOR variable IN (set) DO command
```

Set can be a list of file names, a list of commands, or anything else you want (although most users think that only a set of files can be included).

The CHOICE command

We already used **choice** earlier in this book, but it might be helpful to review how it works. You'll recall that the syntax is as follows:

```
CHOICE /Cxxx /Tdefault,timeout prompt
```

The /C switch is used to provide a list of allowable entries, as a substitute for *xxx*. The /T switch lists the default choice that will be used by DOS if no reply is entered by the *timeout*. *Prompt* can include text of your choice. When a valid key is pressed, DOS assigns an **errorlevel** based on the order of the keys in your /C list. The first key listed receives an **errorlevel** of 1; the second receives an **errorlevel** of 2; and so forth. If you don't specify a set of keys, **choice** uses Y and N.

Here's how I use **choice** in my own AUTOEXEC.BAT file:

```
CHOICE  /T:Y,5 Do you want to load Windows
IF ERRORLEVEL 2 GOTO QUIT
WIN
:QUIT
```

Each time my system boots, AUTOEXEC.BAT pauses at this line and displays the prompt:

```
Do you want to load Windows [Y/N]?
```

If I happen to be away from my computer, DOS waits five seconds and then goes ahead and loads Windows. If I am seated at the computer and want to load Windows, I can press Y immediately to skip the five-second wait. If I want to drop to the DOS prompt and not load Windows, I can press N instead. **Choice** is better than pause because startup won't abort if you're not there, and you have more options.

You could also use choice to load, or not load, individual drivers and programs:

```
@ECHO OFF
PROMPT $p$g
```

```
PATH
C:\D;H:\P;C:\A;F:\w\fh;G:\NDW;G:\W;F:\W2;F:\W\XL;C:\B;C:\U;G:\FAX;C:
\NU;C:\tiga2;C:\

CHOICE /T:Y,5 Load Microsoft Anti-Virus?

IF NOT ERRORLEVEL 2 MSAV

CHOICE /T:Y,5 Load Mouse driver?

IF NOT ERRORLEVEL 2 LH C:\D\mouse
```

Choice could also be used to set up a menuing system for
AUTOEXEC.BAT, much like the one possible for CONFIG.SYS. Instead
of configuration blocks, you would use labels and **goto** commands. Look
at this example:

```
@ECHO OFF

ECHO Do you want to load:

ECHO  1.) Scanner configuration

ECHO  2.) Network configuration

ECHO  3.) David's configuration

ECHO  4.)  Cathy's configuration

CHOICE /C1234 /T:3,10 Enter choice :

CLS

IF ERRORLEVEL 4 GOTO CATHY

IF ERRORLEVEL 3 GOTO DAVID

IF ERRORLEVEL 2 GOTO NETWORK

IF ERRORLEVEL 1 GOTO SCANNER

:SCANNER

...

GOTO NEXT

:NETWORK

...

GOTO NEXT

:DAVID
```

```
. . .

GOTO NEXT

:CATHY

. . .

:NEXT
```

In this example, the user would be shown a menu with four choices. Pressing a key from 1 to 4 would send control of the batch file to the section labeled with the appropriate name. Some additional commands, represented here by the ellipses, would be carried out and then the batch file would branch to the label :NEXT.

Using Environment Variables

Actually, the menu shown previously wouldn't really be required. You can set an environment variable from CONFIG.SYS that can be accessed by batch files. One called %config% is always defined using the name of the block header chosen through a menu system. In our examples in the last chapter, we defined a variable called %user% which contained the name of the user. The preceding menu could be replaced by one of these lines:

```
GOTO %CONFIG%

GOTO %USER%
```

The environment can be useful for other AUTOEXEC.BAT and batch file customizing purposes, so it might be useful to take a few minutes to explain it further.

Exploring Your Environment

The DOS environment is a special area of memory that is set aside to store variables and values as strings of information. The environment can be accessed by batch files, as well as by any program that needs it. The information it contains won't change unless altered by the user's program or batch files, and thus the environment can be used to pass information from one place to another in your system.

The DOS environment starts out as a *Master Environment Block*, which is a block of memory set aside by the operating system to store environmental variables. These are stored as strings of characters in a very simple form, using the following format

```
variable=value
```

where variable is a name defined by you using the set command or by DOS as one of its reserved variables. The value is the string assigned using set.

Reserved Variables—path, prompt, and comspec

As I noted, DOS reserves some variable names and gives them a special meaning. These include **path**, **prompt,** and **comspec**. DOS itself will look in the environment for these variables, and if they are present, will use the value assigned to them in its operations.

For example, **comspec** defines the name of the command processor that will be used whenever DOS loads a second copy with the **command** command. **Path** is the list of subdirectory **paths** that DOS uses when looking for executable files outside of the currently logged directory (these files end in COM, EXE, and BAT). If there is no **path** variable in the environment, DOS will only search the current subdirectory. **Prompt** is a variable that tells DOS what should be contained in the system prompt that is displayed at the DOS command line.

Your batch files can access these variables simply by surrounding the name with percent signs. Here's an example:

```
FOR  %%a in (%path%) DO ECHO  Included subdirectory:
%%a
```

Each time through the loop, DOS would extract another portion of the variable and substitute it for %%a. How did it parse the environmental variable string? Look carefully at the **path** variable defined in the preceding example. I've actually assigned several values to it, separating them with semicolons. DOS will treat each string individually. You can do this with any environment variable, although your program must be set up to do something with the information. DOS knows how to separate individual **path** statements, but if you enter several different **prompt** commands, it will use all of them and incorporate any semicolons you type into the prompt itself.

The Next Step

This has been only a brief introduction to batch file programming and the things you can do with AUTOEXEC.BAT. You'll find these tools useful as you develop special needs for your startup configurations. Now it's time to wrap up with a look at several other utilities included with DOS 6, as well as optional programs from third-parties that provide the features that Microsoft forgot. You'll find discussions of all these in the last section.

Part VII: Advanced Utilities

If DOS 6 has gotten you hooked on utilities, you don't have to stop with the programs covered so far in this book. As long as clever programmers continue to develop new and faster ways of doing things, you'll always find useful utilities that you haven't tried yet. This last section is divided into two chapters. Chapter 29 explains how to use some additional, often overlooked utilities bundled with DOS 6. Chapter 30 outlines some broad categories of utilities that might interest you and explains about the shareware distribution channel.

The key thing to keep in mind when selecting and using these additional utilities is to avoid utility overload. If you have to learn dozens of new commands, it's unlikely that a utility will save you much time. The goal is to increase your productivity, not fill up your free time with new housekeeping tasks that you never bothered with or needed to perform before.

Other DOS 6 Utilities

DOS 6 includes some small utilities that are often overlooked, including a group of them aimed squarely at laptop users. Interlnk and Intersvr provide a way to exchange files between two computers and are especially useful if one of them doesn't have a floppy disk drive. I'll also show you how to use the new **move** and **deltree** utilities, which are new to DOS 6.

Laptop Power

Laptop computers are a symptom of how essential personal computers have become to our working lives. A desktop system has become a basic working tool, so much so that many of us feel lost without access to the programs and data stored on our computers. Executives who once took work home in their briefcases are no longer paperbound; a stack of documents is only a small part of what they do. The applications and files in their computers may be much more important.

Laptop systems provide a way to carry our offices with us when we go home, travel, or commute. However, two conflicting trends are at work.

Users want laptop or notebook-sized computers that are extremely small. Many are only two-thirds the size of a standard desktop keyboard. On the other hand, PC users aren't willing to give up much in the way of functionality. They want tiny computers with large hard disks, full color LCD screens, and powerful 486 microprocessors.

Something has to give. In some cases, laptop computers sacrifice an internal floppy disk. Most of the time, the hard drive is a lot smaller than the one in a desktop main system. In either case, the user has to find some way to get data in and out of the laptop quickly. With the exception of a few workers who use their laptop machine as their main machine (often by plugging in an external monitor and/or keyboard), data must be loaded into the portable computer for manipulation and then exported for other uses.

Floppy Disk Copies

The options haven't always been very efficient. If a laptop has an internal or external floppy drive, data can be copied to a floppy disk and then recopied to another computer. When you're working with a lot of data, that can take three or four disk swaps and a great deal of time. If your laptop uses an external floppy drive, you must take that drive with you as you travel, which defeats the purpose of a small, lightweight system. External Bernoulli drives or hard disks that connect through the parallel port are more weight to carry around.

Built-in modems are another option. Users have been known to log onto an online system like CompuServe, upload files from their computers, then move over to a desktop system a few inches a way, log on again, and download those same files. At 2400 baud, it can take 90 minutes per megabyte—each way—and even if both computers are equipped with 9600 bps modems, the process can still take 45 minutes to transfer a megabyte of data. Keep in mind that you're paying CompuServe a tidy hourly charge for both upload and download.

More advanced users have found software like LapLink to provide a better solution. Special cables can be used to connect two computers, either through the serial or parallel ports, and data is moved at high speed (115K bps or faster) between them. One of these utilities costs more than DOS 6 itself.

Now DOS includes a pair of utilities called **interlnk** and **intersvr** that streamline this method of data interchange. You can also use Interlnk to run programs located on the server computer. The next section explains how to use these utilities.

How Interlnk Works

Interlnk uses a free serial or parallel port on both computers. You must use like ports on each system; you can't connect the serial port of one computer to the parallel port of the other. However, you don't have to use the same port on each; COM1 of one will connect just fine to COM2 of the other. Similarly, you can match LPT1 and LPT2 if they are available.

You'll need a serial cable and a null modem to link two serial ports, and a bidirectional parallel printer cable to connect parallel ports. The null modem is a $5 device available at any Radio Shack and most computer stores. It simply reverses the wires in the serial cable so that the signal sent by one computer is directed to the receive line of the other (otherwise, a serial cable would connect send-to-send and receive-to-receive.)

Note that you don't have to run DOS 6 on both computers for Interlnk to work properly. That's fortunate because you'll find a wide variety of DOS versions running in most environments these days. Users who don't need DOS 6's utilities or who lag behind technology may still be working with DOS 5. Others who never realized how bad DOS 4 was may be using that operating system. There are still many systems out there running DOS 3.3. You should have DOS 6 on one system, probably your laptop, and any version of DOS later than Version 3.0 on the other computer. It's best to have DOS 6 on the client system, because if you use an earlier version, some features of the server (such as larger hard disk volumes) may not be supported by the client machine.

You also must have 16K of free memory on the client and 130K free on the server; but that's usually not a difficult requirement to meet.

You have already encountered *client* and *server* terminology in a networking environment. Microsoft applies the terms to a pair of computers using Interlnk. When you're transferring files, the computer you use to type commands is called the client. This will usually be your laptop computer, or, if you're connecting two desktop machines, one of the two desktop computers. The server is the other computer. When Interlnk is active, the client computer uses the server's disk drives and printers just as if they were attached to the client.

However, to reduce confusion, each of the server's drives is given a new drive letter assignment that the client system uses to reference them. Ordinarily, the drives on the server from A and upward are assigned drive letters that follow the last letter on the client machine. If your laptop has drives A and C, and the server has A, B, C, and D, the server's drives will be accessed as D (drive A), E (drive B), F (drive C), and G (drive D). That may be complicated to remember the first time you do it, but you'll soon get used to the convention.

Setting Up the Client

To set up the client, you must first confirm that INTERLNK.EXE is installed on that system. If it is not, don't panic. Interlnk can copy the necessary files to the other computer if you use a serial connection and have MODE.COM available on the client computer. I'll show you how later.

Next, you must edit the CONFIG.SYS file of the client computer. Use EDIT, EDLIN, or any ASCII text editor. Then, add a line like this:

```
DEVICE=INTERLNK.EXE
```

Include the path to Interlnk if it is not installed in the root directory of the client computer. Place the line last in your CONFIG.SYS file to avoid assigning drive letters to server drives that you normally would want allocated to Bernoulli drives, DoubleSpace volumes, RAM disks, or other peripherals. Then restart the client computer to activate Interlnk. You might want to install Intersrv on the server system and connect the two to allow them to connect automatically.

This sample line will redirect three drives by default. Interlnk will automatically try to connect to the server each time your computer boots up; you won't even need to type the command from the DOS prompt.

Although the simple example line may work in most cases, you can specify quite a few options in the client's CONFIG.SYS file. The complete syntax for this driver is as follows:

```
DEVICE[HIGH]=[drive:][path]INTERLNK.EXE [/DRIVES:n]
[/NOPRINTER][/COM[:][n or address][/LPT[:]
[n or address][/AUTO][/NOSCAN][/LOW][/BAUD:rate][/V]
```

As always, we'll look at each of these options one at a time.

Replace *drive:path* with the full path to INTERLNK.EXE.

/DRIVES:*n* specifies the number of drives you want redirected by Interlnk. The default is three, but you may specify as many drives as you have. If you enter 0, Interlnk only redirects printers. Make sure that your LASTDRIVE command in CONFIG.SYS allows for this number of additional drives.

/NOPRINTER prevents printer ports from being redirected.

/COM tells Interlnk which serial port to use, substituting either 1 to 4 for *n* or the actual *address* of the COM port (useful if you use an address other than the defaults for COM1 to COM4). You'll want to use this switch if you have a serial mouse, to make sure that Interlnk doesn't scan the COM port the mouse is using. If you don't use this switch, or the /LPT switch, Interlnk on the client will interrogate all the serial ports and parallel ports in the system and look for a response from Intersvr on the server. If you use only /COM, with no parameters, it will interrogate only the serial ports in your system.

/LPT specifies LPT1 to LPT3 for Interlnk transfer or tells the program to search only parallel ports for a connection to the server. If you're using a parallel connection and a serial mouse, this switch can prevent Interlnk from scanning the mouse port needlessly.

/AUTO tells DOS to install the Interlnk device driver only if the client can establish a link with the server when the client computer boots. If you don't use this switch, Interlnk is installed in memory regardless of whether the client is connected to the server. The /AUTO switch lets you keep the Interlnk line in CONFIG.SYS all the time, with no sacrifice in memory unless the client and server happen to be connected at bootup time. The downside is that you may need to reboot to establish a connection.

/NOSCAN forces DOS to load INTERLNK.EXE into memory but bypasses the attempt to establish a link.

/LOW tells Interlnk to use conventional memory, even if upper memory blocks are available.

/BAUD sets the maximum baud rate for serial communications. The default is 115,200 bps, but you can also use 9600, 19200, 38400, or 57600. Some older computers and systems with slower universal asynchronous receiver/transceiver (UART) chips don't allow higher speeds through their serial ports.

/V stops most conflicts with a system's timer. You'll know that you have problems if your Interlnk connection halts when you try to access a drive or printer.

Set Up the Server

You do not need to make any changes to CONFIG.SYS on the server. Simply run the INTERSVR.EXE program, which must be installed on the server system. The syntax for this utility is as follows:

```
INTERSVR [drive:][...]INTERSVR.EXE [/X=drive:[...]
[/COM[:][n or address][/LPT[:][n or address][/
BAUD:rate][/V][/B] [/RCOPY]
```

For *drive:*, you may substitute the drive letter(s) of all the drives that are redirected. Intersvr redirects all drives by default; use this parameter to limit the number of drives that are available to the client.

/X excludes the named drives from redirection. If a server has six or seven different drives and you want to exclude only a couple of them, this is a faster way to do it than explicitly naming the drives that *will* be redirected.

/COM defines the COM port that will be used or limits Intersvr to searching only COM ports.

/BAUD sets the maximum baud rate for serial communications. The default is 115,200 bps, but you can also use 9600, 19200, 38400, or 57600. Some older computers and systems with slower universal asynchronous receiver/transceiver (UART) chips don't allow higher speeds through their serial ports.

/V stops most conflicts with a system's timer. You'll know you have problems if your Intersvr connection halts when you try to access a drive or printer.

/B is used with monochrome monitors to switch the display to black-and-white.

/RCOPY copies the Interlnk files from one computer to the other.

Copying INTERLNK.EXE to or from a Floppyless System

If you want to link two computers, one of which doesn't have Interlnk installed, you need to copy the software to that other computer. But what do you do if one of the two doesn't have a floppy disk drive? You can still copy the Interlnk software (only) between the two systems if they can be connected with a seven-wire serial cable and null modem (note that only a three-wire serial cable is needed for ordinary Interlnk communications) and the MODE.COM utility is available on the computer onto which you are installing the Interlnk files.

On the system to receive Interlnk files, log onto the subdirectory that will receive the files. If you are using a port other than COM1, and you are using SHARE.EXE, disable it by removing the appropriate line from your AUTOEXEC.BAT file and rebooting. MODE.COM must be in your DOS path.

Then, type INTERSVR /RCOPY. A remote installation screen will appear. Follow the instructions on the screen to copy the files.

Special Considerations

If you are using Microsoft Windows and a serial mouse, be sure to use either the /LPT or /COM switch to specify the port used. Interlnk's scanning can interfere with the operation of the mouse under Windows. In addition, Windows users will need to redirect LPT1 or LPT2 output to LPT1.DOS or LPT2.DOS. Use the Windows Printer Control Panel, select the printer to be redirected, and then click on the Connect button. Choose either LPT1.DOS or LPT2.DOS as the connection for that printer.

Interlnk does not redirect network drives, CD-ROM drives, or other drives that use redirection.

Running Programs from the Server

You aren't limited to exchanging data with Interlnk. You can actually run programs on the client machines that are located on the server. The program must be configured to operate on the client computer; that is, if you have only CGA display on the client, the program must be compatible with CGA displays. In addition, you cannot run certain DOS 6 commands from the server, including **chkdsk**, **defrag**, **diskcomp**, **diskcopy**, **fdisk**, **format**, **mirror**, **sys**, **undelete**, and **unformat**.

More Power to You

Laptop users will also appreciate POWER.EXE, a utility that works with systems that conform to the Advanced Power Management (APM) specification to conserve power. This TSR can save up to 25 percent of the power normally required, by monitoring activity and turning off certain functions (such as your hard disk drive) when they are not being used.

You must install this driver through CONFIG.SYS, using the following syntax:

```
POWER [ADV[:MAX or REG or MIN] or STD or OFF] /LOW
```

The definitions of each of these parameters is as follows:

ADV activates advanced power management when applications and hardware devices are not being used. You may specify either MAX (maximum), REG (regular), or MIN (minimum) settings. The default is REG. In some cases, if an application is actually active, the MAX or REG settings can hinder performance. For example, if your hard disk is spun down, it may take a few seconds to come back up to speed so that you can access files.

STD tells POWER to use only the power-management features already built into your hardware, if your system supports APM. If it does not, this parameter turns off power managment.

OFF switches power management off.

/LOW loads POWER.EXE into conventional memory.

Note that all these parameters, except for /LOW, may also be used from the DOS command line to control the operation of the POWER driver.

Moving on

The new **move** command has been available previously with many third-party utilities, such as J.P. Software's 4DOS, but it's now become a basic and badly needed part of DOS 6 itself. Move can be used to relocate files from one directory to another and to rename subdirectories. The syntax is as follows:

```
MOVE [drive:][path]filename[,[drive:][path]
[filename][...]] destination
```

For *drive:path\filename,* you can substitute as many files and their paths as you want to move. You can also enter the name of a subdirectory. For *destination,* you must specify the name of the drive and/or directory where the files are to be moved or the new name for the subdirectory.

No check is made to see whether you will overwrite files with the same name in the destination subdirectory. If you move more than one file, the destination must be the name of a directory (you can't rename multiple files while moving them).

The **move** command is a handy way to take the contents of one subdirectory, or an individual file, and place the contents in another location, without needing to first **copy** and then **erase** the files.

DELTREE

The **deltree** command finally gives us a way to delete whole subdirectories and their child directories, along with any files in them, with a single command. Before this utility became available, you needed to log onto the lowest subdirectory in the tree, erase all the files, remove that directory, and repeat for each directory in the tree. Various third-party utilities and environments (such as Norton Desktop for DOS or Windows) let you do this in one step. DOS 6 has finally reached the '90s!

The syntax for **deltree** is as follows:

```
DELTREE [/Y] [drive:][path]
```

The /Y switch tells **deltree** to go ahead and delete the tree without first prompting you to confirm the step. For *drive:path,* substitute the name of the top subdirectory level in the tree you would like to prune. This utility deletes hidden, system, and read-only files, so use it with care.

The Next Step

So far in this book, I've covered every utility included with DOS 6 and a few alternatives you might want to consider. The final chapter will describe some other utility programs you might want to consider that are available from third-party developers.

Beyond DOS 6

Don't think that the introduction of DOS 6 has put an end to the third-party utility industry! The latest version of DOS includes only a basic complement of utilities that Microsoft has found most users request. As you've seen in previous chapters, other utilities are available that do the same things better or more efficiently. In addition, there are still more utilities available that add functions that Microsoft hasn't gotten around to yet. This chapter will describe some of them.

The Ultimate Utility

If Bill Gates had hired Tom Rawson and Rex Conn when he had the chance, we would all be happily using MS-DOS 7 right now. The two innovators behind 4DOS wouldn't have made revolutionary changes to the DOS kernel. Tom and Rex would simply have made "official" DOS more practical, friendlier, and more powerful by giving it a shiny new outer shell. But then, perhaps Chairman Bill *did* know what he was doing. If MS-DOS worked the way we wanted it to, there would be fewer users migrating to graphical interfaces like Windows when all they really wanted was to get some work done.

4DOS, version 4.0 is an alternate command processor that replaces COMMAND.COM under MS-DOS Versions 2 to 6, or DR DOS 3.4, to 6.0. It can function as the command processor in an OS/2 DOS compatibility box, and there is a separate product, 4OS2, that replaces OS/2's CMD.EXE. Symantec thought enough of 4DOS to license a version called NDOS for the Norton Utilities.

Because a command processor interprets every instruction you type, it can enhance each command with new options, faster execution, and a friendlier interface. Even if you run Windows or stick to a few applications, 4DOS is great for those moments when you must face the DOS prompt. However, it was written for those who find it easier and faster to drop to DOS and type a command than scroll through endless directory trees with a mouse.

4DOS can replace your motley collection of oddball utilities with names like PCOPY, SDIR, or SUPEREN. Are you fond of neat little files with names like ASK, LIST, WAIT, BOOT, or TIMER ? 4DOS includes the features of a hundred stand-alone utilities, yet is transparently integrated into DOS. It also lets you perform many expanded functions using the DOS commands you already know.

Under 4DOS, COPY includes a /S switch, just like XCOPY, to copy (and duplicate) subdirectories. It also has a nifty /N (nothing) switch that lets you carry out a mock copying session to see what the results of your actions might be, without actually copying (and overwriting) any files. 4DOS makes it hard to accidentally overwrite files anyway, because you can include /R(eplace) and /U(pdate) switches that ask for confirmation before copying over existing files or newer files.

DEL /Z erases hidden and system files; EXIT can have an optional errorlevel code to pass back to the previous command processor; and SHIFT can accommodate 127 (not 10) replaceable parameters in batch files. Nearly all 4DOS command lines can have 256 characters instead of the DOS-mandated 128-character limitation.

If you want to spend less time at the DOS prompt, 4DOS includes a SELECT command with a point-and-shoot display of filenames you can use with any appropriate internal or external DOS command. Typing

```
select copy  (*.DOC;*.TXT)  C:\BAK
```

creates a screen listing all the files in the current directory ending in DOC or TXT extensions. You can then use the cursor up and down arrows or PgUp and PgDn keys to scroll through the list of files and mark or unmark with the space bar or plus key the ones you want to copy.

The latest version of 4DOS makes some changes for greater compatibility with MS-DOS 5/6 and DR DOS 6.0. It has its own LOADHIGH command for putting memory-resident programs in upper memory, boasts a pop-up command history window you can scroll through, many new switches for existing commands, and a few entirely new commands. However, the best things about 4DOS have been with us for awhile. My nominations for the best:

ALIAS

ALIAS would occupy three of the top slots in any Top Ten list of 4DOS features. ALIAS lets you create your own internal DOS commands and redefine the ones included with DOS or 4DOS. If you don't like how the MD command works, you can create a new version.

Do you sometimes create a subdirectory, switch to that directory, and then perform some task like copy or unzip files? Except, when you're finished, you discover you forgot to type **CD \newdir** and all the files ended up in the parent of the one you wanted?

No problem. Redefine MD with the following line:

```
alias md = '*md %& ^ cd %1'
```

When you type the MD command, it creates the subdirectory specified and then logs onto that directory. Of course, 4DOS lets you create a whole raft of subdirectories at one time by typing them as a list on the command line. We wouldn't want to disable that feature. So, our redefined MD creates all the subdirectories you specified and then changes to the first one in the list.

4DOS alias definitions are placed between back-quote marks if they contain multiple commands or replaceable parameters. (This example has both). The asterisk tells 4DOS that we are referring to the original, internal MD command and not the new one we are defining; otherwise 4DOS would attempt to replace the second MD with the alias. The %& is a replaceable parameter that 4DOS replaces with the rest of the command line, perhaps a whole series of subdirectory names to be created.

The caret symbol separates multiple commands on a single line. Because %1 is used as the replaceable parameter, 4DOS substitutes only the first subdirectory name typed. If you need the old version of the MD command, you can use MKDIR, which is not changed by the alias.

Because aliases are stored in memory, 4DOS executes them immediately, just as it would an internal command. You may use a long list of batch-file type commands, including 4DOS's IFF/THEN/ELSE structures to create commands of your own.

Nor are you limited to fooling around with traditional DOS commands. You can create brand new ones. How about these:

```
alias soundoff = 'echo ATM1 = 0 > com1'
alias windows = 'pushd ^ cdd c:\windows ^ win %& ^
popd'
alias config = 'select (C:\BAT\BOOT*.BAT)'
```

The first alias would turn your modem speaker's sound off every time you typed SOUNDOFF. The second would store the current disk drive and directory on a special stack 4DOS keeps and then change both drive and directory to C:\WINDOWS and load Windows (passing along any command line parameters you might have typed. Then, when you exit Windows, 4DOS would "pop" your original directory off the stack and change back to it.

The last alias might be used by folks who have several sets of AUTO-EXEC.BAT and CONFIG.SYS files, each copied to the root directory by an appropriate batch file, such as BOOTWIN.BAT, BOOT4DOS.BAT, BOOTNIL.BAT, etc.) Typing CONFIG would activate 4DOS's SELECT command and let you point-and-shoot the batch file you wanted to run. Of course, the last command in the file would be REBOOT, which is the 4DOS command to boot your computer.

Could you care less whether, say, COM and EXE files show up in your directory listings? Create an alias that makes them invisible for a moment:

```
alias dirx = 'except (*.COM *.EXE) *DIR'
```

When you type DIRX, 4DOS treats it as a DIR command but uses it's own EXCEPT command to exclude all COM and EXE files. Suppose that you work with image files a lot and want a special directory command that ignores everything but common image file types? Try this alias:

```
alias dirim = '*dir  *.pcx *.tif *.img *.eps *.msp
*.bmp'
```

Or would you like to lock up your computer for a few seconds, perhaps to confuse or thwart troublemakers? Use this alias:

```
alias lock = 'ctty nul ^ delay %1 ^ ctty con
```

Better Batch Files

Long aliases can get unwieldy to type in accurately, and if you have a large collection of them, they can gobble up valuable memory. In many cases, you're better off creating your customized commands using batch files. If you're accustomed to writing batch files using only the available DOS commands, get ready for an education.

With a traditional BAT file, DOS reads in one line at a time, executes the commands on that line and then reads in the next line in the file. That's very slow, at best. 4DOS adds a second type of batch file, called batch-to-memory, with the BTM extension. It reads the entire file into memory at once and is able to execute it five to ten times faster.

4DOS also frees you from command line slavery by providing the tools to create batch files that automate many tasks. It supports BASIC-like IFF/THEN/ELSE, .AND., .OR., and .XOR. logical operators, as well as GOSUB/RETURN control structures; lets you input information interactively while batch files run; and gives those files access to zillions of facts about your computer (from current working directory to amount of free space on a disk) through internal variables and functions. 4DOS also provides commands to read the current cursor position and to move the cursor to any position on the screen you specify. If you want to write a batch file arcade game, 4DOS lets you do it!

Where DOS limits you to comparing strings, errorlevels, or whether or not a file is present (with IF EXIST). 4DOS adds several checks for whether a subdirectory exists and whether a command is an internal command or alias. You can also test for a couple dozen internal variables or use them in batch files in other ways:

```
if "%_cpu"=="486" then echo "You're running a 486!"

if %_env<128 then echo You're running out of environ-
ment space!  Only %_env left!

if "%_win"=="2" gosub WINEnhanced
```

4DOS's variable functions can be used in a similar way:

```
if %@EMS [b]<256 echo Not enough EMS memory!
```

But you can also use them to return useful values, such as the number of seconds since midnight (@TIME), whether a printer is ready, or the DOS attributes (e.g, hidden, system, archived) of a file. Others change strings into substrings, pull out individual words, or convert a string to upper-case.

DESCRIBE

4DOS lets you augment eight-character/three character file names with descriptions of up to 40 characters. Would you rather open every file in a subdirectory to see what it contains, or read a concise description? Descriptions are stored in a hidden file in each subdirectory and are properly updated when the files are transferred or renamed using the internal COPY, MOVE, and RENAME commands.

Configurations

4DOS 4.0 relies on a file called 4DOS.INI, which like WIN.INI, provides control over scads of operating parameters. You can choose a number of screen rows, and foreground and background colors, set environment size, and define whether batch files should start with ECHO on or off. If you want to get really up-close and personal with your operating system, you can include directives in 4DOS.INI that determine cursor size, the frequency and duration of your system beep, and even redefine input keys like backspace, cursor left, and so on.

Of course, there are more options for customization in CONFIG.SYS, and 4DOS always runs a file called 4START.BTM, which can contain SETDOS commands to override the 4DOS.INI settings. SETDOS also lets you turn commands on or off at will from the DOS prompt. So what if nobody can understand how your system works but you—that's an extra security feature, right? J.P. Software, which publishes 4DOS, can be reached at 617-646-3975.

Utility Packages

Although many utilities are available as standalone programs, your most economical collection can be found in packages that combine a whole group of utilities. This section will look at the two leaders, Symantec's The Norton Utilities and Central Point's PC Tools. Both have many features that overlap the utilities provided with DOS 6; indeed, Microsoft drew from each of these companies for its backup, defragmenting, and anti-virus technologies. However, each package has other things to offer.

Both are priced exactly the same at this writing: $179, with a money-back guarantee. The cost could drop as competition from DOS 6's own package heats up in the next few months. Each has mouse support and the kind of easy-to-use graphical interface you would expect. So, how do you compare them? Just look at the individual features and see how they stack up.

Features Found in Norton That PC Tools Doesn't Have

The Norton Utilities include a few features you don't get with PC Tools. You'll need to decide which of these are important to you.

➤ **Disk Editor** Norton's Disk Editor can be used to edit disk sectors directly, including partition tables and FAT. This is heavy-duty, low-level hacking, but the kind of thing many experienced users and programmers require.

➤ **Time/Date Stamper** Norton lets you modify the time/date stamp of files. This is a minor feature that comes in useful if you want all your files to have the same time and date, especially to group all the files from various versions of a software release together.

➤ **Batch File Enhancer** Norton includes a batch programming language, which can be used to create powerful macros and applications.

➤ **Enhanced Command Shell** Norton offers NDOS, a version of 4DOS, that includes the enhancements outlined earlier, plus the capability to change keyboard/mouse/display settings from the Norton Control Panel.

Features Found in PC Tools That Norton Doesn't Have

➤ **Backup** PC Tools includes backup software; Norton Backup is sold as a separate product.

➤ **File Management Shell** Although you can do point-and-shoot file manipulation with NDOS's SELECT utility, only PC Tools has a full-featured file shell included. With Norton, you would need to purchase Norton Desktop for DOS to get the same features.

➤ **Viewers** PC Tools includes viewers that are available on Norton Desktop but not the basic Norton Utilities.

➤ **Appointment Calendar** PC Tools includes a handy appointment calendar utility.

➤ **Dialer** Only PC Tools lets you dial your phone, using a modem.

➤ **File Transfer** Also included in PC Tools is an Interlnk-type file transfer utility.

➤ **Telecommunications** You get basic telecommunications capabilities with PC Tools.

Features They Share

Both programs have the following roughly comparable features:

➤ **Disk Cache** Either one is likely to be a little faster than SmartDrive, and both offer more advanced features.

➤ **Defragmenter/Optimizer** Norton's Speed Disk lives up to its name, and that's the utility Microsoft based its own Defragmenter on. But PC Tools' version is also safe and easy to use.

➤ **Low-Level Formatting Utility** If your hard disk allows low-level formatting, this utility can "refresh" your formatting as required.

➤ **Undelete** Peter Norton invented the unerase utility, but PC Tools does an excellent job, too. Neither one really tops DOS 6, though.

➤ **Unformat** You can do this with DOS 6 now, but the versions provided with Norton, in particular, are likely to be more reliable.

➤ **Diagnose and repair disks** Both Norton's Disk Doctor and PC Tools' DiskFix do a good job at spotting and fixing the most common disk problems, such as damaged FATs. They can each help you locate stray clusters and put broken files back together.

➤ **Make disks bootable** This is helpful if you have a disk that used to boot, and will no longer, or if you need to produce a bootable diskette.

➤ **Encryption and file wiping** If you have sensitive data, you need one of these utilities to hide your data or to reliably erase old information that is no longer needed.

➤ **Menu system** Menu systems make it easy for beginning users to navigate among their applications.

➤ **Prune and graft directories** Until DELTREE, there was no easy way for DOS users to remove whole subdirectories without using one of these tools.

➤ **Search files for characters** The searching utilities with either of these programs are much faster and easier to use than the DOS **find** command.

➤ **Sort and rename directories** DOS 6 still doesn't let you resort directories, although **move** finally adds the capability of renaming them.

➤ **Anti-virus protection** The advantages of Central Point and Norton's standalone anti-virus programs have been described earlier in this book. However, to avoid cannibalizing sales of its standalone Norton Antivirus, the Norton Utilities version only prevents infection to boot-sector viruses.

➤ **Line print utility** Each program has a utility that lets you format and print files to your line printer.

➤ **System information and benchmarks** Norton's System Information utility was the standard long before other benchmarks became available. Now everybody has a version available. MSD.EXE included with DOS 6 does a good job of listing system information, but it doesn't do benchmarks. You need Norton or PC Tools for that.

➤ **BBS support** Both packages are supported with extensive online aids available through CompuServe or their own bulletin boards. When all you need is an upgrade, a quick tip, or a program that enhances a package, these resources are valuable, indeed.

Other Utilities

Many of the features found in the Norton Utilities or PC Tools have been incorporated into so-called "desktop" programs available for DOS and Windows from both companies. To the basic complement of utilities, these packages add icon-driven file management, desk accessories like pop up calculators, screen savers and, in the case of Norton, file viewers (PC Tools already has viewers).

In addition, a broad range of utility programs, some with very specialized functions, can be found as shareware offerings. These utilities, often put together by the authors for their own use. This next section will explain how you can locate shareware utilities.

What Is Shareware?

In a nutshell, shareware is not free or public domain software; shareware is commercial, copyrighted software just like Lotus 1-2-3, and even DOS itself. However, as anyone who has paid $695 for a box containing two disks, a thin manual, and five inches of foam padding can attest, packaging, marketing, and overhead can raise the price of useful packages beyond the reach of many who could benefit from them.

Most shareware is not distributed through normal retail channels. Instead, these programs are made available through electronic bulletin board systems, user group libraries, mail order shareware outlets, and often just between friends. You may elect to print your own manual from the file supplied with the program. Often, however, when you register the program, you receive a fancier bound manual.

For shareware programs that have no retail distribution, the type of distribution is the only difference between a shareware program and a program sold through retail channels. Many fancy non-shareware programs you see in stores were written entirely by a single person or a relatively small team of software engineers (you would be astounded at how small the Ventura Software organization was before it was acquired by Xerox Desktop Software). Shareware, too, is often created by individuals or small companies.

And, just as there are some retail-distributed programs that are turkeys, you may find some really bad shareware. In either case, such programs tend to have a relatively short life. Word gets around that a given package performs poorly. Retailers won't carry bad software long; bulletin boards won't let bad shareware occupy valuable hard disk space; and unhappy users won't make copies to pass along to their friends.

Another similarity between shareware and retail software is that you are expected to pay for it if you use it. With shareware, however, you can try the software first to make sure that it works with your computer and is compatible with other software. If you continue to use it after a trial period, then you're required to register (purchase) the software. Because retail software packages that have been opened are rarely returnable, your only option there is to try the software at the store or on the computer of a friend who happens to have it. Which approach would you say is more convenient?

What shareware does is give new and interesting software a fair shot at success. You might be hesitant to pay $300 for software that does something you didn't know you needed. You would, however, probably be willing to invest in a disk, some online time, or a book like this one for an opportunity to try a package that sounds interesting. Because the shareware vendor doesn't have huge amounts of money tied up in packaging, advertising, and distribution, the vendor can give you that opportunity.

Because shareware often has the same features and functionality as conventionally distributed software, it sometimes ends up in retail channels. A package recognized as superior, like ProComm, can reach many more potential users when sold at retail, because everyone just doesn't have access to a BBS, a user group, friends who collect software, or another shareware outlet. You pay for shareware by registering your package with the author or publisher.

How Do You Find Shareware?

There are several ways to obtain the latest shareware offerings. These are described below.

Write or Call the Authors

If you see a review of a shareware product in a magazine and are ready to register, call the author directly. You can sometimes use your Visa, MasterCard, or American Express card to charge the registration fee. The author will often send you a printed copy of the manual and a copy of the latest version of the software on diskette.

Use Your Modem

You can download software from a computer bulletin board system (BBS). A local bulletin board has the advantage of allowing you to get a copy of any shareware program for free, if the board doesn't charge a user fee, and the phone call is toll-free for you.

Some BBS systems are specialized, serving only certain computer systems or interests, such as desktop publishing. Nearly any general interest, IBM-oriented BBS will have a copy of the best shareware. If you're not familiar with the BBSs in your area, a local computer user group, high school computer club, or the staff at a friendly computer store can help you out. (Radio Shack Computer Plus stores often have transient employees who actually like and use computers.)

If you can't find the shareware you want on on a local board, purchase a copy of Computer Shopper. Each monthly issue of this massive tabloid includes a list of the major bulletin board systems and user groups, arranged geographically.

The BBS method does not guarantee you will get the absolute latest version of any shareware product, because many BBSs depend on their users to upload the software. In larger cities, the most frequently accessed BBSs will have very recent copies of popular shareware and public domain programs.

You can also obtain the very latest version of most shareware from some of the online information services, such as the CompuServe Information Service (CIS). Shareware on these major networks is often uploaded by the authors themselves, so you can be assured of getting a complete copy only days after its release. In the case of 4DOS, J.P. Software also distributes the program to qualified beta testers over CompuServe through a special system, so you'll find a lively, knowledgeable group of users and developers who can answer any questions you might post. There is a forum for 4DOS users that you'll want to explore. Just type GO PCVENB and look for the JP Software area.

The only disadvantage to downloading shareware from the information services is that the service isn't free. CompuServe, for example, charges $6.30 per hour for 300 baud connect time, and $12.60 per hour for 1200 or 2400 baud service. You can also connect at 9600 bps for $22.50, which can be a bargain when you are downloading files; transfers will take place four times as fast, so your net cost will be half. Most services also charge a signup fee.

Logging onto CIS, finding shareware you want, downloading it, and reading some of the interesting messages from other users might take you an hour or so. However, the $6 to $15 it will cost will be well spent. Remember that although you pay for the connect time, you still receive the shareware version of of these programs, so you will need to register your copy if you decide to continue using it.

When you download shareware from an information service or BBS, it will probably be in compressed, or archived format. You'll need a program like ARCE.COM, PKXARC.COM, or PKUNZIP to reconstruct the file. These can be downloaded from the same source or obtained from one of the following outlets

User Groups

These are another excellent source of shareware. Computer Shopper can lead you to some local groups, many of which maintain shareware libraries of disks that users can borrow and copy. You may not even have to join, or you may be able to get a friend who is a member to borrow shareware for you. Again, local computer stores can help you locate user groups in your area.

Many smaller computer stores and even some book stores that carry computer book titles "sell" shareware disks. I've purchased shareware disks from a Book Warehouse outlet in Rochester, N.Y., and from a struggling computer store here in my home town (population 11,000). There is a restriction, (suggested by the Association of Shareware Professionals) on how much such organizations can charge for shareware disks, so you'll usually see these disks priced at $8 or less. The store makes a small profit (their costs are more than the 19 cents they paid for the disk; remember, commercial operations have overhead). The shareware gets wider distribution. It's a good system.

Mail Order

There are dozens of public domain/shareware mail order firms that manage to eke out enough profits from selling software to pay for toll-free 800 numbers, computerized disk duplicating systems, and floor space on which their operators can stand by. Expect to pay from $2 to $6 for each disk. The quality of the product varies all over the place. Some of the low-price firms provide only one or two programs per disk for your two bucks. Others pack them full of compressed software for the same price. Just remember that if you deal with an unknown firm, you have no way of knowing whether or not you're getting the latest version.

For that reason, I deal with the mail-order companies that have good reputations. Lately, I've been using Public Brand Software—800-426-3475, 800-727-3476 in Indiana—almost exclusively, even though, at $5 per disk, their charges are at the high end. However, there is no surcharge for 3.5-inch disks. I also like their catalog. Some of the mail-order firms send out catalogs that are so poorly organized that I throw them away rather than waste time trying to find something useful (with the enormous income I make as an author, I don't have to waste much time to eliminate the savings on a few $1.99 disks).

PBS catalogs, on the other hand, group the various types of software together. New and updated disks are highlighted, so you can find them easily. The descriptions of the programs are complete and accurate.

Top Offerings

There are thousands of shareware utility programs available. Here are some of the top contenders you might want to look for. Windows shareware, another whole category, is not included. (If you're interested in Windows shareware, check out my column "The Other Channel" in *Windows User* magazine each month.)

➤ **AnaDisk** Utility to analyze, inspect, edit, repair and copy floppy disks.

➤ **Cutter** Slices up files into smaller sizes for copying to floppies with limited space.

➤ **Cleanup** McAfee's virus removal tool.

➤ **DirNav** Navigates directories from a menu.

➤ **DiskPix** Shows a pie chart of free disk space and the percentage backed up.

➤ **DiskOrGanizer** A shareware defragmenter that compares well with DOS 6's offering.

➤ **EMMCache** A disk cache that optionally uses expanded memory.

➤ **FEd** A simple byte editor that's better than DEBUG.

➤ **FFF** A fast file finder that searches across subdirectories.

➤ **Flash Light** If your computer is located under your desk, this utility can help: it flashes on your screen whenever your floppies are accessed.

➤ **FormatMaster** Format from two floppy disks cyclicly.

➤ **Guardian** Disk file and password locking.

➤ **Handsoff** Screams when your system is touched!

➤ **NewPath** Adds a disk or subdirectory to the environment path.

➤ **Mouse Cursor** Adds mouse capabilities to DOS programs that don't normally have them.

➤ **MSwitch** Turns mouse on and off from the command line.

➤ **Power Batch** Enhances batch file language with new commands.

➤ **Patriquin's Utilities** A collection of DOS utilities that includes PreBack (shows which files need backing up), PCopy (a better file copying utility), PDaily (runs selected programs from AUTOEXEC.BAT only once each day).

➤ **Scan** McAfee's virus scanning utility, updated frequently.

➤ **Setrows** Sets the number of rows on EGA/VGA monitor screens.

➤ **Speech** A synthesized speech program.

➤ **Stowaway** Frees up hard disk space by cataloging and archiving files to other media.

➤ **ViewCMOS** Looks at your CMOS settings.

➤ **XTree** The shareware version of the popular XTree Gold file manager/shell.

➤ **WPHD** Write protects hard disks.

The Next Step

The next step is up to you. You've read all about DOS 6's exciting utilities, and learned about many of the alternative channels available for third-party utilities. Select the utilities that can help you most and make them a regular part of your repertoire. Utility programs can help you get a lot more enjoyment from your computer, because they make your system easier to use, faster, more powerful, or more efficient.

MS-DOS/Utility Glossary

Here are some brief definitions of many of the technical and semi-technical terms used in this book. You'll also find some common words that don't appear in previous chapters but which are likely to crop up in conversations about MS-DOS.

AccessDOS Special extensions to MS-DOS that meet the needs of people with disabilities.

Advanced Power Management (APM) specification   A standard used for laptop computers that makes it possible for MS-DOS to control power consumption of components like the hard disk and LCD screen.

Ambiguous In computer parlance, anything, such as a file name, that is not defined explicitly. Wildcards can be used in file names to provide a specification that can refer to more than one MS-DOS file.

ANSI.SYS An installable device driver that gives extended keyboard and screen control to the PC.

Anti-Virus A utility that guards against infection by computer viruses, detects them if they have infected one or more files in your computer, and assists in removing the virus from the affected file.

Application program Software such as a word processing program, spreadsheet, or database manager that performs useful work not directly related to the maintenance or operation of the computer.

Applications program interface (API) A common interface that allows software engineers to write programs that will operate with a broad range of computer configurations.

Archive A way to compress or store files that are no longer active. Programs like ARC.EXE or PKZIP.EXE combine and compress files into archive files for more compact, easier storage.

Archive bit A bit within a file's attribute byte in the file allocation table, which is set to a value of 1 or 0 to indicate whether or not the file has been backed up by XCOPY, BACKUP, or some other utility program designed to reset that bit. An archive bit can be modified using the ATTRIB command.

Argument A variable included on the command line that passes information to the command or alias.

ASCII The American Standard Code for Information Interchange (although the International Standard Organization has included this standard under one of its ISO descriptions.) A standard code for representing the most common alphanumeric characters, codes such as line feeds, punctuation marks, and symbols used in computer text.

Strictly speaking, ASCII is a seven-bit code that defines only 127 characters. However, an extended ASCII code with an additional 128 characters is also in common use.

ASP The Association of Shareware Professionals. An industry group that sets standards for authors of shareware programs.

ASPI Advanced SCSI Programing Interface. A standardized way of addressing SCSI devices through the device driver. Supported by CorelSCSI software and many SCSI interface vendors.

Assembler A program that allows the user to write software using a higher level language than machine language, called assembly language. After the program is written, the assembler translates it into machine language.

Assembly language The language used by an assembler, which allows using mnemonic commands such as MOV and INT instead of machine language. The programmer can apply labels to certain sections of code and call these instead of keeping track of where specific modules are located. When the program has been finished, the source code produced can be assembled into machine language object code.

Asynchronous A communications method under which the exact timing of signals is not critical; the next set of information is sent whenever a confirmation signal is received. This is the opposite of the synchronous method in which data is sent within an exact block of time. IBM PCs most commonly use asynchronous communications, as with modems, to exchange data over distances of more than a few feet.

Attribute byte A byte in the file allocation table that stores certain information about a file, such as whether it is read-only, invisible, or a system file or has been modified since it was last backed up. Under DOS, ATTRIB can change only the read-only and archive bits; MS-DOS lets you change any of the attribute bits with a simple ATTRIB command.

AUTOEXEC.BAT An ASCII file placed in the root directory of the boot disk. It contains a list of commands that will be carried out by the command processor automatically during the boot-up operation. This file allows you to load memory-resident programs, specify a PATH to be used by DOS to search for system files, and perform other tasks that configure the system. AUTOEXEC.BAT is not run in a secondary shell.

Back up To make a copy of computer data as a safeguard against accidental loss. The copy that is made is called the backup.

Backup set The set of files spanning as many individual disks or other media as required for a given backup. Each backup session produces a separate backup set.

Base memory A term sometimes applied to the first 640K of memory in a system, which is all that can be accessed by MS-DOS under ordinary conditions.

BASIC Beginner's All-Purpose Symbolic Instruction Code. The high-level language built into IBM PCs and furnished with DOS in compatibles. BASIC.COM is the simplest version with disk I/O capabilities. BASICA.COM and GW-BASIC.EXE are the most widely used versions.

Batch A set stored for later processing as a whole. Batch files, for example, contain sets of DOS commands that can be interpreted and carried out by the command processor one after another when the batch file is called.

Batch processor An interpreter that executes a batch file. Usually, COMMAND.COM is your batch processor, but other enhanced batch processors are available.

Baud A data transmission rate of 1 bit per second, used to measure asynchronous communications speed. The term is derived from J.M.E. Baudot, who invented the Baudot telegraph code.

Bernoulli drive A mass storage device that uses flexible magnetic media and relies on the Bernoulli effect to keep the disk and read/write heads separated by a thin cushion of air. These drives offer the same storage capacity as smaller hard disk drives and have access times that are somewhat slower, but they have the advantage of removable media and freedom from data-damaging head crashes.

Binary Base-two arithmetic, which uses only 1s and 0s to represent numbers. 0001 represents 1 decimal; 0010 represents 2 decimal; 0011 represents 3 decimal; and so on.

Binary file A non-text file, such as a program file. May contain characters beyond the 128 represented by 7-bit ASCII text.

BIOS The Basic Input/Output System of a computer is a set of computer code, provided on read only memory (ROM) chips and used to govern basic system-level functions.

Bit A binary digit, either a 1 or a 0.

Bits per inch Abbreviated bpi, used as a measure of data density along a track.

Boot To start a computer, either when the power is turned on or when the system is reset (through Ctrl-Alt-Del).

Boot drive The disk drive used to start up the computer.

Boot sector virus A type of virus that infects the portion of your hard disk used to initially load MS-DOS.

Bootstrap A very short set of computer instructions, usually designed to do nothing but load into the computer a longer program that carries out the actual loading of the operating system. On disks, the boot sector is found on the first sector of the first track of the first surface to be read by the system.

Buffer An area of memory used to store information temporarily.

Bug An error in a program that results in some unintended action.

Byte Eight bits, which can represent any number from 0000000 to 11111111 binary (0 to 255 decimal).

Cache A memory buffer used to store information read from disk, to allow DOS to access it more quickly. Cache programs use various schemes to make sure that the most frequently accessed sectors and the most recently accessed sectors remain in the buffer as long as possible.

CD-ROM Compact Disk-Read Only Memory. An optical disk mass storage device that, like all optical disks, uses pits stamped on the disk and read by a laser. CD-ROMs are encoded with information during manufacture and cannot be written to by the user. They provide a means of distributing large databases on a compact medium.

Character An alphanumeric character, punctuation mark, or other symbol available from the PC keyboard.

Checksum A number derived from information about a file, which can be stored and compared with current checksums to determine whether the file has been changed, particularly by a virus.

Child directory A directory created below a parent directory. C\ is the root directory of drive C; C\WP is a child directory of C\, and C\WP\LETTERS is a child directory of C\WP.

Client In a network, the computer you use to type commands is called the client, and the one that supplies the file or which controls the peripheral you are accessing is referred to as the server.

Client-server A type of network architecture in which individual desktop system *clients* generally access many or most of the files, peripherals, and sometimes programs from a remote computer called a server.

Cluster The smallest unit of disk space that can be allocated by DOS. For hard disks, a cluster is usually 4 sectors (512 bytes each), 2048 bytes, or 8 sectors for a total of 4096 bytes. Cluster size has a bearing on how efficiently DOS operates. Smaller clusters waste less space on the disk, but larger clusters allow DOS to find information on the disk more efficiently.

COM file A disk file, limited to 64K for its code and data (although such files can have overlays tacked onto the end which make them much larger), which is a DOS executable program.

Command A word or phrase used to tell a computer what to do next.

Command History The MS-DOS feature that allows you to recall the list of commands you have typed, so you can re-use them or modify them.

Command line A set of DOS commands and parameters typed at the DOS prompt.

Command processor A program like COMMAND.COM or 4DOS that serves as an interface between the user and the DOS files that actually carry out various functions.

COMMAND.COM The DOS command interpreter, which takes the commands supplied by the user or software and determines what DOS services are needed to carry them out. 4DOS is a replacement for COMMAND.COM.

Commit A command to tell a cache like SmartDrive to write to disk any sectors that have changed but have not yet been previously updated on your hard disk.

Common A block of commands within CONFIG.SYS that are carried out for all configurations, designated by a [common] label within the file.

Compatibility test An examination of your system's usability with a particular program or hardware component. DOS 6 runs a compatibility test when setting up Backup to determine whether the fastest disk access methods can be used with your computer.

Compiler A program that translates source code written in a higher level language into machine language object code.

Compressed volume A logical hard disk that has had its files reduced in size with DoubleSpace or another file compression utility.

Compression A way to reduce the amount of space taken up by a file by replacing redundant strings of characters with shorter codes that represent the same thing. Your computer can reconstruct the original code during decompression to restore the file to its original state for access or execution. For programs and data, *lossless* compression must be used, which squeezes files with absolutely no loss of the original information. Image files, can be compressed with *lossy* methods, because some ommited information cannot be detected by the human eye.

Compression ratio A comparison between the amount of space a file occupied before compression, and after. Some types of files, such as ASCII or text files, can be compressed 4:1 or more. TIF and other image files that have already been compressed by their applications may produce only a 1.25:1 or lower compression ratio.

COMSPEC An environment variable that tells the command processor where to find the program that is to be used as a secondary command processor.

Concatenate To add together.

CONFIG.DAT A copy of your original CONFIG.SYS file created by DOS 6's Uninstall utility. It can be used to restore your system if you elect to uninstall the new operating system.

CONFIG.SYS An ASCII file, interpreted by DOS on booting, if present in the root directory of the boot disk. CONFIG.SYS is acted on before AUTOEXEC.BAT but cannot contain anything other than commands that specify device drivers to be used or set other system configuration factors such as the number of buffers to be allocated and the size of the environment or to set the SHELL to be used.

Configuration The collection of parameters and components that make up a given application or operating system.

Configuration block A configuration block is a set of CONFIG.SYS commands that are carried out together. Each block begins with a *block header*, a single-word name surrounded by brackets. You may use up to 70 characters but no spaces (use an underline to separate "words"), slashes, commas, semicolons, equal signs, or square brackets.

Console The PC keyboard and display, which are the standard input and standard output device, respectively.

Contiguous In reference to hard disks, contiguous sectors are those that are arranged consecutively on the disk. DOS tries to allocate sectors to a file contiguously so that the disk drive can read as many sectors of a file as possible with a minimum of read/write head movement. However, as a hard disk fills, the unallocated sectors gradually become spread out and fragmented, forcing DOS to choose more and more noncontiguous sectors. Fragmented files can be much slower to access.

Control character A nonprinting character used to send information to a device, such as the control characters used to communicate special commands to a printer.

Conventional memory Another name for base memory, or the first 640K of memory in your computer, which is all that MS-DOS can use to run applications programs.

Coprocessor An additional microprocessor used in tandem with the main processor. IBM PCs and compatibles typically have sockets for an 8087, 80287, or 80387 math coprocessor designed to offload number crunching tasks from the main microprocessor, producing much faster operation for applications involving much computation, such as spread sheet recalculation. The 80486DX processor has a math coprocessor built in, but the 80486SX processor's math capabilities are absent or disabled.

Current directory The default directory that DOS assumes you mean unless you explicitly type some other directory name within a command. The directory a user is presently logged into.

Current drive The disk drive a user is presently logged into.

Cursor An on-screen symbol that indicates the current display position.

CVF Compressed volume file. A read-only, hidden, system file that contains a compressed drive's files, subdirectories, and other contents. A CVF is stored in the root directory of its host drive and has a filename such as DBLSPACE.000.

Cylinder The "stack" of tracks on all the platters of a hard disk drive that can be read simultaneously by the read/write heads.

Data transfer rate The speed at which data is moved from the disk between an external device and memory.

DBLSPACE.BIN A file that gives MS-DOS access to compressed drives. It is loaded first into the top of conventional memory, before CONFIG.SYS is processed, and then moved to a final location by DBLSPACE.SYS.

Debug The process of removing errors from a program and the name of a program in DOS, DEBUG.COM, which allows changing the value of bytes stored in memory and on disk. MS-DOS uses SID instead of DEBUG for these functions.

Defragment To reorganize a hard disk so that all of each file's sectors are located on contiguous hard disk clusters, eliminating the need for the hard disk to skip all over the disk surface to access the file.

Device driver A software module that tells DOS how to control a given piece of hardware, such as a printer, monitor, disk drive, or keyboard. ANSI.SYS and VDISK.SYS are device drivers supplied with DOS. Others are supplied by manufacturers of peripherals.

Diagnostic A utility that tests components of a computer to locate potential defects and problems. When the PC is turned on, built-in diagnostic programs in ROM perform the power-on self-test.

Differential backup A backup in which only the selected files that have been created or changed since the last full or incremental backup are copied. Like the incremental version, a differential backup is fast, because only new or modified files are involved. However, it does not reset the archive flag and mark a file as being backed up. You can use this type of backup to copy the latest versions of files, without affecting any later incremental backup.

Direct Memory Access Abbreviated DMA. The movement of data directly from memory to some other device, such as the disk drive, without first being loaded into the microprocessor.

Directory The list of filenames stored on a disk, along with the size of the file, date and time it was created or last changed, and the type of file.

Disk drive A mass storage device that can read and write information. Disk drives can be floppy drives, hard disks, optical disks, Bernoulli devices, or other types.

DOS Disk Operating System. The control program of the computer that oversees how the system interfaces with the user and the peripherals, including disk drives.

DOS Protected Mode Interface (DPMI). A standard way for multitasking programs and extended memory to communicate with each other, developed by Microsoft. See also *Virtual Control Program Interface.*

Double-buffering A technique used by SmartDrive to provide compatibility with some SCSI and ESDI hard disk controllers that are unable to use memory provided by EMM386 or Windows in enhanced mode. DOS 6 can usually identify these controllers for you automatically and install double-buffering commands in CONFIG.SYS when needed. It creates a special memory 2.5K buffer in conventional RAM, in which physical and virtual addresses are identical. The only "cost" is the small amount of RAM and the overhead required to shuffle data in and out of the new buffer. On a 386 or higher system using virtual 8086 mode (either under Windows or with a memory manager), the read or write address the controller passes along to DOS may not be the same as the actual physical address. Microsoft's Virtual DMA services standard is designed to avoid this problem, but not all bus mastering controllers support it.

Drive specification The letter used by DOS to identify a disk drive, from A to Z.

Dual boot A capability of OS/2 to boot from more than one operating system. One of these can be DOS 6.

Dynamic RAM A type of memory that must be electrically refreshed many times each second to avoid loss of the contents. PCs and compatibles use dynamic RAM to store programs, data, and the operating system.

EBCDIC A code system like ASCII, used with IBM mainframes and some software, such as DisplayWrite.

EDIT MS-DOS's ASCII text-editing and creation program.

EMS Expanded Memory Specification. A special kind of memory that uses hardware and software drivers designed for it. DOS sees this memory in pages, using a window located in conventional memory. MS-DOS can convert extended memory into EMS memory on 80386 and 80486 computers through the EMM386 driver.

EMS swapping Any scheme in which information is placed in EMS memory to make room for other data in conventional memory.

End of file marker A character used to mark the end of a file. DOS uses the Ctrl-Z character (ASCII code 26).

Environment An area of memory set aside to keep track of information, such as the system prompt. You can define variables to be placed in this environment through the SET command.

Environment variable The name of an entry stored in the environment. Some variable names, such as PATH or COMSPEC, are reserved by DOS.

Escape (ASCII code) A special key that produces the ASCII code 27, which represents the Escape character. Many programs use this code to back out of, or escape from menus. The escape character can also be used to send information to the ANSI.SYS device driver.

EXE file A more complex type of DOS executable file, compared to COM files, which allows running programs that require more than 64K of memory.

Exit code A value stored in a memory register when an external command or program is completed. This code can be accessed with the IF ERRORLEVEL test in a batch file. Functions that return errorlevels (DOS external commands like REPLACE supply an exit code), return an errorlevel of 0 if the command has been carried out successfully and a non-zero if there is some other result. Sometimes, these codes can be put to work by the user. For example, REPLACE returns a value of 2 if no source files were found, 3 if the source or target path is invalid, and 5 if access is denied to the file or directory. Your batch file can test for these and recover from the error.

Express setup An installation option for DoubleSpace, MemMaker, and other programs that allows the setup program to determine the best configuration for your particular hardware and software.

Extended BIOS Data Area (XBDA) An area of memory for storage of BIOS data, normally located at the top of conventional memory. EMM386 usually moves it into an UMB. Some programs won't work properly if you allow EMM386.EXE to move this data area to upper memory.

Extended memory Continuous memory from 1M to 16M, which can be used by 80286 and 80386 based computers with applications written to take advantage of this form of memory.

Extended partition The second DOS partition, which is not bootable like the primary partition.

External command A command that is not built into the command processor, but which must be accessed through a separate utility program. External commands are executable files like FORMAT.COM and DISKCOPY.EXE.

FAT File Allocation Table. A special area on the disk that tracks the way clusters are assigned to various files.

File A collection of information, usually data or a program, that has been given a name and has disk space allocated to it.

File control block A file management tool that is used only by older software. The number of such blocks of memory that can be made available is specified by the FCBS command in the CONFIG.SYS file.

File infector virus A computer virus that adds code to program files.

Filename The name given to a file. Under DOS, it consists of eight characters and a three-character extension.

File-oriented backup Any backup system that stores information in files, just as they are stored on the disk. Such a system allows easier access to and restoration of a particular file.

Filter A DOS program that accepts data from the standard input device, modifies it, and then sends it to the standard output device. DOS filters SORT, FIND, and MORE sort, locate specific strings, and display the output in pages, respectively.

Fixed disk Another name for a hard disk drive, so-called because such disks are not commonly removed from the computer while in use.

Floppy disk drive A type of disk drive with removable media. Today, most floppy disks are 5.25 or 3.5 inches square; an earlier type was 8 inches square.

Floptical disk A kind of special 3.5-inch floppies that have had tiny markings placed on them, often burned by a laser. The read/write mechanism of the floptical drive can then use these markings to track much more precisely and, therefore, record data more densely than with conventional floppy disks, up to 21M.

Formatting Preparing a disk for use by writing certain information in magnetic form. Formatting divides the disk into tracks and sectors and sets up a directory structure.

Fragmentation The scattering of file sectors throughout your hard disk as new files are written to the "holes" left by smaller erased files and to other unallocated sectors.

Full backup A full backup is a complete backup of all selected files, most often all the files on a given hard disk, and frequently all the files on all your hard disks. Strictly speaking, a backup of everything is called a *total backup*. A full backup is really nothing more than a complete backup of the selected files without regard for other factors, such as whether they have been backed up or not. In other words, this type of backup copies files without regard to whether or not their archive flags are set. That is, even if some of the files have already been backed up, a full backup will back them up again, anyway. After a full backup has been performed, all the archive flags of the affected files are reset to indicate that the files have been safely backed up. A full backup creates a single history file, which can be used to completely restore a subdirectory, hard disk, or set of hard disks.

Full path The entire description, including disk drive and all subdirectories from the root directory down, of the location of a particular file. C\DOS\TEMP\SWAP.TMP is the full path description of SWAP.TMP.

Hard error An error in reading or writing data caused by hardware. Because such errors are usually the result of damage to the computer, they are more difficult to recover from than soft errors.

Hardware The physical components of a computer system, including the CRT, keyboard, microprocessor, memory, and other peripherals.

Hardware interrupts The signals used by peripherals such as modems, your keyboard, disk drive, etc., to force the CPU to stop processing and to receive a request for services.

Hexadecimal The base-16 number system used with PCs to make binary information easier to interpret by humans. The numbers 0 to 16 are represented by the numerals 0 to 9 plus A, B, C, D, E, and F. An 8-bit byte storing a number from 0 to 255 can readily be represented by the hexadecimal values 0 to FF.

Hidden file A file whose attribute byte is marked so that it will not be displayed by the DOS DIR command unless you specifically say so.

Hierarchical In hard disk terminology, the structuring of directories so that each subdirectory has one parent but can have several child directories, branching out in a tree-like structure.

High-density disks Floppy disks that store more than the standard 360K of information. For example, 5.25-inch high density floppies can hold up to 1.2M of information; high-density 3.5-inch microdisks can store 1.44 to 2.88M.

High-level format The disk preparation performed by FORMAT, in which information needed by DOS to use the disk is written.

High-level language A language that allows representing machine-level operations by mnemonic keywords rather than 1s and 0s. BASIC, COBOL, PASCAL, C, and FORTRAN are all high-level languages.

High Memory Area Abbreviated HMA, the high memory area is the first 64K of extended RAM above the 1M barrier.

When a special memory manager is loaded, this memory can be accessed by certain programs, reducing the amount of conventional or base memory required by that program. MS-DOS loads part of its own kernel into HMA.

History File/Catalog All backup programs keep a history file or catalog of backup sets, which tracks what files are included with a given set of backup disks. The restore function uses this file to put the backed up files on the hard disk where they belong. Microsoft Backup, in both its Windows and DOS versions, keeps a master catalog that stores information about all backups you've performed, as well as individual catalogs about each backup set.

Host drive The original disk volume on which a compressed DoubleSpace volume is stored.

IBMBIO.COM Another name for IO.SYS, the DOS system file that contains low-level information for handling the hardware and which directs the computer to load IBMDOS.COM during bootup.

IBMDOS.COM Another name for MSDOS.SYS, the file that contains the program code needed to carry out various DOS services and which directs the computer to load COMMAND.COM during bootup.

Image-oriented backup Any backup system that creates a mirror image of the disk, without regard to the files themselves. With such a system, the entire disk must be restored from the backup medium to allow access to the files.

Incremental backup An incremental backup copies *only* the selected files that have been created or changed since the last full or incremental backup. This type of backup is used to quickly copy the new or modified files. These files are added to the full backup history file, giving you, in effect, an updated version of your full backup, which can then be used at any time to fully restore your directories or hard disks. An incremental backup resets the archive flags of the copied files to show that they have been properly backed up. An incremental backup is a little like updating a catalog/price sheet by adding new pages to the end and then changing the table of contents to point to the added pages. The old pages don't have be ripped out, and you don't need to reprint the whole catalog, but you end up with an up-to-date publication. The downside is that you need to retain your full backup and all the incremental backups to have a complete copy of everything on your hard disk.

Induce To cause an electrical field to be generated. As the read head of a disk drive passes over the media, the flux changes that have been written to the disk induce an electrical signal that can be interpreted by the drive controller to reconstruct the original information written to the disk.

Input Incoming information. Input can be supplied to the computer by the user or to a program by either the user or a data file.

Instantaneous cache hit rate A ratio that compares the number of SmartDrive cache hits to the total disk accesses in a given period of time.

Instructions The basic set of capabilities of a microprocessor, which allows the chip to load information in registers, move it to other registers, increment the data, add or subtract data to or from registers, and so forth.

Intel 8086 The microprocessor used in the IBM PS/2 Models 25 and some Model 30s and other systems. It processes information internally in 16-bit increments and has a 16-bit data path to memory.

Intel 8088 The microprocessor used in the IBM PC, PC-XT, PCjr, PC Convertible, Portable PC, and many clones. It processes information internally in 16-bit increments but has only an 8-bit path to memory.

Intel 80286 The microprocessor used in the IBM PC-AT, PS/2 Models 50 and 60, and many compatible computers. It has both a real mode, which emulates the 8086 chip and a protected mode, which allows access to more than the 1M of memory that can be addressed by 8088 chips.

Intel 80386 The microprocessor used in the IBM PS/2 Model 80 and other systems. It uses full 32-bit processing and memory and can access the real and protected modes provided by the 80286. In addition, the 80386 chip has built-in sophisticated memory management capabilities that allow setting up virtual 8086 machines, each with access to a full 640K of conventional memory.

Intel 80486 The microprocessor that preceeded the Pentium, which has all the features of the 80386, plus an on-chip floating point processor (equivalent to the 80387), cache memory, and greater speed.

Intelligent Having sufficient programming built-in to carry out certain tasks independently. An intelligent disk drive can accept requests from DOS, locate the data, and deliver it without detailed instructions on how to do the physical I/O.

Interactive Allowing user input during run-time.

Interactive start The DOS 6 bootup sequence initiated when the user holds down the F8 key, in which he or she is prompted to enter Y or N before each device driver is loaded.

Interleave The alternating of logical disk sectors to allow the hard disk time to process the information from one sector before the next is presented. Without interleave, a slow controller would allow the reading of only one sector per revolution.

Interpreter A program that interprets and carries out each line of another program written in a high-level language like BASIC or COBOL. These languages can also be compiled so that DOS can carry out a program's commands directly.

Interrupt A signal that tells the microprocessor to stop what it is doing and do something else. A simple process like pressing a key generates an interrupt.

I/O Input/Output. Used to describe the process whereby information flows to and from the microprocessor or computer through peripherals such as disk drives, modems, CRT screens, and printers.

IO.SYS The DOS system file that contains low-level information for handling the hardware and which directs the computer to load MSDOS.SYS during bootup.

Joint Photographic Expert Group (JPEG) compression A compression scheme that works particularly well with continuous tone images. It is efficient but still retains most of the valuable image information through quantization and discrete cosine transformations on the image.

K In computer teminology, 1024 bytes. 16K represents 16,384 bytes; 64K equals 65,536 bytes; 512K corresponds to 524,288 bytes; and so on.

Label On a hard disk, the volume name applied immediately after high-level formatting, if the /V switch was specified, or by use of the LABEL command. In batch files, a label is a line prefixed with a colon and is used to direct control from other parts of the batch file using the GOTO subcommand.

Lempel-Ziv (LZ) or Lempel-Ziv-Welch (LZW) compression A scheme that replaces frequently used strings of numbers with fixed-length codes. This system uses statistical analysis to determine what sets of numbers appear most often.

LIM Abbreviation for Lotus Intel Microsoft expanded memory specification, another name for EMS, used by Digital Research and others.

Logical Any feature not physically present but defined anyway for convenience. The logical sectors on a hard disk are arranged contiguously. Physically, they can be arranged in alternating fashion through interleaving.

Logic bomb A type of trojan horse, triggered by some logical condition on your computer. Unlike a simple trojan horse that operates every time you activate the host program, a logic bomb remains inert until some specific condition is met. It may wait until you insert a disk in your floppy drive and then erase all the data on that disk, a logic bomb may affect only printer output. Like other trojan horses, a logic bomb can remain with its host program or act as a virus and spread.

Lower memory The first portion of DOS memory, into which the DOS kernel and device drivers are usually loaded. MS-DOS allows placing part of this information to either high memory or upper memory blocks.

Low-level formatting The most basic formatting done on the hard disk to prepare it for partitioning and high-level formatting. This is often done by the manufacturer, which locks out bad sectors at this time.

Macro A series of commands that can be triggered at the press of a key or two. Many applications programs, and utilities like SuperKey and ProKey, allow users to develop their own macros for frequently used command sequences. MS-DOS 5.0 and higher includes macro capabilities in its DOSKEY utility.

Mass storage Permanent storage of computer information, usually on magnetic disk but can also include magnetic tape, optical disk, bubble memory, and other nonvolatile storage media.

Master catalog A listing of all the backup catalogs created during a backup cycle, allowing the user to choose the most current or an earlier set of backup files.

Megabyte 1024K, generally abbreviated as M.

Memory-resident program Also called a Terminate-and-Stay-Resident program (TSR). Utilities loaded into low conventional memory (or into high memory plus extended or expanded memory if you have a memory manager like MS-DOS's EMM386.SYS or Quarterdeck's QEMM) and that remain active while DOS executes other programs. They can be called by pressing a hotkey (as in SIDEKICK) or can work in the background (as in FASTOPEN).

Microprocessor The computer-on-a-chip that is the brains of a personal computer.

Millisecond One-thousandth of a second.

Mount To put a disk device in service, such as a DoubleSpace compressed volume file (CVF). Generally, all your hard disk CVFs will be mounted automatically when DOS boots. You might want to unmount one for security or other reasons and later remount it with this command. However, Mount is most often used to enable DOS to use compressed volumes that have been stored on removable media, such as floppy disks.

Multitasking The capability of a computer system to handle several different chores simultaneously. Because a microcomputer has only one main processor, this is usually done by "slicing" the processor's time into individual segments and allowing the programs to use them in rotation. DOS is not generally a multitasking operating system, although third-party enhancements can give it these capabilities.

Multiuser The capability of a computer system to handle several different tasks done by several different users simultaneously. UNIX is the best-known multiuser system among microcomputer users, although it is also available for larger systems.

Overlays Portions of a program that are called into memory as needed, overlaying a previous redundant section of the program. Using overlays allows programs to run that are much bigger than what could fit into memory all at once.

Parallel Moving data several bits at a time, rather than one bit at a time. Usually, parallel operation involves sending all eight bits of a byte along eight separate data paths at one time. This is faster than serial movement.

Parameter A qualifier that defines more precisely what a program such as the command interpreter is to do.

Parent directory The directory immediately above a child directory.

Parsing Examination of the command line to extract the keywords, parameters, aliases, and variables by the command processor, which then determines which internal or external commands to carry out.

Partition A part of a disk drive, usually set aside for use by a particular operating system. One partition on a hard disk is bootable. One of the others, if any, can become active through use of the FDISK program.

Password A capability of MS-DOS that allows you to prevent access to files or subdirectories unless the user enters a one- to eight-character string of characters. You can differentiate different levels of protection, allowing users to read, write, copy, or remove files, some combination of these priviledges, or to deny access completely.

Path A listing of directory names in order that defines the location of a particular file.

Peripheral Any component of a computer system other than the microprocessor itself and its directly accessible memory. We usually think of peripherals as printers, modems, etc.

Physical Existing in reality.

Pipe DOS's way of making the output of one program the input of another.

Pixel A picture element of a screen image one "dot" of the collection that makes up an image.

Polymorphic virus A kind of virus that is able to mutate, changing its code at random, making it more difficult for virus-scanning software to look for tell-tale sequences of code called signatures. Viruses also can encrypt themselves in random ways, using only a small unencrypted piece of code that does nothing except extract the rest of the code and load it into memory.

Port A channel of the computer used for input or output with a peripheral. The serial and parallel ports of the PC are the most widely used.

Primary partition With DOS 3.3 or later, the bootable DOS partition.

Primary shell The command processor that loads when the system is booted.

Program Code that instructs the computer on how to perform a sequence of functions.

Prompt A character or series of characters that lets the user know that the program is waiting for input. PROMPT is also a DOS command.

QBASIC The version of BASIC furnished with MS-DOS since version 5.0, it is a simpler version of QuickBasic.

Read-Only A file attribute that allows most DOS commands to read the information in the file but not to change it or overwrite it.

Read-Only Memory Memory that can be read by the system but not changed. Abbreviated ROM, read-only memory often contains system programs that help the computer carry out DOS services.

Redirection Re-routing input or output to or from the device for which it was originally headed. For example, you can send screen output to the printer using a command like DIR>>PRN or to a file DIR>>MYFILE.ASC.

Registers The basic memory locations of a microprocessor, through which all information that is processed passes.

Resident portion The part of a program that permanently resides in DOS memory and facilitates loading the transient portions as needed.

RISC Reduced Instruction Set Computer. A computer system that has a special microprocessor which has a smaller instruction set and therefore operates faster. Such systems depend on the software for functions that are handled by the microprocessor in other computers.

Sector The smallest section of a track, containing 512 bytes of data.

Segment A 64K section of memory that is manipulated as a block by DOS.

Serial Passing information one bit at a time in sequential order.

SETUP The MS-DOS program used to change the configuration of the operating system. Other programs, including Microsoft Windows, also have their own utilities with the same name.

Setup files In the realm of disk backups, these are files with the definitions for each type of backup that you want to perform. A setup can include the names of the entire disks or specific files that should be backed up, the media or path to back up to, and various options such as verification, password protection, and so forth.

Shadow RAM Memory between the 640K and 1024K boundaries that is used to duplicate the code and data contained in slower ROM which has the same addresses. When ROM is copied to shadow RAM, the system is usually able to execute the instructions and access the data much more rapidly.

Shell The command processor, such as 4DOS or COMMAND.COM. Also, a program layer designed to simplify things for the user. It often uses menus in place of a harder to learn command-line interface.

SID DR DOS's debugging tool, equivalent to DEBUG under MS-DOS.

Signature The unique piece of code that can be used to identify a particular strain of virus.

Software interrupt A message sent by software to the CPU to force it to stop processing and accept a request for services.

Source The files used by a COPY, MOVE, RENAME, or REPLACE command to perform their functions. For example, the source files are copied to a destination drive, path, and/or filename.

Source code The program code generated by the programmer, which can not be directly executable by the computer. If not, it is translated by an assembler or compiler into machine language object code.

Stack Any "pile" of information that is loaded and accessed on a last-in, first-out basis (like a stack of plates in your pantry).

Static RAM Memory that does not need to be refreshed and which, therefore, does not lose its contents when power to the computer is turned off.

Stealth Virus A virus that does its best to conceal itself from anti-virus software. The first step down this road came in the form of viruses that managed to modify files without changing the date stamp. Others were developed that intercepted requests for information about files from the system. They then subtracted their own length from the length of the file reported to the system. There are now viruses that don't invade files at all but, instead, reside on your hard disk as hidden files. They lie in wait until the time comes to spring into action and destroy your data.

String A series of characters.

Subdirectory A directory created within another directory, which stores its own separate files.

Substrate A base material that is coated with another. For example, flexible polyester forms the substrate onto which a floppy disk's magnetic coating is placed. For hard disks, the substrate is most frequently a rigid aluminum platter.

Swap To exchange one piece of information, generally data stored in memory or disk, for some other information. Swapping allows you to use the same area of memory over and over by moving data into and out of the swap area as it is needed.

Swap file A disk file used to store information swapped from memory. Sometimes an unwanted swap file can remain behind on your hard disk if a session is terminated unexpectedly (your computer locks up or loses power, for example).

System attribute A file attribute indicating that the file belongs to the operating system and should not be moved, erased, or modified.

Target The destination for an operation, such as COPY.

Text file Usually an ASCII file.

Time bomb A kind of specialized logic bomb, activated solely by the elapse of time. Some may wait until so many days or hours have passed (thereby disguising the time of entry to your system) or activate only on a specific day. The infamous Michaelangelo virus, which supposedly was to devastate PCs worldwide on Michaelangelo's birthday, is a time bomb.

Timeout The time limit set by DOS for response to a command.

Track One of the concentric circles on a disk platter, made up of sectors of information, and marked by the read-write head through a series of changes in the direction of the magnetic poles on the disk.

Transient The portion of a program that is loaded into memory only as it is needed.

Tree-structured The hierarchical directory structure of a DOS disk that uses parent and child directories.

Trojan Horse Code hidden inside an otherwise useful program, which springs into action when the program is run. The main program may function perfectly well while the trojan code does its dirty work. Trojan horse is a very broad term that encompasses many different kinds of programs that do something—harmless or not—that you don't expect them to do. A simple trojan horse stays resident in its host program; when the hidden code actively begins to reproduce itself, it enters the more specialized realm of the virus.

Unfragmented A hard disk that has most of its files stored in consecutive sectors and not spread out over the disk. Such an arrangement allows more efficient reading of data with less time required to move the read/write head to gather the information.

Unmount To remove a disk drive from those currently available to the operating system. Compressed disk volumes can be mounted and unmounted by DOS 6.

Upper Memory Block A section of memory between the 640K and 1024K boundaries.

Utility A program that performs some useful system or maintenance function, as opposed to an application program.

Video memory The area of upper memory used by your monitor's display card.

Virtual Control Program Interface (VCPI) This is a specification formalized in 1988 as a standard way for multitasking programs, which use extended memory, to communicate with each other. Desqview and several products called DOS extenders use this specification. Microsoft independently developed its own extended memory specification, called DOS Protected Mode Interface (DPMI). Today, most new software is DPMI compliant, but you may still have some VCPI programs. These may cause problems under Windows.

Virtual disk An electronic or RAM disk created in memory to mimic a real disk drive — only much faster. DOS 3.x and later versions are supplied with VDISK.SYS, a device driver that allows you to create multiple virtual disks in memory.

Virus So-named because they bear a remarkable resemblance to biological viruses that can infect humans. Like biological viruses, they can reproduce themselves and rely on another entity, such as a computer program or data file, to infect another system. Unlike worms, viruses don't actively seek out actual transport to the other system. You must download an infected program, copy it from a floppy disk, run it from a disk or over a network, or otherwise import the virulent code into your system.

Virus signature A unique set of numbers that indicate the presence of a particular virus; a fingerprint, if you will.

Volume The largest hard disk entity that DOS is able to deal with.

XMS Extended Memory Specification, which defines how high, upper, and extended memory can be accessed on computers with Intel 80286 and higher microprocessors.

Windows Microsoft's graphical user interface, which runs on 286 and higher microprocessors.

Wildcard Characters used in a filename to specify a single character (?) or any sequence of characters (*).

Winchester Another name for a fixed disk drive.

Worm   A bit of program code that can reproduce itself and move through programs and systems, and even into other systems. Some worms can wander through your PC's memory or hard disk space until all of it is consumed. Others know how to attach themselves to electronic mail or other data that moves from system to system and, thus, can actively spread on their own. The 1988 Internet Worm, which affected 6000 computers worldwide, is an example of this type of invader.

Resource Directory

This appendix provides information about the vendors of some of the third-party DOS add-on products mentioned in this book. List prices were current when this book was published in mid-1993 but are subject to change.

Anti-Virus Products

AntiVirusPLUS
T.C.P. Techmar Computer Products, Inc.
98-11 Queens Blvd., Rego Park, NY 11374
800-922-0015, 718-997-6666
fax 718-520-0170
List price: $99.95

Central Point Anti-Virus for DOS and Windows
Central Point Software Inc.
15220 NW Greenbrier Pkwy., #200, Beaverton, OR 97006
800-445-4208, 503-690-8090
List price: $129.00

Detect Plus
Commcrypt Inc.
10000 Virginia Manor Rd., #300, Beltsville, MD 20705
800-334-8338, 301-470-2500
fax 301-470-2507
List price: $129.00

Dr. Solomon's Anti-Virus Toolkit
Ontrack Computer Systems Inc.
6321 Bury Dr., #15-19, Eden Prarie, MN 55346
800-752-1333, 612-937-1107
fax 612-937-5815
List price: $150.00

F-Prot Professional
Command Software Systems
1061 Indiantown Rd., #500, Jupiter, FL 33477
407-575-3200
fax 407-575-3026
List price: $49.00

InocuLAN/PC
Cheyenne Software Inc.
55 Bryant Ave., Roslyn, NY 11576
516-484-5110
fax 516-484-3493
List price: $49.00

The Norton Anti-Virus
Symantec Corp.
10201 Torre Ave., Cupertino, CA 95014
800-441-7234, 408-252-3570
fax 408-255-3344
List price: $129.00

NOVI
Symantec Corp.
10201 Torre Ave., Cupertino, CA 95014
800-441-7234, 408-252-3570
fax 408-255-3344
List price: $129.00

PC Rx
Trend Micro Devices Inc.
2421 W. 205th St., #D-100, Torrance, CA 90501
800-228-5651, 310-782-8190
fax 310-328-5982
List price: $69.00

Pro-Scan
McAfee Associates
3350 Scott Blvd., Bldg. 14, Santa Clara, CA 95054
408-988-3832
fax 408-970-9727
BBS 408-988-4004
List price: $89.95

Untouchable
Fifth Generation Systems Inc.
10049 N. Reiger Rd., Baton Rouge, LA 70809-4562
800-873-4383, 504-291-7221
fax 504-295-3268
List price: $99.00

Vaccine
The Davidson Group
20 Exchange Pl., New York, NY 10005
800-999-6031, 212-422-4100
fax 212-422-1953
List Price: $129.00

Victor Charlie
Computer Security Associates
738 1/2 Meeting St., West Columbia, SC 29169
803-796-6591
fax 803-796-8379
BBS 803-791-5421
List price: $50.00 (shareware registration)

Virex for the PC
Datawatch Corp.
3700 Lyckan Pkwy., Suite B, Durham, NC 27707
919-490-1277
fax 919-419-8312
List price: $49.95

ViruCide Plus
Parsons Technology Inc.
One Parsons Dr., P.O. Box 100, Hiawatha, IA 52233-0100
800-223-6925, 319-395-9626
fax 319-393-1002
List price: $69.00

ViruSafe
XTree Co.
4115 Broad St., Bld. 1, San Luis Obispo, CA 93401-7993
800-333-6561, 805-541-0604
fax 805-541-4762
List price: $99.00

Virus Alert
LOOK Software
P.O. Box 78072 Cityview, Nepean, Ontario, Canada K2G5W2
800-267-0778, 613-837-2151
fax 613-837-5572
List price: $39.95

Virus Buster
Leprechaun Software International Ltd.
P.O. Box 669306, Marietta, GA 30066
800-521-8849, 404-971-8900
fax 404-971-8828
BBS 404-971-8886
List price: $129.00

Vi-Spy Professional
RG Software Systems Inc.
6900 E. Camelback Rd., #630, Scottsdale, AZ 85251
602-423-8000
fax 602-423-8389
List price: $149.95

IBM AntiVirus
IBM Corp.
Old Orchard Rd., Armonk, NY 10504
800-551-3579
List price: $29.95

VirusCure Plus
International Microcomputer Software Inc.
1938 Fourth St., San Rafael, CA 94901
800-833-4674, 415-454-7101
fax 415-454-8901
List price: $99.95

VirusNet
Safetynet Inc.
14 Tower Dr., East Hanover, NJ 07936-3320
800-851-0188, 908-851-0188
fax 908-276-6575
List price: $49.95

Panda Pro
Panda Systems
801 Wilson Rd., Wilmington, DE 19803
800-727-2632, 302-764-4722
fax 302-764-6186
List price: $79.95

Data Physician PLUS
Digital Dispatch Inc.
55 Lakeland Shores Rd., Lakeland, MN 55043
800-221-8091, 612-436-1000
fax 612-436-2085
List price: $49.00

Backup Software

Central Point Backup
Central Point Software, Inc.
15220 N.W. Greenbrier Pkwy., Suite 200, Beaverton, OR 97006
800-445-4208
fax 503-690-8083
List price: $129.00

Distinct Back-Up
Distinct Corp.
P.O. Box 3710, Saratoga, CA 95070-1410
408-741-0781
fax 408-741-0795
List price: $129.00

FastBack Plus
Fifth Generation Systems
10049 N. Reiger Rd., Baton Rouge, LA 70809
800-873-4384
fax 504-295-3268
List price: $189.00

Norton Backup
Symantec Corp.
10201 Torre Ave., Cupertino, CA 95014
800-441-7234
408-252-3570
List price: $129.00 Norton Backup for DOS
              $149.00 Norton Backup for Windows

Sytos Plus File Backup
Sytron Corp.
508-898-0100
fax 508-898-2677
List price: $225.00

Back-It for Windows
Gazelle Systems
305 N. 500 West, Provo UT 84601
800-786-3278, 801-377-1288
List price: $99.95

FastBack Express
Fifth Generation Systems
10049 N. Reiger Rd., Baton Rouge, LA 70809
800-873-4384, 504-291-7221
List price: $99.00

SitBack for Windows
SitBack Technologies
9290 Bond, Suite 104, Overland Park, KS 66214
800-873-7482, 913-894-0808
List price $99.00

SitBack Lite for Windows
SitBack Technologies
9290 Bond, Suite 104, Overland Park, KS 66214
800-873-7482, 913-894-0808
List price: $19.95

Memory Managers

386Max
Qualitas, Inc.
7101 Wisconsin Ave., #1386, Bethesda, MD 20814
800-733-1377, 301-907-6700
List price: $99.95

Memory Commander
V Communications, Inc.
4320 Stevens Creek Blvd., #275, San Jose, CA 95129
800-648-8266, 408-296-4224
List price: $99.95

NetRoom
Helix Software Co., Inc.
47-09 30th St., Long Island City, NY 11101
800-451-0551, 718-392-3100
List price: $99.00

QEMM-386
Quarterdeck Office
Systems Inc.
150 Pico Blvd., Santa Monica, CA 90405
310-392-9851
List price: $99.95

QMAPS
Quadtel Corp.
3190-J Airport Loop Dr., Costa Mesa, CA 92626
800-748-5718, 714-754-4422
List price: $99.95

Disk Optimizers/Defragmenters

Disk Optimizer Tools
SoftLogic Solutions, Inc.
800-272-9900
fax 603-627-9610

FastTrax
FastTrax Int'l
510-525-3510

The Norton Utilities
Symantec Corp.
800-441-7234
408-252-3570

OPTune
Gazelle Systems, Inc.
800-786-3278
fax 801-373-6933

PC-Kwik Power Disk
Multisoft Corp.
800-759-5945
fax 503-646-8267

PC Tools
Central Point Software, Inc.
800-445-4208
fax 503-690-8083

Vopt
Golden Bow Systems
800-284-3269
fax 619-298-9950

Backup Hardware

Alloy Computer Products Inc.
One Brigham St., Marlboro, MA 01752
800-800-2556
fax 508-481-7711

Backtrax
21800 Oxnard St., #700, Woodland Hills, CA 91367
800-669-3506
fax 818-704-7733

Colorado Memory Systems Inc.
800 S. Taft Ave., Loveland, CO 80537
303-669-8000
fax 303-669-0401

Core Int'l Inc.
7171 N. Federal Hwy., Boca Raton, FL 33487
407-997-6055
fax 407-997-6009

Maynard Electronics
36 Skyline Dr., Lake Mary, FL 32746
800-821-8782
fax 407-263-3555

Mountain Network Solutions Inc.
240 E. Hacienda Ave., Campbell, CA 95008-6623
800-458-0300
fax 408-379-4302

Tallgrass Technologies Corp.
11100 W. 82nd St., Lenexa, KS 66214
800-825-4727
fax 913-492-2465

Tecmar
6225 Cochran Rd., Solon, OH 44139
216-349-0600
fax 216-349-0851

Wangtek Inc.
41 Moreland Rd., Simi Valley, CA 93065
805-583-5255
fax 805-583-8249

Index